MOUNTAINEERING

THE FREEDOM *of the* HILLS

FOURTH EDITION

Plate 1. Cirque of the Unclimbables, Logan Mountains, Northwest Terr. (Galen Rowell)

MOUNTAINEERING
THE FREEDOM *of the* HILLS

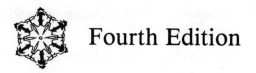 Fourth Edition

Editor: ED PETERS

Revision Committee:

ROGER ANDERSEN
DAVE ENFIELD
LEE HELSER
BOB SWANSON
JOHN YOUNG

Illustrations:

ROBERT CRAM
and
RAMONA HAMMERLY

THE MOUNTAINEERS
Seattle, Washington

THE MOUNTAINEERS
Organized 1906

To explore and study the mountains, forests, and watercourses of the Northwest;

To gather into permanent form the history and traditions of this region;

To preserve by the encouragement of protective legislation or otherwise the natural beauty of Northwest America;

To make expeditions into these regions in fulfillment of the above purposes;

To encourage a spirit of good fellowship among all lovers of outdoor life.

Published by The Mountaineers
306 2nd Ave. W., Seattle, Washington 98119

Published simultaneously in Australia by A.H. & A.W. Reed Pty. Ltd.
2 Aquatic Drive, Frenchs Forest, Sydney, N.S.W. 2086

Published simultaneously in Canada by Douglas & McIntyre, Ltd.
1615 Venables Street, Vancouver, B.C. V5L 2H1

Published simultaneously in New Zealand by A.H. & A.W. Reed Ltd.
68–74 Kingsford-Smith Street, Wellington

Distributed in the United Kingdom by Cordee
3a DeMontfort St., Leicester LE1 7HD

Manufactured in the United States of America
First edition, April 1960; Second edition, December 1967; Third edition, January 1974
Fourth edition, January 1982; second printing, June 1983; third
printing, March 1984; fourth printing, December 1984

Library of Congress Cataloging in Publication Data
Main entry under title:

Mountaineering, the freedom of the hills.

Includes index.
1. Mountaineering. I. Peters, Ed. II. Mountaineers (Society)
GV200.M688   1982   796.5'22   81-18787
ISBN 0-89886-001-6   AACR2

*

PREFACE

THE ORIGINS of *Mountaineering: The Freedom of the Hills* may be said to be lost in antiquity, or at least in early decades of the 20th century, when Puget Sounders began regularly venturing into the wilderness that surrounded their young cities and towns.

The first definable step toward the book occurred in 1934 with organization of the Climbing Course, a school since presented annually by The Mountaineers. Though European works, particularly Young's classic *Mountaincraft*, were required reading, they did not cover various subjects unique and important to American and Pacific Northwest mountaineering. To fill the gaps, outlines prepared by Course lecturers were distributed to students; eventually these were fleshed out and gathered together as the *Climber's Notebook,* subsequently published, in 1948, as the *Mountaineers Handbook*.

By 1955 tools and techniques had changed so drastically, and the Course had so grown in size and complexity, the need was felt for a new and more comprehensive textbook. Thus was undertaken the lengthy effort that culminated in 1960 with publication of the first edition of *Freedom*.

Members of the First Edition Editorial Committee were: Harvey Manning, chairman; John R. Hazle, Carl Henrikson, Nancy Bickford Miller, Thomas Miller, Franz Mohling, Rowland Tabor, and Lesley Stark Tabor. A substantial portion of the then relatively small Puget Sound climbing community participated, some 75 as writers of preliminary, revised, advanced, semifinal, and final chapter drafts, and another hundred or two as reviewers, planners, illustrators, typists, proofreaders, financiers, promoters, retailers, warehousemen, and shipping clerks. Rare was the Mountaineer climber of the period who did not have a hand in making or selling the book.

The first-edition team retired from the scene confident it had written for the ages, the sport and Course seeming to have gone about as far as they could go. However, the final wisdom of the 1950s became the archaic nonsense of the 1960s. Army and navy surplus gear from World War II wore out, replaced by sophisticated new parkas, packs, tents, boots, crampons, ropes, pitons, and whatnot. Old techniques thought to be the embodiment of perfection were refined out of all recognition; new ones were invented. Consequently, in 1964 there began another extended, strenuous effort leading in 1967 to publication of the second edition of *Freedom*.

Members of the Second Edition Editorial Committee were: John M. Davis, chairman; Tom Hallstaff, Max Hollenbeck, Jim Mitchell, Roger Neubauer, and Howard Stansbury. Though much of the first edition was retained intact, again the task force was of impressive proportions, numbering several dozen writers, uncounted reviewers and helpers. Rickety survivors of the previous committee, notably John R. Hazle, Tom Miller, and Harvey Manning unretired briefly to provide continuity. As he had with the first edition, Harvey Manning once more edited the entire text and supervised production.

The necessity for a continuous updating of *Freedom,* urged by previous editorial committees, was again stressed in late 1970 by Max Hollenbeck, then president of The Mountaineers. Chairman Sam Fry, with Fred Hart, Sean Rice, Jim Sanford, and Howard Stansbury, spearheaded the Third Edition, which was published in 1974.

By this time, those involved were beginning to suspect that some sort of monster had been created, and the Revision Committee retreated, muttering about future editions.

Freedom 4, as it has been referred to during preparation, has been drafted, reviewed, and polished by a cast of hundreds. Comments from many climbers have been received, considered, and incorporated or rejected. The final product must be termed a major revision since many chapters have been completely rewritten, notably the entire Ice and Snow section.

A climber imparts knowledge to a novice, the years pass, the novice with the head start of knowledge becomes the expert, often returning to teach the teacher. So it has been in this case. The words of thousands who helped with previous editions may have been lost, yet the knowledge those words provided was the cornerstone necessary to create *Freedom 4*.

A team of technical editors selected to be responsible for overall guidance consisted of Ed Peters, chairman; Roger Andersen, Dave Enfield,

Lee Helser, and John Young, with Dave Anthony and Robert Swanson each serving over part of the two-year period.

Each chapter was assigned to a "writer," responsible for ensuring its completion. Subsequent drafts were reviewed by the technical editors and returned for rewriting until satisfactory.

"Preparation" was updated by Dave Enfield with help from Clint Kelley; "Clothing and Equipment" was updated by John Moen, assisted by Clint Kelley, Paul Measel and Greg Varney. "Camping and Sleeping" was reworked by Fay Pullen; "Alpine Cuisine" and "Food Requirements" were brought up to date by Joan Firey and Cynthia Young, with help from Lee Helser. "Navigation" was completely rewritten by Bob Burns with considerable help from Clint Kelley. "Wilderness Travel" was updated slightly by Mary Sutliff and Dave Enfield. The chapter on routefinding was deleted in favor of distributing the major information in other chapters where appropriate. "Ropes and Knots" was updated by Erhard Wichert and Ed Peters; "Belaying" and "Rappelling" were rewritten by Roger Andersen. The rock climbing section was reorganized, with "Rock Technique" written by Robert Swanson, "Protection" (previously called Free Climbing) written by Ken Small and "Pitons and Aid Climbing" written by Ed Peters with help from Bill Sumner, Rick LeDuc, and Bob Williams.

The Snow and Ice section was reorganized somewhat with "Basic Snow Travel" written by Roy Ellis with help from Dave Enfield and Roger Andersen. "Snow Climbing" was completely rewritten by Jeff Snow (appropriately); "Ice Climbing" was completely rewritten by Tamara McCollom with critiques of various drafts by Yvon Chouinard, Jeff Lowe, Kevin Donald, and Bill Sumner, and "Glacier Travel" was updated by John Young. "Climbing Safety" was updated by Clint Kelley, "Leadership" by Jim Sanford with help from Del Fadden, "First Aid" made current by Gerald Sabel, "Alpine Rescue" revised by Don Goodman with help from then Seattle Mountain Rescue chairman Al Errington.

"Mountain Geology" was reviewed with a few corrections by Ed Vervoort, "Cycle of Snow" condensed by Ed LaChappelle with help from Ed Peters and Lee Helser, and "Mountain Weather" updated by Mark Albright. Although the people mentioned all made substantial contributions, many other climbers provided valuable help through critiques of subsequent drafts; each chapter represents the efforts of at least ten people.

As drafts of chapters began to emerge, Peggy Ferber, editor of the Third Edition, was impressed to make sentences from the jumble of words, to provide at least some consistency in spelling, and to ensure that all participles were properly belayed. Glenn Brindeiro, Dick Erwood, and Duncan Kelso read final drafts for technical accuracy and consistency and to make certain no vital information had been lost in the whiteout of verbiage.

All new artwork was prepared by Bob Cram and Ramona Hammerly. Thanks must go to Recreational Equipment, Inc. and The Swallow's Nest, outdoor climbing equipment suppliers in Seattle, Washington, who provided the latest climbing equipment items for the artists to sketch.

Although those intimately involved for the first time in revising a text of such wide application and such impressive historical background as *Freedom* may have been too inextricably committed to withdraw by the time they realized the magnitude of the undertaking, they, like the veterans of previous editions, saw their duty clearly and responded accordingly.

One issue raised for consideration was that masculine pronouns had been used throughout previous editions. Although the authors, editors, and publisher of this edition, as well as previous ones, are well aware that women climb as well as men, conventional masculine pronouns are used in this edition also (though perhaps with less emphasis), to avoid awkward construction or stilted phrases that impede the flow of words and thought.

The authors, editors and publisher trust that the readers will also recognize the love of mountains and wild places implicit throughout the book. Although neither sociological treatise nor conservation tract, this book represents the efforts of many who sincerely love the out-of-doors, and wish to share that love with others who will cherish and protect it.

> I must hurry,
> for there they go
> and I am their leader.
> (unknown)

*

CONTENTS

*

PLATES

 PART ONE

Approaching the Peaks

Plate 2. Daybreak, Eldorado Peak, North Cascades. (Bruce Gaumond)

1 *

PREPARATION

A MOUNTAINEER is one who seeks the freedom of the hills, full wilderness citizenship, with all its privileges and rewards, its responsibilities and demands. For though mountaineering at best is exhilarating, at worst it is frustrating, discouraging and punishing, even disastrous to those who ignore nature's stern and impersonal rules.

Freedom of the hills lies largely in the ability of a party, whatever the size, to handle every problem of travel and living, including emergencies, with nothing more than the members can carry conveniently on their backs, using their physical resources and the knowledge and judgment they have gained through experience. Implicit is the responsibility each individual must have to the environment, to the party, and to himself.

Though distant views of mountains may speak of adventure, they seldom more than hint at the multitudinous joys and hardships awaiting in the high places. Early on, of course, aspiring mountaineers will assess their fondness for the totality of nature — mosquitoes as well as birds, wicked brush as well as pretty flowers, cold rain and cruel wind as well as warm sunshine and soft breezes. They will weigh the exhilaration of the summit against the exhaustion of the lengthy training and strenuous effort required to reach the heights. They must decide whether the pleasures are really worth the pains, and some individuals will properly conclude at this point that they would be happier in a less demanding recreation.

There are as many mountaineering experiences as there are mountains and mountaineers, too many to summarize except in a thick volume of philosophy, poetry, craft, religion, or whatever. No attempt will be made here to explore the spiritual and aesthetic profundities of the sport: this book is intended rather as a passport for those who wish to safely and confidently enjoy the freedom of the hills.

Responsibility to the Environment

Throughout man's history mountains have epitomized remoteness, wildness and the unknown. Tarns and meadows have symbolized delicate beauty; rugged spires have represented durability and timelessness. Yet today tarns are being polluted with human waste, meadows trampled by boots and crushed by sleeping bags.

If fragile ecosystems and structures are to be preserved, for meanings and values far beyond those of "sport," and for generations yet to be born, the mountaineer must study and understand the character of the land he travels, comprehend the vulnerability of its plants and soils and creatures, and must utilize new techniques of camping and climbing.

The true mountaineer—climber or hillwalker—walks softly through the wilderness striving to leave not the slightest trace of his passage. This individual accepts the fact that privilege entails responsibility, without which freedom is only license.

Physical Preparation

The mountaineer, in order to fully enjoy the exhilaration of the mountain experience, must work diligently to maintain the most important item of equipment—the body. The informed individual knows that the human body derives its energy from the oxygen-dependent burning of stored chemical fuel, that prevention of dehydration is essential for the functioning of the entire system, and that the processes involved utilize materials which are replenished during periods of inactivity or sleep. In brief, the mountaineer recognizes the importance of food, water, and rest to maintain physical and psychological strength, and in extreme cases, life itself.

As the novice quickly learns, the ease of coping with physical and mental stress depends largely on the efficiency of organs and muscles: the better the physical condition, the better the body can supply necessary fuel and the better the chance of avoiding hazardous exhaustion. The nature and intensity of the climber's conditioning program will vary with each individual. Maintenance of physical condition is the personal responsibility of the conscientious mountaineer. Proper physical conditioning will ensure that the individual will be an asset, not a liability, to the party as well as permitting the individual to realize and enjoy the personal rewards to be derived from the experience.

Knowledge to Cope with a New World

Mountains are a foreign environment, not necessarily hostile, but certainly indifferent. It is necessary, therefore, that mountain travelers be knowledgeable about many things uncommon to the urban dweller or the weekend sightseer. Mountaineers, whether beginning or experienced, must diligently acquire familiarity with the conditions and techniques of travel in the mountain wilderness in order to be assured of safe and successful trips.

Wilderness travelers carry navigation aids and have mastered their use. Before the trip they study maps and descriptions of the route and surrounding terrain. Mountaineers strive by experience to become successful at the art of routefinding. They climb with their eyes, observing the route constantly, looking for those general characteristics of the terrain that are no longer apparent when they are engulfed by trees or surrounded by crevasses or have their noses pressed to the rock. Many summits are lost due to errors in routefinding, often during the approach to the peak, long before the climbing becomes difficult.

Experienced mountaineers are mindful of the weather, having not only knowledge of the predicted outlook, but also an eye on the sky to observe changes early. Through prudence and often bitter experience, they journey into the mountains always equipped for the most severe conditions conceivable. Wilderness travelers must understand that the human body functions within narrow limits and that it cannot, for example, withstand more than slight variations in internal temperature. The problem of decreasing internal temperature — hypothermia — is especially serious in areas where the approach of cold, wind-driven precipitation is often rapid and unpredictable. Deterioration due to hypothermia may be rapid and uncontrolled. Trained individuals know that wet clothing transmits heat from the body much faster than dry clothing; that, when everything is sodden, wool and certain non-absorbent synthetics insulate far better than other materials; that wind alone can kill and windproof shell clothing can be a lifesaver; that an uncovered head dissipates a great deal of heat.

Knowledgeable mountaineers know that dehydration leads rapidly to deteriorating health, and perhaps death, and have, therefore, noted availability and location of water, whether from streams, lakes or snowfields; their water bottles will never be allowed to go dry.

When entering the mountains, they always have a planned but flexible itinerary, including one or more objectives, and an expected time of return. Emergencies, although occurring infrequently, may necessitate a late return, most often a day or two beyond that expected. Such delays often coincide with adverse weather, for which wise individuals are educated in survival techniques and equipped accordingly. The need for an unexpected bivouac may result from an accident: although most injuries occurring in the mountains are, fortunately, relatively minor, trained mountaineers know the importance of a working knowledge of first aid, have studied to acquire and maintain it, and are equipped to render assistance if necessary.

The mountain world provides variety appropriate for any interested individual, from trail users to aid climbers. It is the responsibility of *each* mountain traveler to be experienced in the climbing techniques necessary to negotiate the terrain to be encountered, to have studied and practiced these techniques and to continue to refine them. On any trip, although the objective and route may be challenging, the wise individual knows that the mountain wilderness is not the place to foolishly experiment with new and unfamiliar techniques.

Wise mountaineers never stop learning more about themselves and their new, foreign environment, steadily and assiduously enlarging their knowledge as if happiness and health depended on it — as indeed they do.

Judgment and Experience

A mountaineering textbook can outline the basics of equipment and techniques, and perhaps also suggest how to learn from experience. However, judgment, the most important of all qualities, develops only with time, from the successes as well as the failures. The more one travels in the mountains the broader his knowledge, yet repeatedly new situations arise for which there is no trustworthy precedent, times when no confident response can be automatically made, when judgment must be exercised. In this uncertainty lies much of the charm of mountaineering — the infinite variety, the elusive perfection perpetually sought but never quite attained. But in this uncertainty also lies the potential for many tragedies.

With the best of intentions it is often difficult for anyone, particularly the beginner, to apply proper judgment in unanticipated circumstances. For this reason there has been developed, over many years, a standard of judgment — a mountaineers' Climbing Code — based on careful observation of the habits of skilled climbers and thoughtful analysis of accidents. With only slight adaptation the Code serves not merely climbers but all wilderness travelers.

A Standard of Judgment: A Climbing Code

A climbing party of three is the minimum, unless adequate prearranged support is available. On glaciers, a minimum of two rope teams is recommended.

Rope up on all exposed places and for all glacier travel. Anchor all belays.

Keep the party together, and obey the leader or majority rule.

Never climb beyond your ability and knowledge.

Never let judgment be overruled by desire when choosing the route or turning back.

Carry at all times the clothing, food, and equipment necessary.

Leave the trip schedule with a responsible person.

Follow the precepts of sound mountaineering as set forth in textbooks of recognized merit.

Behave at all times in a manner that will not reflect unfavorably upon mountaineering.

By no means a step-by-step formula for conquering summits, the Code is rather the key to safe and sane mountaineering (see Chapter 17, Climbing Safety). Climbers have sometimes questioned the necessity of a set of rules for a sport in which much of the appeal rests in the absence of formal rules. Nevertheless, each year serious accidents continue to occur because these principles were violated. The Code rests on the premise that sensible mountaineers want strong chances of safety and success even in risk-filled or doubtful situations; they want safeguards in case they have misjudged those chances; and they want the ability to control and minimize their exposure to grave danger and death. Admittedly, there will be circumstances in which the veteran mountaineer may, based on sound reason and experienced judgment, knowingly overstep the boundaries presented in the Code. Even so, adherence to the Code is recommended for newer climbers who have not yet developed the judgment through years of experience. It may cost them some summits, but will significantly increase the chances of their achieving the rank of veterans.

Plate 3. Rani Col on Himalchuli, Gurkha Himal, Nepal. (John Cleare)

2 *

CLOTHING AND EQUIPMENT

A COMPREHENSIVE SURVEY of the garb and gear in current favor among mountaineers would require as many pages as a fair-sized encyclopedia and would try the patience of the most painstaking scholar. Witness mountain shop catalogs, invaluable guides to the newest advances in design (and price), yet often giving such a variety of choices that reading a single catalog may lead to confusion, two to bewildered irresolution, and three to catatonia.

This chapter and the one following do not pretend to be definitive, but rather offer a brief summary of opinion and guidelines on what is most desirable in the basic outfit of a climber, the gear necessary for even the most elementary trip. Other basic tools—and more specialized equipment—will be discussed later in context of use.

Equipment carried on any trip must be kept to the safe minimum and must be just as light as is consistent with durability and versatility. Modern materials and methods of manufacture have made possible great saving in weight with no sacrifice of utility; unfortunately, very often the lower the weight the higher the price.

Given unlimited funds a person can visit a mountain shop and walk out later fully and superbly outfitted for the high country. The novice of ordinary means must proceed more cautiously to avoid financial disaster. However, if one has a background of hiking and camping, many of the major expenditures lie behind, and even the lifelong urbanite finds much in his closet, basement, and kitchen that can be converted to mountain use, though perhaps only as a stopgap.

The beginner can avoid confusion and/or bankruptcy by taking one trip at a time, one purchase at a time, remembering there is no economy in buying cheap. Boots come first, necessary for even the simplest alpine excursion, plus warm clothing, a clutter of small and inexpensive essentials, and a rucksack to carry them. For an overnight trip, shelter and kitchenware can be improvised at small cost, but the required frame or soft pack is a substantial investment and the indispensable sleeping bag a painful purchase. Before venturing onto steep snow, a person must have an ice axe. The climbing rope comes fairly late in the timetable since the novice will be—or should be—making his first roped climbs with an experienced companion who owns one.

The governing rule is, then, never to buy anything until the next climb demands it. By improvising, modifying, borrowing, and renting, the basic outfit can be budgeted over the entire first climbing season. In succeeding years stopgaps can be gradually replaced, all the more wisely for the delay, and specialized tools accumulated.

FOOTGEAR
Boots: Foundation of the Climber

One day of climbing may involve travel through and over streams, mud, logs, brush, meadow, and scree, stepkicking in snow, and delicate footwork on steep rock. A single pair of boots usually must suffice for all these conditions; a good climbing boot, therefore, represents a happy compromise among a number of conflicting requirements. It should be tough to withstand the scraping of rocks, stiff and solid for kicking steps in hard snow, yet comfortable enough for the approach hike. The upper must be high enough to protect the ankles in rough walking, yet permit them to flex to the extreme angles required by cramponing and slab climbing. The sole should provide traction on both slippery heather and smooth rock. There must be room to wiggle the toes, but the fit must not be so loose that the foot can slip around inside, causing blisters while hiking and loss of control on small holds. It is important to remember when trying on boots for size that they should be fitted with the number of socks to be worn, keeping in mind the fact that socks which seem to fill the boot to overflowing at first will pack into place around the foot in a very few minutes. However, boots that are too tight may constrict blood circulation, causing feet to be very cold, and thus more susceptible to frostbite. If boots seem to fit well in the store, consider coming back later to try them again. If the fit is still good, wear them around the house for a few days to be sure.

The compromise currently found best by most climbers (Fig. 2-1), is a 5½- to 7½-inch-high boot with a lug sole of fairly hard rubber and a three-quarter-length steel shank. The lug sole grips well on snow, provides excellent insulation from the cold and cushioning from the discomfort of travel on rough terrain. It is also satisfactory for most alpine rock climbing.

Fig. 2-1. Typical boots. *Left to right,* light boot with scree cuff, heavy climbing boot with gusseted tongue and stiff sole, and specialized rock shoe.

Dozens of boot styles are available which fall within the limits of the recommended compromise. Whichever is chosen must meet still further tests of acceptability. The welt should be narrow (Fig. 2-2), lest it bend on small holds and cause a slip. The top should open wide so that even when the boot is wet or frozen it can be put on with minimum struggle. Reducing the number of seams decreases the points of entry for water and lengthens boot life, since seams are susceptible to abrasion and are frequently the first part to fail. Minimizing seams adds to the expense of construction but increases durability, as do double and triple layering in areas exposed to roughest wear. Especially desirable are hard toe and heel counters to prevent bruises, uncomfortable compression by crampon straps, and to protect the feet during stepkicking.

Price is usually a fair measure of leather quality: very inexpensive boots sometimes fall apart in a season or two; a good pair of boots will, with proper care, last several years. To prevent mildew and rot, boots should be washed off after each use, stuffed with a boot tree or paper, then thoroughly dried in a ventilated, moderately warm storage place. High temperatures are as damaging to leather as to human skin (remember, leather *is* skin), and the boot lacks nerve endings to warn of harm being done. The boots seen roasting by the campfire are the very ones that mysteriously disintegrate on some future climb.

Water can enter the boot not only over the top but also through the leather or seams. Boots of good quality leather, well waterproofed, particularly at the seams, and having a tongue gussetted to the top (Fig. 2-1) can exclude water for a long while even when slopping around in wet snow (assuming none enters over the top). Waterproofing is best applied a day or two before a climb to allow the preservative to soak into the leather. The type of preservative used depends on how the leather was tanned (be sure to find out when buying): for chrome-tanned (dry-tanned) leather use silicone-based wax; for vegetable-tanned leather, oil or grease. To preserve the cemented bond between the layers of the sole, be sure to keep this area absolutely free of any oil-based treatment. The welt should be treated with a coating of shellac and wax, or one of the commercial preparations available specifically for this purpose.

Besides the "compromise" boot described, other options are available for special purposes. A boot with a soft-leather upper and flexible sole, is most comfortable for trail walking and easy alpine terrain. A stiffer, double upper, heavier sole (one-half- to three-quarter-length steel shank), and a hard toe are more desirable for scree and snow and moderate climbing. Boots with very stiff uppers (Fig. 2-2) and full shanks (steel or wood), though difficult to break in and somewhat uncomfortable on open trail, are preferred for alpine rock and ice climbing. A careful fit can ameliorate these difficulties. Double- and triple-insulated boots are used for very cold weather and expeditionary climbing.

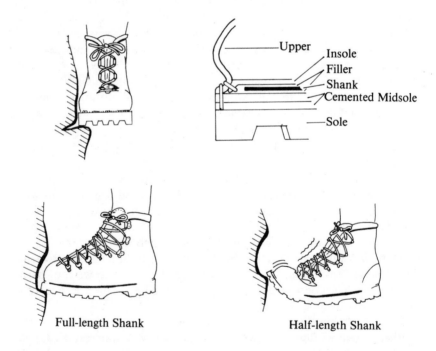

Fig. 2-2. Boot features. *Top left,* narrow welt, for small footholds. *Top right,* Norwegian welt, noted for stiffness and solid construction. *Bottom,* shank length determines flexibility of the boot sole.

Socks

Socks perform four vital functions: cushioning, insulation, absorption of perspiration, and reduction of foot/boot friction. Wool has been proved to be superior material for socks. A light, smoothly woven pair is usually worn next to the skin and a heavy, rough-woven pair over these. People with tender feet sometimes add a pair of light cotton or synthetic socks next to the skin. The toes must always be free to wiggle: three tightly packed pairs of socks give less protection from cold than two looser layers, since compression of fibers reduces the dead-air space which is the the chief source of insulation.

Insoles can be added to provide extra insulation and cushioning and to gain a snugger fit. Insoles of woven synthetic materials are nonabsorbent, do not become matted or damp, and have a loose structure that helps ventilate the foot. Other materials are felt, leather, and lambskin—all of which absorb moisture and must be taken out when drying boots. Insoles must be in place when fitting boots for size, or can be substituted for the layer of socks they replace.

Other Footgear

Some mountaineers carry camp footgear for comfort and to give boots a chance to air or dry. Tennis, training, or running shoes are popular in summer, down booties for cold weather bivouacs and winter tenting. On certain climbs, with long sections that will be done using friction, many prefer to wear special rock shoes (Fig. 2-1) to secure a better footing. These should be deferred to a later purchase, after consulting with other climbers who wear the different types available.

CLOTHING

Man is a warm-blooded creature and, therefore, must maintain a compatible micro-environment next to his skin by the use of suitable clothing. Various combinations of cold, wet, and windy conditions can destroy this layer of warm air; if the process is not corrected, body heat is lost, eventually leading to a condition known as hypothermia, a dangerous lowering of the body's core temperature.

Food and muscular activity are the main sources of body heat; the sun, fire, and hot food and drink are external sources of heat. Body heat may be lost through five different mechanisms: radiation, conduction, convection, evaporation and respiration.

Radiation, the movement of heat rays from a warm object to a colder object, is a great cause of cooling. An uncovered head can radiate one-half of the body's heat production at 40°F. At 5°F, up to 75 per cent of the total heat production can be lost. Parka hoods and balaclavas are vital to prevent this huge heat loss.

Conduction—touching cold objects such as cold metal, sitting on ice, snow, and cold rock, and especially wearing wet clothing—causes considerable heat loss. Wet clothing can conduct 240 times as much heat from the body as dry clothing. Wet clothing acts much as a wick and if exposed to a cold wind will drain much more heat than a climber can ever generate.

Convection is the movement of air. The body continually warms the air next to the skin by radiation to a temperature nearly equal to that of the skin. This layer of warm air must be controlled by the use of insulative clothing, and if necessary, windproof garments.

Evaporation of sweat causes some heat loss. Sweating can soak clothing and thereby contribute to heat loss by conduction. Ventilation will reduce sweating and aid in keeping clothing dry.

Respiration also cools. Inhaling cold air, especially at high altitude during strenuous climbing can significantly affect body temperature.

Acute hypothermia, an insidious killer, proceeds from uncontrollable shivering to increasing clumsiness and loss of judgment, and unchecked, to a fairly rapid lapse into unconsciousness and death. It can and does occur at moderate temperatures of 45°F during wet and windy conditions in people who are not aware of this possibility and lack proper clothing. Refer to Chapter 19, First Aid, for the signs, symptoms, and treatment of hypothermia.

The character of a climb or outing determines the clothing and equipment to be taken, and the climber must select and use his clothing with great care to ensure that adequate shelter, dry insulating clothing and food are available to survive, although not necessarily in comfort.

The novice climber usually asks what is the minimum amount of clothing that will ensure survival during a bivouac. There is no simple answer to this question since clothing is only one of the factors in survival. Others involved include experience, physical condition, mental attitude, physique and nutrition. Bivouac survival cannot be purchased from an outdoor store. The experienced alpine mountaineer who does 150,000 feet elevation gain in a year, who is in fine physical condition, and has a positive mental attitude, may be able to do several planned and perhaps a couple of unplanned bivouacs each year without difficulty, and even enjoy them (probably more so after the fact). Only through experience does this person know what is necessary and sufficient for his own survival. He can distinguish that fine line between carrying too much and carrying too little. The novice, however, can attain this wisdom only through a continuous and energetic climbing program and up to that point must ensure safety by erring in the direction of carrying too much, only eliminating items as he finds that doing so will not threaten his survival.

Clothing best serves its most essential purpose of preserving body heat when worn in multiple layers with ventilating material next to the skin, insulating layers to trap warmed air, and outer shells to protect against wind and rain. Because of the rapid changes in temperature, wind, and exertion usually experienced, garments must be quickly and easily put on or removed even under difficult conditions. Ventilation is always necessary when the body is working, since enclosing the system within an airtight layer results in condensation of perspiration and thus wet clothing.

Thickness is warmth. Table 2-a is a rough guide to the total thickness of insulation, of whatever kind, for comfort at various temperatures and activities. However, the kind of insulation used determines the actual heat-preservation value in real-life situations.

Table 2-a. Insulation for Various Situations.

	Total Thickness of Insulation (in inches)		
Temperature	*Sleeping*	*Light Work*	*Heavy Work*
40°F	1.5	.8	.2
0°F	2.5	1.3	.35
−40°F	3.5	1.9	.5

Cotton readily absorbs water and has virtually no insulating value when wet. Wool, also quite absorbent, retains its dead-air structure when wet; the weight and bulk of woolen clothing, though, make it impractical as the sole source of insulation at very low temperatures. Nylon pile is warm, even when wet, dries quickly, and weight for weight, is warmer than wool. Nylon pile, though expensive, makes a versatile and practical garment.

Noncellular synthetic filaments such as polyesters and acrylics absorb very little water and dry quickly. Spun synthetic filament (Dacron Hollofil II®, Polarguard®, Thinsulate®) is lighter for equivalent dead-air thickness than wool, and unlike down, does not collapse when wet; thus it is an excellent alternative insulation in areas with a moist climate. Although there are differences among the synthetics, they do in general have the disadvantage of being heavier and less compressible than down.

Windproof garments are essential to minimize heat loss (Table 2-b), and a waterproof shell is necessary to keep insulating layers dry, though it is difficult to keep moisture out and still maintain adequate ventilation. A parka made of Gore-Tex® provides some ventilation as well as protection from wind and rain.

Table 2-b. Wind Chill Chart.

Wind Speed MPH	Temperature (°F)										
	50	40	30	20	10	0	−10	−20	−30	−40	−50
	Equivalent Chill Temperature										
Calm	50	40	30	20	10	0	−10	−20	−30	−40	−50
5	48	37	27	16	6	−5	−15	−26	−36	−47	−57
10	40	28	16	4	−9	−21	−33	−46	−58	−70	−83
15	36	22	9	−5	−18	−36	−45	−58	−72	−85	−99
20	32	18	4	−10	−25	−39	−53	−67	−82	−96	−110
25	30	16	0	−15	−29	−44	−59	−74	−88	−104	−118
30	28	13	−2	−18	−33	−48	−63	−79	−94	−109	−125
35	27	11	−4	−20	−35	−49	−67	−83	−98	−113	−129
40	26	10	−6	−21	−37	−53	−69	−85	−100	−116	−132
above 40	little additional effect										

Little Danger | Great | Extreme

Danger of Freezing Exposed Flesh if Dry and Properly Clothed

To use this table, which illustrates the intensely chilling effect of from frostbite. The zones shown on the table indicate the danger of wind, find wind speed (in miles per hour) in left-hand column and frostbite to any exposed flesh of an average person in good condition temperature (in degrees F) in top row; the intersection of these is the whose body is properly clothed for the conditions. When the effective equivalent temperature. For example, at a temperature of 0°F a temperature is −25°F or less, care should be taken to minimize breeze of 15 mph has the cooling effect of a temperature of −36°F on exposure of bare skin to wind. a calm day and precautions should be taken to protect exposed flesh

Clothing should be of a loose fit for minimum restriction of body movement and blood flow and should overlap at all points of junction (waist, wrist, ankle, and neck) to reduce heat loss. The types of clothing chosen will vary somewhat depending on severity of the worst possible weather, always allowing for the unexpected.

Below the Waist

Climbing trousers should be loose-fitting and of a closely woven, hard-finish fabric for abrasion resistance and windproofness. Wool is much preferred in a cool, wet climate. The life expectancy of pants can be extended by reinforcing the seat and perhaps the knees with patches of nylon or cotton canvas or leather, all of which are slow to dry if untreated (leather patches may be waterproofed with a good wax polish). A seat patch of coated nylon packcloth, coated side in, provides a moisture-resistant barrier during a sitting belay or sitting glissades. Large pockets sewn onto trouser thighs are useful for carrying small items in frequent demand, such as mittens and snacks. Knicker-style trousers usually offer more freedom of knee movement and reduce snagging while fighting brush. Opening the leg straps and rolling down the socks will allow cooling ventilation for the legs.

For the hardy, shorts travel well in the rain and are good for deep stream crossings, keeping the long pants dry in the pack for camp.

Wind pants, made of light, tough, very closely woven nylon, are used for protection from wind, snow, and wet brush. They are cut large enough to be put on without removing boots; with side-zippers they can be easily donned even while wearing crampons. Though weighing only a few ounces and stuffing easily into a pocket, wind pants over regular trousers reduce heat loss considerably in a hard blow and shed snow easily in winter conditions. As a fringe benefit, they help to keep trousers dry during sitting glissades but provide a fast running surface which has the disadvantage of being an absolute hazard on steep snow or ice.

Waterproof rain chaps are pant-legs that protect the legs below the parka, poncho, or cagoule—sans seat to provide some ventilation. The trouser seat will be exposed to rain if the parka does not have sufficient length.

Long wool underwear is desirable for winter travel (and sleeping) and cold alpine conditions. Long underwear, just as climbing trousers and boots, should not be considered to be extra clothing. The convenience and versatility of the layer system are lost if the climber, faced with a sudden and severe storm, must strip to the skin and remove boots to put on long underwear to gain some insulation from the cold. Some climbers carry, when conditions are marginal, a thinly insulated overpant, with full length leg zippers, (such as ski warm-up pants) to be donned if conditions are severe. Down or synthetic pile underwear can also be carried and worn as outer wear during a bivouac.

The boundary between trousers and boots is an important area. Gaiters (Fig. 2-3) made of tough nylon with elastic top and bottom fit snugly over pants and boot tops to keep snow and trash out of the boot. Short gaiters, 5 or 6 inches, are sufficient for most summer climbing and help keep gravel out of boots when short pants are worn. When deep snow is anticipated or when knickers are worn, long gaiters, to above the calf, are better. Waterproof nylon is preferred by some but is hot and causes sweating underneath, especially in the longer styles. A strap under the instep and a boot lace hook hold the gaiters down; a full-length zipper, lacing, or Velcro®, allows them to be donned without removing boots. Gaiters should be snug to avoid catching on crampon points. On winter and high-altitude climbs wet zippers, especially the small toothed variety, may freeze overnight and be very difficult to work. Supergaiters (Fig. 2-3), an insulative covering extending from the welt to above the boot top, leave lug soles exposed for climbing, keep out snow, and also provide some protection from frostbite.

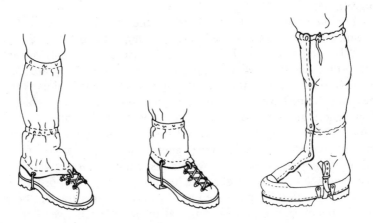

Fig. 2-3. Gaiters. *Left to right,* full, short length, and supergaiter.

Above the Waist

A warm torso helps warm toes and fingers. The layer system is superbly adapted to the quick fluctuations of cold and heat typical of alpine regions: layers are added or removed one by one to keep pace with changing conditions. The layers should fit loosely to ensure freedom of motion.

An undershirt of open-weave material permits ventilation to evaporate perspiration and when closed in by other clothing traps an additional insulating layer of air. Cotton fishnet is popular, but like all cotton clothing is cold when wet. Wool undergarments are preferable though more expensive. A nylon T-shirt, although having an unusual feel when damp, absorbs little water and dries readily; it thus works well as the first layer in many conditions, and also relieves the scratchiness of a woolen second layer.

Shirts and sweaters provide insulation mainly by trapping air within and between themselves. Several light, loose-fitting layers are therefore more effective than one heavy garment. Shirts and sweaters should be entirely wool or nylon pile, slow to get wet and even then retaining much of their insulating value. At least one of the shirts should have a long tail so it will remain inside the pants and protect the midriff. Cotton sweatshirts absorb water like sponges and rapidly become worthless as insulation.

Though two layers above underwear — wool or nylon pile garments — are sufficient in most climbing, Table 2-a shows it is impractical to depend solely on traditional wool garments at very low temperatures: the bulk and weight become too great. Down clothing has two properties — lightness and compressibility — which makes it indispensable in severe cold. A down garment can be squeezed into an incredibly small volume and yet quickly regain full loft. Of course down must never be allowed to become wet since it then loses practically all its insulating value and is virtually impossible to dry while in the mountains (as mentioned above, Dacron Hollofil II®, Polarguard®, or Thinsulate® are alternatives to down, though not as compressible).

Unless the temperature is very low, down clothing is seldom worn while in motion but many climbers carry a parka, sweater, vest, or underwear (down or synthetic pile) for emergencies, bivouacs, and/or added comfort during cold hours in camp. A vest or sweater is often adequate even in winter in mild coastal climates. For cold-weather expeditionary trips, down parkas weighing 2 to 3 pounds are frequently used.

Insulation is the role of shirts, sweaters, down, or synthetic fill clothing. Over these in foul weather comes the parka (Fig. 2-4), whose function is to break the wind and shed water. Except for light work in heavy rain, a completely waterproof parka is undesirable, because it does not breathe, that is, perspiration cannot evaporate through it. The ideal parka is wind and waterproof and breathes. The uninsulated parka is most versatile, insulative layers being added underneath as needed. A garment made of Gore-Tex® approaches this ideal, but is expensive and must be carefully maintained according to the manufacturer's instructions. And in *no* parka, even one made of Gore-Tex®, can a climber carry a full pack up a mountain in a warm rain without condensation.

Fig. 2-4. Parkas. *Left,* pullover design (anorak) with snap closure cuffs. *Right,* parka for more severe conditions, with face tunnel, two-way zipper and snap front, Velcro ® cuff.

Parkas of cotton or polyester-cotton blend (65–35 cloth) are tough and wind resistant, but repel water only in light rain for short periods even when treated with waterproofing substances. Furthermore, they are relatively bulky and heavy, weighing about 1½ to 2 pounds.

Unlined nylon wind shirts with attached hoods are tough, wind resistant (but not wind proof), light, and compact enough to stuff into a pocket, but tend to leak at least a day before any rain falls. They are excellent for high altitudes, where rain is not a problem. However, many imports are loosely woven and more appropriate when worn for style around a ski lodge than for warmth on a windy ridge. Quality can be determined by trying to blow through the material and observing resistance. Additional raingear is a desirable supplement to either a cotton, polyester/cotton blend, or uncoated nylon parka.

Essential to any parka is a hood that protects the head, neck, and face. The hood should be roomy enough for additional hat(s) inside and should come well up over the chin. A drawstring can close a face tunnel so that only eyes and nose are uncovered. The skirt should extend to the bottom of the hips and there should be a drawstring at the waist and full sleeves with snaps, elastic, or Velcro® tape for wrist closure. Large slash pockets, with buttons or zippers, are useful for warming hands and storing mittens, goggles, and candy bars. Some climbers prefer the pullover design (anorak), for though a front zipper allows easy control of body temperature, a zipper can jam and a parka which cannot be closed will not give full protection when really needed. Parkas equipped with snap or

Velcro® closures in addition to the zipper, offer more versatility and safety. Large-toothed nylon zippers are superior to small-toothed or metal zippers; though they occasionally catch material they rarely tear it and show very little tendency to freeze in cold conditions.

When hiking or climbing in the rain the choice lies between getting wet quickly with cold water from the sky or more slowly with warm water from the body. A variety of light, compact, and fairly durable raingear is available; each presents the same problem in some degree. Many have found raingear made of Gore-Tex® to be very satisfactory.

Full-length ponchos shed the rain and allow more air circulation than parkas; their major faults lie in being so cumbersome as to be restricted to camps and open trails, and almost totally useless in wind. Ponchos are also a trip hazard, especially on rough trails. A coated-nylon poncho which can double as a tarp weighs about ¾ pound.

A rain parka and chaps, or a cagoule (a roomy, knee-length pullover anorak), can be used for protection while moving in a hard rain. Although the cagoule can provide emergency shelter, especially where there is only room to stand, it is a nuisance around the knees and should not be longer. Coated nylon fabrics are lightweight though delicate, and lose their waterproofness with heavy use; plastic is cheap but tears too easily to be reliable; rubberized fabric is durable and waterproof but much too heavy.

Headgear

An unprotected head can account for from one-third to one-half of the body's heat loss. The head, therefore, is the first part to cool when over-heating, and equally important, the most vital part to insulate when chilling (when your feet are cold, put on your hat).

Two to three types of headgear are often carried by climbers for protection of the head from sun, rain, and cold. A white cotton glacier hat is excellent for sun and also cool weather. For warm, rainy trips, a lightweight rain hat keeps rain off the head while allowing some ventilation for the neck area. However, a warm insulative cap of wool, orlon, nylon pile or other synthetic, to fit under the parka hood or hard hat, is necessary for cold weather, emergencies, bivouacs, and warmer sleeping. A wool or orlon balaclava can be rolled up or down to cover the entire head and neck and, even when wet, prevents much loss of body heat.

In the sun many use only a sweat band or a handkerchief knotted at the corners and dampened periodically with water. Others need the more complete protection of a brimmed hat with a handkerchief "tent" hanging down to protect neck and face; many "sheiks" appear in the intense sun of glacier travel.

Mittens and Gloves

Mittens are better than gloves for warmth, allowing the fingers to snuggle together. A pair of synthetic pile or heavy wool mittens, worn inside wind- and water-repellent overmitts when the situation demands, suffices for most climbing. Ideally either the inner mitt or overmitt covers the wrist and laps under or over the parka sleeve. Nylon mittens insulated with 100 per cent polyamid/nylon pile can be wrung out when soaking wet and still retain their insulating loft. If using wool mittens, carry an extra pair in case they become soaked in rain or snow. Some ski mitts have foam insulation which is effective when wet. Leather gloves are vital for belaying and useful in thorny brush but are difficult to waterproof and next to impossible to dry. At very low temperatures (about 0°F), exposed fingers freeze to metal; in these circumstances light silk or nylon gloves worn under mitts allow tasks to be performed without exposing the skin. Fingerless wool gloves may be useful in cold-weather rock climbing; attacking army surplus wool gloves with scissors is an economical approach. If needed, a pair of heavy wool boot socks can be used in an emergency to substitute for lost or wet mittens. To prevent loss, mittens should have a security cord that fastens around the wrist.

PACKS

The climber usually owns two or three packs: a rucksack large enough to hold the necessities for a one-day climb, a large soft pack for weekend trips and/or a frame pack with a bag sufficient to carry camping gear and supplies for a week or more. Most important, any pack should be designed to carry the load high and close to the back (Fig. 2-5); a slight for-

Fig. 2-5. Carry weight high, close to the shoulders. *Left,* pack on hips, forcing a crouch. *Right,* pack high, allowing comfortable upright stance.

ward lean brings the load directly over the feet so that balance is not disturbed. Packs constructed from waterproof materials are not necessarily waterproof. Individual plastic bags can protect the contents of the pack from water but one large plastic bag used as a liner is better and more simple. Dry things are kept inside the liner and wet clothing can be stored between the liner and the outside pack.

Rucksacks

In choosing a rucksack (also known as a summit or day pack) one must be sure it fits well and the capacity is suited to the individual needs (Fig. 2-6). The so-called mini pack (less than 1400 cu. in.) has little use in the mountains. For glacier and winter climbing a bag of 2600 cu. in. may not be large enough to hold the clothing needed for the severe weather often encountered.

The waistband, whether padded or not, adds significantly to comfort and load carrying capacity and is necessary to prevent unpredictable lurching. A double bottom of nylon or leather, haul strap, and ice axe carrier are desirable for alpine climbing. Other accessories on the outside such as side pockets, flap pocket, straps for attaching rope, crampons, and skis are matters of preference and anticipated use. However, a smooth profile (absence of projections) may prevent the pack from catching in chimneys and brush.

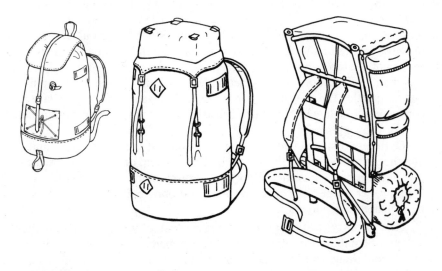

Fig. 2-6. Packs. *Left,* summit rucksack without exterior pockets to snag when hauling up rock faces. *Center,* soft pack, with padded hip band and without protruding pockets to catch on brush or rock. *Right,* external-frame pack with contoured metal frame and padded hip band.

Soft Packs

For weekend climbs some prefer the soft pack, a large rucksack (3000–4000 cu. in.) which usually has an internal frame or stays to maintain shape and transfer the weight of the load to the hips through a substantial waistband (Fig. 2-6). There are many different styles of soft packs available with various combinations of compression and chest straps for added stability. The use of compression straps on a large pack provides both the capacity for the carry into base camp and the capability to reduce the pack size suitable to carry to the summit. Because of its versatility, a pack of this type may be an economical initial investment for the beginning climber. With a proper fit, large rucksacks can carry loads of 35 pounds; even as much as 50 pounds can be supported by some designs, but they do make the back hot and sweaty. Care must be exercised when loading these packs to ensure that the center of gravity is both forward and high in the pack.

Frame Packs

For loads of 30 pounds or more a frame pack (Fig. 2-6) may be more desirable. Consisting of a long, rigid frame held away from the back by taut nylon or mesh backbands, it allows the load to be carried high and shared among shoulders, back, and hips on well padded shoulder straps and a wide, easily adjustable waistband. The waistband performs the vital function of controlling the distribution of load; a snug belt places most of the weight on the hips; a loose belt loads the shoulders more heavily. The frame should be fitted or adjusted so the waistband comes to the top of the hip bones when snugged up, for if the frame is too long the waistband will be too low, restricting leg movement when going uphill and not putting the proper load on the hips. The waistband should have a convenient buckle which must be released before entering an avalanche area or crossing streams.

Optimum distance between shoulder straps at the top of the frame, and the correct length of the straps, both dependent on the skeletal structure of the packer, are other important features in fitting a pack correctly. With proper frame size for torso length and body build, most packs can be adjusted to fit anyone.

New pack styles appear on the market constantly, offering an infinite variety of combinations of pockets, compartments, and closure arrangements, and designed to load through the top, front, or both. Top loaders hold cargo securely but lack the convenience of the front loader. Packs that depend on zippers for load-carrying structure or crucial closures should be approached with caution since failure of a zipper could disable the pack. A full-length sack is preferred by some in order to have a single unit and further protect the sleeping bag from rain and brush. For long trips, the basic frame pack is supplemented by a summit pack for climbing, carried around the sleeping bag during the long-haul backpack to base camp.

MISCELLANEOUS EQUIPMENT

A catalog of sometimes-useful miscellany could easily run to many volumes. This chapter suggests many items that need no elaboration; a few are discussed below, others are discussed in later chapters.

The Mountaineers began their annual Climbing Course in the 1930s, and after a number of incidents, it was determined that many difficulties could have been avoided if each individual climber had been properly equipped to meet emergencies. As a teaching aid, a list of items that must be carried by each climber on every climb was suggested. The list, the bare essentials that an experienced climber would not be without, eventually became known as the Ten Essentials:

1. map of area (in a case)
2. compass
3. flashlight with extra cells and bulbs
4. extra food
5. extra clothing
6. sunglasses
7. first aid kit
8. pocket knife
9. matches in waterproof container
10. firestarter

Map and Compass

A map of the area to be traveled and a suitable compass are complementary essentials; Chapter 5, Navigation, describes both in detail.

Flashlights and Headlamps

Climbs frequently begin before dawn and often end after dark. Every climber must therefore carry a reliable flashlight or headlamp on every climb. A suggested safe minimum for most trips is a flashlight using two C-size carbon-zinc cells and a .27 amp (PR4) bulb plus a spare set of cells and bulb, a combination giving up to six hours of light in continuous use. (A wise precaution is to reverse one cell until the light is needed to prevent accidental discharge in the pack.)

A hand-held flashlight is relatively light and fully satisfactory if hands are not otherwise occupied. The headlamp has important advantages on climbs where rope and ice axe place priority demands on the hands; in emergencies where the climbing party must move over difficult terrain during darkness it can be a lifesaver.

Alkaline cells are 50 per cent heavier than standard carbon-zinc and cost about three times as much, but have a useful life two to four times longer in continuous use. D-size cells have more capacity per unit weight, and thus greater efficiency, than C-size cells. High-amperage bulbs draw more current; low-amperage bulbs give dimmer light but last longer. The use of such bulbs may be considered when extended battery life is desired.

Nickel cadmium rechargeable batteries are being used by some climbers. Although more expensive than alkaline cells, they can be recharged at home between trips up to 1000 times, thus saving a considerable amount of money. Two NiCad C-size cells provide four hours of light, which is adequate for most around-camp situations, but not for long approaches or returns in the dark. The combination of NiCad cells in use plus backup of alkaline cells is economical and provides a margin of safety.

Some climbers are now using lithium cells, which have the attractive features of long shelf life and of maintaining their potential well in the cold. Currently available types, however, are pressurized and if shorted may explode, or more commonly, lose pressure and are dead when needed. Lithium cells are considered to be hazardous material.

Innovative climbers make their own headlamps (Fig. 2-7), but craftsmanship must be of a high order or these assemblies fail in the field. The most common failure is associated with the switch. Properly installed phone plugs and jacks provide positive on-off function and permit a quick and simple change to a fresh battery pack. The battery pack, buried in a warm pocket, will provide a steady flow of current during cold temperatures.

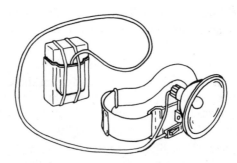

Fig. 2-7. Headlamp. Home-assembled unit with cigarette box as battery pack; suitable for C-cell systems.

Extra Food

It is difficult to be more than forty-eight hours from some kind of civilization in the contiguous United States; however occasionally, due to foul weather, faulty navigation, lost party member(s), or accident, a climbing party does get delayed. A one-day supply of extra food is a reasonable minimum for the generation of energy and heat. This emergency food should require no cooking, be light in weight and easily digestable (such as carbohydrates), and store well in the pack for a long period of time without deterioration. A combination of meat bars, nuts, mint bars, tropical chocolate will work well. To boost morale during such unpleasant delays, some people also prepare cocoa, soup, coffee or tea in a metal cup if a small flame can be sustained.

Extra Clothing

Clothing has been discussed above but the climber must ask himself how many layers of useful clothing can be counted on in an emergency. The garments used during the active portion of a climb and considered to be the regular climbing outfit are inner and outer socks, boots, underwear, trousers, shirt, sweater or second shirt, parka, hat, mitts and/or gloves, raingear etc. These garments will suffice over a wide range of temperature and weather as long as the climber is active. If activity ceases due to delay or forced emergency bivouac, extra clothing is needed to retain as much body heat as possible. Extra food will generate some heat but vital body heat must be retained with warm clothing and shelter.

During a strenuous climb, perspiration can soak clothing and destroy its insulation value. It is important to be able to remove a soaked undershirt and put dry clothing (pile is excellent) next to the skin and then add dry insulation such as a down or synthetic fill garment, along with the other clothing in layers. Protection for the head and neck can be gained by wearing a balaclava. Clean, dry socks will help to warm feet. Polyester or pile mitts are needed for the hands. For winter and expedition climbing, where conditions may be very severe, more insulation above the waist may be needed along with insulated overpants for the legs. The parka (regular clothing) is worn for protection plus a shelter such as a plastic tube tent or trash bags. The various garments should be sized to go on easily without restriction. An insulating seat pad will reduce heat loss through conduction.

A climber may use some of his extra clothing during an extended break from activity such as lunch, but care must be taken to keep them dry. To ensure survival in an emergency, the amount of extra clothing should be adjusted for each trip according to the worst conditions that might be encountered, and the weight and use of each item of clothing carefully evaluated. On extended climbing trips of seven or more days, allowing 2 pounds for food per day, overnight gear, clothing, plus 5 to 10 pounds of technical climbing equipment, the total weight is considerable and every useless ounce must be eliminated.

Glasses — Sun and Prescription

Eyes are particularly vulnerable to the brilliance of mountain skies or light reflected from snow, and if unprotected can quickly be painfully burned or even permanently damaged. The experience is so excruciatingly painful that when once snowblinded, one will never let it happen again. Since the damage occurs before the pain is felt, it is essential for the climber to have sunglasses which greatly reduce the amount of visible light, invisible ultraviolet and infrared rays striking the eyes: passage should be no more than 10 or 15 per cent. Remember: dangerous radiation penetrates even clouds and fog.

The lenses should be very dark, but careful shopping is necessary, since many inexpensive sunglasses offered for sale on the American market are more for style than eye protection. The design should keep light from entering at the sides and bottom, yet give adequate ventilation to prevent fogging. Extra pairs of goggles are worth their weight to any party venturing into the blinding glare of a snowfield or glacier.

In emergency, a piece of cardboard with small slits can save eye damage, though providing minimal vision.

Climbers who need prescription glasses to obtain any clear view of their surroundings encounter special problems. Any climber so nearsighted as to have difficulty traveling treacherous terrain must always carry an extra pair in his rucksack. A good combination in bright conditions is a pair of large, well ventilated ski goggles with very dark lenses worn loosely over prescription lenses; less cumbersome but again more expensive are prescription goggles.

Many climbers carry two degrees of eye protection for differing conditions: an average pair for cloudy weather, trail and meadow travel and rock climbing, and a pair of "dark-dark" goggles for intense glare of snow and high-altitude glacier travel.

First Aid Kit

Many people who continue to hike and climb carry a first aid kit inadequate to treat the injuries that will sooner or later be encountered. Refer to Chapter 19, First Aid, for a summary of common problems and recommended items for a climber's first aid kit.

Knife

In food preparation, in firebuilding, in first aid, in high-angle rock climbing — everywhere in alpine life — a knife is so essential that every climber must carry one. The traditional Boy Scout knife with two folding blades, can opener, combination screwdriver and bottle opener, and sometimes an awl, is handiest and least expensive. The similar Swiss Army knife is superior in every respect but costs more.

Matches and Firestarters

An *emergency* supply of matches, waterproofed or stowed in a watertight container, must always be carried, on each and every trip, in addition to the matches or butane lighter used for routine purposes. Since "waterproof" matches are frequently fireproof as well, an alternative is wooden matches stored with a strip of sandpaper in an absolutely waterproof container. A stub of plumber's candle or a bit of solid chemical fuel ("heat tabs," "canned heat") is indispensable to ignite wet wood, start a fire quickly in an emergency, or, on a glacier when other fuel is lacking, to warm a cup of lifesaving water or juice.

Water Bottle

High peaks are usually bone-dry or solidly frozen, so each climber must carry water. A 1-quart capacity water container generally suffices, but is not enough on more sun-blasted climbs. Wide-mouthed poly bottles are most popular because they can be refilled with snow or from trickles more easily than small-mouthed bottles. With a poly bottle a climber can enjoy fruit juices untainted by the metal salts generated in containers of steel or aluminum.

Sunburn Preventives

Sunlight at high altitudes has a burning capacity many times greater than at sea level—so much greater, especially with reflection from snow, that it is a threat not only to comfort but to health. A tan can be developed painlessly only by controlling the length and intensity of exposure, and since climbers cannot avoid long exposure, they must reduce the intensity of sunlight reaching their skin by the use of clothing wherever possible and sunburn preventives on exposed skin. Individuals vary widely in natural pigmentation and thus in toleration to exposure and in degree of protection needed. There is only one rule: the penalty for underestimation is so severe that no amount of protection can be excessive. Tanned skin, whatever its cosmetic value, offers minor protection against the intense burning of high altitudes.

By far the best sun protection is clothing; even on a hot day the discomfort of covering up is well justified. For areas that cannot be protected with clothing, sunburn preventives containing PABA (p-amino benzoic acid) are being used with success. As with any product, it is important to follow the directions on the container and heed any warnings. Clear preparations require thoroughness to ensure complete coverage, and perhaps repeated application during the day. There are commercial products available which, if not sweated off, effectively block ultraviolet rays. Alcohol-base "suntan" lotions offer little protection even at moderate altitudes.

Actors' grease paint (clown white) or zinc-oxide pastes give virtually complete protection, and a grease base ensures against their being washed off by perspiration. One application is good for the entire climb, except where fingers and equipment rub the skin bare. The major disadvantage of these preparations is that they are somewhat difficult to remove.

The area around the mouth is particularly susceptible to fever blisters resulting from exposure to sun. The lips should be covered with a total-sun-blocking cream or zinc-oxide that resists washing, sweating or licking.

Insect Repellent

Wilderness is the occasional abode of man and the permanent habitat of insects. The more lush the flowered alpine meadow, the greater the profusion of insects. There is no record of malaria or yellow fever contracted from alpine mosquitoes and, except in sub-Arctic ranges, little danger of being bitten to death. The bite is painless and the itching an irritation at worst, so that the hazard is chiefly mental. The ideal remedy for mosquitoes and every other flying bug is a steady breeze. Given a choice between hungry insects and a cold wind the latter is infinitely preferable.

Smallest of the fly family is the "no-see-um" (gnat), usually found in dank river bottoms. Though invisible except in the dusk with the light behind it, this tiny insect gets off a most amazingly painful chew, the more unpleasant because one cannot see the creature to punish him.

On approach marches in western ranges ticks are a nuisance if not a serious health menace. They are most abundant in the springtime of dry lands — local inquiry is advisable. The majority can be thwarted merely by fastening the pants tightly around the boots and then watching for hitch-hikers on pants legs.

A tick discovered during preliminary prospecting will leave the area at a touch. Even after an hour or so of serious drilling a gentle straight-forward pull may still bring it entirely out into the open. Once it is deeply imbedded only surgery by razor blade or physician will do the trick. It may be less painful to take antibiotics and leave the head in the flesh like a thorn to fester and come out days or even weeks later. After camping in infested areas preventive measures should include inspection not only of bodies, but clothing, sleeping bags, tents, packs, and other equipment.

Complete coverage by heavy clothing, including gloves and head nets in extreme conditions, may keep out mosquitoes and flies but not "no-see-ums" or ticks, and in warm weather is most uncomfortable. Insect repellents may therefore be necessary. For general-purpose use the chemical N, N-diethyl-metatoluamide (diethyl toluamide) has been judged most effective. Acting on the principle that the "touch" repulses the insect — it will land but not bite — one application to the skin of one of the stronger concentrations is effective for several hours. Protection is good against mosquitoes, flies, gnats, chiggers, and ticks. Diethyl toluamide in alcohol solution is marketed under several brand names with differing potencies (75 per cent active ingredients being the most potent) and in differing forms such as cream, stick, aerosol spray, and foam. Concentrated solutions do, however, sometimes dissolve the paint on ice axes and other equipment.

Repair and Improvisation

All climbers through experience accumulate emergency kits composed of odd bits and pieces wonderfully versatile in times of trouble: an assortment of wires, tape, safety pins (from blister-puncturing size up to sailors' awls for piercing leather), thread, razor blades, yarn, squares of patching fabric, coils of nylon string, small pliers — the list could be extended indefinitely. Generally climbers — with 20-20 hindsight — carry those items they wish they had carried on some past climb.

Ice Axe

The numerous uses of the ice axe and its specifications are discussed in Chapter 6, Wilderness Travel, and Chapter 13, Basic Snow Travel. It is mentioned here because of its indispensability on snowfields, glaciers and snowcovered alpine trails in spring and early summer. It has great value in traveling steep heather, scree, brush, crossing streams by log or ford, and digging sanitation holes. An axe is nearly useless and can be dangerous if carried on steep snow by a person who is not practiced in its use.

EQUIPMENT CHECKLIST

It is difficult on journey's eve to remember everything that may be needed. The more quickly one packs, the more easily an item may be forgotten. Seasoned climbers have learned, often as not through sad experience, that a systematic run through a checklist is the only sure way, no matter how many times they have packed their sacks for past trips. The following example is representative, though by no means either universal or complete; each person should make his own list, building upon the Ten Essentials. For more technical climbing climbers will choose specialized equipment which best satisfies their requirements and fancy. Items that may be shared in small groups are indicated by an asterisk — *; those in parentheses are optional, depending on personal preference and the nature of the trip.

All Trips

In Pack   *Other*

Ten Essentials   ice axe
 1. map of area (in a case)   emergency shelter
 2. compass   metal cup
 3. flashlight with extra   (insulating seat pad)
    cells and bulbs   water bottle
 4. extra food   lunch
 5. extra clothing (socks,   sunburn preventive
    mitts, sweater, shirt,   (lip protection)
    balaclava, down or   handkerchief
    synthetic fill garment,   toilet paper
    etc.)   whistle
 6. sunglasses   insect repellent
 7. first aid kit   (nylon cord)
 8. pocket knife   (altimeter)
 9. matches in waterproof   (inexpensive watch)
    container   (camera and film)
10. firestarter   (binocular)

Clothing

boots   (gaiters)
socks, inner and outer   (wind/rain pants)
underwear   (long underwear)
pants   (raingear)
warm sweater and shirt   (shorts)
parka, wind/rain   (hot weather shirt)
hats (wool, rain, sun)
mittens, gloves
down or synthetic garments

Additional for Overnight and Longer Trips

frame pack/soft pack,   *(water container)
   rucksack   (personal hygiene)
sleeping bag and stuff sack   *repair kit — pliers, wire,
sleeping pad or mattress   cord, needle, thread,
*shelter — tent and   pins, clevis pin and
   accessories, tarp,   split ring
   groundsheet   (spare clothing)
*food   (spare underwear)
spoon   (camp footgear)

*stove, accessories and
    fuel
*pots, accessories,
    scouring pad

(down booties)
(pack cover)

Additional for Glacier or Winter Climbs

ice axe
crampons
carabiners
slings (chest, prusik)
seat harness
(hard hat)
(avalanche cord)
*climbing rope
*rescue pulley
*(flukes, pickets, ice
    screws)
*(wands)
*snow shovel
*(igloo saw)
(snowshoes or skis, poles)

additional warm clothing
    mitten shells
    extra mittens, socks
    balaclava
    long underwear
    (down or synthetic fill
        clothing)
extra goggles
(extra candles)
(stove and fuel)
additional leader gear
    (alarm timepiece)
    (group first aid)
    (headlamp and batteries)

Additional for Basic Rock Climbs

hard hat
carabiners
belay gloves
runners
seat harness

*climbing rope
*(chocks)
*(pitons, hammer)

Plate 4. Mt. Formidable from campsite at Kool Aid Lake, North Cascades. (Bob and Ira Spring)

3 *

CAMPING AND
SLEEPING

A CLIMBING CAMP is not always a comfortable, snug, alpine haven, but if proximity to the summit is the determining factor, a bivouac on a ledge of the mountain itself may be dictated, since the way to gain an extra hour for the climb is to camp an hour higher on the mountain. Forests ordinarily provide easy and excellent camps but often are too far below the peaks for reasonable summit attempts. Meadows above timberline offer the best sites in terms of esthetics, but because of their brief growing season are the most fragile of the mountain ecosystems.

Whatever the goal, concern for the environment should have equal weight with concern for comfort. Heathers must bloom, seed, and add their fraction of an inch of growth within a brief two-month period, and at their exceedingly slow growth rate damage done to plants by an overnight stay may require many years of recovery. Grasses are more resilient, yet a tarp or tent left on a meadow turf for a week may wipe out an entire growing season for the covered patch; moving a permanent camp every few days reduces the harm done any one spot. A rock slab is least vulnerable, and thus from this point of view, best; a sandy or gravelly flat, and open, plant-sparse areas in deep forest, in that order, are slightly less ideal.

A large proportion of long-established campsites in American mountains are on the banks of lakes and streams. However waterside plant life are so especially delicate, and water pollution such a growing problem with the backcountry population explosion of recent years, that in many areas camping already is officially banned within 100 or 200 feet of highland lakes and creeks.

Charms of the view and the immediate locality often influence choice of site, but microclimatology also must be given consideration: wind is the most active cooling agent and its capricious alpine behavior can be quite exasperating. Patterns of flow are often highly localized, with a full gale blasting one patch of meadow, while a few yards away the flowers droop in still and sultry air. Also to be considered is the relationship of wind to tent: pitched with the wind blowing in the open end, the tent distends, interior pressure equalizing exterior and minimizing "flap." But alpine winds are instantaneously reversible without warning—a tarp strung as a windbreak in afternoon may become a balloon after sunset. One consolation of foul weather is that storm winds are fairly consistent.

Frequently an up-slope afternoon breeze reverses at night to an icy down-slope draft from snowfields. Cold air is heavier than warm air and in settled weather flows downward like water, following valleys and collecting in depressions. Thus there is often a chill breeze down a creek or dry wash and a pool of cold air in a basin. Night air is often degrees cooler beside a river or lake than on benches or knolls above.

SHELTER

In most mountains the weather is untrustworthy and huts are scarce, and therefore many alpine travelers carry portable shelter. *Tents* and *tarps* both have virtues and vices, and each for some conditions is unquestionably superior. Certainly a tent is the only shelter worthy of the name above timberline, for glacier camps, winter, in strong winds, and in mosquito country. Of prime importance, it can be erected almost anywhere, being a self-contained unit. The main criticism of tents is that they are either heavy or expensive, and no serious mountaineer can afford the burden of a cheap, heavy tent.

Curiously enough, shelter is often more necessary on a clear night than on a cloudy one: whenever two opposing surfaces differ in temperature, the warmer radiates heat to the colder. Since the human body is usually warmer than the night sky, exposed portions of the body or sleeping bag radiate heat and grow cold. Any shelter at all serves as a baffle: a climber sacked out under a tree may sleep cozy and warm while companions a few feet away shiver under the stars, where, under certain conditions, their problems may be compounded by a heavy dew saturating their sleeping bags. Clouds often reflect heat back to earth and thus have the effect of a huge tarp between sleeper and sky; the clear nights are the cold ones.

Tarps

A tarp is both light in weight and low in cost, and offers adequate shelter from all but extreme weather in lowland forests and among subalpine trees. It gives less protection than a tent from heat loss and wind, and none at all from insects, but allows more convenient study of natural science and scenic splendor. On the debit side, setting up a tarp demands human ingenuity and some co-operation from the landscape.

Tarps of polyethylene are inexpensive and though not as durable as nylon, the cost is so small that frequent replacement is economically feasible (carry every shred home for disposal!). Coated nylon tarps come with reinforced grommets sewn into sides and corners for easy rigging. Tarps lacking grommets can be rigged by tying off each corner around a small cone or pebble or with a Visklamp®—a small rubber ball and a dumbbell-shaped metal gadget (Fig. 3-1). Another method is permanently attached loops of nylon tape.

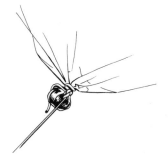

Fig. 3-1. Tarps without grommets can be secured by wrapping tarp edge around a small object and tying as shown.

The most versatile size is about 9 by 12 feet, providing luxurious living room for two people and their gear and adequate for three, or even four if they are small people or very good friends. An 11- by 14-foot size will house four more comfortably. In smaller sizes the usable space approaches the vanishing point, since the outer margins of tarp-covered ground are usually only half-protected, if that.

Rigging a tarpaulin shelter is an art using only a few basic designs but unlimited variations: the architect needs imagination and experience to become a master.

The weary climber who wraps himself in the tarp as if it were a large blanket is protected from wind but generally finds himself damp from his own perspiration by morning.

The A-tent design (Fig. 3-2a) resembles a true tent, the tarp being draped over a line stretched between two supports, its edges fastened down on either side. Trees, large boulders, or telescoping tent poles can be employed as end supports, but if these are lacking, either one or two bipods can be improvised, as shown in the illustration. Maximum protection in wind-driven rain is gained by rigging the tarp as close to the ground as needs for head room will allow, edges flush to the ground, anchored with a large log, rocks or ridge of snow (Fig. 3-2b). The windward foot or two will be wet, so ample overhang should be allowed. In calm weather the edges may be raised some distance in the air for spacious and gracious living.

The *shed roof* (Fig. 3-2c), with four corners tied to anything handy, covers more floor area than the A-tent; though of no value in high wind it is ideal in mild weather or gently falling rain.

Other designs can be improvised (Fig. 3-2d and e), but whatever the design, a tarp must be rigged with tight lines to reduce flapping in the wind and to provide proper roof drainage. Tarp campers customarily carry a considerable quantity of strong, light nylon cord to enable them to use any conceivable kind of anchor points.

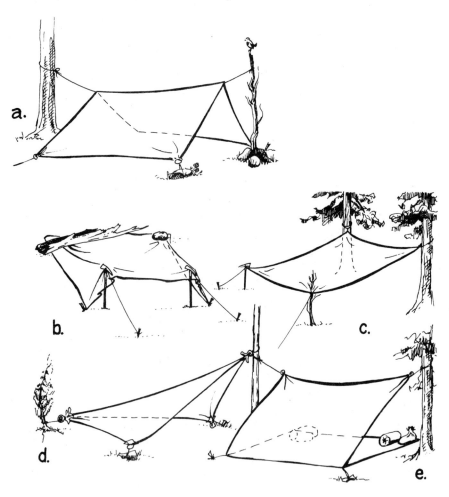

Fig. 3-2. Shelters improvised from tarps.

When terrain allows two tarps to be pitched together the waste area is much decreased, whether the two be overlapped at or along the ridge in a giant A-tent or side by side in a shed. With such "circus tents" vast regions may be covered, so that even a prolonged rain or drizzle can be outwaited in comparative freedom and comfort.

Polyethylene ground sheets are necessary under a tarp. Normally water stays below the sheet, but sudden rains sometimes cause floods not foreseen when camp was made. Ditching, that is digging drainage channels around tents or tarps, is not an acceptable practice: meadow turf is usually a tangle of struggling roots, severance of which can damage plants several feet away. If ground water is a problem, moving camp, though a nuisance, is the best solution.

Equipment as well as climbers needs shelter. Whenever space is cramped within tent or under tarp it is well to carry a number of large plastic sacks and sheets of plastic for dry storage outside. In wet mountains the few extra ounces are worth the weight.

Tents

Tents offer greater protection and comfort than tarps, though of course at greater cost. The choice of a tent depends upon its intended use and individual preferences. Will it be used only in the summer or for three or four seasons? above or below timberline? Will it need to accommodate two people or three or four? Is luxurious space desired, or just the bare minimum? Is the lightest weight available required or will a few extra pounds be tolerated? How much to spend? With the proliferation of tent manufacturers over the past few years, almost any combination of size, shape, weight and design features is now available, and the choice can be almost overwhelming. Many hours of poring over mountain shop catalogs are required. Better still is observation of tents in use; owners are generally willing to discuss the advantages and shortcomings of their models.

Tents are constructed with either single or double walls, of either waterproof or breathable materials. A completely enclosed unit must be well ventilated and preferably should "breathe." If the tent is made of completely waterproof material, the moisture exhaled by occupants condenses on the cold walls and runs down to collect in puddles on the floor. In a single night two persons can expel enough water vapor from lungs to drench sleeping bags. Nevertheless, some very inexpensive tents are constructed of one layer of waterproof material. Such tents cannot be recommended except for the mildest of conditions below timberline where the door and windows can be left open for ventilation. Even so, some condensation inside must be expected.

The ideal material for a tent is one which will both breathe and keep out a driving rain. With the recent development of Gore-Tex®, a thin membrane of polytetrafluoroethylene laminated to various fabrics, the dream of a generation of tent users seems to have come true. But it is not without its disadvantages: it must be kept scrupulously clean. Once contaminated by dirt or body oils, the membrane will leak, although proper cleaning will restore the original waterproof properties. There have also been some reports that at low temperatures Gore-Tex® will ice up and thus cease to breathe. Nevertheless, most of the lightest—and most expensive—tents for their size are made of Gore-Tex® and evidence to date seems to confirm that they do work under most conditions and with proper care.

Before the development of Gore-Tex®, the dilemma of a waterproof yet breathable tent was solved by using a double wall—a breathable layer covered by a waterproof layer, usually in the form of a separate rain fly. The majority of mountain tents are still designed using this principle.

The rain fly of a double-wall tent should be designed not to touch the inner walls when properly rigged; where it touches, the condensation effect is the same as in a waterproof tent. The fly should also come fairly close to the ground to adequately cover the tent and entrance and minimize exposure to wind-driven rain. Some models have a built-in rain fly rather than a separate one. Although many climber-years of experience prove that the double-wall design lets moisture out but not in, it should be kept in mind that under certain conditions some condensation will occur in any tent, regardless of construction. Condensation commonly forms on waterproof side panels which extend a foot or more up from the floor in some tents; sleeping bags should be kept away from these damp areas.

Another rather recent design uses two very lightweight layers, the outer one waterproof, and a carefully designed ventilation system to prevent condensation. These tents are even lighter for their size than Gore-Tex® tents, but as might be expected, are also very expensive.

Shapes of tents vary widely (Fig. 3-3). The trend has been to tunnel and free-standing dome-shaped styles, which make maximum use of available space and minimize the number of stakes and guylines needed. In fact the free-standing tents need no guylines at all and can be picked up and moved as a unit, but must still be staked out in a hard wind to prevent their blowing away.

The old standby, the A-frame tent can still be found. Although not giving as much internal space for the same dimensions as a tunnel or dome tent, it is a simpler, hence generally less expensive, design and has proven its worth over the years. Some A-frame tents have been redesigned to eliminate the frequently annoying entrance guyline.

The two-person tent is probably the most popular size, offering the greatest flexibility in weight and choice of campsite. Many two-person tents are large enough to accommodate three people in a pinch, yet light enough to be used by one person occasionally. However, there is no denying that the larger space of three- and four-person tents, especially those high enough to stand in, are profoundly helpful to morale during a long stormy spell. Some of the three- and four-person tents are light enough to be carried by two people — really luxurious living.

Various entrance designs offer zip doors, tunnels, alcoves, vestibules and hoods. Careful scrutiny of the entrance is in order to determine that a minimum amount of rain or snow is admitted when entering or exiting; some designs are notably lacking in such consideration. Many options are also offered in the arrangement and type of ventilation holes, windows, mosquito netting and other features.

Fig. 3-3. Mountain tents. *Top,* free-standing dome tent. *Bottom left to right,* tunnel tent, and A-frame tent.

In general, cooking inside a tent cannot be recommended, particularly with gasoline stoves. Besides the danger from combustion fumes, any spilled fuel or flare-up is a very real fire hazard. Cooking also adds greatly to inside condensation. Nevertheless, under certain circumstances cooking inside a tent is unavoidable; in such cases, a cook hole or cooking alcove and well placed ventilation holes can lessen the danger.

The psychological and esthetic value of tent color is a consideration. Brighter hues are more pleasing to the tent-bound and have practical value to the climber seeking camp in fog or dark. On the other hand, more subdued hues blend into the background, lessening the intrusion upon the landscape.

Snow Camps

A snow camp can be warm and comfortable, but in no other camp is insulation so important or shelter so essential. Every person who goes

into the mountains must carry or be able to improvise the minimum requirements for a comfortable night — or at the very least for survival — on
snow.

The most convenient shelter is a *tent* installed on a stamped-out platform slightly larger than the floor. Regular stakes may be replaced by
"deadmen," bags filled with snow or rocks. Stakes themselves can be used
as deadmen by burying them in a trench in a horizontal position and perpendicular to the guyline; more serviceable deadmen can be prepared in
advance by drilling holes in a stake or metal plate and attaching a bridle
to which the tent guyline is then tied (Fig. 3-4).

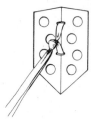

Fig. 3-4. Deadman tent stake.

Heavy, wet snow should not be allowed to pile up on the tent or fly:
forces on the rigging may become excessive and bring the whole structure
down on the occupants. Continual shaking of tent walls and even
shoveling out along the sides are often required.

In forests a natural shelter can often be found in a *tree cave*; some
snow engineering, a tarp, and lots of ingenuity make a snug hideaway in
the worst blow or heaviest rainstorm. In the absence of trees similar shelter can be improvised by digging a *trench* in the snow some 4 to 6 feet deep
and large enough to accommodate the party, then stretching a tarp over
the top, perhaps gaining a slight pitch by anchoring one side to a ridge of
snow. Though excellent in windy or rainy weather, a heavy snowfall can
easily and disastrously collapse a roof so nearly flat.

A *snow cave* (Fig. 3-5) requires more time but provides more protection during a storm. There is absolutely no comparison between the comfort of a calm, quiet cave and a flapping, gale-swept tent. In emergencies,
snow caves have so often meant survival that mountaineers consider
knowledge of the construction technique mandatory.

Although a snow cave can be dug by hand, the job is made much
easier by a lightweight shovel, with which a cave for four can be dug in an
hour or so, depending on snow conditions. All that is necessary in fairly
firm snow is a minimum depth of about 6 feet; a steep slope such as along
a riverbank or snowdrift is desirable. The first step is to dig an entry-way
into the slope deep enough to start a tunnel. Continue to dig inward about
3 feet to form the entrance, then upward to make the living area large
enough for the party. The floor of the sleeping area should be above the

top of the entry tunnel to trap warm air inside. The upper surfaces should be smooth and concave so that any melting snow will run down the walls rather than drip on occupants. To avoid asphyxiation, a ventilation hole is made to the outside and enlarged as necessary if the interior becomes too warm. A ground sheet on the sleeping area is necessary to keep things dry and prevent loss of equipment in the snow.

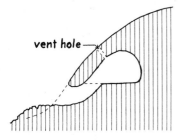

Fig. 3-5. Snow cave.

Under some conditions unsuitable for snow caves, *snow-block shelters* can be constructed. The trench igloo (Fig. 3-6) can be built on either a flat area or in a hillside as a quick emergency shelter for one or two people. A narrow trench is excavated by cutting blocks, roofed over A-frame style with the blocks. Then the interior can be enlarged by digging. The traditional igloo requires proper snow consistency or preparation and a certain amount of expertise for success.

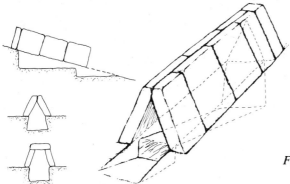

Fig. 3-6. Trench igloo.

The environmental impact of snow camping is often not immediately recognized; tin cans, leftover food and human wastes are obliterated by falling snow, only to reappear, unsightly, with the spring thaw. *Pick up immediately any litter that drops in the snow and stow it away to be packed out.*

SLEEPING BAGS

Warmest and lightest of all conventional designs is the mummy bag (Fig. 3-7), tapering toward the feet, hooded to fit over the head, and with a small face opening that can be closed with drawstrings to shut out wind. The unfortunate few suffering from claustrophobia use a rectangular bag, despite its extra weight and broad, breezy opening. A lighter combination than a conventional bag is a half bag and insulated parka, since many climbers regularly carry a parka anyway.

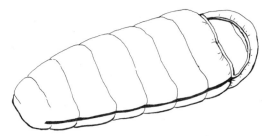

Fig. 3-7. Mummy bag.

Zippers are the almost universal means of closure even though they sometimes snag the fabric or go off the trolley. Heat loss through the zipper is reduced by backing it up with a tube of insulating material. Bags without zippers thus reduce weight and eliminate closure problems, but complicate access.

The warmth, weight, and cost of a sleeping bag are chiefly functions of the kind and quantity of insulation—down or a synthetic polyester. No one has yet improved on nature: down is still the most efficient insulator per unit weight for a sleeping bag. Its chief disadvantages are its high cost and its absorbency. Once wet, down loses most of its insulating value, and is for all practical purposes impossible to dry out in wet mountains. Polyesters, on the other hand, are resistant to moisture, retain most of their loft when wet, and dry relatively quickly. They are also much less expensive than down. Bags made with polyester are still slightly heavier than comparable down styles and do not compress quite as easily, thus making a bulkier load. But polyester bags are becoming more popular as research developments improve the material and as down continues to increase in price.

The warmth of a sleeping bag depends on the entrapment of dead air. The loft, or inches of thickness, determines the effectiveness of insulation: more loft, more dead air. The amount of fill a bag requires for a certain loft depends on the style, the method of construction, the size and the type of insulation of the bag. Therefore two bags with the same weight of fill may have quite different comfort ranges. Sleeping bags can be categorized as recommended for summer, three-season, or winter expedition use. Most manufacturers rate their bags with optimistic minimum comfort temperatures, but these ratings are at best an educated guess and not even entirely consistent from one manufacturer to another. Whether or not a particular bag will be comfortable for a particular person at a given temperature depends upon a number of factors: shelter (if any), ground insulation, additional clothing worn, and whether the individual is a husky young adult sleeping off a steak or a frail senior citizen who skipped dinner.

Three basic construction methods are used in down bags to keep the fill uniformly distributed: sewn-through, slant tube, and overlapping tube (Fig. 3-8). Sewn-through construction is just that: the inner cover is stitched directly to the outer, a simple and inexpensive method, but one with substantial heat loss at the seams. The majority of down bags are made with slant tube construction, which eliminates cold spots at the seams. The most efficient design, overlapping tubes, is used only in the most expensive bags. In addition many designs use channel blocks, baffles that prevent down from shifting.

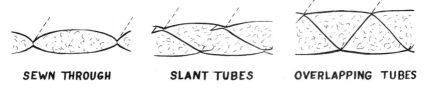

SEWN THROUGH   SLANT TUBES   OVERLAPPING TUBES

Fig. 3-8. Construction of down bags.

Most polyester bags are constructed with sandwiched layers of polyester batts, but some inexpensive summer-weight bags have sewn-through construction — and cold spots along seams — similar to those described for down. The more sophisticated shingle construction method uses batts of polyester stitched alternately to the outer shell and the inner lining (Fig. 3-9).

SEWN THROUGH   SANDWICH   SHINGLE

Fig. 3-9. Construction of polyester bags.

Dirt decreases the insulating capability of any sleeping bag. A removable washable liner, which adds a few ounces, or spot cleaning of soiled areas, especially around the head of the bag, prolongs the time between cleanings, but a thorough cleaning may eventually be necessary. A durable outer cover of breathable material adds weight but also some insulation and protection from moisture and abrasion.

Both down and polyester bags can be hand-washed at home with any mild soap, or with one of the special down soaps now available, which do an excellent job of cleaning. Rinsing should be thorough to remove *all* traces of soap. Excess water can be squeezed gently out by hand or the bag can be spun gently in the spin cycle of an automatic washing machine. (A down bag must be handled carefully when wet to prevent damage to the inner structure.) The bag can then be dried at the lowest heat setting in a dryer or air-dried outside, with more time allowed for a down bag, and frequent shaking and turning to break up lumps of wet down. A down bag can also be dry cleaned, but only by a professional who knows how to handle down, and only if thoroughly aired afterwards to remove all traces of toxic fluids which can cause illness or even death. Polyester bags should not be dry cleaned.

Every effort should be made to keep the sleeping bag dry, particularly if it is down. Polyester bags are not quite so difficult to dry, but in the absence of good weather, or time to spread and turn and fluff the bag, or a fire (and attendant sparks), a wet polyester bag is still a wet polyester bag, and not as warm as a dry bag. Most sleeping bag stuff sacks are not waterproof and should be additionally covered or lined with waterproof plastic bags, particularly if the bag is to be carried on the outside of a frame pack.

Wearing wet clothing to bed can result in some drying, but at the expense of a cold sleep and wet bag, and is therefore not advisable. (In good weather clothing will dry more effectively next day over a bush in camp or hung from the pack while traveling, and in bad weather it will in any event get wet again very quickly.) In cold conditions *small* clothing items, such as mittens and socks, can be taken into the bag to dry. In very cold weather boots should be taken inside the sleeping bag, wrapped in a plastic bag, to prevent freezing.

Closing the bag around the face allows more immediate warming of the interior, a process also speeded by undressing inside the bag. A wool hat provides additional insulation for the head, and dry socks help warm cold feet. Heat loss from exhalation can be reduced by breathing through a sweater; pulling the head inside the bag warms both quickly but adds considerably to interior moisture.

GROUND INSULATION

Since down, and to a lesser extent polyester, compresses under body weight to almost nothing, additional insulation underneath is desirable for a warm bed. On wet ground or snow it is essential. Extra clothing, pack frame, rope, and boots can be used for improvised padding but a foam or air mattress is more comfortable (Fig. 3-10).

An *air mattress* provides the softest bed for its weight and bulk; however, on snow or cold ground convection currents within the air chambers carry heat away from the body. A thin foam pad on top of the mattress increases warmth.

Fig. 3-10. Sleeping on pack and gear.

A relatively thin (⅜-inch) pad of *closed-cell foam,* such as *ensolite* (more durable) or polyethylene foam (lighter weight) provides good insulation under the bag. An 1½-inch-thick pad of open-cell foam is also often used. Less Spartan than ⅜-inch sheets on hard ground, it makes a bulky roll and must be protected from absorbing water. Some foam products are not adaptable to temperatures below 0°F. The self-inflating air mattress, such as Therm-A-Rest®, combines the insulation of open-cell foam and the cushioning of an air mattress.

A 4-foot-long pad or mattress is adequate under most conditions, since items of equipment can be used to support and insulate feet and legs.

In spite of tradition, the destruction of alpine plants and the strewing of resultant dead foliage are so repugnant that bough beds are not to be considered an alternative except in the direst of emergencies. Retaining their insulation and comfort so briefly, they rarely justify the time, effort, and vandalism necessary for their construction. Modern materials are so light, versatile, comfortable, and inexpensive as to render bough beds obsolete.

BIVOUACS

In American terminology a bivouac is a camp made in the course of a climb using only materials that can easily be carried in a rucksack. For long ascents bivouacs are often planned and their rigors lessened by down or polyester clothing, a special bivouac sack, cagoule, or perhaps merely a tarp and extra clothing. Although a planned bivouac ordinarily occurs only on a difficult climb where the weight of special equipment must be kept low, a pound or so extra per person is worthwhile for safety and additional comfort.

Shelter from wind and/or rain is most essential. Every climber should carry an emergency shelter consisting of a lightweight plastic tube (or two very large plastic trash bags). Better yet for a planned bivouac is either a cagoule, which is large enough to cover the whole body when the knees are drawn up to the chest, or a *bivouac sack* — a large, tent-like envelope of tightly woven fabric, just large enough to accommodate one or two persons, needing no poles or stakes, but equipped with strong loops for anchoring to rocks or pitons. A Gore-Tex® sleeping bag cover, used without a sleeping bag as a bivouac sack, is efficient enough for regular use in place of tarp or tent for ordinary camps too. For insulation in cold weather a half-length down or polyester bag weighing about a pound can be used with a jacket. Another alternative is fitting a *bivouac sleeve* inside the pack; the climber puts his feet in the pack and pulls the sleeve up over his legs and hips, protecting upper torso and extremities with waterproof parka or poncho. Body heat should always be utilized and the entire party should huddle together as much as possible for warmth.

More common is the bivouac forced by such unanticipated delays as an accident or loss of route. At low altitudes extra clothing, a small (12- to 14-inch) square insulating pad (sit-upon) and a hot drink prepared over a stove or *small* fire will dispel most discomfort.

In organizing a bivouac on a peak anything or anyone liable to fall — packs, bivouac sack, and climbers — is anchored. Body heat is conserved by brushing snow from clothing, exchanging damp garments for dry, removing (and carefully anchoring) wet boots, placing feet with dry socks in the rucksack, loosening belt and items of clothing that impede circulation, and donning all warm clothing such as hats, scarf, and mitts.

In reasonably good weather a high-altitude bivouac can be a memorable experience, with physical miseries more than repaid by a sky that reveals a wealth of unsuspected stars, but in bad weather that same bivouac can be dangerous in itself and leave the party seriously debilitated by morning.

A bivouac can be made any place with minimum equipment and time and extracts the maximum possible comfort from terrain and materials available. Every climber, in planning every trip, should consider what he takes in terms of a bivouac, asking, "Could I survive in bad weather with only this equipment?"

Plate 5. Twin Sisters, North Cascades. (Bruce Gaumond)

Plate 6. Lyman Glacier, below Chiwawa Mountain, North Cascades. (Bob and Ira Spring)

4 *

ALPINE CUISINE

CLIMBERS EAT PRIMARILY to provide fuel for reaching summits. In theory, therefore, some standard menu could be devised, such as cube sugar, margarine, dried beef, powdered milk, prunes, and vitamin supplements, which would serve for every excursion, short or long. It is even possible that these ingredients or their chemical equivalents could be homogenized and pressed into compact, durable bars imprinted with the recommended daily dosage.

However, the mountain experience is considerably more complex than a track meet, and includes not only victories on peaks but such small joys as a nice cup of tea. Good food gives a festive touch, improves the scenery, and keeps up spirits during days of storm and fog. Bad food makes trails steeper, beds lumpier, sunsets paler, and friends harder to get along with.

Nonetheless, few people go into the wilderness primarily to eat. If fueling the body quickly and simply is the first aim of alpine cuisine, the enjoyment of meals is at least a worthy secondary objective.

COOKING

Little or no physiological basis has been found for addiction to hot food. However, the habit is hard to kick for much more than a weekend, so most climbers heat some of their food. The alternative is demonstrated by the peakbagger munching sandwiches and raisins.

The warmth of flames and hot food can be lifesaving, but in the many wilderness areas that prohibit fires, building one may be justified only in a survival or search-and-rescue situation. Similarly a stove or chemical fire may be invaluable when weather, darkness, or accident force a halt on glacier or cliff. The Complete Wilderness Traveler is always prepared with adequate clothing, heat-conserving survival techniques, and food reserves that require no cooking. This same Traveler is never caught without dry matches in a suitable weatherproof container, and has the ability to start an emergency fire in adverse conditions.

The contemporary mountaineer generally cooks meals over one of the currently available special-purpose stoves, gaining the advantages of speed, simplicity, and lessened impact on the environment with a relatively small amount of extra weight in the pack.

Solid fuels carried primarily as firestarters are light and cheap, but serve only for limited cooking, such as providing hot drinks on a bivouac. A stove with a pressure tank, burning kerosene, gasoline (petrol or benzine), or liquefied gas, is indispensable for a normal amount of cooking, or if the only available water is melted snow.

A number of ingenious, lightweight, and reliable backpacker-oriented stoves are available (Fig. 4–1). Each has advantages, each has special tricks. The climber should make first acquaintance with the stove at home, and then escalate the relationship through steadily less ideal conditions. Kept in good working order these stoves last for years.

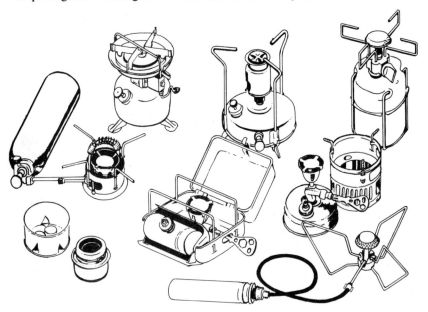

Fig. 4-1. Top: left to right, white gas stove, kerosene stove, butane stove. *Middle: left to right,* multi-fuel stove with pump, white gas stove with enclosure, white gas stove. *Bottom: left to right,* can for hexamine tabs, alcohol burner, and lightweight stove using butane lighter refill canister.

Mountaineering stoves typically weigh 500 gms empty (1 + pounds) and burn about an hour on 0.3 liters of fuel (approximately ½ pint). Stoves are available either with or without pumps. In non-pump versions pressure is initially built up by burning a small amount of fuel in a priming cup on top of the tank, then is maintained by heat from the burner. Stoves having fuel pumps are generally started more readily. The stoves using pressurized liquid petroleum gas — butane or propane — ignite directly without preheating or pumping. Use only specially refined or white *gasoline* prepared for pressurized stoves in all gas stoves. All automotive gasoline, including "unleaded" gas, must be avoided. Fuel prepared for pressurized stoves is preferred as being less likely to clog jets, build up excessive pressure, or emit toxic fumes. *Kerosene* produces about the same heat per equal weight as gasoline, but is less volatile. Kerosene-burning stoves are pressurized with a pump, in addition to being primed with alcohol or gasoline.

Stoves fueled with disposable cartridges of *liquid butane gas* are comparable to gasoline stoves in weight and heating capacity. They are much simpler to operate, but low temperatures can reduce efficiency to the point of non-functioning unless the fuel is warmed. At higher elevations, because atmospheric pressure is less and the pressure within the cartridge relatively more, butane can be used at lower temperatures. Table 4-a summarizes representative altitude/temperature limits.

Table 4-a. Typical Butane Stove Lower Temperature Limits.

Elevation		Temperature	
sea level		0°C	32°F
5,000 ft	1525 m	−5.6°C	22°F
10,000 ft	3050 m	−10.6°C	13°F
15,000 ft	4575 m	−15.6°C	4°F

The choice of a climber's stove should take into account fuel preferences and availabilities, altitude and temperatures of intended use, and, finally, personal preference and confidence in its use and reliability.

When a self-pressurizing stove is set on snow it must be insulated to prevent tank pressure from falling. A small square of masonite or ensolite is adequate for insulation and stability.

The chief enemy of any stove is wind, which reduces efficiency. A protected flame — for example, in a tent — may be closed down for efficiency, but an unprotected stove must be kept roaring to combat wind — very wasteful of fuel. Various combination wind shields and cooking pot supporters are available for mountaineering stoves; pot lids also conserve heat. Most of the mountaineering and backpacker type stoves will boil approximately 1 liter (1 quart) of water at sea level in 7 to 12 minutes. Wind can increase this to 18 to 25 minutes, or even prevent boiling entirely.

A strong cautionary note on stove and lantern safety is appropriate at this point: tents have been blown up, equipment burned, and people injured by careless stove and lantern handling. Apply rules of safety and common sense: never change pressurized fuel cartridges in a tent or near other burning stoves. Fuel occasionally escapes and can be ignited or trapped in the tent, exploding when the stove or lantern is relit. Always fill and start liquid fueled stoves and lanterns outside the tent and away from other open flames. Fuel can be spilled and stoves or lanterns often flare up when first started or restarted.

On a long trip when fuel must be conserved, stove-cookery requires careful planning to ensure that something is always on the flame and that the flame is always kept low, never licking up the sides of the pot.

Melting snow for all of one's water *or* cooking outside a tent can require *twice* as much fuel as cooking inside a tent. Extra fuel should be carried in a tightly closed metal container, with a screw top backed up by a rubber gasket, plainly marked to avoid confusion, and stowed in an outer pocket of the bag to prevent food contamination. Fuel stored in polyethelene containers gradually diffuses out through the plastic.

HOUSEKEEPING

Cooking and Eating Utensils

Aluminum cooking pots have nearly replaced the various sizes of tin cans once found at every campsite. Bails are desirable for handling and carrying and pot lids to keep in heat and steam, improving efficiency.

Typically a meal is cooked in two pots: one 3-liter (1 liter = approximately 1 quart) size for the main-dish "stew" for four people and a smaller 1½-liter size for tea and other drinks. The large pot is the "grease pot" and the smaller is kept grease-free, seldom requiring cleaning. For two people the 1½-liter size is adequate for the main course; for a party of six a 4-liter size is best.

The simplest eating utensils are a single large cup (or small pot) and a spoon. Some people like to use a bowl besides.

Dishwashing

On weekend trips it is easiest to carry dishes and pots home dirty; a chore that is rarely better than inconvenient in the hills is quickly done in a kitchen. On longer trips where utensils are used more than once they must be kept reasonably clean. As soon as emptied, cooking pots should be filled with water and left to soak, or cleaned immediately.

Teflon-coated pots are easier to clean, but greater care is required, as the coating may be easily damaged with metal or abrasive cleaners. In general, woven plastic or metal scouring pads are useful weapons against burned-on stew and add negligible weight to the pack. Cleaning pots with sand, gravel, or grass leaves unsightly bits of food solids around lakes and streams to attract flies and rodents. Uneaten foods are a problem and should be carried out or disposed of well away from the water supply. Too much food indicates poor planning.

Soaps or biodegradable detergents are used cautiously if at all. Parties commonly remain healthy on week-long trips without so much as a pinch of soap by taking moderate care in cleaning pots with hot water after each meal. Utensils on which soap has been used must be thoroughly rinsed to avoid unpleasant symptoms in the lower digestive tract — better a bit of grease. Soapy water must not be disposed of near stream or lake, but added to the ground where it will do the least harm.

Frustrating Animals

Hungry rodents and bears will gnaw through plastic bags, packs, and even tents to get an easy meal. A food sack or pack hung from a tree or suspended from a pole must be farther from the trunk and higher from the ground than a bear can reach, and recent generations of bears seem to have evolved telescoping forearms. Considerable ingenuity is needed also to keep food safe from mice, which can walk a tight line and drop from astonishing heights.

Food caches are generally not acceptable in the wilderness except as officially designated and maintained for emergencies. Animals' discovery of an improperly protected cache merely results in a large mess and brings them back again and again with all their relatives.

Garbage Control

Responsible hikers and climbers maintain garbage sacks at camp, and on the trail stow every particle of paper, glass, plastic, or metal in their packs for later disposal.

And so the rule: *If you can carry it into the wilderness full, you can carry it out empty.* The rule applies universally to trips lasting one day or several weeks; the garbage, burned or unburned, is carried home in a heavy-duty plastic bag brought along for the purpose. On long trips a fire can be built occasionally to burn waste food, paper, and plastic, if allowed by regulations and conditions. However, the burn site or firepit should be cleaned to remove the unsightly aluminum foil flecks resulting from contemporary food packaging.

Leaving a clean camp and cleaning up a filthy camp may have the effect of stimulating subsequent visitors to think it over before tossing trash in the brush, stream or lake. Many persons will leave garbage where they find other garbage, but not cast the first trash where the field is clean.

Water Pollution and Human Wastes

It is becoming apparent that much supposedly virgin water, however clear and cold, may be so contaminated by thoughtless humans and their uncontrolled domestic animals that it could be as dangerous as any city sewer. For personal protection, therefore, wilderness travelers must now and increasingly in the future inspect carefully the water they propose to use, and when in doubt give it preliminary treatment, with water purification tablets or by boiling 10 minutes — longer at higher altitudes.

The rules of good wilderness sanitation are simple and absolute. Use the facilities provided by the managing agency for the use intended (*never, never,* put cans and garbage in latrines). If no latrines exist, dig a hole 20 to 25 cm (8 to 10 inches) in diameter, and no deeper than 15 to 20 cm (6 to 8 inches), and at least 60 meters (200 feet) — farther if possible — from any open water, allowing for maximum water level around lakes. After use, fill the hole with loose soil and tamp the sod back in place. Used non-biodegradable items of personal hygiene, such as sanitary napkins, should be carried out in sealed, air-tight containers, unless provisions are available for a fire which will reduce them completely, finally, and absolutely to ashes.

SHORT-HAUL EATING: WEEKENDS

On trips of two or three days, or even longer if basecamp is close to the road, weight is not a major factor in planning meals. Any food on the grocery store shelves, tinned, fresh, or frozen, is a candidate for consideration; the modern abundance of processed foods allows great scope for the imagination.

Supper

Some alpine gourmets plan sensational suppers, such as a tossed salad of fresh lettuce, tomatoes, and cucumbers, imported egg drop soup, corn on the cob, broiled sirloin steaks with fresh mushrooms and onions, a shortcake made of hot brown-and-serve biscuits and frozen strawberries, and for beverages, fresh milk, or perhaps liebfraumilch, followed by coffee and liqueur. However, the typical climber frequently arrives in camp at 6 or 7 p.m. and must be in bed by 8 to be cheerfully away at 3 a.m. or earlier, and remembering the old adage that "though the food is cold, the inner man is hot," often contents himself with a supper of sandwiches and fruit juice.

Between menus of steak and salad at one extreme and sandwiches and juice on the other lie many meals both nourishing and delicious yet easily and rapidly prepared. The *grocery store stew* is concocted from various items selected at random or by intuition. A safe but pedestrian example is a can of meat and gravy mixed with a can of whole kernel corn. In any combination a dash of grated cheese or a chunk of margarine may enormously improve flavor. Bread, a hot drink, and a dessert of pastry or instant pudding round out a satisfying meal. Another simple supper is built around *hot sandwiches*: hamburgers, hot dogs, or minute steaks fried or broiled, combined with salad greens or relish, supplemented by drinks and dessert.

Cup cookery is particularly suitable for one-person meals, especially in cold and windy camps. Having at hand a stove, two large metal cups, and a pot of water, the climber heats each course in sequence: a cup of soup from an envelope of dehydrated soup mix, a cup of meatballs eaten with bread and butter, finally a nice cup of tea and a Danish roll, and off to sleep. An alternative is the freeze-dried entree, to which only boiling water need be added. Much of this preparation can be managed from within a sleeping bag.

Breakfast

When time is crucial, breakfast is merely the first installment of lunch. A tiny can of fruit cocktail, or a doughnut and a swallow of milk, are typical menus. Some persons are convinced their legs won't work without hot food; their neurosis can be quickly pampered with instant hot cereal or cocoa.

Lunch

As soon as breakfast is completed the mountaineer commences lunch, which is eaten continually through the remainder of the day, pausing briefly for supper. Food in the rucksack and nibblies in the pockets are main courses for the summit lunch, morsels for rest-stops, and sweets to suck while walking.

Few trips are conducted so austerely that one cannot eat for pleasure as well as physiological efficiency. Most hikers or climbers eat whatever delicacies suit them personally and which they are clever enough to carry. Some people require a high-carbohydrate diet with many candy bars; others thrive best on a high protein/fat intake including cheese, sausage, and nuts. Smaller amounts of food eaten several times during a long day are the rule, since a feast followed by violent exertion sets up a competition between the digestive and muscular functions of the blood that leads to indigestion or weakness or both.

The range of alternatives for lunches can be much greater on short hauls than the semi-expedition lunches discussed later in this chapter. Sandwiches made before leaving town, wrapped first in plastic and then in foil, remain fresh and tasty through a weekend. Apples, oranges, bananas, grapes, cherry tomatoes, cucumbers, celery—fresh fruits and vegetables in general—are never quite so delicious as high on a hot, dry cliff. The choice, actually, is limited only by imagination and the time available before the trip for browsing through groceries, natural food stores, and delicacy shops. A sound rule for short trips is to carry a variety of foods, even if this means carrying home a slight surplus; the appetite often becomes tricky in a quick transition from city life and the beginner may not be able to predict what will be tempting during the climb, when nourishment is mandatory but unappealing.

Water

The notion lingers that because it is a pleasure to drink when thirsty, it must be harmful, and therefore one should resist the devil by sucking a stone, or perhaps a prune pit. Water is as vital to life as oxygen; the body can lose as much as a gallon of water without lasting physical damage, but efficiency is substantially lowered well before this point. Authorities recommend an average daily intake of 2 liters (2 quarts) of water during active exertion, and twice that in hot weather. Salt lost by sweating must be replaced to avoid a deficiency and subsequent heat cramps; in addition to that gained from foods, about 2 grams of salt per quart of water drunk may be taken, most conveniently in the form of salt tablets.

The old superstition does, however, have some basis in fact; as beginners frequently learn the hard way, even when water is plentiful thirst should be slaked in moderation. Tossing a large volume of liquid onto the stomach slows one down; if the person is very hot and the water is very cold it can even knock him out. Drink little, drink often, is the rule, and to this end mountaineers often carry loaded canteens even when they could, strictly speaking, survive from one creek to the next. A canteen supply of pure water should always be available in the party for first aid purposes. Powdered drink mixes added to the canteen are standard and on short trips cans of juice may be carried.

The same subterranean tradition that recommends sucking stones for-bids eating snow. But this prohibition is cheerfully ignored by climbers, whose only caution is moderation, melting snow in the mouth before swallowing it, just as a child learns to lick rather than chew an ice cream cone.

HIGH-ALTITUDE EATING
Water

Far above timberline water is often at a premium. As soon as the campsite is located, one or more members of the party begin collecting a reservoir, since at sundown the high mountains generally freeze tight. Sometimes a tongue of snow dribbles into a stream, but more often only dampens the rock or makes mud. In the latter case a depression may be dredged, the water allowed to clear, and the resulting spring channeled into a pot with a twig. Another common source of water is overhanging eaves of snow. Their drips vary in volume; a number of pots under a number of drips may be required to fill party needs.

In the absence of streams or drips, "water machines" can be devised if the sun is shining, or has been recently. A dark tarp spread thinly with snow makes great pools of water with little effort. Plastic bags filled with snow are slower but steady. Both produce an unpalatable, plastic flavored liquid that should not be called "water" but by its proper name "melted snow," suitable for cooking and hot beverages, but a nauseous drink taken straight. A warm rock with a flat, tilted surface will work. If there is no sunshine the only source of water is snow melted on a stove. Water machines seem to work poorly at high elevations—above 15,000 feet—due to sublimation of snow directly into water vapor.

When a single night is to be spent at high camp and prospects for sunshine are poor, it is best to carry a large canteen supply from lower altitudes. In long stays at high altitude, dehydration is a major problem; there is evidence that some symptoms of altitude illness derive from dehydration and potential salt deficiency.

The climber's last thoughts before bed are to protect his precious water supply from freezing, usually by storage next to or in the sleeping bag. There is no more cheerless beginning for a climb than a canteen of ice.

Food

In the gales characteristic of high camps cooking is difficult if not impossible. The most suitable foods are those that require only warming or may be eaten cold if worse comes to worst. Fuel must always be carried and its weight is another argument for simple menus. Boil cookery is a problem: for every drop of 5°C (10°F) in boiling temperature, cooking time is approximately doubled. Table 4-b shows the drastically inverse ratio between boiling point and altitude.

Table 4-b. Boiling Point of Water.

Elevation		Temperature		Cooking Time (*sea level* = 1)
sea level		100°C	212°F	1
5,000 ft	1525 m	95°C	203°F	1.9
10,000 ft	3050 m	90°C	194°F	3.8
15,000 ft	4575 m	85°C	185°F	7.2
20,000 ft	7000 m	80°C	176°F	13.0

Short visits to high altitude are documented by more than a century of experience. A typical quick gain in elevation is the weekend ascent of Mt. Rainier in the western American Cascades, where climbers normally spend Friday night near sea level, Saturday night at 3050 meters (10,000 feet), and perhaps only 20 hours after leaving tidewater reach the 4392-meter (14,410-foot) summit. A majority feel symptoms of mountain sickness ranging from a slight malaise to violent vomiting and severe headaches. The eating habits proven successful on Mt. Rainier by past generations are obviously valuable in all less demanding situations, and apply up to approximately the 7000-meter (20,000-foot) level.

In the abrupt ascent to high altitude there is not time for physiological acclimatization and the entire circulatory system is laboring merely to supply oxygen to the body. Large meals and foods difficult to digest demand attention the system simply cannot spare, and illness results. The climber therefore eats light and often, never loading the stomach with a heavy meal. The menu stresses carbohydrates which are easiest to digest, and scants fats and proteins, which are most difficult — though a good (*not* excessive) meal of fat and protein the night before the ascent is helpful in stoking the body later on.

Only trial and error can teach a person what foods the individual body can tolerate at high altitude. Some individuals seem unaffected and with great relish eat smoked oysters and pepperoni at high elevations — partly, no doubt, for the benefit of their bilious companions. The climber in doubt should depend chiefly on carbohydrates, but at all costs and at whatever effort must continue to eat, lest the loss of energy reinforce the debilitating effect of oxygen lack; even when thoroughly ill, one often can take nourishment in the form of fruit juice.

LONG-HAUL EATING: THE SEMI-EXPEDITION

The "semi-expedition" is an extended outing with all food and equipment hauled on the party members' backs. The limit is about two weeks, since few people are capable of carrying, at any one time, the loads necessary for longer. Logistically at least, longer trips become true expeditions requiring relay packing, porters, or airplane drops.

Though even today there are wildernesses in Alaska, Canada, and the Antarctic large enough to require true expeditions, in western America, where only relatively small enclaves of primitive nature remain, the semi-expedition is the most characteristic wilderness experience.

One factor contributing to the success of a semi-expedition is menu planning. Too much food means too much weight and too few peaks. Too little or improper food means not enough stamina and too few peaks. Unpalatable food in any quantity means low morale and unpleasant memories.

Planning and Packaging

Dividing the Group

Since meals are social events, many small groups plan all food together. A common, carefully planned menu also requires the least weight. However, on other occasions tastes are so divergent that breakfast and lunch are left to the individual and only supper, the most complicated meal of the day, is a group effort.

The size of cooking units should rarely exceed six. Beyond that number the efficiency of group preparation is outweighed by complications of large pots and small stoves.

Selecting the Menu

Packs are not significantly heavier on short hauls if food quantities are estimated high by one or several pounds, nor is there any real hardship if vital ingredients are overlooked, since anyone can get by for a weekend without sugar in his cereal. Semi-expeditions, on the other hand, demand precise planning, both to save the unnecessary ounces that pyramid to staggering pounds and to ensure that right down to the last meal there is salt for the potatoes. The climber who groans at hoisting a ponderous pack on Day One feels justifiable bitterness when arriving back at the road on Day Fourteen carrying an unused pound of margarine. And the climber who must endure bland tea night after night can never forgive the blundering fool who forgot the lemon crystals.

Meals are sometimes planned by the group sitting in committee, sometimes by an elected individual. In either case the same procedure is followed. First, menus are written down for each meal. From this is compiled an ingredients list with estimated quantities, and from this the shopping list. Estimation comes easily for the experienced semi-expeditioner who knows that a certain amount of a certain ingredient is just about right for so many companions of long-expressed tastes. The less experienced can benefit from study of Appendix 1.

The dietician must plan meals to remain within the maximum load limit the party can reasonably carry for the trip in question. A ration of 680 to 910 gms (1½ to 2 pounds) per person per day will fuel active climbers and feed them quite well if dehydrated products are used. A diet allowing 680 gms (1½ pounds) per person must be exceedingly well planned to provide enough calories; a careless planner can easily exceed 910 gms (2 pounds) without providing enough calories. It is much easier to plan on the low side and add extras than to think big and be forced to subtract a soup here, a dessert there.

Packaging

The elaborate packages of commercial foods are too bulky and heavy for the strained back of the semi-expeditioner. Therefore, after all foods have been gathered, they should be repacked for carrying—a considerable but worthwhile chore. Many types of plastic sacks and sheets are available for the purpose, including some with air-tight seals, but the average semi-expeditioner gets by with plastic sacks of various sizes, tied or rubber-banded at the mouth. As an additional refinement, label and instructions for the contents may be included in the bag. For finely powdered items, such as powdered potatoes or jello, double-sacking is wise and adds insignificant weight. Plastics have an odor that can permeate dehydrated foods, particularly dairy products, and make them unpalatable, but the effect is not noticeable until well after two weeks. Items such as honey and mustard can be safely stowed in refillable plastic tubes or flexible freezer containers with tight lids.

Though requiring considerable work at home, the greatest ease in camp comes from packaging specific meals before packs are ever hoisted. By doing so one can avoid the problems of too much rice at some meals and hardly enough for the last—as can happen when one has a single "rice sack" for the entire trip. Small kitchen scales greatly aid in this repackaging task. A labeling system is also to the cook's advantage (felt pens mark efficiently on plastic). Smaller packages can be placed in larger ones of heavier-ply plastic, and lumped (and labeled) as "Breakfast," "Supper," "Drinks," "Desserts," "Soups," "Spices," and so on. When planning is not so critical from the standpoint of weight, it may still be useful to gather food into logical groupings to eliminate any crisis if a party separates and the "other group" has all the raisins.

Note about Measurements

The recommended amounts in this chapter are educated estimates, and conversions are approximations rounded off to avoid unwieldy fractions. One solid ounce is, of course, 28.352 grams, but is herein rounded out to 30 grams for convenience. Similarly, 1 quart and 1 liter (liquid measure) are used interchangeably. After all, alpine cuisine is not an exact science, but a true art form.

Lunch

For the climber lunch is a critically important meal, beginning early and continuing late—and in the case of a bivouac, replacing suppers and breakfasts. Frequently, therefore, nearly half the daily ration is allotted to lunch—340 to 450 gms (12 to 16 oz.).

Lunching and munching preferences vary so widely that it is prudent for every party member to share in the planning; those who love their kippered herring or Italian salami may not be able to abide blue cheese and provoloni. One popular staple is "gorp," or "squirrel food," a mixture of nuts, candy, raisins, and other dehydrated fruits; one handful makes a snack, several make a meal; fastidious eaters may prefer the constituents served separately. Another grain-based staple is granola. Gorp and granola are generally available premixed at natural food stores. The menu shown in Table 4-c takes a bit more trouble to plan but usually pleases most palates for several days. The protein constituents should be included in every lunch; one or more of the others can be omitted on easy days. The "special" delights" are a matter of personal taste.

Table 4-c. Basic Semi-Expedition Lunch.

Category	Amount per person-day (gms)	(oz.)
meat	60	2
cheese	60	2
nuts or peanut butter	60	2
dried fruit	60	2
bread	90	3
(or crackers)	(60)	(2)
chocolate or candy bars	60	2
hard candy	30	1
dried mixes and special delights	60	2
	480	16

Supper

Main Course

With half the person-day ration of weight allotted to the nondehydrated foods of lunch, the other half makes up breakfasts and suppers consisting largely of dehydrated foods. Commercially prepared freeze-dried dinners offer tempting meals complete in one package—beef stew, chili con carne, and many others—at luxury prices. The industrious can concoct their own meals with substantial monetary savings and excellent results, though at considerable expense in time.

In every climbing area of the world, parallel evolution has produced the same magnificent meal, variously called "one-pot-supper," "mulligan," "hoosh," or "glop." By any name its virtues are extraordinary. A large number of compatible ingredients are cooked in a single pot with a saving of equipment, time, and fuel. The blended components have a flavor greater than the sum of the parts; the result is a complete, satisfying, colorful, and memorable meal.

Table 4-d. Meats for Semi-Expedition Glops.

Category	Amount per person-day (gms)	(oz.)
tinned	120	4
chicken (boneless)		
chopped meat		
corned beef		
ham		
roast beef		
salmon		
tuna		
sausage	120	4
chipped beef	60	2
dried, compressed	45–60	1½–2
meat bars		
bacon bars		
vacuum-dried meats	30–60	1–2
freeze-dried		
meat	40–45	1⅓–1½
shrimp	15–30	½–1
ham	15–20	½–⅔

The complete glop begins with a base of spicy flavor provided by a dehydrated soup or sauce mix placed in the pot along with the water. At appropriate later times, depending on the meal, starches and meats and various other things are added. Tables 4-d and 4-e give the principal alternatives available in meats and starches, and the amounts in each category.

Soups and Side-Dishes

A cup of soup is always a welcome prelude to the main course, and should be planned whenever considerations of time, weight, and fuel allow—always remembering, though, that whatever weight and fuel are expended on soup may be at the expense of the glop. Many "instant soups" of diverse international origin are on the market. One package, added to water at one cup per person serves a party of three or four; with the addition of a bouillon cube, four or five.

Table 4-e. Starches for Semi-Expedition Glops.

Category	Quantity Weight (gms)	(oz.)	Amount Dry Measure (cups)	(ml)
rice				
pre-cooked (5-minute soak type)	70	2⅓	⅔	160
quick-cooking (10–15-minute cooking type)	60	2	¼	60
potatoes				
mashed, powdered	30 to 60	1 to 2	¼	60
mashed flakes (bulkier, easier mixing)	30 to 60	1 to 2	1 shaken down	240
sliced, diced, cubed (slow cooking, may be soaked)	60	2	–	–
wheat, processed ("Ala." Slow cooking—15 minutes. Good change of pace.)	60	2	⅓	80
pasta (macaroni, spaghetti, noodles. Choose thin varieties cooking in 7 minutes or less.)	60	2	–	–

If the weight of a genuine soup cannot be afforded, bouillon is an old favorite that weighs little, has minimal food value, but is helpful in replacing water and salt, warming cold bodies, and stimulating appetites of the exhausted.

Though bulky and expensive, freeze-dried vegetables weigh little and become amazingly appealing to some people after a few days of potatoes and sausage. Freeze-dried fruits are excellent but too expensive for frequent use; fruits and vegetables dried in home dehydrators are much less costly. It is not a bad plan to slip in a side-dish of vegetables once every several days; often they are greeted more enthusiastically than dessert.

Pre-cooked soy beans or processed soy products (in powder or textured forms) are excellent low-cost protein additions to meals. For those more intimately concerned with nutrition and healthful foods many types of supplements and "organic" foods are often found packaged in natural food stores and easily incorporated in a backpack diet.

Bread or biscuit can rarely be planned for supper on a semi-expedition, but scraps left over from lunch are welcome.

Drinks and Desserts

Drinks and/or desserts are also added according to the weight allotment available. The total ration per person-day usually does not allow soup, vegetable side-dish, drink, and dessert for every supper. Planning one or two trimmings for each day provides a good balance; not all, and maybe none, are wanted each day and the extras can accumulate for the light days and rest days, including periods of storms when there is nothing to do but eat and sleep.

After a dry day on the peak or trail a cold flavorful drink is immensely delightful, and ideally the first order of business on reaching camp is mixing a pot of punch — lemonade, orange juice, grape juice, or whatever — from powdered mixes. The artificially sweetened drinks are inferior both in taste and aftertaste but are so light they can be used more liberally.

Tea is another no-weight item that can be planned for every supper, allowing one bag per person per day, or carrying bulk tea if preferred. Instant coffee can also be carried to allow addicts to maintain their habit. Where the weight mounts up in these drinks is the addition of sugar. Before the trip, count the members of the party who use sugar in their tea or coffee and figure about 10 to 15 gms (⅓ to ½ oz.) per serving; on the trip, watch the sugar-users to make sure they don't consume the entire supply in a couple of days. Tea drinking can be varied by use of spiced varieties or a bit of dried mint or some lemon crystals; tea with brown sugar or honey is an abomination to purists but ambrosia to others. A powdered cream product should be included for those who can't endure black coffee, or even coffee with milk. Cocoa, and also coffee-cocoa, a half-and-half mixture of instant powders of the two, are as much desserts as drinks. The same is true of hot jello.

Full-scale desserts — pudding being the standard — are usually planned only once every several days. The time and fuel required by cooked puddings have made them rather a rarity in mountain camps. Instants of many types are available and though most seem somewhat synthetic, some are quite acceptable and dependable. On a cold day any pudding — even instant — may be more appreciated served hot.

At camps where snow is available, and a good amount of salt for the freezing mixture, ice cream can be made from powdered mixes. Such an exotic dessert as Neapolitan ice cream should stun even the most chronic malcontent into awed silence.

Staples and Seasonings

Sugar is a matter of preference. Brown is one-third again as heavy as white because of moisture, but is much preferred by many for flavor.

Instant powdered *milk* is indispensable in the mountain diet for nutritional value.

Margarine (preferred to butter on long trips for its keeping qualities) makes every other food taste better—bread, potatoes, glops, oatmeal, even cocoa. It also has the most calories per pound of any food in the climbing larder; when weight is extremely critical and the party is trying to shave a few ounces from the 1-kgm (2-pound) ration, the margarine allotment can be raised at the expense of other items.

Salt is essential to the body as well as the palate. Cooked cereals are virtually inedible without it, and individuals may want to salt their glop to taste. Relatively little is needed, since other foods (such as a soup mix used as a base for glops and the salt tablets swallowed while sweating during the day) supply most of the physiological requirements.

As for seasonings—packages of dehydrated onions, green peppers, and herbs, and shakers of pepper and garlic salt and chili—their total weight is insignificant beside that of a chock or carabiner, but they can transform survival rations into banquets.

Breakfast

Breakfasts are a major semi-expedition problem. Cold-and-fast meals save time and fuel but are heavy and bulky; mush-and-cocoa meals take time but slip down easily in a freezing pre-dawn. The usual procedure is to plan fast breakfasts for the long days, hot for the medium days, roughly half-and-half, and add one or two luxury breakfasts for layover days of rain or recuperation. Another aspect of the problem is that most parties include a mixture of farm-type hearty-breakfasters and urbanized late-starters who can barely tolerate the thought of solid nourishment until the sun is high. A happy medium will strike the former as starvation and the latter as nausea; when there is any argument the farmers must give way in the interests of group efficiency, consoling themselves with the thought that lunch will begin shortly.

For the fast start, many mountaineers prepackage a standard meal before the trip, measuring a prepared cold cereal (such as granola), sugar, raisins or other fruit, and powdered milk into a "breakfast bag." Stir in water—cold for a cold meal, hot for a hot one—and breakfast is ready.

A hot drink is a pleasant addition to a cold meal and a standard element of a hot one. Common choices are cocoa, coffee-cocoa (mocha), instant breakfast drinks, plain or chocolate malted milk, all pre-mixed with powdered milk. Some favor hot jello, and just plain milk isn't bad.

Mush—oatmeal, farina, or whatever—is the standard hot breakfast; the instant or quick varieties really take no time at all beyond heating water. Sugar, milk, margarine, and bacon bar can be mixed into the cooking pot or added by the individual to taste. Wheat germ can be added to the mush—or to cold cereals—for additional protein and B vitamins.

Freeze-dried, instant, and powdered eggs produce highly variable results. Experimentation at home prior to their use in the wilderness can allow development of acceptable omelet-like dishes. Bits of cheese, vegetables, freeze-dried meat, etc., are recommended in these omelets. A less conventional but comparable protein breakfast is dried chipped beef in cream or cheese sauce served on crackers. Either of these is more efficient than cereals in terms of calories per ounce.

Fruits, dried by sun or vacuum, can be soaked or cooked the previous night for quick reheating in the morning, then eaten separately or combined with mush. A powdered citrus drink, often warmed for a predawn start, adds variety; so, also, do the luscious freeze-dried fruits, which for the weight are the equivalent of eating pure money.

Into almost every rat-race a day of rain must fall, and with it opportunity for the luxury breakfast—which actually need not weigh a great deal, the luxury lying in the time of preparation. Hotcakes can be delicious or unpalatable depending on the experience of the cook and the elapsed time since the party ate a civilized meal. A small, lightweight skillet that can double as someone's eating dish or a pot lid (as in some cooking sets) is almost a necessity; a small spatula is helpful. Syrup can be made from brown sugar, or lunch jam can be used.

Bacon is an old favorite with either hotcakes or scrambled eggs; canned meats or sausages are magnificent. Whatever the main course, the ideal luxury breakfast includes cold orange juice for a start, stewed fruit, hot beverage, and bread or biscuit spread with margarine and jam or honey. When all this is eaten, it is noon or nearly so, and time to take a short walk before lunch.

Plate 7. Breakfast at White Rock Lakes, North Cascades. (Bob and Ira Spring)

Plate 8. Mitre Peak from northwest, Karakoram, Pakistan. (John Cleare).

5 *

NAVIGATION

NAVIGATION IS THE PROCESS of determining one's present position and the location of the objective, and of selecting and following the route between these two points. Most wilderness navigation is done by inspection, that is, by looking at the surrounding terrain and relating what is seen to prior knowledge of the locality or to features described on a map. The area of navigational concern for a mountaineer is small, seldom larger than can be seen from a vantage point. When resort to instruments is necessary or desirable, the only ones essential should be simple, self-contained, easily mastered, and virtually foolproof. With good maps mountain navigation can be easy and exact. Skill is very largely a function of experience, though the basic tools and procedures can be quickly mastered in the relative safety of back yard or local park.

THE TOOLS

Nature offers several rudimentary indicators of direction. In the north temperate zone the summer sun rises somewhere between northeast and east, is due south at noon, and sets between west and northwest. South slopes are sunnier and thus drier than north, with vegetation sparser or of an entirely different type. North slopes are snowier and because of more intense glaciation in past ages often are steeper. Persons stranded in the wilderness without equipment may be completely dependent on such information. However, they can simplify orientation by always carrying a map and an artificial direction finder, i.e., a compass.

The Map

Navigation is aided by verbal descriptions of an area from conversations or correspondence with previous visitors, or from published sources such as alpine journals and climbing guides. The value of photographs, particularly those taken from airplanes, is obvious, though compared with the human eye a camera lens gives at best a distorted view of the world. Aerial photographs — even when available — are bulky, expensive, and difficult to interpret and to keep in good condition, but are well worth the trouble and expense when extremely precise knowledge of the terrain is needed. For terrain description a climber generally depends chiefly on a map, a symbolic representation of an area that relates places to one another by distances and bearings and by convenient shorthand conveys a wealth of information in a form easily carried and easily understood.

Types of Maps and Their Uses

Sketch maps are usually prepared for the special purpose of providing graphic notes of particular routes and features. They are not always drawn to scale, seldom show any surrounding detail, and may not indicate directions and elevations accurately. But one should not sneer at sketches; many mountaineers use them. When used as supplements to proper navigational maps — which never include interesting and useful details like "cedar growing sideways in rock crevice by small waterfall" — they are very useful as routefinding aids. There are still remote areas where sketch maps obtained from preceding climbers are the only detailed information available.

Forest Service maps, and comparable ones issued by other governmental agencies, are invaluable. These comprehensive maps are revised periodically in the light of news brought in by rangers walking over the country and are the best guides to the current state of roads, trails, shelters, and other human works. Drainage patterns and divides are carefully traced and some elevations are given. Few Forest Service maps show the vertical shape of the land; the stream which appears on the map paralleling the trail may be in a gully 200 feet below. The few which do are not published to meet National Map Accuracy standards, and thus can occasionally be confusing. These maps can be obtained — usually for a small fee — at ranger stations or by writing to headquarters offices of the various National Forests. Similar maps transcribed more or less carefully from Forest Service maps and other sources are produced commercially for some areas. These are commonly called "county" or "sports" maps and are sold in stores catering to hunters and fishermen.

Hunters' maps distributed prior to each hunting season by several of the large timber companies are revised yearly and are excellent for finding passable routes through the growing maze of logging roads. Their perusal frequently reveals a new or shorter approach than those described in guidebooks or shown on other maps.

Topographic maps are the prime tool of the mountain navigator. Their name is derived from their depiction of topography, the shape of the earth's surface. On these maps the description of the works of humans is subordinated to terrain details. Topographic maps published by the U.S. Geological Survey and of interest to the mountaineer occur in three scales referred to as "series."

Maps on a *scale of 1:250,000,* the *United States series,* are issued for all states including Alaska, for some portions of which they are the only maps. The scale, about ¼ inch to the mile (or 4 mm to the km), is of little use to the mountaineer afoot. However, this series is superb for broad orientation, and far superior to highway maps in that with just a bit of practice one can soon name and describe hills and dales better than most local residents; from a summit they allow identification of peaks and ranges in the haze far beyond the boundaries of localized maps. Many are offered in three-dimensional molded plastic editions, splendid for home study of mountain range structure and drainage patterns.

Many maps are published using a *scale of 1:62,500,* nearly 1 inch to the mile (or 16 mm to the km) in the *15-minute series,* each covering about 12 by 18 miles (20 by 30 km) in the northern United States. For the mountaineer this series gives sufficient topographic information for route selection, and each sheet includes enough area to make orientation easy. (The corresponding maps for Alaska are printed with a *scale of 1:63,360,* exactly 1 inch to the mile, and have an east-west dimension which is actually greater than 15 minutes of longitude.)

The newest mapping in the contiguous United States and much of the reissuing of older maps is proceeding on the *scale of 1:24,000,* about 2½ inches to the mile (or 40 mm to the km) in the *7½-minute series,* each sheet covering an area of about 6 by 9 miles (10 by 14 km). The greater detail of these maps makes them ideal for cross-country route planning; however, because more maps must be carried to cover the same area, they may not always be as desirable as 15-minute maps for field use.

Topographic maps for areas west of the Mississippi River can be purchased at mountain shops or ordered directly from the U.S. Geological Survey, Federal Center, Denver, Colorado 80225. For the east, maps can be ordered from the U.S. Geological Survey, Washington, D.C. 20242. Index maps for each state are free on request.

Similar topographic maps are available for much of Canada. Indexes to maps published by the Canadian government are free on request from the Map Distribution Office, 615 Booth Street, Ottawa, Ontario. Indexes

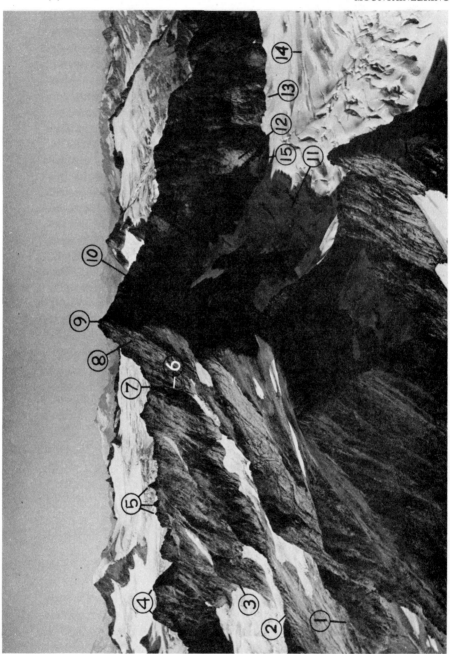

Fig. 5-1. Photograph of a mountainous area with features keyed.

1. Basin: flat area, water, camp spots.
2. Snow or ice line: dashed line ends on cliffs, rock.
3. Buttress: change in features of wall may provide approach to ridge.
4. Twin summits: which is higher?
5. Gendarmes, aiguilles, or pinnacles.
6. Gully or couloir.
7. Saddle, pass, or col.
8. Rock face.
9. Summit: highest point on map.
10. Ridge or arete.
11. East slope: note shadows and ice accumulation.
12. Cirque wall: glacier occupies this cirque.
13. Moat.
14. Crevasses: indicated by irregular contours, not smooth as near buttress, 3. above.
15. Bergschrund: not seen on map but inferred possibility when rock and snow are steep.

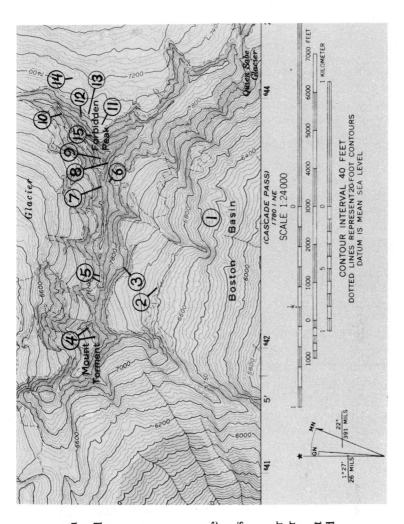

Fig. 5-2. Topographic map covering same area as that of Fig. 5-1.

CONTOUR INTERVAL 40 FEET
DOTTED LINES REPRESENT 20-FOOT CONTOURS
DATUM IS MEAN SEA LEVEL

(CASCADE PASS)
1780 I NE
SCALE 1:24000

to maps issued by the individual provinces may be obtained, at no cost, by writing to the appropriate government office in each provincial capital.

Interpretation of Topographic Maps

Topographic maps show the shape of the terrain with contour lines, which are drawn to represent constant elevations above sea level on the surface of the earth. The interval between contour lines always represents an equal vertical distance, generally 20 to 250 feet (or 5 to 100 meters), depending on the scale of the map and the steepness of the terrain. For convenient reading, usually each fifth contour line is wider, and its elevation is printed periodically along its length. Interpretation of topographic maps is quite simple. Widely spaced lines indicate a gentle slope; lines that run close together show a cliff. A valley or a gully makes a pattern of "V"s pointing upstream or uphill. A ridge appears as downhill-pointing "V"s or "U"s depending on the sharpness of the crest. When the direction of travel crosses lines of succeedingly higher numbers it is going uphill; when it crosses lines of succeedingly lower numbers it is going downhill. If the line of travel does not cross contour lines, it is not going up or down, but *traversing* the slope with no more variation in elevation than one contour interval.

The value of topographic maps lies in the ability they give one to predict the main terrain features by looking at the general shape of groups of lines. Thinking of contour lines as resembling stair steps, a hillside represented on the contour map has an appearance similar to that of a wide staircase viewed from above; a ridge, the appearance of two wide staircases back to back; and a very steep hillside, the appearance of a staircase with very narrow treads. A cliff is represented by contour lines very close together or on top of each other. A cirque, or head of a mountain valley, resembles the end of a football stadium. Finally, a mountain peak is represented as a circular-shaped staircase ascending in a series of closed contours to the innermost circle or point indicating the summit. Fig. 5-1 and 5-2 give a comparison between a photograph of a mountainous area and a topographic map covering the same area.

Vegetation features can usually be inferred to some degree from an inspection of the map. Green generally is used to depict *marketable timber*, i.e., forest areas of reasonably large trees (though such green coloring often does not define the exact borders of these areas). Mottled green and white is often used for scrub vegetation, sometimes in marshy or swampy places. The lack of green color on a topographic map generally leaves only the brown contour lines; thus, areas without substantial timber appear as various shades of brown. Such areas may or may not be vegetated. For example, one brown area on a map may be a high-elevation rocky ridge, the only vegetation being an occasional scrub fir or some heather. Another brown area may be an avalanche gully, devoid of any timber but filled, in the summer, with a nearly impenetrable thicket of slide alder or other brush. Another area of almost identical appearance on a map may be a gully covered with a rockslide, which may be ascended with comparative ease. Thus, when studying a map for a climbing route, one cannot assume that the lack of any green color means that the area is totally devoid of all vegetation—only that it does not contain commercially valuable timber.

Glaciers and permanent snowfields are white on topographic maps, but the contour lines for such areas are blue. Gentle slopes on glaciers appear to be mostly white, while considerably steeper areas appear to be predominantly blue.

Other features shown on topographic maps are readily discernable because of their color. Black, for example, is almost always used to denote human features such as roads, trails, bridges, buildings, railroads, and power lines. Blue, on the other hand, is used for water features such as lakes, streams, springs, glaciers, and permanent snowfields.

One must not overlook other information given on maps which, though seemingly unimportant, may nevertheless be very significant in determining the route up a mountain. Such features include the date of the survey from which the map was made (usually printed in the lower left-hand corner), the revision date of the map (generally in the lower right-hand corner), the reference names of the adjacent maps for other areas, the contour interval, and the scale, usually at the bottom of the map.

One of the more significant map features is the *magnetic declination diagram* normally printed at the bottom of the map, and showing its orientation to both true north (the direction from any given point on the earth to the geographic north pole) and magnetic north (the direction to which a magnetic compass needle points). Magnetic declination (referred to as "declination" in the remainder of the text) is the angle of difference between true (geographic) north and magnetic north, and varies from place to place throughout the world. This will be discussed in further detail in relation to the use of the compass.

Contour maps offer much information about the landscape but do not tell all. In the older surveys contour lines were sketched more or less freehand. Even with modern maps it must be remembered that a 60-foot cliff will not be evident at all if it lies between lines at 80-foot intervals.

Regardless of the value of topographic maps, no one map tells the whole story, and all sources should be thoroughly studied before entering unknown territory. Thus, useful as they are for showing the topography of an area, the principal value of topographic maps lies in their unique ability to represent the shape of the natural geographic features, rather than human works, for which up-to-date Forest Service maps are usually far superior. Topographic maps are updated only at relatively infrequent intervals, and logging roads, logged areas, and other such human features are often not shown on the latest topographic map. It is therefore useful to compare a Forest Service map with a topographic one, and to add information on roads, trails, and other human works onto the older topographic maps. In this way, maximum benefit can be obtained from both types of maps.

Map Protection and Modification

Inexpensive, easily replaced maps are expendable, but not during a climb. Enclosure in a clear plastic bag or map case is adequate protection and allows use without damage, even in wet weather.

Sometimes an area of interest lies near the corner or edge of more than one map. In such cases the pertinent area of each map can be cut out and the sections joined together with tape. More durable composites can be made by mounting the sections of maps on lightweight cloth backing with photographers' dry mounting tissue or spray mounting adhesive. Such composites can be made to cover any area of interest to the climber.

Some topographic maps are confusing even to an expert; it is helpful to outline the ridge structure with pencil lines along the main crests. More laborious but even more valuable is *shading* a map to simulate shadows cast when the sun is low in the northwest. Such techniques speed development of the stereoscopic vision characteristic of a practiced map reader.

The Compass

A compass is a magnetized needle mounted so that it can respond freely to the earth's magnetism. It is by far the quickest and most accurate means of establishing direction since the needle always aligns itself with the magnetic field of the earth — almost always, that is. Hidden ore bodies ("magnetic anomalies") and some innocent-appearing rocks may deflect the earth's gross magnetic field. In addition, magnetic items in the climber's outfit, such as ice axes, knives, belt buckles, and other metal, can attract the compass needle and must be kept away from the compass while it is in use.

The small, round, inexpensive pocket-watch type of compass marked only with the cardinal directions indicates little more than the general direction of the sunset, and is inadequate for mountaineering use. A compass to be used for wilderness navigation should enable one to determine a bearing, or a direction, to within a very few degrees, and the dial of the compass should be graduated in 1- or 2-degree increments in a clockwise direction. A 5-degree error in 1 mile of travel would lead the navigator about 460 feet astray from the intended destination (about 85 meters away in 1 kilometer of travel). If no landmarks are visible, as in fog or dense timber, a more accurate reading is often necessary. A liquid damped needle eliminates excessive oscillations of the compass needle and permits fast and accurate readings, or even continuous readings while walking, whereas an undamped needle always vibrates while being held, thus introducing unacceptable errors.

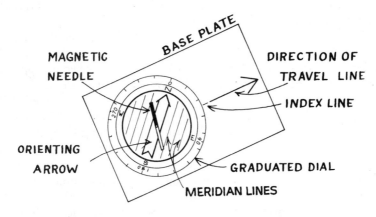

Fig. 5-3. Essential features of mountaineering compass.

Fig. 5-3 shows the essential features of the typical mountaineering compass. The *magnetic needle* is the heart of the instrument. Generally one end of the needle is a different color than the other, to avoid any possible confusion as to which end is the north-seeking one. Sometimes this end of the needle is made luminous, as an aid in nighttime navigation. The *graduated dial* on a *rotating housing* enables one to read bearings or to set the desired compass course at the *index line*. The line from the center of the magnetic needle to the index line and beyond is called the *direction of travel line*, sometimes indicated with an arrow on the baseplate. (Some compasses do not have an index line as such; on such instruments, the bearings can be set and read at the direction of travel line.) Within the rotating housing is an *orienting arrow*, within which the magnetic needle must lie in order to achieve precise alignment between the graduated dial and the magnetic needle. These features are necessary to take and follow bearings accurately. Also within the rotating housing is a set of *meridian lines*. These are simply a few lines which are parallel to the orienting arrow, and thus can be used to align the compass with a map. A transparent *base plate*, whose edges are parallel with the direction of travel line, is also an essential part of the mountain traveler's compass, for use with the map.

Other features are more or less optional, depending on the desires and budget of the individual. A *sighting mirror* on a folding plate can be used as an aid in simultaneously aligning the magnetic needle, the orienting arrow, and the object being sighted. This feature can sometimes enable one to obtain slightly more accurate readings than without a mirror. Some compasses are equipped with an *automatic declination offset* adjustment. This is a useful feature which eliminates the need to correct for the effects of declination, though it usually adds considerable cost to the device. Instead of such an addition, there are other ways to correct for declination, as discussed below.

Declination, as described earlier, is a measure of the difference in direction between true and magnetic north. Where the declination is zero a compass needle points to true north, i.e., toward the geographic north pole. Because of the different locations of the geographic and the magnetic north poles and the complexities of the earth's magnetic field, however, the compass needle rarely points to true north. The amount of this difference, or declination, is different for various places on the surface of the earth. In parts of Michigan, Indiana, Ohio, Kentucky, Tennessee, and the Carolinas, magnetic north is exactly in line with the true north pole, and therefore the compass needle does point directly to true north. In these areas, the correction between true and magnetic north, or the declination, is zero. In areas of North America to the east of these states, the magnetic needle points west of true north, so these states are said to have a *western declination*. States west of the above-mentioned ones, on the other hand, have an *eastern declination*, since from these states magnetic north appears to be east of the true north pole. Maps are usually printed and routes are often described in terms of directions related to true north. Any compass-aided navigation must therefore take declination into account.

Bearings

A *bearing* is simply the direction from one place to another, measured as an angle with respect to the direction of an accepted reference line. For the purposes of this text, the word "bearing" will mean the angle measured clockwise in degrees from the line to true north (parallel to the local meridian) around to the direction of interest. Since the complete circle of all possible directions is divided into 360 units called *degrees*, with zero lying at true north, 90 is due east, 180 is south, 270 is west, and 360 is north again (360 and zero degrees are the same). If some object is due west of one's position, it is said that the bearing from one's position to the object is 270 degrees. If another object is halfway between north and east, i.e., northeast, then its bearing is halfway between zero and 90 degrees, or 45 degrees.

To *take a bearing* means to measure the direction from your position to some other object. With a compass, it is very easy to take a bearing on any object. First, suppose that you are along the line of zero declination, such as some place in Ohio or Kentucky where the declination is zero. In this case, the compass can be held level so that the north-seeking end of its magnetic needle points directly to true north. The compass can then be rotated until the "360" or "0" mark lines up with the north-seeking end of the magnetic needle. The compass is then aligned with the earth's true directions, and "90" on the compass is aligned with east, "180" with south, and so on. To "take a bearing" on any given object then only requires sighting across the compass at the object of interest and judging what number on the dial best corresponds to the object's position. In theory, this should be an acceptable method, but in actual practice it has the potential for quite large errors. For this reason, compass manufacturers have added a few features which can greatly increase the accuracy of the instrument. These features are the *direction of travel line,* the *orienting arrow,* and the *index line.* All of these features serve to increase the accuracy of the bearings taken: the direction of travel line, by providing a long line which can be pointed at an object with far more accuracy than can be obtained by simply sighting across a compass; the orienting arrow, which allows the magnetic needle to be merely aligned parallel with it, rather than the less accurate technique of trying to point it at a specific number; and the index line, at which the resulting bearing is read. To make use of these features in taking a bearing, simply point the direction of travel line toward the object for which the bearing is desired. Then, while holding the base plate level and in place with one hand, turn the rotating housing with the other hand until the orienting arrow is aligned with the magnetic needle. Once this is done, read the *bearing* from the graduated dial at the index line. In Fig. 5-4, for example, the bearing is read as 270 degrees.

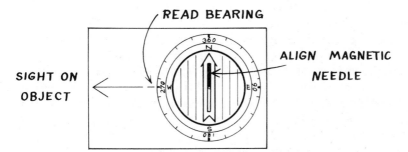

Fig. 5-4. Example of "taking a bearing" on an object at 270 degrees.

For accuracy and ease when performing the operations described above, the compass should be held at arm's length, at or near waist level, unless it has a sighting mirror. In the latter case, it should be held at eye level, its sight pointing at the objective, and the needle and the orienting arrow observed from the mirror. The housing is then rotated to make the needle and the orienting arrow line up in the mirror, while the objective remains lined up with the sight. In either case, the compass base plate must always be *level*.

Correcting for Declinaton

In the above-stated example, it was assumed that a bearing was taken in a place where the declination was zero. When the declination is not zero, the procedure for taking a bearing is identical, except for a minor correction. Fig. 5-5 helps to explain the reasoning behind this correction. It shows the relationship between the true north pole and magnetic north in the contiguous United States. Anywhere along the zero declination line, the bearing read on the compass will be a "true" one, since no correction for declination is necessary. However, east or west of this line some amount of correction is required. Consider, for example, a mountain navigator in Colorado, where the declination is 14 degrees east. The navigator "takes a bearing" on peak "B" from his or her present position at peak "A." The bearing that the navigator wishes to determine is the angle between the line "A–B" and the direction to true north, indicated in the figure as the "true bearing." However, the compass actually measures the "magnetic bearing," i.e., the angle between line "A–B" and the line from the observer to magnetic north. It can be seen from the figure that the "magnetic bearing," is 14 degrees *less* than the true bearing. Accordingly, 14 degrees must be *added* to the "magnetic bearing" in order to obtain the "true bearing." Thus, anywhere west of the zero declination line, the declination must be added to the bearing read on the compass in order to obtain a true bearing. In Washington State, about 22 degrees must be added; in central California, about 18 degrees must be added to the bearing read on the compass.

In areas east of the zero declination line, the opposite situation occurs. Consider, for example, a wilderness traveler in Maine, where the declination is about 20 degrees west. The observer is at point "C" and wishes to take a bearing on point "D." This bearing is the angle between line "C–D" and the line from the observer to true north, and is labeled as the "true bearing" in the figure. What the compass reads, however, is the angle between line "C–D" and the line from the observer to magnetic north. This bearing is indicated as the "magnetic bearing." From the figure it is apparent that the magnetic bearing is 20 degrees *greater* than the true bearing. Thus, 20 degress must be *subtracted* from the compass reading to determine the true bearing. Varying amounts of correction must similarly be made in other places east of the zero declination line. In

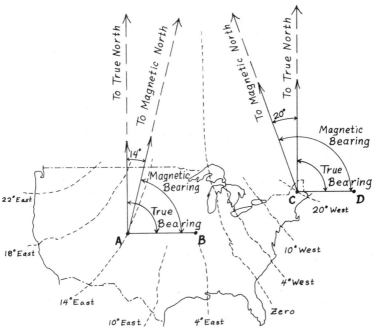

Fig. 5-5. Relationship between true and magnetic north in the United States.

Virginia, 4 degrees must be subtracted from all readings taken with the compass; in New Jersey, about 10 degrees must be subtracted.

Some of the more expensive compasses with built-in declination correction adjustments make it possible to correct for declination for any given area by aligning the magnetic needle with an adjustable *declination arrow* rather than with an orienting arrow; true bearings can then be read directly, and no addition or subtraction is necessary. The same effect can be produced in less expensive compasses by reading all bearings at a specially marked point (referred to as a "declination mark") to the right or left of the index line, as shown in Fig. 5-6a and 5-6b. Such a mark can be made by scratching the plastic base plate with a sharp instrument and darkening this mark with a pencil. (If the owner wishes not to deface the instrument permanently, a piece of tape on the base plate next to the rotating housing can be used instead.) To take a bearing with the compass so marked for declination, the compass is then used in the same way as described above, except that the bearing is read at this declination mark instead of at the index line. In central Colorado, the declination mark would be 14 degress to the right of (or clockwise from) the index line; its location could be found by setting zero at the index line and making the required mark on the base plate adjacent to the "14" line, as shown in Figure 5-6a. In Washington State, the declination mark would be about

22 degrees to the right of the index line. Similarly, in areas east of the zero declination line, a scratch or tape mark can be placed on the left side of (or counter-clockwise from) the index line, as shown in Figure 5-6b. In this figure, the compass has been altered to read true bearings directly for Maine, with a declination of 20 degrees west. The exact location of this mark can be found by setting 20 degrees at the index line, and making the declination mark at the zero degree line. (Some compasses have numbers and an index line on the *inside*, rather than the outside, of the dial. For such compasses, the declination mark should be placed on the back side of the compass, behind and inside the rotating dial.)

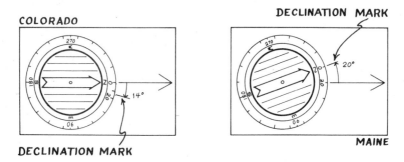

Fig. 5-6. Compass corrections. a. For area west of zero declination line. b. For area east of zero declination line.

The use of the declination mark as described above is not the *only* way to account for declination; indeed, the navigator can add or subtract the declination correction instead, without altering the compass, as was explained earlier. Both methods produce the same result; however, the use of the declination mark is always dependable, whereas climbers and wilderness travelers, particularly when tired, cold, or in a hurry, have been known to add instead of subtract and vice versa, thus doubling their error. For this reason, the use of the declination mark is highly recommended.

Practice in the Use of the Compass

The ability to take accurate bearings does not come naturally; only practice and great care achieve good and repeatable bearings. Practice is best done where the orientation of one's directions is known and the results can be checked instantly. First, modify the compass with a declination mark, as explained above. Next, choose a place to practice where the directions are accurately known. One of the best places for practice is an intersection where the streets run exactly north-south and east-west. Point the compass with its direction of travel line aligned as closely as possible with the curb, sidewalk, or edge of the road, in, say, an easterly direction. Next, rotate the compass housing until the magnetic needle is centered within the orienting arrow. Finally, read the true bearing at the declination mark. The resulting bearing should agree to within 2 degrees of its known value (2 degrees is the best accuracy obtainable with this type of compass). Thus, if the compass is pointed due east, the reading should be between 88 and 92 degrees. If it is not, then the entire operation should be repeated, with more care. Repeated practice exercises such as this can quickly develop skill and self-confidence in the use of the compass. Proficiency in taking compass bearings is essential to off-trail navigation, and is also a starting point for other navigational skills.

Following a Desired Bearing

To follow a given bearing, simply reverse the process. For example, to travel in a westerly direction, rotate the compass housing until the 270 degree mark is adjacent to the declination mark. (If the compass is not marked, then the declination must be added to the desired bearing if east of the zero declination line, or subtracted if west of it. This corrected bearing is then set in at the index line.) Then, without moving the housing any more, rotate the entire compass until the north-seeking end of the magnetic needle is lined up with the pointed end of the orienting arrow. The direction of travel line will then point in the desired direction, i.e., due west. In order to gain experience and confidence with this operation, practice following all four of the cardinal directions at a street intersection.

The Compass as a Protractor

In addition to being used to take and follow bearings, the compass can also be used as a protractor, i.e., to measure angles from one place to another on a map. To do this, place the compass on the map with the edge of its base plate aligned with the two points which define the direction to be measured. If a bearing from "A" to "B" is desired, then the direction of travel line should be pointed in the direction of *from* "A" *to* "B." The compass is then held in position on the map while the rotating housing is turned to make the compass meridian lines parallel to the north-south lines on the map, with the orienting arrow pointing to the top of the map. The true bearing from "A" to "B" is then read *at the index line*. (When using a compass with an automatic declination correction, the adjustable declination arrow will not be exactly parallel to the north-south lines of the map, but it must nevertheless point in the general direction of the top of the map.) In Fig. 5-7, for example, to measure the bearing from Panic Peak to Deception Dome, the compass has been placed with its edge on a

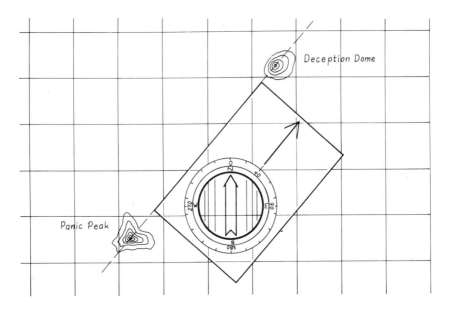

Fig. 5-7. Example of measuring a bearing from a map using the compass.

line joining the two peaks, and with the direction of travel line parallel to the direction from Panic to Deception. The compass housing has been rotated until the compass meridian lines are parallel with the north-south lines on the map, and the orienting arrow is pointing to the top of the map. The resulting true bearing is then read at the index line as 40 degrees. Note that no mention has been made of the magnetic needle, nor of declination. In this operation, when the compass is merely being used as a protractor, the magnetic needle and the effects of declination are entirely ignored.

In much the same way, bearings can be plotted on the map, using the compass as a protractor. Suppose that a friend has left a camera along a trail at a point from which he had measured the bearing to Mt. Magnificent as 135 degrees. In planning our trip to the same area we wish to mark this spot on our maps. To locate this position, 135 is set in at the index line and one edge of the base plate is placed on Mt. Magnificent, as shown in Fig. 5-8. The entire compass is then rotated until the compass meridian lines are parallel with the north-south lines of the map, and the orienting arrow points to the top of the map. Once it is lined up, the desired location is somewhere along the line indicated by the edge of the base plate, the line "A–B." This line intersects the trail at point "C," so this is the point from which the bearing to Mt. Magnificent is 135 degress. It is here that we should look for our friend's camera. (Some maps do not

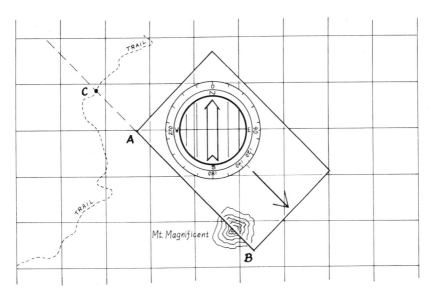

Fig. 5-8. Example of plotting a bearing on a map using the compass.

have north-south lines. In this case, draw them in, at intervals of about 1 inch − 2½ cm − or so.)

Cautions to be Observed When Using the Compass

There is a crucial distinction between the use of the compass in map and in field work. When measuring bearings and plotting them on a map, the magnetic needle is entirely ignored. Furthermore, when performing these operations, the desired angle, or bearing, is set in or read *at the index line*, i.e., the small mark that is in line with the direction of travel line. When using the compass in the field to take and follow bearings, however, the compass needle *is* used, and the desired bearings are read or set in *at the declination mark* as explained above to correct for declination (unless the compass has an adjustable declination arrow, or unless the navigator wishes to add or subtract declination instead of marking the compass).

Should you disagree with your compass, remember that a compass, when properly used, is almost always right, whereas individual judgment is sometimes clouded by fatigue, confusion, hunger, dehydration, lack of time, or other factors. For this reason the compass should usually be trusted over one's own intuition. If the indicated direction of travel disagrees sharply from yours, first check to ensure that the proper compass techniques are being used. If in doubt, consult other members of the party. But once it is determined that the compass is being used properly, it should then be trusted over blind guesses, hunches, and intuition.

Iron, steel, and other magnetic metals can sometimes cause significant compass errors. When using a compass to take and follow bearings, be careful not to let metal objects such as belt buckles, ice axes, and other such objects get too close to the compass. If a seemingly nonsensical result is obtained from a compass, perhaps some metal object is affecting the reading.

Two common mistakes, in both map and field work, are to use the wrong end of the orienting arrow, or the wrong orientation of the direction of travel line; either results in an error of 180 degrees. It must be remembered that in field work the north-seeking end of the magnetic needle must be aligned with the pointed end of the orienting arrow, and that the direction defined by the line from the center of the magnetic needle to the index line must be pointed to the objective. Similarly, when using the compass as a protractor, the pointed end of the orienting arrow must always be pointed towards true north on the map. It is quite possible to make the meridian lines parallel with the north-south lines of the map — as they should be — while forgetting that two possible orientations of these lines are possible: one that is correct, and one that is totally reversed. Always double-check to make sure that the pointed end of the orienting arrow is towards true north on the map (usually the top of the map).

The Altimeter

It is essential that every member of a climbing party carry a map and compass. In addition, at least one party member should carry an *altimeter,* a special kind of barometer which is calibrated in altitude instead of pressure. (Since atmospheric pressure decreases at a uniform rate with increasing altitude, it is possible to use a standard barometer for measuring altitudes by fitting it with a scale labeled in feet or meters instead of units of pressure.)

Properly used, an altimeter can help to verify location as determined by the map and compass (or other means), and indeed may on occasion be the only means of knowing when the desired elevation or position has been reached, particularly in foggy weather or on a glacier.

If, as a peak is ascended, the altimeter is frequently consulted, the group obtains a true indication of its progress, and no one is surprised when, upon attaining a viewpoint, considerable distance is seen to remain between the party's location and its objective. In addition, the amount of remaining elevation gain can easily be determined, thus simplifying the decision as to whether to continue or to turn back.

A most useful application of the altimeter is in descending, when many routefinding errors are made. Frequently, a climbing party goes up a hillside to a ridge crest, then up the ridge to the summit. On the descent, they follow the ridge to the place where it was first encountered. If this place is not marked, or if it is on windswept snow where previous footprints have been obliterated, then the correct place at which to leave the ridge may be difficult to find. With an altimeter, however, they can make a note of the elevation at which the ridge crest was first attained. Then, in making the descent, they can follow the ridge until the altimeter again registers the same reading.

Since an altimeter responds to changes in atmospheric pressure, and since atmospheric pressure, in turn, is dependent on weather and other factors, it must be recognized that an altimeter cannot be accepted as an absolute indicator of elevation in the same way that a thermometer can be used as an indicator of temperature. Instead, its most useful purpose is as an indicator of *changes* in elevation over short periods of time and relatively small distances. For this reason, the altimeter should not merely be consulted when an elevation reading is desired, but should be checked and reset at every specific reference point – a trailhead, a lake, a col, or a known point on a ridge – at which the elevation is known (generally by reading it from a map). When camp is reached, look at the altimeter and remember or jot down the indicated altitude. Then, when leaving camp the following day, check the altimeter to see if the reading has changed during the night. If so, reset it to the elevation previously indicated upon arrival in camp. In addition to ensuring accuracy in altimeter readings, this process also reveals the barometric changes that foretell weather changes. An apparent increase in elevation corresponds to a decreasing barometric pressure, which is often an indication of deteriorating weather. An observed decrease in elevation, on the other hand, means an increase in barometric pressure, and thus a possible improvement in the weather.

Altimeters are only as accurate as the skill and experience of the user. Even the best of altimeters is subject to variations caused by weather and temperature changes, so the buyer of such an instrument should not be misled by the apparent precision of the more expensive instruments when choosing among the alternatives. Under the best of conditions, an altimeter can seldom be expected to be more accurate than to within about 100 feet (30 meters) of its indicated altitude.

ORIENTATION

By orientation, the first step in navigation, mountaineers find where they are, or if they already know where they are, they determine bearings from their position to other landmarks. If a quick look around does not

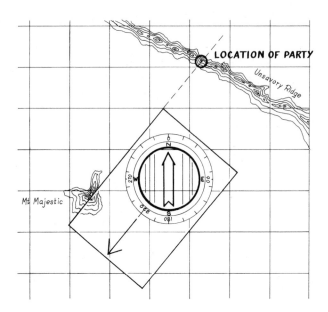

Fig. 5-9. Example of orientation with line position known.

accomplish the job of orientation, they resort to their maps and compasses.

When a party's *point position* (summit, pass, lake outlet, fork of a river, etc.) is known, they are sure of wherever they are, and can identify on the map any visible feature in the landscape, or can identify in the landscape any visible feature shown on the map. Referring to Fig. 5-2, assume that a group of climbers is atop Forbidden Peak. To identify an unknown peak, they can sight on its summit with their compasses and determine the bearing of their line of sight to that peak. A quick plot on the map now shows that this compass bearing from Forbidden intersects an easily identifiable mountain. For example, if the bearing were found to be 275 degrees, the unknown mountain would be found to be Mt. Torment. If, on the other hand, the climbers did not know where Mt. Torment was, and they wished to see it, they could measure the bearing from Forbidden to Torment on the map and would find this to be 275 degrees. They could then set this bearing at their declination marks, rotate their compasses until the magnetic needle was aligned with the orienting arrow, and then observe the direction pointed out by the direction of travel line. This line would point to Mt. Torment. By these methods, any feature visible from the peak can be identified, and any visible feature shown on the map can be pointed out.

With *line position known* (ridge, trail, river, contour line, etc.) and one visible feature recognized, point position can be found. Assume the climbers know they are on Unsavory Ridge (see Fig. 5-9) and in the distance they recognize Mt. Majestic. They use their compasses, and determine that the bearing from their position to Mt. Majestic is 220 degrees. They can then plot the line of this bearing through Mt. Majestic on their maps and extend this line in the opposite direction to intersect Unsavory Ridge. The point of intersection tells the climbers where they are.

With only *area position known*, at least two visible features must be recognized to find point position. Assume that the climbers know only that they are in the Fantastic Crags. They take a bearing on Mt. Majestic, find it to be 40 degrees, and draw a line "A–B" indicating this bearing on the map (Fig. 5-10). They also recognize Unsavory Spire, find its bearing to be 130 degrees, and draw a second line ("C–D"). Where the two lines intersect on the map (point "E") indicates the location of the climbers. However, if they happen to be on the top of a ridge and the lines of the map intersect in Fantastic River, then something is wrong. Perhaps they now recognize Imposing Peak and the third bearing line intersects one of the others at a more reasonable location. (The closer to 90 degrees is the angle between any two bearing lines, the more accurately their

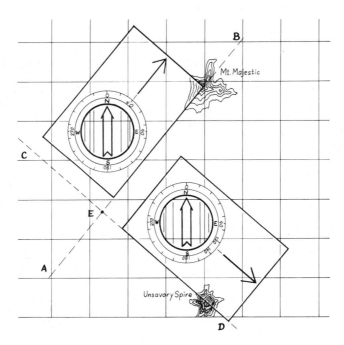

Fig. 5-10. Example of orientation with area position known.

intersection indicates position.) If several bearing lines agree on a location with no similarity to the terrain, then the climbers suspect it is a crazy old map, that there must be some magnetic anomaly in the rocks, or maybe that those peaks are not Majestic, Unsavory, and Imposing after all.

With only area position known and only one visible feature recognized, only line position (along the bearing line) can be found. However, suppose the climbers still feel certain of good old Majestic, and also know they are near a river, not on a ridge. They therefore know that they are at or near one of the several points where the Majestic bearing line intersects Fantastic River. Perhaps, from a comparison of the map and the terrain, they can find only one possible location that fits all the facts. This is a good example of an orientation problem which might be solved with an altimeter. If the climbers are on a hillside at some known bearing from Mt. Majestic, and someone in the party has an altimeter, the intersection of the Mt. Majestic bearing line with the contour line for their elevation gives enough information to enable the party to determine its position. In situations such as these, all the pieces of information at the disposal of the group should be employed to determine its position. Common sense, in addition to quantitative information from instruments, should be used as much as possible in orientation.

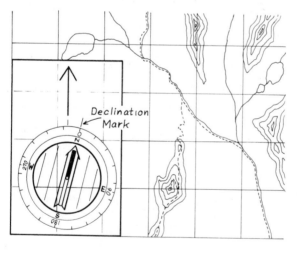

Note that the magnetic needle is parallel to magnetic north ("MN"), while the direction of travel line is parallel to true north ("*") on the map.

Fig. 5-11. Use of the compass in orienting the map.

Occasionally, it is helpful to *orient the map* in order to obtain a wider understanding of one's surroundings. Though this is not an essential aspect of navigation and orientation, it is nevertheless sometimes helpful to individuals for whom the other orientation methods do not provide a clear enough picture. To orient the map, place it on a flat surface with the base plate of the compass aligned with the north-south lines on the map, and its direction of travel line pointing to the top of the map (true north), with 360 degrees set at the declination mark, as shown in Fig. 5-11. Then, while holding the compass in place on the map, rotate both the map and the compass together until the north-seeking end of the magnetic needle is aligned with the orienting arrow. When this occurs, the magnetic needle will be aligned with the declination diagram on the map. (If a compass with an adjustable declination arrow is used, 360 degrees should be set at the index line, the compass placed on the map, and both rotated together until the magnetic needle is aligned with the declination arrow.) There will now be a direct uniformity between lines of sight read from the map and those observed in the area covered by the map. Such map orientation should only be used for broad, general orientation, and not for precise position determining or exact navigation, because wet, dirty, uneven and/or ferrous surfaces in the field usually create errors. Precise orientation should be achieved by taking accurate bearings, and then carefully plotting them on the map using the compass as a protractor as described above.

NAVIGATION

By *navigation*, mountain travelers get where they want to go. Even while pounding a trail or following a leader, the navigator, unlike others in the group, does not find the way purely by trail signs and summit registers, nor entirely by boot heels. At every step the look of the country changes a bit; at every step the navigator, with a sharp and roving eye, updates the last certain fix. At a pass, or around a bulge in the ridge, or through a break in the clouds, whenever new landmarks appear, the navigator pauses to connect them mentally with the map.

Mountain navigators know how amazingly different the country looks on the return trip. While eager apprentices gaze to the summit, experienced navigators frequently glance over their shoulders toward camp, not because they wish they had never left but because they hope to get back. Particularly at critical turns they fix in their minds the *over-the-shoulder shape of the route*, such as: opposite a waterfall, at a moraine with an iron-stained boulder perched on the crest, the route bursts through a cedar thicket and down a mossy slab to a gnarled snag.

When the route is complex, and particularly if a late return is anticipated, the navigator may find a small *notebook* valuable for entering times, elevations, landmarks, and compass bearings as navigational aids (as well as for writing memoirs in later years).

The mechanics of navigation by map and compass are quite simple once the elementary principles of compass use and orientation are mastered. Initially, and preferably before the trip, the overall route is defined. Much of this may be on obvious trails where the map alone gives adequate guidance. These parts will be connected by or connected to sections without such localized markings. These sections may well be met under conditions—dense brush, forest, or clouds—such that instrumental guidance is called for; major landmarks cannot be monitored. Before embarking on such a section of travel the first step is to determine one's point position on the map, either by having carefully followed the route marked on the map or by using the techniques described above. Next from the map, or by sighting from a viewpoint in the field, the objective of the route section and its bearing are determined. In order to follow this bearing, the desired number of degrees is set at the declination mark, and the compass is then rotated until its magnetic needle is aligned with the orienting arrow. The direction of travel line then points to the objective, and to identifiable intermediate points on the same bearing. An example of this process is shown in Fig. 5-12. A party's location has been found to be point "A," and the objective is point "B." First, the true bearing from "A" to "B" is measured with the compass, as in Fig. 5-12a. The angle is thus found to be 285 degrees, as read *at the index line.* This value is then set in *at the declination mark*, as in Fig. 5-12b for a compass used in Washington State with a declination of 22 degrees east. Finally, the entire compass is rotated until the magnetic needle is aligned with the orienting arrow, as shown in Fig. 5-12c. The direction of travel line now points to the objective.

When the view of an objective is blocked by cliffs, forests, or other obstacles, navigation is accomplished by the use of intermediate objectives. If these are not visible because of fog or dense forests, there are several ways to travel a predetermined bearing. One way is to walk in the direction of the desired bearing with continuous reference to the compass, or to sight landmarks within the limit of visibility and walk towards them. In this case, the accuracy of the method is increased when the distance from point to point is as far as possible. Where fog or whiteout leaves no visible intermediate landmarks a member of the party may serve this role. This surrogate landmark moves ahead to near the limit of visibility and is guided by voice or hand signals to a point along the desired bearing. As an added benefit of this approach the person serving this role can take back bearings on the rest of the party as a further check on the proper choice of location. This is done repeatedly until the objec-

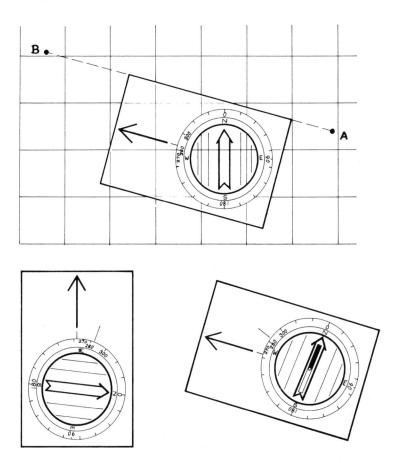

Fig. 5-12. Example of navigation using the map and compass. a. Measuring the bearing from "A" to "B." b. Setting bearing at declination mark. c. Following the bearing.

tive or an intermediate objective is reached. This method, if carefully used, can be quite accurate, since the two measurements taken at each place tend to counteract any compass errors.

This use of "intermediate objectives" is best adapted to situations in which the primary target can be seen initially (or its bearing can be found by measurement from a map), but this target cannot be seen during much of the course. It is assumed, however, that the course can be followed directly, and that intermediate objectives can be seen and selected along that course. This works well in forests, hills and valleys, many stream crossings, and a few other situations.

When, however, the route itself is blocked — by cliffs, lakes, swamps, or rock towers — so that an on-course objective can neither be seen nor followed, recourse is often made to moving a paced distance at 90 degrees to the chosen course, then going past the blockage on a bearing parallel to the original course, and finally returning to the original course by another 90 degree movement paced the same distance as the earlier one, but in the opposite direction, as shown in Fig. 5-13.

When landmarks are lacking or obscured by fog or night, or may be on the return, the route may be *marked*. On snow and glaciers, wands are used, as described in later chapters. For most other terrain, the best marker is brightly colored crepe paper in thin rolls, durable enough not to disintegrate in the first rain or wind, as does toilet paper, but perishable enough to vanish without a trace over the winter. Whether they are degradable or not, remove them on the return; climbers who decorate the hills with brightly colored strips should in all justice be condemned to spend eternity untying these ugly eyesores in whatever place is reserved for them and other despoilers of the wilderness.

The navigator should at all times keep in mind which way to go if completely baffled: the appropriate compass bearing to be followed which will lead to some long, unmistakable line, such as a highway, trail, or lake, which forms one boundary of the climbing area. For example, anywhere along or near the route shown in Fig. 5-13, following a bearing of about 200 degrees will eventually lead to the highway. Such a *baseline* always lies in roughly the same compass direction wherever the party is

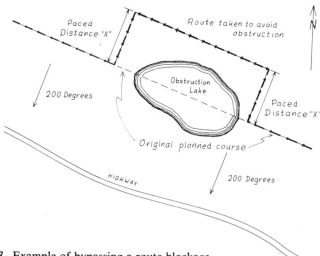

Fig. 5-13. Example of bypassing a route blockage.

within the climbing area. Though following a compass bearing to a baseline may not always be the quickest way out, it is at least an ultimate way out.

Navigators of ocean and air often travel great distances to an exact destination entirely by instrument. Mountain travelers also occasionally navigate entirely by instruments for great distances, and sometimes even get where they want to go. If a party is traveling in a straight line towards a given peak, and it becomes obscured by clouds, a quick compass bearing taken on the peak prior to losing sight of it gives the party a compass bearing to follow, even in the absence of any visibility. One bearing is enough for this purpose, and since the better quality liquid damped compasses give accurate readings even when held in the hand while walking, the navigator can advance with confidence that the objective will be reached. The reliability of this technique is further enhanced when each member of the party travels compass in hand.

It is quite common to encounter situations in which the objective is a specific point on a line. One such example is on the return from a climb, while navigating to the place where the car is parked on a road. If the direction of travel is roughly perpendicular to this line, an error of as little as 1 or 2 degrees can be enough to cause the party to miss its destination, thus necessitating an additional walk along this line to the destination. This annoyance, however, is considerably compounded when the direction of the error is unknown. In this case the route must be found by trial and error, with a fifty-fifty chance of choosing the wrong direction. Of even more serious consequence is the case in which the desired point is at the *end* of a line; in the event of missing this destination due to a small navigational error, it is sometimes possible to miss the line entirely, and to spend hours trying to find it again. One way to prevent these irritating occurrences is to choose and follow a course which intentionally leads to the right or left of the actual destination, so that when the line is reached, there is no doubt as to which direction to travel.

LOST

A good navigator is never lost, but having learned humility, always carries enough food and clothing to survive hours or even days of temporary confusion. Stated differently, there is no such thing as being lost — only varying degrees of uncertainty about one's position. Therefore, apprentice navigators must master techniques for minimizing confusion, and must be prepared to handle the situation in which the uncertainty of their position becomes too great to allow an easy and fast return.

The first rule is, *stop*. Particularly on the weary return with nightfall approaching, when caution is most vital, the temptation to plunge hopefully forward is strong, and errors increase with every step.

If orientation cannot be quickly regained, but was certain a short time earlier, the route should be retraced to the previously known point; an hour groaning upward may save a bitter night out. If the last certain orientation is hours away, and the present position can be approximately determined, it may be best to move ahead cautiously, alert for landmarks. But if night and exhaustion are near at hand, the best navigation technique might be a bivouac.

Climbing history reveals the significant fact that a party of two or more, even if the greenest of novices, rarely gets dangerously lost or confused. It is the unintentionally lone person, overwhelmed by a sense of human fragility and the immensity of the wilderness, who throws away his life. Fear in the face of nature is no sign of cowardice, but rather is a healthy reaction; it is entirely proper, when alone, to treat every step as a life or death matter.

If due to whatever reasons, one does become hopelessly confused while alone, extreme caution is most advisable. Terror must be overcome by reason or it can kill. As with a confused party, the first rule is to stop. Look around for other members of the party, shout, and listen for answering shouts. If none are heard, sit down, try to relax, and calm down. Consult the map to determine approximate location and to plan a route out of the area if the rest of the party is not found. Panic should be resisted, along with wishful thinking. The old, discredited rule of following a stream out of the wilderness should be forgotten: a stream may lead deeper into the wilderness, and certainly will lead away from the search area and often into dense timber or thick brush. Once cool and collected, though perhaps still confused, mark the present location with a cairn or toilet paper, then scout in all directions, each time returning to the marked position. Well before dark, stop scouting and collect water and firewood, if available. If the weather is bad, seek shelter before dark, and spend the night keeping the fire going, singing cheerful songs, and rehearsing out loud the funny story this will make some day.

If the confused or lost climber behaves in this manner, and his companions are similarly sensible, they are likely to be reunited in the morning. If there is no sign of search activity the next day, through some misunderstanding such as a divided party, the lone climber must once again fight down panic. He may decide, after a day or so, that it is best to proceed cautiously to the baseline, but if the terrain is prohibitively dangerous for lone travel he should concentrate on letting himself be found. It is far easier to find a person who stays in one place in the open, builds a fire, periodically shouts, or all of these, than one who thrashes on in hysterical hope, steadily weakening.

FREEDOM OF THE HILLS

Routefinding in the high country is not a science, but an art. Some travelers have the gift and some do not, but all must learn the use of the tools and all can improve with practice. Indeed, it is in large part the subject of this entire book, since skillful routefinding is so essential to safe off-trail travel.

In medieval times the greatest honor a visitor could receive was the rights of a citizen, the freedom of the city, sometimes symbolized by presenting the visitor with the "keys to the city." For the modern alpine traveler, routefinding is the key to wandering at will through valley jungles, green meadows, steep cliffs, and broad glaciers, earning the rights of a citizen in an alien land, a mountaineer with the freedom of the hills.

Plate 9. Howser Spires beyond Warren Glacier, Bugaboo Mountains, B.C. (Galen Rowell)

6 *

WILDERNESS TRAVEL

OVER THE CENTURIES civilization has gradually crept up the approaches to many mountain ranges. Armies and elephants have crossed the Alps, and the Himalaya is isolated more by politics than nature. In such ranges it is possible to be purely a climber, trusting a native guide or railway conductor to lead the way to the first rocks or ice.

There is another sort of mountain range that lies deep in wilderness. When a climbing party leaves its automobiles at a trailhead in a valley of the Cascade Range in Washington State or is deposited on the beach of a British Columbia fjord it may face long hours or days of wilderness travel before enjoying alpine pleasures. The technique of muddling through brush is not as glamorous as class 5 rock climbing, but many a peak has been lost in thickets of slide alder. Indeed, the major defenses of a wilderness mountain frequently lie below snowline and the final scramble to the summit is anticlimactic after the epic approach.

ROUTES AND NON-ROUTES

Routefinding, an art not to be confused with the science of navigation, involves locating a route that can be followed within the limitations of the climbing party. While the principles of routefinding can be studied at home, only by applying them in actual practice in the mountains can one develop any significant skill, and only then do the principles become meaningful; only then can one develop the integrated sense of terrain and distance necessary for skillful routefinding. As with other climbing skills, the best way for a neophyte to learn is by climbing with experienced mountaineers, observing their technique and asking questions. A skillful (lucky) routefinder is an asset to any party.

Successful routefinding begins at home with assembly and study of as much information as possible. Route descriptions found in guidebooks or climbing journals are helpful whether the objective is to repeat a previous route, to avoid it, or to establish a new one. One must be aware, however, that sometimes the trivial-sounding description may pertain to a route having major difficulties and appalling exposure. Guidebook descriptions often can be supplemented by drawings or photographs in such references as hiking guides, picture books or geological reports. Of course, various maps can provide extensive route information, but one must be aware of the limitations of each type, as described in Chapter 5, Navigation.

No one set of immutable laws governs choice of wilderness route; each range has its own peculiarities of geology and climate. The Canadian Rockies mountaineer accustomed to broad, meadowed valleys and open forests is horrified when he encounters the narrow canyons, totally occupied by jungles and cataracts, of the Coast Range in British Columbia. The Cascades mountaineer used to deep snow in June everywhere above 4000 feet feels parched when he visits the Sierra Nevada in California and must climb thousands of feet higher to find more than scraps of snow.

Prolonged mountaineering in a single range fills one with the lore of routefinding in that range, but even the wiliest traveler should enter each new range humble in spirit. He is not utterly ignorant, for in knowing any mountains well he knows something of all mountains. This knowledge can be extrapolated, and supplemented by information from guidebooks, journals, maps, and acquaintances. None of these is a substitute for firsthand experience, but all at least prepare him to be a good student.

Climate and geology make mountains what they are. Knowing that the west slope of the Olympic Mountains in Washington State receives in excess of 150 inches of annual precipitation with a frost level that extends in winter to sea level prepares the experienced mountaineer for dense brush and a low snowline and miserable weather. Knowing that the Tetons in Wyoming are comparatively arid and hot prepares him for a relative absence of brush, snow, and water. Knowing that the Olympics are composed mostly of weak sediments leads him to anticipate wearisome scree and easy ridge-running. Knowing that the Sir Donald group of the Selkirks in British Columbia is quartzite gives advance confidence in the soundness of the rock, however steep. The mountaineer who knows the major outlines of a range's climate and geology can learn a great deal more by map study.

Frequently, local authorities, including park or forest rangers, geologists, and other climbers, can give valuable advice on routes or local conditions. Climbers' trails, undisclosed by any official map but well known to locals, can immeasurably expedite the approach. In an unfamiliar area a brief visit with a forest ranger may save substantial time.

Whether the mountaineer's travels are in familiar or foreign territory, on trails or off, he must continuously be watching for the way back (viewed from the opposite direction a route may be remarkably unfamiliar), for changes that may occur during the day, such as a stream rising from snowmelt or rainstorm, and for emergency campsites, a water supply, and even for materials from which he could build an emergency fire in a downpour. These observations become second nature as the result of conscious practice.

Approach Observations

Getting to the mountain is the first critical problem of routefinding and errors in solving it have frequently resulted in loss of summits long before any technical climbing was encountered. Throughout the approach the peak is constantly studied for details of possible climbing routes, since the distant view reveals gross patterns of ridges, cliffs, snowfields, and glaciers as well as average angle of inclination. As the party closes in on the peak, details of fault lines, bands of cliffs, and crevasse fields become apparent. It generally holds that gross patterns seen from afar are repeated in fine detail when viewed closer. Ledges revealed by snow or shrubs from a distance often turn out to be "sidewalks" with numerous smaller ledges interspersed between. The major fault lines, or weaknesses, of the mountain visible at a distance, are usually accompanied by finer, less obvious repetitions.

If the party's approach skirts the base of the mountain, the peak can be viewed from various perspectives, sometimes revealing piece by piece portions of a climbing route not apparent from any single direction. A system of ledges not highlighted by snow or shrubs, and indistinguishable against background cliffs, may be seen with startling clarity from another angle with the sky behind. Changing lighting as the sun traverses the sky often creates revealing shadows across a mountain face even when viewed straight on. Just a few minutes of studying lengthening or shortening shadows may be sufficient to disclose that apparently sheer cliffs are only moderately angled slopes.

The presence of snow, except perhaps during or immediately after a storm, discloses an angle of inclination permitting easy climbing, for snow will not long remain on slopes exceeding 40 degrees. Beware nature's tricks, though: rime adhering to vertical or even overhanging cliffs can at first appear to be snow, and deep high-angle gulleys often retain snow or ice year around, especially when shaded. Snow may glisten and sparkle, but does not shine: brilliant, shining snowfields high on the mountain are sheathed in ice and will no doubt call for the party's best ice climbing technique.

As the party nears the peak, keys to its defenses are sought: ridges with lower average inclination than the faces they divide; cracks, ledges, and chimneys leading up or across the faces; snowfields or glaciers offering easier or predictable pitches. Not only are possible routes identified, but climbing hazards are noted. Snowfields and icefalls are observed for avalanche activity. Rock faces are studied for signs of rockfall — snowfields readily reveal any recent activity on cliffs above by rock-filled "shell craters." If the route must go through such hazards, it may be better done in the cold hours of night or very early morning, before the warmth of the rising sun begins to melt the icy mortar bonding precariously perched boulders or seracs, setting off the daily bombardment of slopes below.

Throughout the approach the skilled routefinder repeatedly "climbs with his eyes," seeking continuous routes and evaluating difficulties and hazards. When the routes become so lengthy or complex as to tax the memory, quick sketches may be taken during rest stops. Such memory aids sometimes prove invaluable later in the climb when the critical exit gulley is lost from view. No matter how sage the foregoing advice, however, it will not apply to every climb. There will always be those peaks that are climbed "from the other side."

Trails

A trail by definition is not wilderness even though it be a corridor of civilization barely a foot wide. Usually there is something of a trail between the roadhead and terra incognita, a track that starts bravely and dwindles to nothing. In many a present wilderness the traveler comes upon useful remnants of a past penetration by civilization, fragmentary trails of long-vanished miners or trappers.

Even in ranges with heavy traffic and well posted with signs a moderate degree of alertness is required to find and keep on the correct trail. The beginning may be obliterated by logging operations or highway construction. Parties often stagnate mentally on a long monotonous walk and miss their proper turnoff. A good many more, awaiting an intersection with a prominent sign that has been flattened by winter snows or carried off by a souvenir hunter, find themselves at nightfall far up the wrong creek. Signs are poor substitutes for the methods of orientation discussed in Chapter 5, Navigation.

The climber must remember that very few trails were engineered for his use. Miners build trails to ore, fishermen to the high lakes, trappers along valleys, pioneers over passes, and animals pursue their own special interests. Frequently the mine or the lake or the pass is a splendid basecamp, and any old remnant of track is worth following if it goes reasonably near the right destination. Inevitably, however, there comes the painful moment when a pleasant trail must be abandoned because it goes to a lake or a prospect hole many miles up the wrong valley.

A human trail is often blazed in the forests and indicated above timberline by rock cairns; some are, unfortunately, marked with the ultimate abomination — pressurized spray paint. Following a marked trail requires some skill and much care: the tree with the critical blaze grows old and topples, an avalanche carries away a cairn. Also many marks are made by confused climbers on the wrong route.

An important principle in choosing off-trail routes is always to follow the course that a trail would follow if there were one. Trail builders generally find the easiest going; by studying their work one can more quickly and wisely navigate the pure wilderness.

Brush

Wherever there is running water and/or sliding snow, brush thrives. The classic example is a low-altitude gully swept by avalanches in winter and a torrent in summer. Coniferous trees cannot mature but conditions are perfect for supple shrubs which flourish during the short summer season, usually bend undamaged under the snow, and even if stripped to the ground quickly sprout again from the roots. Coniferous forests, if allowed to mature, reach high and steal all the sunlight, eventually throttling deciduous trees; along riverbanks brush keeps a window on the sun and builds a narrow dense thicket. A river that changes course frequently prevents conifers from gaining control and has a wide belt of alder bottoms. At subalpine elevations the entire valley floor may be a tangle, winter avalanche snow lasting late into summer and thus preventing forests but encouraging brush.

Large conifers are on the side of justice and the traveler, but small ones are poor friends. The second-growth timber that springs densely up after a fire or windstorm or logging is at its worst when about 20 feet high, the branches completely filling the space between trees, the overhead cover not yet so thick that lack of sunlight has caused these lower limbs to die and fall away. Moreover, at this age deciduous brush is still very much in the contest. Even more difficult to negotiate are blowdowns, avalanche fans, and logging trash where the jumble is so chaotic that frequently a quarter-mile an hour is an heroic velocity. A single such obstacle only a few hundred feet wide may justify major modifications of route and schedule.

The scrub growth at timberline, where wind forces conifers to huddle next to the ground, usually stands alone or in small clumps, but occasionally it forms a continuous belt. Another subalpine horror is scrub cedar that clings to bands of rocks and cliffs. These nearly impenetrable thickets of tough twisted trunks and branches are to be avoided entirely if possible by seeking breaks in the cliff bands.

If a skirmish with brush must be accepted there are a few techniques for getting through with a minimum of effort. Inspect the brushy area as much as possible on the approach and choose the shortest route across to a clear area beyond, using any fallen trees with long straight trunks as elevated walkways. Overlapping bushes may be parted vertically—wearing gloves if the vegetation is a type covered with thorns—to allow passage, and in some cases, such as slide alder, horizontally, stepping on some of the lower limbs and raising the higher ones to provide a passageway. In steep terrain some brush is helpful if it is well anchored and strong enough to use for handholds and "vegetable belays."

Brush is not without its dangers. Downhill-slanting vine maple or alder gives slippery footing and if one is bouncing along many feet from the ground a lost hold can cause a bad fall. Brush obscures cliffs, boulders, and ravines, and more than once has led a traveler to mischief. The manzanita (California's State bush) may grab a rope with such tenacity that one can recover it only with the bush in tow.

The best policy of all is to avoid brush. So bald a statement seems much like forthrightly condemning Hell, yet even in ranges where brush is a frightful menace an alert traveler often can thread an easy path. The following principles are helpful:

1. Use trail as much as possible; 5 miles of trail may be less work than 1 mile of brush.
2. Travel above the brush on early season snowcover. Some valleys are easy going in May when the party walks on 10 feet of snow but are almost impossible in July when the party must burrow under 10 feet of brush.
3. In summer avoid avalanche tracks. When following a long valley the best route may be on slopes with a south or west exposure where the snow does not avalanche so ferociously as on the opposite side. When climbing a valley wall stick to the "timber cones" between avalanche paths.
4. Always aim for the heaviest timber.
5. The ridge spurs between creeks and the valley walls above rivers may be dry and brushless while the creek bottoms and valley floors are nightmares.
6. As a final alternative consider going right into the channel of the stream. Gravel and boulder beds may provide a clear tunnel through the brush, though wading may be the price. Streams flowing in deep canyons, however, are usually either choked with fallen timber or interrupted by waterfalls.

7. If the valley bottoms are hopeless and the valley sides scarred by myriad avalanche tracks, it may be worthwhile to climb as directly as possible to timberline and take a high route above the brush. The difficulties of the rocks and ice must of course be weighed against those below.
8. In alpine valleys travel on scree and remnants of snow rather than adjacent thickets.
9. Seek game trails. Animals dislike brush as much as man does. Their intelligence is less than human but their experience greater.

Talus

The rocks of the peaks constantly crumble and tumble and pile up in the valley as talus. Most of the rubble emerges from gullies and spreads out below in fan-shaped cones which often merge into one another, forming a broad band of talus between the valley greenery and precipice. Talus fans also often alternate with timber cones.

Talus slopes build gradually over the ages. In the oldest heaps, soil has filled the interstices between boulders, making smooth pathways. "Newer" rock piles without vegetation can be dependable where the climber can leap about lightly, guarding against the occasional teetering stone by his very momentum.

In volcanic and younger mountains talus can be dangerous. Rapid disintegration of the rocks leaves even huge boulders delicately balanced, and the traveler must always be ready to skip nimbly aside when his foothold suddenly shifts. Occasionally a talus slope, and frequently moraines, which are very recent piles of sand and rock, are so insecure that kicking loose one key stone will destroy the precarious equilibrium, setting off a disastrous rock avalanche. The slopes of smallest fragments, called *scree*, may be securely anchored by vegetation or may be as loose as sand, requiring great patience and energy to climb.

The most careful person on the stablest scree cannot avoid loosing an occasional pebble or boulder and therefore routes are preferred which allow each climber to avoid the fall line of climbers above and below. When the choice of route is restricted, as in a narrow gully, each member must tread gently and instantaneously give a warning shout should he start a stone rolling. Frequently it is essential for a party to travel one at a time or closely bunched up so that rocks cannot attain dangerous momentum between members.

On descent, loose scree is sometimes sought rather than avoided, for the sport of "screeing." The object is to start a minor slide of pebbles and then ride it down, in a standing glissade, shuffling the feet adroitly to keep them on the surface, avoiding large leg-breaker rocks, stepping to one side if things get out of hand. Screeing, however, is permissible only where vegetation is totally non-existent; the merits of the sport do not justify wiping out the tiniest struggling plant.

Snow

The techniques of snow travel and climbing are the same whether the snow lies on a high spire or in the deep woods. If slopes are at all long and steep, safeguards such as ice axe and rope should be employed even if the party is walking along a trail — a trail buried under a dozen feet of snow.

Not to be overlooked are the advantages of snow in cross-country travel. Talus, brush, and logging slash are paved highways when covered by consolidated snow and for this reason many a peak is best bagged early in the season. During the same season snow bridges may provide quick passage over rushing streams, with the caveat that crossing snow bridges over streams is often much like crossing bridges over crevasses. As spring merges into summer and obstacles emerge, the route along a valley floor may be quite erratic, taking advantage of every remaining snow patch for the few yards or steps of easy walking it provides.

Despite the advantages of walking on the spring or early summer snow patches there are some potential hazards. Logs and boulders covered with snow often have adjacent hidden cavities which can give way under the foot of the unwary traveler. Probe or avoid likely spots, and step wide off logs or rocks.

Streams beneath the snow melt the underside of the snowcover until it can no longer support the weight of a traveler (Fig. 6-1). A careless step may result in a sudden drop and wet feet, or worse, being carried under the snow by a swift stream. Watch for depressions or variations in color or texture of the snow and listen for sounds of running water underneath. The volume of water emerging at the foot of a snowfield may give a clue to the existence if not the size of the cavity beneath.

With experience a person is able to recognize and avoid the hidden dangers lurking under the surface of the snow and use the medium to his own advantage.

Streams

When a party enters wilderness without trail or bridge, water becomes a major impediment. In the Canadian Coast Range or Alaska, climbers may spend more time and energy crossing a perilous river than on their ultimate objective, the mountain.

Finding the Crossing

Whenever the peak lies beyond a respectable river the crossing is a major factor in route selection. A distant view — perhaps from a ridge before descent into the valley—is sometimes better than a hundred close views from a riverbank. When a distant view is unobtainable or unhelpful the party must balance one against the other the merits of going along close to the bank for the sake of finding a footlog or log jam, at the expense of suffering riverbottom brush, and walking high on open ridge slopes, then striking directly for the river.

Fig. 6-1. Snow bridge over stream.

In deep forest a party may find easy passage over even the widest river on a semipermanent log jam wedged together during some past flood. Higher in the mountains footlogs are harder to come by, particularly when the river changes course periodically, preventing the growth of large trees near its channel. If such footlogs are not available and wading is inevitable, one sound, though not entirely obvious bit of advice is to seek always the widest part of a river: the narrows of a watercourse, though seemingly offering the shortest duration of suffering, are the deepest and the swiftest, and hence the most dangerous.

Making the Crossing

Before attempting any stream crossing that would require swimming in case of slip, unfasten the waist strap of the pack. Frequently it is possible to cross a stream by hopping from one boulder to another. The sequence should be closely studied beforehand and every stride and leap rehearsed mentally. Often safety lies in smooth and steady progress, the stones being too unsteady and slippery to allow balance for more than a moment in transit to the next. An ice axe or pole for an added point of support may be almost indispensable.

At low altitude footlogs are relatively plentiful and require a second thought only when slippery, awkwardly thin, or steeply inclined. Again an ice axe or pole, or a tightly stretched handline, is helpful in maintaining balance on an unstable log crossing.

The efforts of a wilderness traveler are directed toward finding a dry crossing by stone or log but the wet crossing must often be accepted. If the water is placid and the stones rounded, Spartan climbers carry boots and lower garments dry in the pack. In more severe conditions an excellent plan is to remove socks before wading and wear boots in the water; on the far side the boots can be drained and dry socks replaced. The climber must consider the advantages and disadvantages of removing trousers or other clothing in deeper crossings. Any loose clothing increases the drag from rapidly moving water, but clothing reduces the chilling factor of icy water and may permit a longer crossing before the legs or feet become numb.

The force of moving water is easy to underestimate. A swift stream flowing only shin-deep boils up against the knees. Knee-deep water may boil above the waist and give the traveler a disconcerting sensation of buoyancy. Whenever water boils above the knee it is dangerous — the rocks underfoot are also buoyant and easily dislodged, and one false step turns the brave climber into a frightened swimmer bounding in white water from boulder to boulder. It is well to remember that frothy water contains so much air that though wet enough to drown in, it may not be dense enough to float the human body. Water milky from glacier-milled rock flour presents the added difficulty that one cannot see the bottom but must probe blindly with the feet.

Sometimes if the stream is fairly deep but not too swift, a crossing can be made quite easily by angling downstream at about the same speed as the current. Usually, however, it is best to face upstream on the crossing, leaning into the current and stabbing the ice axe or a stout pole upstream for a third point of suspension. The leading foot probes for solid placement on the shifting bottom, the following foot advances, and the the axe or pole is thrust into a new position. Sometimes the crossing is best made in pairs, one person bracing the other while he advances to a secure stance. Team crossing with a pole is a method in common use in some parts of the world. Team members line up facing across the stream with the pole parallel to the stream. Each member grasps the pole securely. As the team advances across the stream the upstream member breaks the force of the current while the others help support him. If one person slips, the others can support him until he regains his footing.

On a very hazardous crossing it is only common sense for the leader to be belayed. Skill in belaying is essential, supplemented by visualization of a body caught in stream flow. Obviously it is best for the belay to be placed as far above the crossing as possible, for in a "fall" the leader will pendulum in the current to the near bank. The higher upstream the belay, the shorter the fall. Rescuers poised on the bank at the end of the pendulum swing can often save a life by swift action. Once the leader has attained the far shore his companions can be safeguarded by an anchored handline. They should stay on the downstream side of the handline and either move hand-over-hand or grasp a short sling clipped to a carabiner which slides along the line. When there is any doubt every member should be belayed, with due respect for potentially entangling snags.

Some rivers are quite perfectly impassable. If the headwaters are fed by snow, early morning is usually the time of minimum flow and a party may camp overnight awaiting lower water. Sometimes it is necessary to hike hours or days seeking a vulnerable point. Very rarely a Tyrolean traverse (see Chapter 12) can be rigged if one member is capable of swimming or wading the flood to fix a line on the far bank. For the widest and deepest rivers rafts are the only alternative short of hiking to the headwaters, which in some cases would make a very long outing indeed.

EFFICIENT WALKING

In generations past, walking was so necessary a human activity that nearly everyone was expert. Nowadays, with the advance of mechanized transportation, walking has become so rare an art that usually a person taking up the sport of wilderness mountaineering must first learn to walk before he can climb. Though the technique is not at all complicated, and can be performed in a rough and ready fashion even by infants, a little study and practice are needed to become proficient.

Preparing to Walk

Conditioning

Any physical activity is most easily performed by a body in good condition from frequent exercise. Through a sustained high level of muscular exertion the capacity for exertion is increased, as discussed in Appendix 1. Mountaineering being predominantly a sport of those with sedentary occupations, most persons undergo the annual agonies of "getting in condition." On an extended trip conditioning comes naturally and easily. During the first days the heart pounds and the lungs gasp and the muscles ache, but the system steadily adjusts and eventually begins to attain that splendid and exhilarating state when extraordinary feats are possible and enjoyable. Weekend mountaineering is frustrating: the body "tunes up" during the weekend and on Monday—back in the office—is ready for marvelous things; by Thursday, disappointed, it begins to relax. Generally the early part of a season requires considerable mental resolve and some physical discomfort, for it takes several months of weekend outings to attain the physical fitness gained in one good week of hard walking. A schedule of training exercises helps immensely in developing endurance.

Going Light

If the fault of overloading were not so universal it would be banal to declare that one can walk faster with a lighter pack. Most novices quickly learn to do without pajamas, parasols, and cast-iron skillets but even the experienced sometimes fail to thoroughly analyze their gear. Each item should be considered: Is it absolutely necessary? Was it used on the previous trip? Is there any lighter substitute? Ruthless paring of ounces—but never at the expense of safety and/or climbing essentials— saves pounds of weight and adds miles to the hiking range.

The Act of Walking

It is one thing to walk from the doorstep to the family automobile or from the bus stop to the office; on such short journeys it is not essential to walk efficiently. It is quite another matter to walk many miles through rough wilderness carrying heavy loads. The maximum capacity varies with individuals, depending upon conditioning and general physical size and strength. However, whatever the maximum capacity may be of a particular individual at a particular moment, it cannot be realized without careful attention to practices of good walking.

Pace and Rest

The proper pace is a complex equation between the body's strength, the load it is carrying, the distance to be traveled, and the time available. It is silly to specify 3 miles per hour as good average speed, or 1000 feet of altitude per hour, or 15 miles per day. There is too wide a range between flat sea level trail and steep alpine slopes, between 20-pound rucksacks and 100-pound expeditionary loads, for any average to be meaningful. There are several aspects to pace: first, the speed, or number of steps taken during an hour; second, the manner in which these steps should be taken to conserve energy; third, how frequently the party should cease taking steps—that is, rest.

The most common mistake of the beginner is walking too fast, thinking desperately of the great distance to be covered. It is pointless to travel 1 mile in 4 minutes—or 15 minutes—if the result is such utter exhaustion that the remaining 9 miles to basecamp are impossible. Nor do rational mountaineers keep books listing the "best time from Swamp Camp to

Blowdown Camp as 3 hours 47 minutes 12.5 seconds." Sometimes it may be necessary to make all possible haste from Swamp Camp to Blowdown Camp, as when being pursued by a forest fire, but if an entire day is available for the journey it is far more meritorious to arrive relaxed at Blowdown with memories and photographs of the flora, fauna, and geology en route.

There is a simple test by which any individual at any time can determine if his pace is proper: if it cannot be sustained hour after hour it is too fast. Two departments of the body have separate control. A person can walk only as fast as his legs allow: when it becomes a mighty effort to drag the foot forward the pace is too fast. A person can walk only as fast as his lungs allow: when the lungs are desperately gasping for air the pace is too fast. Either symptom requires a slowdown. Along a flat trail the legs complain while the lungs are still content. At high altitude the lungs are starving for air while the legs are growing stiff from lack of exercise.

Ambition and vanity usually ensure male chauvinists against going too slowly. Some hikers place excessive emphasis on the rule that a pace should be comfortable. The body complains long before it is hurt. The muscles may ache but still have 10 miles left in them; the lungs may gasp but be able to continue gasping another 3 hours. Indeed, the body improves its efficiency most rapidly when driven close to its limits of performance. A certain degree of suffering is inevitable if one is to become a good walker.

Speed fluctuates during the day. At the beginning of a walk, especially in the morning, it is well to go along slowly to let the body become gradually aware of the demands that will be made. With so courteous a start it is more enthusiastic about gearing up to full power. The phenomenon of "second wind" is familiar: after an initial period during which willpower must be exerted to keep going, suddenly the hiker finds himself striding along happy and strong, free to observe with pleasure the sights along the way. Physiologically this means the heart has taken a faster tempo, the blood is circulating more rapidly, the muscles have loosened.

Since the trail is seldom uniform the climber must adjust his pace. On a steep hill he plods slowly and methodically but as the grade lessens his speed increases until on a decline he may be fairly flying along. Late in the day speed decreases, for though adrenalin secretions allow short bursts of explosive exertion there is no "third wind." The body has already done its utmost and the accumulating poisons of fatigue steadily lower efficiency.

If one mountaineering technique had to be singled out as most important, honors would go to the *rest step*, used on any terrain whenever expenditure of energy is so great that either legs or lungs need an interval of recuperation between steps. The pace is slow, since for every step there is a pause. Breathing must be synchronized with the sequence. For example: inhale as rear foot advances to a new position; exhale as the unweighted advanced leg rests, the body entirely supported on the rear leg; repeat. When the air is thin it is the lungs that need a pause, sometimes for two or three or five breaths to each step. At high elevations climbers must make a conscious effort to breathe deeply and frequently. At lower altitude it is leg muscles that need extra time to accumulate energy.

An important element of the rest step is mental composure. When the summit seems to remain constantly distant for hours on end the individual must trust the rest step to slowly but steadily chew up the miles. When monotony impairs morale he must draw on his inner resources, his ability to lose time and place in reflection of other times and places.

A reasonable speed, with the rest step when needed, eliminates nearly all the collapse rests of the novice hiker, who sags in a heap at the slightest provocation. Still, some rests are required by the strongest and most expert walkers. Formulas are frequently proposed for the allowable number of rests per hour and their optimum duration. All such formulas presume uniform human beings with uniform packs walking along uniform trails and therefore they are all nonsense. Their one germ of truth is that "to rest is not to conquer." A party sprawled in the meadows is not getting any closer to its objective, unless its objective is sprawling in meadows. It is simple logic to ask always whether a rest is really necessary, and if not, whether there is time for luxury. A party holding to a tight schedule will not rest nearly so often as members would like. If there is no hurry it will rest whenever the mood seizes.

Mandatory for a large party and desirable for any is a *shakedown* rest during the first half-hour of the day: bootlaces must be loosened or tightened, packstraps adjusted, layers of clothing added or subtracted. In mixed groups party separations should be declared as a matter of course and/or as need and terrain dictate: their omission can cause almost debilitating distress to members too shy to express the need. (Wilderness etiquette and large numbers of weekend mountaineers dictate that the first party separation should if possible be near the trailhead at a service station or privy.) During the early part of a day, while the body is fresh, rests should be infrequent and short: for such *breathers* it is best to rest in a standing or semi-reclining postion, leaning against a tree or hillside to remove packweight from the shoulders, taking deep breaths and a bite to eat. Later on the body demands more complete relaxation and about every hour or two the party staggers into a *sackout* rest. When it is nearing time for a stop members begin watching for some point with special advantages, such as convenient slopes for unslinging packs, a water supply, a view, or pretty flowers. It is all too easy to prolong such moments, but when the camp or summit is still far away climbers should remember how agonizing is the resumption of a march once muscles become cold and stiff. Experienced walkers, knowing the day's itinerary and whether it is easy or rough, automatically include the proper number of breathers and sackouts. They know moreover that at the end of a long hard haul the body, despite all reason and rest-stepping, begins to defy will and demand the *collapse* rest, toppling into snow or mud and lying there utterly inert and content.

Downhill and Sidehill

Downhill walking is nowhere nearly so fatiguing as uphill walking but the blessings of gravity are not unmixed. It is on the downtrail that blisters are raised and knee cartilage displaced, for weight drops abruptly and roughly on legs and feet. Jolts traveling up the spine so shock and jar the entire body that after a long descent the very head may begin to ache. Far sooner the hiker feels his knees coming loose at the hinges and expects them to begin working both ways like those of a rag doll. Even more serious, at every step the toes jam forward in the boot and hot spots develop on the feet.

The first preparation for the downtrail is to stuff the boots full of socks and tie the laces tight to reduce movement of foot within boot. The downhill pace is kept much more moderate than the one urged by gravity. The leg lands on each step with bent knee to cushion the jar and the feet are placed as lightly as possible, as if they were already sore. Such restraint is extremely tiring to muscles of the upper leg, which may begin to quiver under the strain of holding back the weight of the body and pack; in loose pumice or scree a stiff-legged glissade provides welcome relief. Rests on the downtrail are just as essential as on the uptrail.

Sidehill-gouging is one of the ultimate evils of the mountain world; when it cannot be avoided there is no alternative to suffering the agonies of bent ankles and contorted hips. If there is a choice between struggling along a sidehill and dropping into a flat valley—barring valley bottom brush—the altitude loss is often more than compensated for by the saving of legs and ankles. Similarly, if the top of the ridge is rounded the walking may be much easier in the long run even though there are many ups and downs. On a long sidehill gouge it may be possible to switchback occasionally to alternate muscle strain. Any available flat spots such as imbedded rocks, grass or heather clumps, animal trails, and the like offer relief.

Etiquette

Walking is more often than not a social sport and demands a regard for certain social amenities, a trail etiquette which is really no more than common sense thoughtfulness. On the trail it is very bad form to follow the man ahead so closely that he feels pressed; besides, he may respond with equally bad form by bending back the branches of a tree like a catapult and loosing them full in the face of the follower. If one wishes to tie a shoelace or adjust a pack, it is simple courtesy to step aside and not block traffic. In passing another member of the party, social amenities are better served by expressing this desire rather than crowding past, especially on narrow trails or the edges of cliffs. If a member or members of the party cannot keep up with the pace set by the leader, the speed should be reduced. Wilderness is characterized by a small population density, and ill will fostered by stumbling over one another is decidedly unnecessary.

Use of the Ice Axe

Although introduction of the flip-top beverage container has largely relieved the ice axe of its function as a can opener, climbers and hikers still find it an invaluable all-purpose tool. On open trails many climbers strap the axe on the pack, using the ice axe carrier provided or tying it to the frame. In rough country the axe is so useful in the hands, and in the pack snags so frequently on brush and tree limbs, it is better brought out into the open.

Ice axes, like any edged tool, should be kept sharpened to a degree appropriate to the use intended. An axe properly sharpened for climbing ice may be a hazard on a trail or when used as a third leg on a heather slope. At such times it is prudent to install an axe guard.

Even so the ice axe is probably the most dangerous implement of mountaineering. Carrying an axe without the skill to use it properly provides a false sense of security, as well as high risk of injury should the alpine traveler fall on his own axe and impale himself. All too frequently climbers have slipped on hard snow only to discover that the principles of ice axe arrest only vaguely recalled from the pages of a climbing text were not adequate to stop the fall. It is imperative that alpine travelers be skilled in arrest techniques *before* venturing onto hard or crusty snow. The way to acquire this skill is by practice on slopes with safe runout in case of failure to arrest (see Chapter 14).

When the axe is carried in the hand on good trail the shaft is grasped at the balance point, the spike forward and the head to the rear with the pick down. Thus the man behind is safeguarded against accidentally running into the spike, and the pick is less likely to do the owner harm in a stumble. When a climber is weary or footing is poor he can use the axe for a cane, grasped by the head with the pick to the rear. On steep slippery terrain, whether mud, needles, grass, or snow, the axe is grasped by the head with the guard removed and the pick to the rear, in position for a quick arrest in event of a slip.

On any terrain other than a flat and beaten trail the climber may find numerous unsuspected uses of the axe. In stream fording it provides a third leg among the shifting stones. When hopping over talus it gives many a slight touch-and-go balance point. On steep hillsides, just as on steep snow, the axe held diagonally across the body, spike touching the slope, helps hold a stable, vertical stance. Though the ice axe self-arrest is treated in Chapter 14 as a technique for snow, many a climber has been most happy to use it to stop himself in steep meadows and forest.

Fig. 6-2. Carrying ice axe on easy terrain.

 PART TWO

Climbing Fundamentals

Plate 10. First pitch, Cascade Waterfall, Banff, Alberta. (Patrick Morrow)

7 *

ROPES AND KNOTS

THE ROPE, more than any other item of equipment, symbolizes the climber. Since the main purpose of the rope is to limit the fall of a climber when his strength, judgment or the terrain let him down, an inadequate rope or ignorance of its proper use is often worse than no rope at all, due to the false sense of security it conveys. A climber should devote considerable thought to the selection of his rope as well as to its care and proper use.

The climbing rope must be attached to the climbers, and frequently also to the mountain, to be effective; climbers must therefore learn to tie and use a number of knots. The ones described herein have been selected on the basis of strength, adaptability to differing situations, and ease of tying. Knots are also used in constructing seat harnesses, runners, slings and prusiks. These items are described, as well as the knots used in making them or connecting them to rope or mountain. One additional item—the carabiner—is introduced here because although a hardware item, it is used with rope, runners, and harnesses.

ROPES

Climbing ropes may be made from natural or synthetic fibers by either laid or kernmantel construction (Fig. 7-1). Laid ropes are usually composed of three main strands twisted around each other, each strand consisting of many individual fibers which are also twisted around each other. Kernmantel ropes are made of a core of twisted, braided, or parallel strands of nylon enclosed in a tightly woven outer sheath.

For many years laid ropes of natural fibers, primarily manila hemp, were used. Because of low strength and limited shock absorbing properties, manila has no place in climbing today except as expendable training ropes, and then only in situations where they will not be subjected to the high stresses of leader falls.

Fig. 7-1. Climbing ropes. *Left,* laid. *Right,* kernmantel.

More recently laid ropes made of nylon were used, offering greater strength and improved shock absorbing ability. One nylon laid rope, Goldline®, is still available. It is satisfactory for much snow and glacier climbing and for occasional use on rock, and, as a bonus, it ordinarily is the least expensive of ropes. However, because of its principal disadvantages — readiness to kink, a tendency to spin a free-hanging climber, greater friction on rock, and often excessive stretch under body weight — it is seldom seen in use for high-angle rock or ice climbing.

Kernmantel, or core-and-sheath ropes were developed in Europe and introduced in America in the 1960s. Though costing more, these ropes are chosen almost exclusively today for their superior energy absorbing characteristics and handling qualities. Most ropes of this type, manufactured specifically for climbing, have been subjected to the test of the UIAA (Union International des Associations d'Alpinisme), an organization whose membership includes climbers, climbing organizations, and equipment manufacturers. The UIAA test, originally proposed in France during the 1950s, determines the rope's ability to withstand repeated shock-loading while limiting the peak force felt by the falling climber.

Selecting a Rope

In order to intelligently select the rope on which to trust his life, a climber must know which qualities are essential and which are merely desirable. The two essential qualities are breaking strength and shock absorbency: the rope must be strong enough to withstand the forces applied to it in a fall, and at the same time stretch just enough to absorb the energy developed by the falling climber without putting an intolerably high peak force on the body. The rope should not elongate so much (like a rubber band) at the bottom of the fall that unnecessary injuries are sustained from a collision with a ledge or the ground.

All discussion here is of "single ropes," that is, ropes of a diameter or strength which permit their use as a single line in climbing, as opposed to "double ropes," which are smaller in diameter and lower in strength, yet if doubled (two lines) have equal or greater strength than the single rope. Single ropes are generally 10 to 11.5 mm in diameter; double ropes are often 9 mm in diameter or smaller, and are used in Europe, although rarely in America.

Any single rope meeting UIAA standards is satisfactory for climbing. Minor variations in tensile strength or shock absorbency are often ignored and the final decision based on such intangibles as "feel" and appearance. A climbing rope should be purchased only at stores where climbing equipment is sold. To pass today's UIAA tests, a 2.8-meter (approximately 9-foot) sample of the rope must sustain three falls of an 80-kilogram (176-lb) weight without failure. The weight is positioned for a fall of 5 meters (16 feet) with the peak force on the rope not exceeding 1200 kilograms (2650 lbs) for the first fall.

One desirable quality of a rope is its ability to sustain hard falls even after considerable use. In addition, it should be relatively light in weight, resistant to abrasion and kinking, hold knots well, slide smoothly over rock and through carabiners, offer a good grip to the hands, soak up little or no water, and have a reasonably long life expectancy. One other desirable characteristic, resistance to being cut over an edge during a fall, is currently being investigated. It appears likely that in the future a standard test of this characteristic will be developed and this parameter identified for the purchaser. Unfortunately in the design of the rope an improvement in one desirable characteristic likely results in a detrimental effect to another; thus the end result is a compromise.

For all-around use the 45-meter (150-foot) length is normally satisfactory. Rock climbing enthusiasts may prefer longer ropes and snow climbers shorter ones. A 37-meter (120-foot) rope is generally considered the shortest useful length and 50 meters (165 feet) about as long as practical. Backpackers occasionally carry a shorter rope for emergency use when not intending any roped climbing.

Care of the Rope

As with any other piece of fine equipment, a rope deserves care in storage and use to avoid damage. Novices frequently are taken aback by the outraged screams they hear when their feet carelessly land on someone's rope. They may even fear for their lives if their feet wear crampons. While such vehemence may seem unwarranted at first, thought of oneself dangling in an exposed situation from a partly perforated rope may lead to a greater understanding of the experienced climber's attitude. In general, climbers take great care NOT to step on the rope, to avoid snagging it on sharp rocks, and to keep it out of the way while using sharp instruments. Even when the greatest care has been exercised, the rope should be checked over its entire length for cuts and abrasions after use.

During periods between use, the rope should be stored in a clean, cool place, out of the rays of the sun. All knots should be removed and the rope coiled loosely. It should not be stretched or left under tension during storage, and at no time should it be allowed to come in contact with battery acid or other potentially harmful chemicals. The ends should be fused in a flame, taped or whipped to prevent unravelling, and only manufacturer-recommended preparations or procedures should be used for marking the midpoint.

Over a period of time, dirt and tiny rock particles working their way between fibers of the rope may cut them, so the rope should be washed occasionally. Use mild soap and the "delicate fabrics" setting on an automatic washer, rinse well to remove soap, then drip dry.

Even with the best of tender loving care, a rope eventually wears out. When its strength is in doubt, for whatever reason, retire it. A cut in the rope is always grounds for retirement, as is a hard fall. A conservative evaluation is called for: attempts to rationalize continued use of a doubtful rope after a fall could lead to a disastrous failure on the next fall.

Fig. 7-2. Mountaineer's coil.

Various organizations concerned with mountain safety offer "days of usage" estimates of climbing rope life. While a correlation does seem to exist between the number of sustained UIAA falls and its useful safe life, satisfactory statistical proof is still lacking. A kernmantel rope may be considered overdue for retirement when the outer sheath is worn or cut through, anywhere. One rule of thumb is to retire a rope when 50 per cent of the surface strands are worn to fuzz. Certainly a 10-year-old rope could not be depended on; many would say that a 5-year-old rope was too old, and at least a few climbers retire a rope after 2 years of use, regardless of its appearance.

The rope is normally coiled for ease of carrying and storing. A number of coiling methods have been used; the two presented in Fig. 7-2 and 7-3 are relatively easy to accomplish and result in a minimum of later kinks and knots. When coiling, allow each loop to lie as it does naturally except for major kinks, rather than forcing it into a neat-looking coil. This will minimize twists and kinks when it is uncoiled for use.

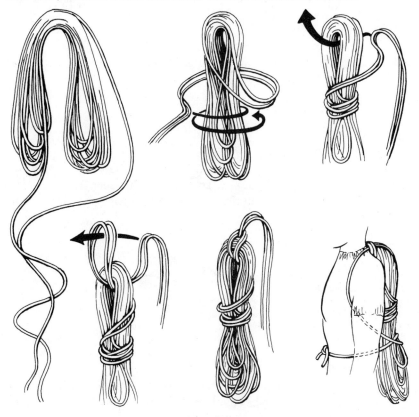

Fig. 7-3. Butterfly coil.

KNOTS

Often there is a need to tie a knot in rope or webbing under adverse circumstances – in the dark, on a steep rock cliff, during a drenching rainstorm, while hanging on with one hand. The climber must know which knot is best (or at least acceptable) for the purpose intended, and must know how to tie the knot well. Repeated practice is the most effective teacher (sadistic climbing instructors recommended practicing knots in simulated climbing conditions – under a cold shower at 2 a.m. without turning on the lights).

The climber should keep in mind that any knot is a temporary connection. Knots depended upon over a long time period have magical ability to untie themselves, possibly with help from the trolls on the mountain. Permanent knots are desirable for some purposes, but no such knot exists. Most knots are intended to be temporary: they must be secure for the moment to anchor a belay, but untied immediately after as the climb continues. All knots must be repeatedly checked, and sometimes retied.

Fig. 7-4. Overhand knot.

Fundamental Knots

The Overhand Knot and Overhand Loop

Perhaps the simplest knot to tie, the overhand knot (Fig. 7-4) is used to secure a loose end of a rope after another knot has been tied. It can also be used to form a loop when tied with a doubled rope or webbing (Fig. 7-5).

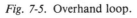

Fig. 7-5. Overhand loop.

Figure-8 Loop

The figure-8 is a simple way of making a loop anywhere on a rope. It is a very strong knot, yet can be readily untied after having been loaded. It is often confused with the overhand knot, but is tied with an extra twist, which gives it its distinctive "8" appearance.

Fig. 7-6. Figure-8 loop.

Figure-8, Rewoven

By tying the figure-8 in this manner, it is possible to use this knot to fasten the rope to trees or places the loop cannot be slipped over (as shown in Fig. 7-7). Because of its strength, simplicity and ease of checking, this knot is used to attach the end of the climbing rope to the climber's seat harness as discussed later. When completed, this knot looks exactly like the figure-8 loop.

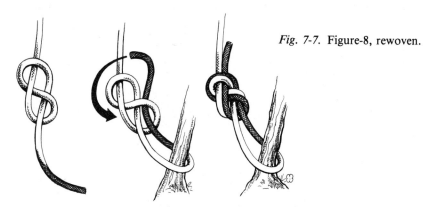

Fig. 7-7. Figure-8, rewoven.

Water Knot

The water knot is used to attach two rope or webbing ends together. Start the knot by tying an overhand knot in one of the ends. Then feed the other end back through the knot, following the path of the first rope in reverse. If tied with webbing, the finished knot should appear as shown in Fig. 7-8. Since this knot has a tendency to creep, as soon as you have tied it, try to pull it apart, using your full body weight, and check it from time to time. This knot is used primarily to tie runners, chest harnesses, and as a tie-off for a homemade harness.

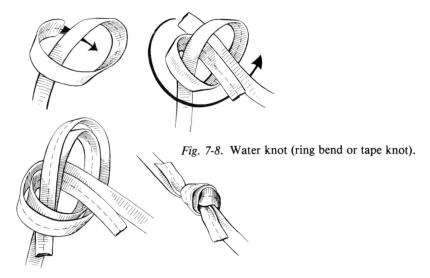

Fig. 7-8. Water knot (ring bend or tape knot).

Double Sheet Bend

This knot is sometimes used instead of the water knot as the tie-off knot for the homemade seat harness described later. The ends of the webbing must be secured with overhand backup knots. The double sheet bend is more easily adjusted for tightening the harness waist loops than a water knot, but has a greater tendency to work loose.

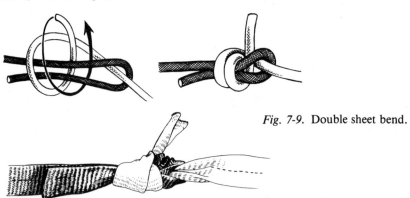

Fig. 7-9. Double sheet bend.

Single Bowline

The single bowline (Fig. 7-10) is used to form a loop at the end of a rope. This knot is quite strong and is used when setting up a belay anchor. It can easily be adjusted and is well suited to applications such as fastening a loop around a tree. As with most knots, the loose end should be tied off with an overhand knot as shown in Fig. 7-4.

Fig. 7-10. Single bowline.

Double Bowline

A loop can be formed in the middle of a rope by using the double bowline (Fig. 7-11). It is tied in the same manner as the single bowline and has similar uses. When using a seat harness, the middle man on a three-man rope team may use the double bowline to attach the climbing rope to the harness. The loop end must be secured with an overhand knot or a carabiner.

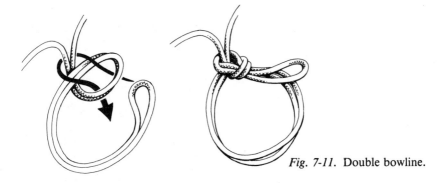

Fig. 7-11. Double bowline.

The Fisherman's Knot

This knot, which consists of two simple overhand knots, can be used for tying two ropes together as shown in Fig. 7-12. It has, to a large degree, been replaced by the double fisherman's knot, and is shown here primarily to provide a clearer understanding of the double fisherman's knot below.

Fig. 7-12. Fisherman's knot.

The Double Fisherman's Knot

Also called a grapevine knot, this secure knot is favored by climbers over the water knot for tying runners and for tying two ropes together because it does not work loose as easily as a water knot. The figure shows the double fisherman's knot for tying two ropes together.

Fig. 7-13. Double fisherman's knot.

Special Purpose Knots

Other often-used knots—the girth hitch, overhand slip knot, and the clove hitch—are shown in Fig. 7-14 tying off partially driven pitons. Other uses are suggested in later chapters.

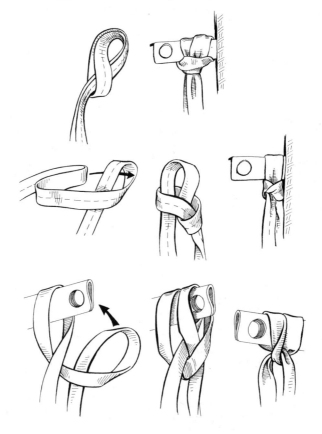

Fig. 7-14. Top, girth hitch; *center,* overhand slip knot; *bottom,* clove hitch.

The Prusik Knot

The prusik knot provides the climber with a practical means of ascending the climbing rope. Under tension the prusik knot grips the climbing rope; with the tension removed the knot can easily be moved along the rope. Note that the rope for tying the prusik should be of smaller diameter than the climbing rope. The knot is also useful on tent or tarp guylines as a means of tightening these lines, using the same principle of increasing or releasing tension.

When tying the knot form a large loop behind the climbing rope. Gather the remainder of the sling material in the other hand and pass it around the climbing rope and through the loop three times. Then straighten out the loops so they lie next to each other, but do not cross (neatness counts!). Two turns around a twisted style rope may hold. However, two turns may not hold on a kernmantel rope—three are generally used. Unusual situations, such as heavy loads or ice-covered ropes, may require more turns.

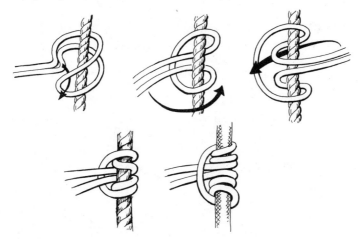

Fig. 7-15. Prusik knot. Tying sequence and three-wrap prusik for kernmantel rope, viewed from the back.

Connecting the Climber to the Rope

The traditional tie-in connecting the climber to a rope, a bowline-on-a-coil, is still known to most climbers and is occasionally used when a seat harness is not available. However, the bowline-on-a-coil and similar bowline-on-a-coil middleman present a serious problem in a fall: the rope coils around the waist ride up partially over the chest, constricting breathing; hanging in this position for 15 minutes or longer can cause suffocation.

The swami belt (four to six wraps of nylon webbing tied around the waist) became popular with rock climbers who wanted to increase the working length of their climbing ropes. It also offers some improvement over the bowline-on-a-coil in distributing the forces sustained in a fall over a larger area of the mid-section of the body, but does not eliminate the problem of suffocation when hanging.

A seat harness with leg loops is the best solution. When used properly, the seat harness will ride comfortably on the hips, and, in the event of a fall, the forces will be applied to the pelvic structure. A seat harness is used for both rock and glacier climbing, and also makes an excellent rappel seat.

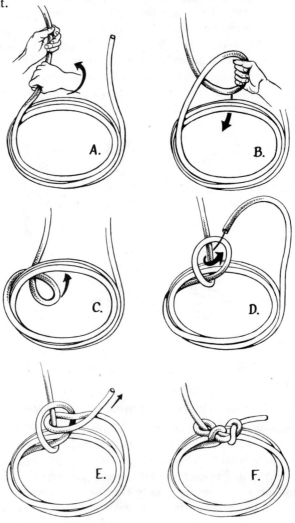

Fig. 7-16. Bowline-on-a-coil, endman.

The Bowline-on-a-Coil, Endman

The bowline-on-a-coil wraps three or four coils around the climber's waist to distribute the shock of a fall. The coils must be wound tightly during tying; otherwise in a fall they will slip up around the climber's chest and interfere with breathing. This knot, like most others, can work loose during normal use, and should be reinforced by tying off the loose end with an overhand knot around the coils as shown in Fig. 7-16f.

Bowline-on-a-Coil Middleman

Bowline-on-a-coil middleman can be used to attach the middleman of a three-man rope team to the climbing rope. The method of tying the knot is very similar to the bowline-on-a-coil at the end of the rope, except that a doubled rope is used throughout. The doubled rope is passed around the body twice, making a total of four strands. Instead of tying off the loose end, the end loop may be clipped to the coils with a carabiner, as shown in Fig. 7-17.

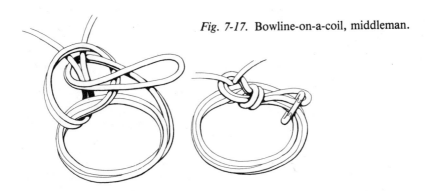

Fig. 7-17. Bowline-on-a-coil, middleman.

SEAT HARNESSES
Homemade Seat Harness

The harness described requires about 22 feet of 1-inch tubular nylon webbing for an average-sized climber. The leg loops are tied as shown in Fig. 7-18. The length of the bridge between the leg loops is about 6-8 inches. The size of the leg loops is important in achieving a proper fit; some tailoring will be required for everyone. The leg loops should be tied so the knot does not ride too high on the hips, but should be large enough to be worn comfortably over the heaviest clothing that will be worn while climbing. The recommended knot for tying the leg loops is the overhand loop knot (Fig. 7-5). Once the leg loops are properly sized they are left in the webbing. Fig. 7-18 shows how the harness is put on and secured. A separate waist loop, made from about 8 feet of webbing, is also worn with the harness as a backup system in case the harness knot should work loose, and to provide a tie-in should the need arise to remove the leg loop portion of the harness for nature calls. Water knots used as the tie-off for both harness and waist loop may be tightened by first tying the knots loosely and then working the excess slack through each knot.

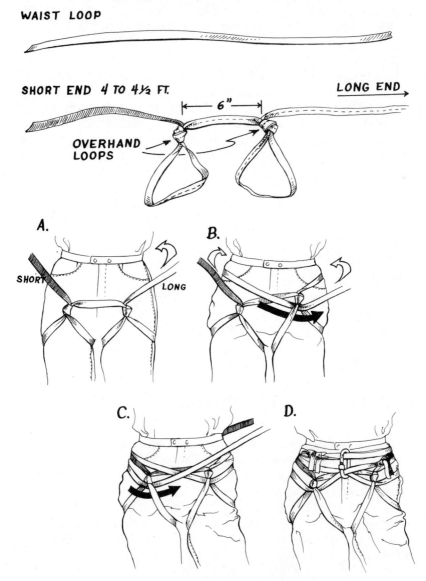

WAIST LOOP

SHORT END 4 TO 4½ FT.

LONG END

OVERHAND LOOPS

A.

SHORT

LONG

B.

C.

D.

Fig. 7-18. Seat harness construction. *Top,* length of material; *bottom,* how it is worn.

Commercial Seat Harnesses

A number of commercially made seat harness types are available, usually made of broader webbing, sewn to form the harness (Fig. 7-19). A purchased harness is more comfortable, but the beginning climber will find the homemade tied harness described previously is a satisfactory and economical start. Before purchasing a commercial harness, consult climbers who use different types and perhaps try several, sitting in them to determine the comfort provided. Read the tie-in directions and follow them. The rewoven figure-8 knot works well for tying in to most of the available types.

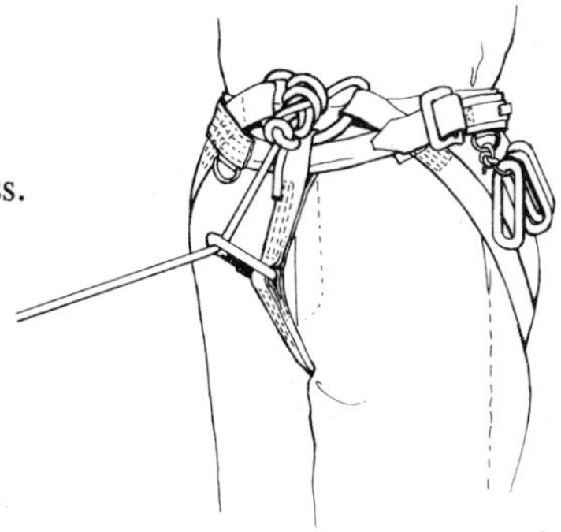

Fig. 7-19. Typical commercial seat harness.

Some commercial seat harnesses are designed to be used with a chest harness (these are termed full body harnesses). Some Europeans use a chest harness only, but this practice is generally considered dangerous by American climbers.

Tying into a Harness

A typical tie-in is shown using a rewoven figure-8 knot (Fig. 7-20). Make certain that the knot is tied close to the body to prevent its catching on rock or getting in the way of climbing. The first "8" is tied approximately 3 feet from the end of the rope, the end passed through all parts of the harness and waist loop webbing in front of the climber, then is completed by reweaving and finished off with an overhand backup knot. The middleman on a rope ties in with a double bowline.

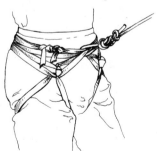

Fig. 7-20. Tying into a harness.

RUNNERS

One of the simplest and most useful pieces of climbing equipment is the runner, a loop of 1-inch tubular nylon webbing, or 8- or 9-mm kernmantel rope. The principal use is to attach the climbing rope to points of protection, and to attach the belayer to the anchor. As protection devices, they may be looped or tied around trees, natural chockstones, rock horns, or anything else the climber's ingenuity may suggest.

Fig. 7-21. Runner tied with a double fisherman's knot.

The single runner is made from a 5½-foot length of webbing. Double or triple length runners (9½ or 14 feet of webbing) are also frequently useful and should be made of material of different colors for ease of identification. After the runner material is cut to the desired length, the ends are fused in a flame and then tied with a double fisherman's knot as shown in Fig. 7-21, or a water knot. If the water knot is used the length of webbing necessary will be 6 inches shorter. Knots should be checked before a climb to make certain they have not partially untied. In general, all rules for the care of climbing ropes apply to runners.

CHEST SLING

A chest sling (Fig. 7-22), worn during travel on glaciers, is connected to the climbing rope only after a fall into a crevasse has occurred, to keep the hanging climber upright. It is actually just a long runner made from approximately 8 feet of 1-inch tubular webbing. Each sling must be adjusted to fit snugly over normal outer clothing. The carabiner connecting the sling in the front should have the gate facing out.

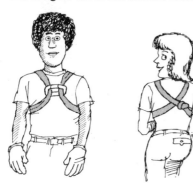

Fig. 7-22. Chest slings on climbers.

PRUSIK SLINGS

Prusik slings are used on all glacier climbs to enable a climber to extricate himself should a crevasse spring open under his feet. Separate slings of unequal length, one for each foot, are made from ¼-inch diameter (6-mm) rope – Dacron, polypropylene with a Dacron braided sheath, or kernmantel. Approximately 22 feet (7 m) of material will be needed (Fig. 7-23).

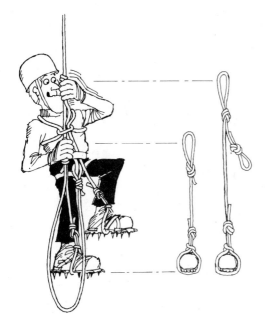

Fig. 7-23. Prusik slings.

The foot loops should be large enough to pass over crampons when putting the loops on, and have slip knots (Fig. 7-24) for tightening onto the boot.

When the long prusik is tied, an extra long "tail" 5 feet long, may be left. This is later made into a safety loop, which can be attached to the seat harness. The safety loop acts as a backup in case the climber steps out of both foot loops. It can also be used to support body weight if necessary, to rest the legs. The exact length of this safety loop is best determined by the individual in a practice situation. Once completed, the prusik slings should have the dimensions (dependent upon the size of the individual) as shown in Fig. 7-23. The total length of the long prusik sling, when the slip knot is snug around the boot, should be from the boot to the ear. The short prusik sling should extend from the boot to the elbow.

Using Prusiks — Prusiking

The longer sling is attached, with a prusik knot, to the rope, above the shorter one. The longer sling is passed through the belt or the loops of the seat harness and to the foot (note in Fig. 7-23 that the rope and the long prusik sling both pass through the chest sling carabiner, permitting the climber to lean back to rest). While standing on one sling, the climber can move the prusik knot for the other sling up the rope. By alternately moving first one prusik, then the other, he can move up the rope and out of the crevasse. (Note: to slide a prusik knot up or down the rope it must be unweighted — simply by lifting the foot.)

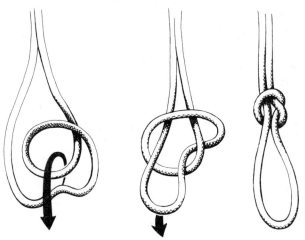

Fig. 7-24. Slip knot for prusik sling for foot loops.

CARABINERS

An extremely useful item of equipment is the carabiner (Fig. 7-25). Carabiners attach belayers to anchors, connect ropes to intermediate protection points, connect aid climbers to their points of direct support, and assemble friction brake systems. The greatest force a carabiner must withstand is that applied at a protection point during a fall. It is generally believed that their test strength should be 3500 lbs. or greater. Most carabiners on the market are made of aluminum alloy in one of three shapes: oval, D shape, or modified (slant) D shape. Since the weakest part of the carabiner is usually the gate, D-shaped carbiners are generally stronger than ovals since the shape permits the largest part of the load to be applied to the solid side, opposite the gate. Nevertheless, ovals are still preferred for all-around use because they are easier to use for carrying other hardware and in carabiner brake rappel systems.

Inspect carabiners closely for cracks and flaws in the metal, and be certain gates open and close smoothly without binding. There should be good side-to-side rigidity in the gate when it is open, and it must be capable of opening when the carabiner is supporting a climber's weight in order to connect a rope during aid climbing. The locking slot should slant or have a notch so the gate will lock shut under the impact of a fall. Check gate pins to see that they are prevented from working out of the holes, which would result in carabiner weakening and failure. A gate pin shorter than the hole where it is placed reduces the potential strength of a carabiner.

Hollow carabiners, which were designed to reduce weight, appear to be more susceptible than solid carabiners to physical damage or manufacturing error.

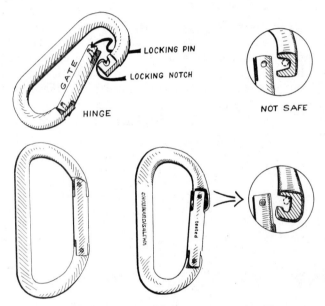

Fig. 7-25. Carabiners. *Upper left,* oval with parts named; *lower left,* "D" carabiner; *center,* modified "D" with gate detail; *upper right,* gate which has developed flared notch is unsafe.

Carabiners should be marked for identification with colored tape or paint. If the gate sticks after having been in use a while, the cause may be a burr on the gate or locking hook, dirt in the hinges or spring, or a bent gate. Burrs can be removed by careful filing. Corroded or dirty gates can be cleaned by applying oil, kerosene, solvent, or white gas or a similar solvent to the hinge spring slot and working until smooth, then dipping the carabiner in boiling water for 20 to 30 seconds to remove the cleaning agent so that more grit will not adhere to the newly cleaned area. Carabiners with bent gates or badly scarred sides should be retired.

One of the recent design changes has been to thicken the metal around the locking notch. This produces a stronger carabiner and helps to identify by feel which end of the gate opens, but also creates the occasionally encountered nuisance of being too thick to fit in some old bolt hangers and pitons.

Fig. 7-26. Locking carabiner.

A locking or "safety" carabiner (Fig. 7-26) has a threaded sleeve on the gate that tightens over the gate opening end to hold the gate closed. It offers some insurance (but no guarantee) against accidental opening of the gate: the locking sleeve has been known to work loose, particularly when a rope moves against it, so the closure needs periodic checking as if it were a knot. Where a locking carabiner is necessary or desirable, a climber can usually substitute two regular carabiners as described in Chapter 9, Rappelling.

Plate 11. Mt. Triumph, North Cascades. (Bruce Gaumond)

Plate 12. Climbers reach summit of Pere Eternal, Mont Blanc Massif, Italy. (John Cleare)

8 *

BELAYING

HIKING AND SCRAMBLING become climbing when progress becomes difficult enough to make falling a real possibility, and when the consequences of a fall would be serious. At that point mountaineers use a rope to continue with security. But unless that rope is used in a safe and knowledgeable manner, it may actually increase the danger rather than reduce it. On crevassed glaciers and sometimes on steep snow, a climbing team routinely ropes up and travels together. In all other situations when the security of the rope is called for, one person is stationary, protecting his partner with the technique known as *belaying*.

Belaying is the procedure by which the stationary climber, the *belayer*, manages the rope that is tied to the climbing member of the team and uses it to stop a fall if one should occur. The belayer takes a position with an *anchor*, an strong attachment point to the mountain, and a *stance,* bracing against the terrain to resist a hard pull on the rope. Rope is let out or taken in as the climber advances, keeping a minimum of slack between the rope partners so that any fall will be stopped as short as possible. If the climber does fall, the belayer tightens up on the rope, braces against the stance and anchor, and absorbs the force of the fall by friction around his body and stretch in the rope.

A climber with a belay from above, referred to as a *follower* or *second,* can make difficult climbing moves in the blissful knowledge that any slip would merely take up the little slack and slight stretch in the rope. What makes *leading*, or climbing above the belay so much more serious, is the distance a falling leader will drop before the rope becomes taut and the belay can begin to hold the fall. Because of the great resulting forces, belaying the leader is as vital and demanding a task as is found in mountaineering. But belaying is boring, and laxness is encouraged by the relative rarity of hard falls. Alertness and appreciation of the importance of the belayer's role are critical. A leader, belayed by a novice without this understanding, or lacking knowledge and training in belay technique, would be wise to climb as if there were no belay at all. Old-timers saying "the leader must not fall" recognized the difficulty of belaying a leader and the inadequacy of equipment and technique then available.

WHEN TO ROPE UP AND BELAY

The Climbing Code urges: "Rope up on all exposed places and for all glacier travel." An exposed place is one where an unroped climber is "exposed" to the probability of severe injury in a fall, but more generally the term *exposure* is also used to describe the distance an unroped climber would fall. Exposure is the most important factor signaling a climbing party to consider using the rope. Other factors are the difficulty of the climb, the experience and strength of each party member, availability of anchors, weather conditions and possible sickness or injury.

A rope offers no help if still in or on a pack when suddenly needed. Tying in is best done at a secure spot, before the party finds itself committed to difficult unroped climbing or to tying in one-handed while clinging to small holds. If the difficult sections are very short, a party occasionally dons harnesses and proceeds unroped, but is ready to quickly uncoil the rope and tie in when necessary.

Although some party members may feel comfortable scampering over an easy but exposed section, the others must feel no peer pressure against asking for a rope and must receive a belay if they request one. Also, part of the leader's job, and the experienced climbers' responsibility, is recognizing when a cocky novice is unaware of his need for a rope.

Merely tying into a rope provides no security unless it is used correctly. Roping only "for confidence" simply guarantees that the confident climber will not fall alone. On rock, to rope up for security means to set up a sound belay. On moderately angled crevassed glaciers, rope partners usually can move together, ready to perform team self-arrest if one person disappears into a snow-covered hole (see Chapter 16). Even there, belays are often set up to protect the climber at points of particular hazard such as snow bridges or crevasse ends. On steep snow and ice, choosing between traveling unroped, roped and moving together, or belaying, is an involved decision discussed in Chapter 14. There too are described the specialized belays used on snow and ice.

The rope often creates its own danger on rubble-strewn slopes where a dragging line may dislodge loose rock. It also may be more hazard than help on terrain offering no adequate stance or anchors, and in areas subject to rockfall or avalanche. A party encountering such problems may have to decide between climbing without the protection of the rope or retreating.

Once a party begins belaying, the climb is divided into segments from one belay position to the next, each called a *pitch*, and each limited by the length of the rope. Ideally, each belay point ending a pitch becomes the belay point for the leader of the succeeding one. Sometimes a section of trivial climbing is encountered between belayed pitches, and rather than take the time to unrope and tie back in again, a climbing team may elect to stay roped up and move together, with each member carrying a handful of rope coils. Since one falling would certainly pull off the other, *moving-in-coils* should be reserved for truly easy ground. Wherever exposed, the team should choose between belaying or unroping.

ORDER OF ROPING

Rope teams of two people are greatly preferred for speed and efficiency on technical terrain, especially for continuously belayed rock climbing. Ropes of three are frequently necessary when a party consists of an odd number of climbers and are often preferable for moderate glacier travel. Experience of the individuals is another consideration, as a party of six with only two adequately skilled rope leaders may have to climb in two rope teams of three. Generally, removing the weakest from a rope team of three results in a stronger team, while removing either of the stronger produces a team weaker than the original three. However, the efficiency advantage of pairs is so great that any reasonable uniformity in ability dictates two-person teams.

Ropes of four or more, seen occasionally for snow and glacier climbing, are extremely cumbersome and aggravate the danger of overwhelming an arrest or belay if more than one climber should fall or be pulled off at the same time.

Each position on a rope team carries quite different responsibilities. The first person up a rock pitch, the *leader*, makes most of the route-finding decisions and takes the greatest risk. The second person can help select the route, but mainly is concerned with providing a sound belay for the leader. On a three-person team, the third climber ordinarily is just along for the ride, but may help by carrying the heaviest rucksack or watching for rockfall.

When all members of a party are approximately equal in ability, positions on the rope are chosen on a basis of personal preference, and it is customary to trade positions to distribute the fun and workload. A rope of two equally skilled climbers ordinarily uses the pleasant and rapid method of *swinging leads*, each climber alternately belaying and leading.

When members are markedly unequal in skill and experience, the most skillful climber usually leads the most difficult pitches on the ascent. Descending, the best climber remains in the uppermost and most exposed position and thus is last down. The second-best climber ideally still should be in position to give the last down a sound belay, but may also need to go first if the route is obscure or tricky. On a traverse the weakest member is given the most protected position in the middle of the rope. Rope order must always be assigned with careful consideration of the pitch just ahead and the current strength of the team members.

THE BELAY CHAIN

Once belaying has begun, a climbing team cannot trust thoughtlessly to running through routine, mechanical procedures. Each belay set-up consists of an interacting system of parts called the *belay chain* (Fig. 8-1). Like a chain, a belay system is as secure as its weakest link, although each belay component may not necessarily be subjected to the same force. In order, the components are (1) the anchor, (2) the means of attaching the belayer to the anchor, (3) the belayer's stance, body, hands, and any arrangements to control the rope, (4) the rope itself, (5) any intermediate protection points, (6) the rope's attachment to the climber, generally a knot and harness, and (7) the climber's body. This chapter covers the first three components. Protection techniques and equipment are described in Chapter 11, where the discussion of how belay system components interact is completed.

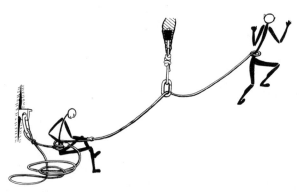

Fig. 8-1. Belay chain includes anchor, anchor attachment, belayer, rope, intermediate points of protection, tie-in to climber, and the climber.

HIP BELAYING

Over the years many belay techniques have been proposed and tested, but at least in North America, the *hip belay* in its various forms has retained its place as the fundamental method even though certain specialized belay devices are finding a degree of acceptance.

Hip belays require no single-use equipment, readily adjust to various anchor configurations, and offer the greatest flexibility to smoothly and quickly let out or take in rope. A hip belay can reduce the peak force on less-than-ideal anchors and stances. Extreme falls continue to be held by hip belays, demonstrating the technique's adequate strength. While care is necessary in establishing hip belay positions, belay devices also require their own special precautions, some of which are not at all obvious. Confronted with an iced-up rope or discovering the device has been forgotten at home or dropped down the mountain, anyone may have to use a hip belay. Beginners should start with this time-tested belay technique. Many climbers find it completely satisfactory for all the climbing they ever do.

Rope Handling

To give a hip belay, the belayer holds the rope from the climber in one hand, lays it around the back of his hips, and grasps it by the other hand (Fig. 8-2). Belaying then involves letting out or taking in rope as needed, always ready to stop a fall at any instant.

Fig. 8-2. Anchored sitting hip belay for a climber below the belay position.

The hand on the rope between the belayer and climber is called the *feeling hand*; its function is to sense the amount of tension or slack in the rope. The other hand is the *braking hand*, the one that does the work of stopping a falling climber. *Under no circumstances may the braking hand be removed from the rope while the climber is depending upon the belay.*

As long as the climber is stationary both hands merely hold onto the rope. To let out rope to a climber moving away, the belayer pulls slack through the braking hand with the feeling hand. The braking hand stays on the rope and shakes any kinks or snarls out of it, occasionally helped by the feeling hand to pull up slack. Although minimizing slack is essential, a climber belaying a leader must be extremely careful to let out enough rope so that the leader is not drawn up sharply by a tight rope from behind while making a delicate climbing move.

When the climber is moving toward the belayer, the sequence of hand movements is carefully synchronized, as diagrammed in Fig. 8-3. The two hands, working together, take in rope, removing slack as it develops. At the end of each sequence the feeling hand usually is closer to the belayer's body than the braking hand (Fig. 8-3b). To begin the next sequence, the feeling hand slides out along the rope (the breaking hand does not move) until both arms are fairly straight and the hands side-by-side (Fig. 8-3c). The braking hand lays the rope beyond the feeling hand to where it may be grasped by the thumb and fingers (Fig. 8-3d). The feeling hand grips both strands of rope and the braking hand slides back along the rope toward the hip, but not too far back or it may be pulled behind the belayer's back if the climber suddenly falls. The feeling hand releases the strand of rope running from the braking hand and the process is repeated (Fig. 8-3e) until the climber has joined the belayer. The movements are not entirely instinctive and novices must practice them until the sequence is quick and automatic with either hand serving either function.

Belay Signals

Effective communication between climber and belayer is essential for safety and efficiency. The belayer particularly needs to be advised whether to take in or let out rope as the climber moves upward or downward. If a fall occurs, the climber must not allow embarrassment to deprive the belayer of the earliest possible warning.

Over the years American climbers have developed a set of universally accepted signals, each quite distinct, so that even wind-garbled words can be interpreted correctly (Table 8-a). They must be used properly, clearly and loudly enough to be heard. Bellowing, however uncouth, may be necessary on windy days or when the climber is out of sight. Such conditions may also require shorter leads. Where other climbing teams are within hearing, belayer and climber should use each others' names to avoid confusion.

These signals are verbal. Sometimes when a belayed climber will clearly be out of sight or sound it is necessary to prearrange a set of silent signals using tugs on the rope. No standard set of these exist and climbers usually work them out in advance.

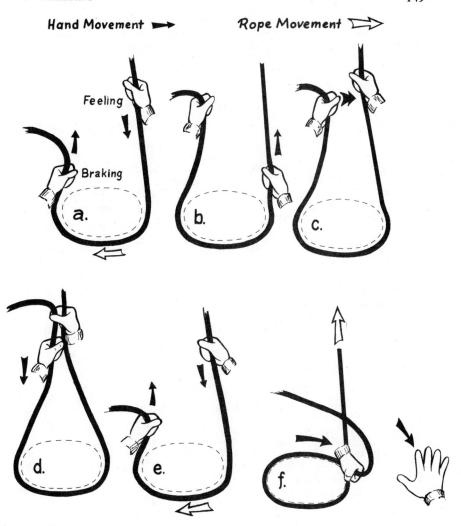

Hand Movement ➤ **Rope Movement** ➪

Fig. 8-3. Taking in rope: left hand is braking hand; right hand is feeling hand. Dashed oval is cross-section through the belayer's hips. Note — black arrows indicate hand movements; white arrows indicate rope movement.

a. Pull in rope with both hands on rope until braking hand is fully extended.
b. Hold rope with braking hand and slide feeling hand out.
c. Bring hands together.
d. Hold both parts of rope with feeling hand. Slide braking hand toward body, keeping it ready in case of a fall.
e. Repeat cycle.
f. Holding a fall. Arrest position: braking hand wraps rope around body and tightens grip to hold fall. Feeling hand is off rope, helping to brace belayer.

Table 8-a. Belay Signals.

Belayer	Climber	Meaning
	"On belay?"	Is the belay ready yet?
"Belay on"		All set. The belay will now catch you if you fall.
	"Climbing"	I am ready to climb.
"Climb"		Go ahead. The rope length between us will be controlled accordingly.
	"Up rope"	˙There is slack in the rope. Take in all loose rope.
Takes in rope. No verbal answer required.		
	"Slack"	I need some slack in the rope.
Gives a little slack. No verbal answer required.		
	"Tension"	Take up all slack. My weight is coming onto the rope.
Takes in any slack, assumes arrest position, and holds the rope tightly.		
	"Falling!" (or scream)	Self-explanatory.
Assumes arrest position to stop fall.		
	"How much rope?"	Generally a leader asking how much rope the belayer still has to be paid out.

"Twenty feet"
(or whatever rope length
remains to be paid out)

	"Off belay"	I am secure and will no longer need the belay.
"Belay off"		Echoed to ensure there is no misunderstanding.

Holding a Fall

When a fall occurs everything is up to the belayer. The climber can do little except make desperate grabs at ledges and vegetation. The belayer must promptly assume the *arrest position*, in which the body is braced with the feeling hand and the rope is wrapped completely around the hips with the braking hand (Fig. 8-3f and 8-4). If the fall catches the belayer completely by surprise, the hip wrap must be completed before the braking hand clamps down even if the rope runs slightly. It is the friction between the rope and the belayer's body that reduces the load on the braking hand to a manageable force.

Fig. 8-4. Sitting hip belay in arrest position, holding a climber fallen below.

Wearing belay gloves is essential; hard falls have held bare-handed, but at a cost of reducing the palm of the braking hand to hamburger.

When the climber is following "with a top rope," a fall may be instantly held by the belayer. The resulting force on the belayer is small as long as he has remained attentive and not allowed slack to creep into the system.

A falling leader, however, rapidly develops great energy of motion which must be absorbed in or transmitted through each link in the belay chain and ultimately dissipated as heat while the force of the fall is held by the belayer, stance, and anchor.

For years climbers used manila and other rope of low breaking strength and little shock absorbency. To absorb the energy of a fall without breaking either climber or rope, the belayer had to check a leader fall gradually by deliberately allowing the rope to slide several feet as the fall was slowed to a halt. Such a *dynamic belay* can reduce the peak force on each belay chain link by lengthening the short period during which the total energy must be absorbed, though at a cost of a somewhat longer fall. The very rapid judgment necessary to make a dynamic belay effective, knowing how quickly to wrap the rope and clamp down with the braking hand, was learned by thorough training and practice. Stopping too fast could produce great peak forces; too slowly and the climber could strike a ledge or obstruction before the fall was stopped.

With the introduction of synthetic ropes, *deliberate* dynamic belaying became less necessary. It remains important, however, whenever a leader fall may have to be held by a belay with an anchor suspected to be inadequate. In these situations, the belayer must anticipate the need for purposely making the belay dynamic to limit the load on the anchor.

The dynamic ropes, nylon with a sheath-and-core construction (commonly called "kernmantel"), stretch under the force of a severe fall, thereby spreading out the time of energy absorption and reducing the maximum force applied to the rope. With a *static belay*, in which no rope slippage is allowed, this peak force is termed the *impact force*. Although they have necessarily high breaking strengths, modern dynamic ropes are designed to transmit relatively lower forces while holding falls; the lower a rope's published impact force, the softer is the shock effect on people and equipment. Even so, the peak force in a hard leader fall continues to exceed the force that a hip belay can hold completely statically, and it becomes an *involuntary* dynamic belay.

With almost universal use of dynamic ropes, belaying as statically as possible has become accepted practice. Much less judgment is required, since the belayer simply clamps down and concentrates on holding on. Short falls can be held statically and much more softly than was possible with the old, unyielding ropes. On longer falls where greater forces develop, it is not possible to stop a falling climber quite as quickly: the rope slips through the belayer's tightest grasp, and, like it or not, the belay is dynamic. The belayer, knowing the sliding of the rope is the result of forces that cannot be controlled instantaneously, must stay calm and remain confident that the technique *will* work. The rope will slip a short distance, but if the belayer perseveres the energy will be dissipated and the fall will be held, with a peak force much less than any completely static belay can provide.

BELAY SECURITY

Location

Finding belay positions, associated anchors, and stances is an important element of routefinding. Climbers need to keep their eyes open for good belay points as well as climbable lines. Indeed, the two go together — often a delicate lead is a reasonable risk only if a solid belay can be established.

Sound anchors and strong stances are not the only considerations. The belayer, not having free movement, is particularly vulnerable to falling rock and must be provided as much protection as possible. In gullies or other areas of particularly heavy rockfall, every effort should be made to place the belay stance either around a corner or under an overhang. To disturb as few rocks as possible, climbers above the belay should exercise care in keeping the rope away from loose rubble.

Anchors

A secure anchor for the belay is the ultimate foundation of roped climbing: if everything else fails the entire rope team may end up hanging from it. The Climbing Code emphasizes "anchor all belays." The goal is a "bombproof anchor" — a supporting point capable of holding more than any possible load, more than the impact force of the rope, or a "free-falling Mack truck!" One obviously solid large tree or rock horn is more reliable than any collection of hardware and should be used wherever possible. Unfortunately such welcome objects are not always available, and thus the climber frequently must devise his own anchors where nature has failed to provide.

The placement and use of artificial anchors on rock — runners, chocks, pitons, and bolts — is detailed in Chapters 11 and 12. Snow and ice anchors — bollards, ice screws, and snow flukes — are covered in Chapters 14 and 15. Accepting an artificial anchor as adequate is a matter testing each climber's judgment and common sense.

A safe climber anchoring a belay seeks at least two separate and very strong anchors. *Multiple* anchor points drastically reduce the chance of disastrous failure of this last line of defense, but each separate anchor point must be *sound*. One secure anchor plus one or four or fifteen obviously insecure ones equal only one anchor point.

Single fixed pins and bolts are similarly untrustworthy. Most were placed by the early 1970s before the onset of "clean" and usually hammerless climbing and have been rusting and loosening, perhaps even holding falls, ever since. Documented cases of defectively manufactured bolts suggest that not only is a two-bolt anchor necessary but that they should also be of different sizes and/or manufacturers.

Additionally, each of multiple anchors must be rigged *independently* so the failure of one cannot cause the failure of others, and *snugly*, so the failure of one cannot "shock load" another by taking up the slack with a tremendous impact rather than smoothly transferring the static load.

The force of a leader fall can come unpredictably upward or downward on a belayer if protection point(s) fail. An anchor system must, therefore, be capable of holding a force in either direction. This is accomplished using artificial chocks by rigging two "in opposition." Since the pair are not independent, they equal only one anchor point. A single chock is never an adequate belay anchor.

When an adequate anchor cannot be constructed with the available equipment, keen judgment is required. There is great temptation here to cut the margin of safety too fine, since it is fairly probable that no accident will occur. Retreat may well be the only safe option, possibly by the leader down climbing while still belayed from below. If the decision is to push ahead, the possibility of making a leader belay deliberately dynamic should be considered. This is one of the situations where pitons may still have a role; on remote or seldom-climbed routes, one hammer and a small selection of pitons may allow a party to quickly continue in safety where a group with only runners and chocks could proceed only by flirting with disaster.

Stances

The *stance* is the place and posture the body assumes to resist the possible hard pull on the rope. Considerations in its selection include the range of directions from which the pull could come, terrain advantages like ledges or supporting projections, the anchor's ability to support a particular stance, and the belayer's comfort.

Concern for comfort may seem selfish on the part of the belayer, but unless a position can be maintained over a long period of time it is a poor one, however otherwise solid and safe. Contorted stances should be avoided, as well as those that press sharp objects into the body. Though initially the belayer may not be disturbed by the discomfort, eventually alertness will be impaired and the urgent necessity to change stance may coincide disastrously with the climber's moment of greatest need.

The soundest stance, ideal on rock, snow, brush, anywhere, is the *sitting hip belay* (Fig. 8-2). The belayer sits in a comfortable position with legs spread well apart for stability, feet braced against projections. If the climber falls, the rope must run *between* the belayer's feet to pull the belayer into his foot braces, ensuring the stability of the stance (Fig. 8-5). If the rope runs outside the legs the sideways force can quickly tip over the entire stance. The low center of gravity provides additional stability by keeping the force down where the bracing can effectively resist it.

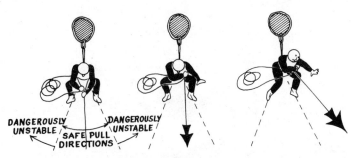

Fig. 8-5. Left, stable direction of pull for sitting hip belay. *Center,* a pull on the belayer between the foot braces increases position's stability. *Right,* a pull on the belayer outside tripod formed with foot braces can tip the belayer out of position.

Test braces to be sure they deserve trust. If good projections cannot be found for the feet, their unreliability can be compensated for by an extraordinarily strong hip brace, such as a hollow in the ground where the belayer sits as if in a well. Indeed, if the pull will be downward, the belayer may sometimes sit on a narrow ledge with legs dangling over the edge (Fig. 8-6). This position is often quite strong, especially if the ledge backslopes a bit.

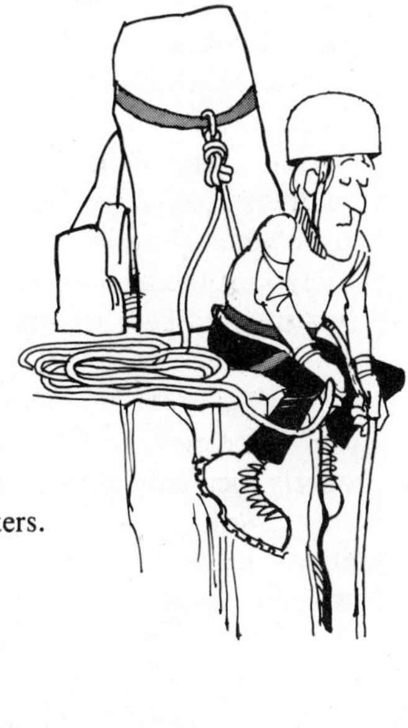

Fig. 8-6. Sitting hip belay in tight quarters.

Sometimes a sitting belayer can straddle a tree or rock; a fall then tends to pull the belayer into the single support. If sufficiently large, such support points are extremely strong and may even double as the anchor (Fig. 8-7), but the belayer can be pulled sideways and the belay dislocated when the support is small. The belayer's free hand can be used effectively as an extra brace, and such use is planned before the need arises.

Fig. 8-7. Large rock horn serving as both anchor and brace for sitting hip belay.

The *standing hip belay* is not as stable as the sitting position. In its simplest form, the belayer stands facing the direction of expected pull, with one leg forward, and securely braced, and the rope, during a fall, running close inside this leg and around the hips (Fig. 8-8). Useful in small belay positions this stance requires substantial anchors to hold hard falls.

A very versatile stance allowing tripod stability at very small and steep belay positions is the *semi-hanging hip belay* (Fig. 8-9). The belayer, tied into the anchors directly in front, braces his feet on the best available footholds to either side of the anchor, and leans backwards against the anchor. Stability is assured by "aiming the belay" with the rope running through a carabiner at the anchor and on to the climber. A fall draws the belayer securely into the anchor while his braced feet and weight at the hips resist twisting and keep the stance straight.

Attaching to Anchors

A sound anchor can make a shaky stance bombproof, provided care is taken to properly locate the stance relative to the anchor and to properly connect belayer with anchor. There are many adequate attachment schemes, but even more that are not as strong as they should be, and some that are downright dangerous.

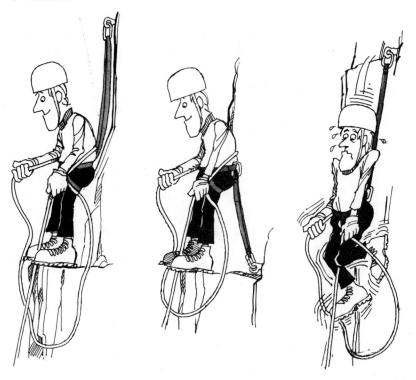

Fig. 8-8. Standing belays — used when terrain too steep for more stable positions. *Left,* high anchor supports position. *Center,* anchor is low, belayer can be jerked off as shown on *right.*

The anchor should be rigged in line with the stance and the direction of the expected pull of the rope in a fall. In addition to providing ultimate support for the entire chain, the anchor should assist the belayer in maintaining the stance and should restrain him from being pulled out of position. Using the idealized sitting hip belay "aimed" toward the expected pull directly in front, the anchor should be directly behind the belayer, above the stance if the expected pull is down, and below when the force will be upward. An anchor rigged off to one side can cause the belayer to be swung sideways out of the stance (Fig. 8-10), while one rigged below when the pull comes downward is certain to be "shock-loaded" if the stance cannot hold the peak force (Fig. 8-8). Either, of course, is better than nothing.

There should be no slack whatsoever between the belayer and the anchor points. A tight anchor connection can make a shaky stance bombproof; a loose one can only begin to help after the stance has failed. When the anchor must be some distance away, the belayer can obtain proper

Fig. 8-9. Semi-hanging hip belay. Note the belayer is independently affixed to more than one good anchor with the belay "aimed" through the upper anchor. A third anchor would increase security but is not shown for clarity.

tension by adjusting the connection length and/or moving the stance forward.

The belay position should be as close as possible to the anchor to minimize the distance the belayer can be swung sideways or lifted if the pull does not come directly opposite the anchor (Fig. 8-10). Also, the elasticity of a long anchor attachment might allow the stance to be broken.

Tying into at least one of the anchor points with the climbing rope is strongly recommended. Not only does it provide one of the strongest possible connections, but also has the climber on a "pre-tie-off" if, as a result of a fall, the belayer completely runs out of rope. Since the climbing rope is attached at the front of the harness, the belayer can be rotated out of position, with complete loss of belay, during a fall, unless the rope passes around the hip on the same side as the feeling hand to reach the anchor behind, as shown in Fig. 8-11. (If the belayer is facing the anchor this problem does not exist.) Similarly, the rope can be flipped over a rock formation too large for runners, quickly making an otherwise unusable formation into an ideal anchor (Fig. 8-12).

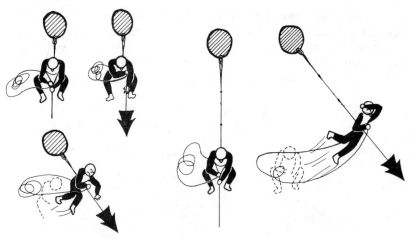

Fig. 8-10. Relationship between belayer and anchor. *Left,* short anchor in line of pull is best; even if pulled to side, belayer is moved only a short distance. *Right,* long anchor is poor; belayer can be pulled far to side or lifted up.

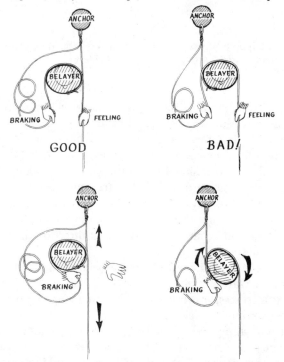

Fig. 8-11. Using the climbing rope tied to front of belayer's harness to attach to anchor. *Left,* rope loop to anchor correctly runs around belayer's feeling hand side. In fall, anchor restrains belayer from being rotated. *Right,* rope loop to anchor around braking hand side spins climber under force of a fall.

A belay chain should not depend absolutely on a single, regular, non-locking carabiner. Besides the possibility of unobserved damage or manufacturing flaw, its gate may be held open by clothing, webbing, rope, or rock, drastically weakening it. Chains of three or more carabiners should never be used because of their amazing ability to unclip themselves.

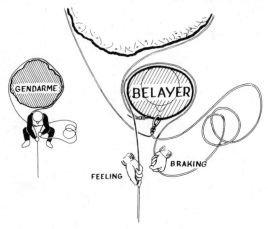

Fig. 8-12. Using a loop of the rope to anchor to very large rock formation. Note anchor attachment must go around feeling hand side.

Controlling the Rope

Often an inexperienced or thoughtless belayer will prepare to hold a force from one direction when the circumstances of the pitch can readily result in a force from quite another. Even more insidious, as the climber changes position the potential line of fall may also change. Along ridges falls can occur down either side. Protection points can fail, confronting a belayer expecting an upward pull with a tremendous downward force. The alert belayer will always view the climber as a person about to become a falling object, and think seriously about where that object will fall, how the rope will behave, and from what direction the force of the fall will reach the stance.

Several steps may be taken to help the belayer control the rope and widen the range of safe aiming direction for a given stance. They are not a substitute for alertness, however, since the changing climbing situation affects the precautions as well.

Since the hip wrap provides the friction needed to hold a fall, the belayer must take great care to ensure that a pull from an unexpected direction does not strip it away (Fig. 8-13). Climbers should practice belaying "either handed" so that the hand on the opposite side of a belayer's body from the expected pull may always be the braking hand. Alert manipulation by the feeling hand can often place the rope where any fall will wrap the rope about the belayer even more tightly.

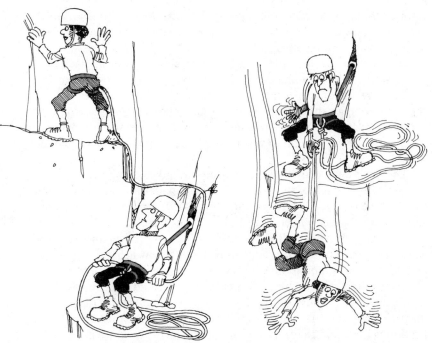

Fig. 8-13. Leader, traversing above belayer and falling, can strip away the hip wrap. A single chock anchor is inadequate.

Clipping a carabiner into the feeling hand side or front of the belayer's harness and passing the rope to the climber through it assures a good body wrap for frictional control (Fig. 8-14).

If the expected pull is down, the rope can be controlled by having it run above the anchor attachment behind the belayer. Similarly, the rope running under the anchor can help handle an upward force. However, the belayer must be aware that placing the rope above the anchor can readily allow it to ride up onto the sensitive waist, creating intolerable pain. In that case a positive guarantee of a downward direction, or padding with

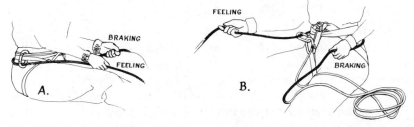

Fig. 8-14. Control carabiners. Belay rope running through carabiner clipped to belayer's harness before passing around feeling hand side ensures hip wrap if force should come from unexpected direction. *Left,* on feeling hand side of hand-tied harness. *Right,* on front of commercial harness.

extra clothing, is necessary. Wrapping the rope under an anchor attachment can allow the rope to be torn out underneath the belayer if a force is applied downward unexpectedly.

If the anchor is attached by a carabiner clipped into the back of the harness, the belay rope can run directly through that carabiner to control a force upward or downward. However, anywhere one piece of nylon rope or webbing rubs against another under tension, the stationary nylon is rapidly melted through. Reasonable caution avoids any contact where the belay rope might tend to saw through the harness or anchor connection.

There are several advantages in using two linked carabiners to clip the anchor into the back of the belayer's harness, with the belay rope running through the one nearest the anchor (Fig. 8-15): the anchor immediately supports the stance under any load, without significantly reducing the friction around the hips. The rope remains controlled against either upward or downward loads, is constrained to stay low around solid muscle and bone, and cannot abrade harness or anchor nylon. Since this scheme does absolutely depend upon two carabiners behind and out of the belayer's sight, they must be checked carefully to be certain that they are properly clipped into harness, rope, anchor, and each other, that the connection is taut, and that nothing can open one of the gates accidentally. At least the anchor carabiner with the belay rope, if not both, should be a locking carabiner. This attachment may be backed up by additionally tying the belayer's rope, with slack, into an anchor.

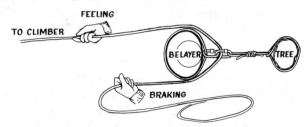

Fig. 8-15. Connecting belayer to anchor with two linked carabiners into the back of the belayer's harness.

It is frequently wise to predetermine the pull direction by establishing an artificial aiming point (Fig. 8-16). Any solid protection point directly in front of the belay position will do to ensure that the pull of a fall will come from the direction the belayer is best prepared to cope with. Like a belay anchor, it must be multi-directional as well as sound. Indeed, in some situations an anchor can be used as the aiming point (Fig. 8-9).

Recovering From a Fall

Belaying does not end with successfully holding a fall: the climber must regain a secure position on the mountain. If uninjured, the climber

Fig. 8-16. Aiming belays. *Top,* naturally aimed belay: belayer faces direction of pull. *Center,* unaimed belay: belayer not facing direction of pull, which would twist him around; he might lose control. *Bottom,* artificially aimed belay: direction of force remains constant.

will probably swing back onto the rock and try again, or move to a resting spot. Terrain and available rope permitting, the belayer may be able to lower a fallen climber to a ledge. Otherwise preparations made before the pitch began will determine whether or not the team is immobilized until outside help can arrive.

A climber dangling under an overhang while his partner hangs on like grim death will wish he had carried prusiks or sling material from which they could be improvised. Many experienced climbers are never parted from two short loops of 6- or 7-mm perlon with which to tie effective prusik knots. These can then be extended with regular runners.

If the climber has been knocked unconscious, is injured, or is hanging beneath an overhang, the belayer must *tie off* the rope before rescue efforts can be initiated. The simplest means of doing so requires a sling of 6- to 7-mm rope or ⁹⁄₁₆ to 1-inch webbing. A standard runner will work, although rope makes better prusik knots than webbing. The sling or runner must be handy, preferably carried attached to the harness, since a reach of more than 2 feet from the stance while holding the fallen climber is often impossible.

While the braking hand securely holds the fallen climber, the feeling hand ties a prusik knot around the belay rope with the sling or runner, and secures it to the anchor (Fig. 8-17). Slack is slowly let out until it is certain the prusik will hold firmly. No longer trapped by the fallen climber's weight, the belayer can get out of the stance and immediately tie the belay rope directly into the anchor so as not to leave the climber hanging by a single prusik. This accomplished, additional help may be summoned or rescue measures begun.

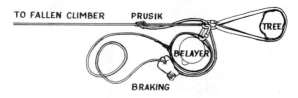

Fig. 8-17. Tying off belay rope after a fall for belayer using two-linked-carabiner anchoring scheme.

Anyone falling tied in only with a waistloop or bowline-on-a-coil will immediately recognize the value of harnesses with leg loops. A victim hanging freely must somehow relieve the pressure on the lower rib cage before the diaphragm is compressed, causing suffocation, unconsciousness, and eventually death. Flipping over backward can momentarily help, and the *baboon hang* (Fig. 8-18) can be used to convert a standard length runner into an emergency seat. These maneuvers are likely beyond the ability of an injured climber, whose prospects, hanging only by the waist, are very poor indeed.

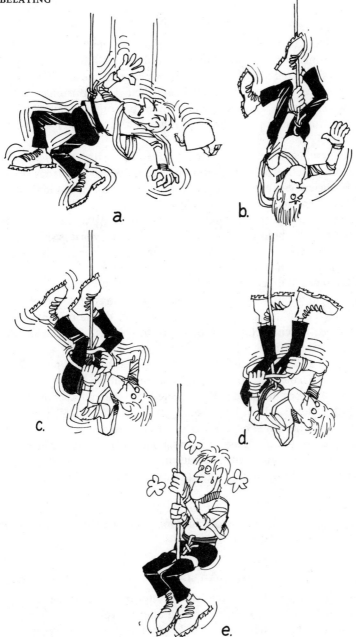

Fig. 8-18. Baboon hang sequence.
a. Argh . . .
b. Tip upside down, hook foot around rope.
c. and d. Slide runner over feet in front of rope — no need to twist runner.
e. Sit up.

EFFICIENCY

A climbing team must be concerned with minimizing wasted time in the mountains. A slow party will often fail to reach its summit, and frequently is subjected to hazards which a faster team can avoid completely. Next to poor routefinding, inefficient belaying consumes more "5 minutes here and 15 minutes there" than any other element of roped climbing, time that by mid-afternoon will add up to the loss of success and safety.

Of course, each belay needs to be set up correctly as well as quickly. Only from practice on real climbs can the necessary efficiency develop. Belay proficiency is as much conditioning as the more familiar physical training or experience with exposure.

There are several procedures which can improve a team's efficiency. The first is to climb unroped or move-in-coils wherever it is safe to do so. A few moments spent seeking an easier way up the next pitch can save a lot of time wrestling with the rope.

A balanced pair can "swing leads," each member leading and following alternate pitches. The same belay that brings up a follower, after an exchange of hardware, continues to protect the same climber as he leads the next pitch. Belay positions must be selected that can shift from belaying downward for a follower to belaying upward for a leader.

Delays searching for anchors can be avoided by stopping leads short of a full rope length if a bombproof anchor is immediately available.

Once having established and connected into the first anchor at the end of a pitch, a leader should immediately signal "off belay!" The belayer, knowing that the climber has secured the rope to the mountain, can immediately get out of the stance, retaining one anchor until the new belay is ready, and start dismantling the old anchor while the climber above is finding additional anchor points, taking a stance, and drawing up the slack in the rope.

To save much tedious "up-roping," the new belayer should pull all the slack up hand-over-hand, before running it around the hips and clipping into any control carabiners.

BELAY DEVICES

Hand in hand with synthetic kernmantel ropes has come a series of mechanical belay devices and proposed alternatives to body belays. Encouraged by the belief that the kernmantel ropes themselves can adequately soften the force of a fall, these innovations are intended to offer a simpler, more foolproof system by catching falls statically, preferably with the belayer's body removed from the belay chain. All these devices must be used only with kernmantel rope: they can badly damage, even break older style laid ropes, even those of nylon.

Most popular is the Sticht Belay Plate (Fig. 8-19), although some prefer the figure-8 descender for belaying. Numerous other manufacturers have, and will, come up with "the answer." Carefully study all the manufacturer's instructions and warnings *and* independent discussion found in mountaineering journals and accident reports.

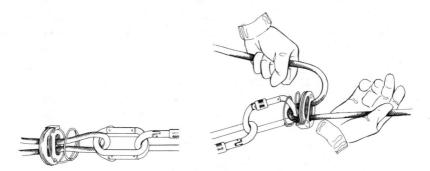

Fig. 8-19. Sticht Belay Plates. *Left,* in use letting out rope; *right,* holding a fall. If the spring should pass over a single, non-locking carabiner it could open the gate.

Enough climbers have adopted the Sticht Belay Plate to justify a description of its use here. Use of a locking carabiner or two carabiners with correctly positioned gates (Chapter 9, Rappelling) with the Sticht Belay Plate is critical. A tendency of early models to unintentionally "lock down" on the belay rope has been cured to a degree by an attached spring holding the device away from the carabiner except under the force of a fall.

Considerable experience with this device has demonstrated some advantages: a small belayer finds it easier to handle the load of a much heavier climber; rescue situations can require a belay to hold three people and a litter — more than a hip belay can hope to hold, but a load that a Sticht Belay Plate directly off an absolutely bombproof anchor can restrain.

There are also problems. Rope handling takes considerable practice. Leaders wishing to advance smoothly can be maddeningly slowed to the rate the belayer can work slack through the device. Nor can a belayer very rapidly take in rope to shorten a low-angle, sliding fall. Worse still are the accumulating indications that the device allows unacceptably high peak forces during hard falls. As static a belay as mechanical belay devices provide has been cited as a factor in anchor bolt failures and rope damage, especially when used directly off the anchor. And although the belayer's body may not need to sustain this force, there is no way to remove the falling climber from the belay chain.

BELAYING PRACTICE

Although the rope is all a climber needs to learn rope handling, belaying is a skill that can only be perfected through practice. In years gone by, to provide experience with the forces present in leader falls, one climber would set up a belay and two, three or four others would grab the end of the rope and run down a hill or steep slab while the belayer tried to stop the simulated fall. Other groups built towers and brave members took turns jumping from them, thus adding a bit of realism to the practice. More recently, belay towers using weights and hauling lines have been designed (Fig. 8-20). The weight-lifting power is furnished by a group of climbers, or lacking a large enough group, perhaps a car. A 100-pound weight falling from a well-oiled pulley is surprisingly difficult to arrest.

Fig. 8-20. Belay practice on tower, and *right,* the real world.

SUMMARY

1. A climbing route is generally divided into pitches according to the location of good belay stances. The full length of the climbing rope need not necessarily be the length of the pitch.
2. Anchor the belay, preferably with two or more good anchor points. The climbing rope can be used for this purpose and the anchor should be kept as close as possible to the belayer. The line between belayer and anchor must be snug.
3. Aim the belay so that the force of a fall will pull the belayer against his anchor and braced limbs. A "manufactured" aiming point prevents unexpected changes of direction of pull.
4. If no aiming point is used, be alert for changes in direction of pull.
5. Never, never, never take the braking hand off the rope during a belay.
6. Learn the climbing signals thoroughly and use them correctly.
7. Wrap the rope around the hips as far as possible when assuming the arrest position, and before gripping the rope tightly.
8. The belayer must remain constantly alert to his responsibility for the safety of the team as a whole, and must have the grim determination to hold any possible fall.

Plate 13. Rappelling off The Maiden, Eldorado Springs Canyon, Colorado.
(Robert McQuilkin)

9 *

RAPPELLING

RAPPELLING IS DESCENDING by sliding down a rope, controlling speed and progress by friction against the rope. A climber can move down nearly any pitch, even an overhanging one, *en rappel*; in fact, some pitches can be descended only by this technique. Although relatively easy to accomplish correctly and safely, rappelling is statistically among the most dangerous thing climbers do. A rappelling climber is often hanging out over a long potential fall, totally dependent on the anchor and ability to use equipment properly. Easy repetition develops overconfidence and carelessness, and exhilaration encourages hazardous technique. Constant vigilance toward each detail is the price of each safe descent.

When a climbing party is descending, a choice must sometimes be made between climbing down and rappelling. The choice is made on many considerations: safety, speed, convenience, nature of the terrain, weather, time available, and condition of the party. Rappelling may be the fastest and safest means to descend a particular pitch, but frequently, however, it is not, even when the essential prerequisite, an adequate rappel anchor, is readily available. Knowledge of rappelling does not make downclimbing skill unnecessary. Rather it is a method to be used when downclimbing presents particular difficulties. Even very difficult sections must sometimes be downclimbed, as when a rope leader must retreat from a pitch with no reasonable anchor. If the decision is to rappel, it must be done efficiently as well as correctly. Hours flash by while an unpracticed party fumbles with a series of rappels.

RAPPEL SYSTEMS

All rappel systems involve a substantial anchor through which a rope is doubled into strands of two equal lengths; the rope is retrieved by pulling one end from below later. The rope is secured to the climber by either wrapping it around his body to provide friction, or by passing through a friction device attached to the climber's harness. In all rappel systems, the climber's hand grasping the rope controls the speed of descent. To prevent rope burns, gloves are a wise precaution. Keeping the legs spread improves stability and turning the head downhill permits a view of the route.

The *arm rappel* (Fig. 9-1) is useful for negotiating low-angle slopes. The climber lays the rappel rope over his shoulders, then wraps it once around both extended arms. Rate of descent is controlled by hand grip and by friction on shoulders and arms.

Fig. 9-1. Arm rappel.

The simplest all-purpose rappel is the *dulfersitz* (Fig. 9-2) which requires no special equipment and should be mastered by every climber. The climber faces the anchor and steps into the dulfersitz by straddling the rope, bringing it forward around one hip, up across the chest, and over the opposite shoulder, then down the back to be held by the braking hand on the same side as the wrapped hip. The guiding hand holds the rope above the climber to maintain an upright position. A hazard with the dulfersitz, especially on high-angle rappels, is unwrapping the leg. This possibility is reduced by keeping the wrapped leg slightly lower than the other. Collars should be turned up where the rope runs over the shoulder to protect the neck. Padding and careful control are advisable since friction of the rope around the hip and across the shoulder can become extremely uncomfortable, especially on very steep rappels.

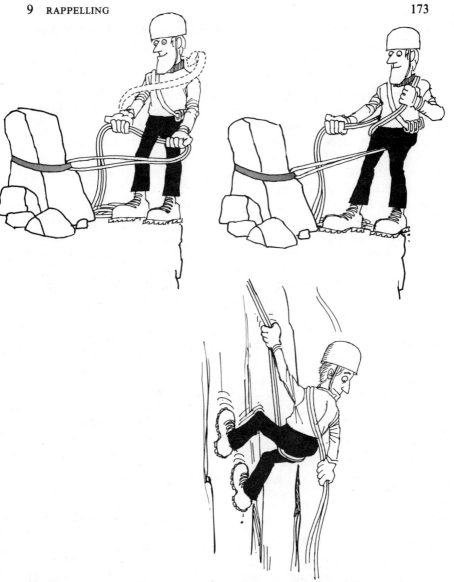

Fig. 9-2. Dulfersitz rappel: straddle rope facing anchor, pass rope diagonally across chest and over shoulder (braking hand is on same side as hip over which rope passes).

Friction brakes permit comfortable rappels and are easy to control. Free rappels (from overhangs), rappels with bulky or heavy packs, and rappels on single strands or small-diameter ropes are more easily controlled when using brake systems. The principal disadvantage of brake rappels is that they introduce additional pieces of equipment into the rappel system, each of which becomes a point of potential failure. While most experienced climbers have adopted brake rappels, their use requires great care.

Brake systems all operate on the same principle: the climber's weight is attached to the hanging rope by a friction device capable of sliding. The braking hand controls the rate of descent by adjusting the amount of friction so the rope slides through the brake at the desired speed. The braking hand accomplishes this by wrapping the rope partly about the body or gripping it more firmly. The guiding (uphill) hand merely slides along the rope to help maintain balance. Obviously, the braking hand must never release the rope.

Brake rappels require a seat harness, such as the tied webbing seat harness described in Chapter 7. Commercial harnesses for climbing are especially comfortable; however, the attachment point on certain models is dependent on stitching, making a webbing backup waistloop a wise precaution. Some climbers prefer to improvise diaper or figure-8 rappel seats. Never rappel with a simple waistloop, as this practice is subject to the same dangers of diaphragm constriction and unconsciousness as the waist tie-in, discussed in Chapter 7.

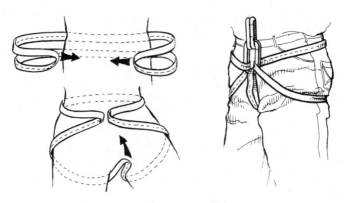

Fig. 9-3. Diaper sling.

A diaper sling (Fig. 9-3) requires about 10 feet of webbing sling rope tied into a large loop: starting with the loop behind the back, one end is pulled to the front from each side and a third end from between the legs. The three loops are clipped together in front with carabiners. This sling may also be clipped to a waistloop, if one is worn.

A figure-8 seat (Fig. 9-4) is improvised from a standard length runner or any other suitable length of webbing or small-diameter rope. This seat must be clipped to a waistloop to help maintain stability.

The brake system is attached to the seat harness with one locking or two regular carabiners. Any place a regular carabiner may be subjected to

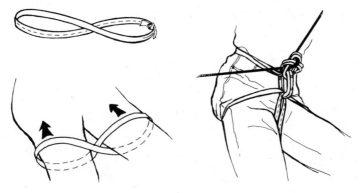

Fig. 9-4. Figure-8 sling.

a twisting or side load, two should be used with gates correctly positioned as shown in Fig. 9-5 to prevent their being forced open and accidentally unclipping.

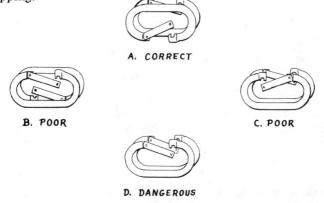

A. *CORRECT*

B. *POOR*   C. *POOR*

D. *DANGEROUS*

Fig. 9-5. Doubled carabiners. Example d. can unclip under a twisting or sideways load as readily as a single carabiner. Should one of the carabiners in example b. flip end-for-end, a real possibility, the result is d. Any load coming on a gate in example a. is also supported by a solid carabiner back, as it is not in example c.

The most commonly used brake system is the carabiner brake (Fig. 9-6). Although somewhat complex to set up, it has the advantage of not requiring any special equipment other than carabiners. A pair of carabiners is clipped into the harness carabiner(s). Facing the anchor, the climber lifts a loop of the rappel rope or ropes through the outer carabiner pair and clips the loop off across the carabiners with one or more braking carabiners. Three precautions must be carefully observed:

1. The gates of the carabiner pair must be correctly positioned to ensure that where a braking carabiner presses against the side of a carabiner gate, that gate is supported by a solid side of the other carabiner.

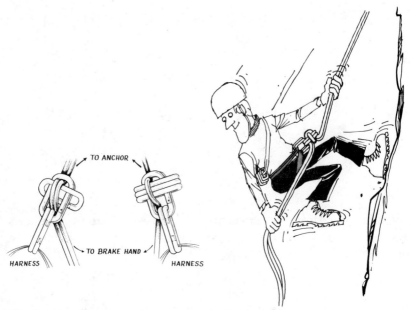

Fig. 9-6. Carabiner brakes: for normal double rope rappel, with added carabiners for greater friction with single or small diameter rope, and in use.

2. The rappel rope must run over the solid side of the braking carabiners, never under any circumstances across a gate.
3. The rappel rope must run from the anchor into the outer end of the carabiner pair and out by the inner end, so that the climber is not attempting to rappel up the rope.

One braking carabiner provides sufficient friction for most rappels on doubled 11-mm climbing rope. Very steep or free rappels, or those done single strand, with a heavy pack, or by a heavy climber, may require the additional friction of a second braking carabiner. As many as five braking carabiners have been used to control single strand rappels on small-diameter rope. Although not common, grooves can be created where the rope runs against the carabiners, particularly if rappels are performed with a dirty, gritty rope. Inspect your carabiners occasionally.

A simple brake system consists of a single carabiner with attached brake bar clipped into the harness carabiners. Loops of each rope strand are pushed through the carabiner and the bar latched to the gate so that rope tension holds the brake bar against the carabiner, locking the gate closed. As with a carabiner brake, the climber must be careful to rig this system with the rope positioned correctly, holding the bar against the carabiner, as shown in Fig. 9-7. Additional friction can be obtained by adding a second brake bar system (or more) in series. Although brake bar

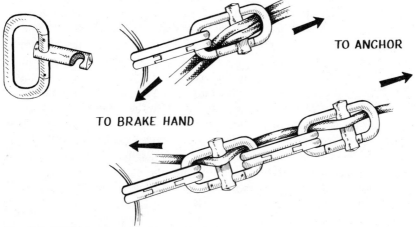

TO ANCHOR

TO BRAKE HAND

Fig. 9-7. Brake bars on carabiner, single bar used for double rope rappel, and multiple brake bars for single rope rappel.

systems have been used safely for many years, concern has often been expressed about the side forces the bar may place on the carabiner gate. Newly designed carabiners will not permit the bar to slide over the gate end. The popularity of brake bars appears to be diminishing in favor of other brake systems for rappelling.

The carabiner wrap system uses only a single locking carabiner clipped into the harness carabiners. This carabiner's gate should be as shown in Fig. 9-8. The rappel rope runs through the outer carabiner end, opposite the harness, and is wrapped around the carabiner's solid back, with more turns for more friction. Two turns of each of two rope

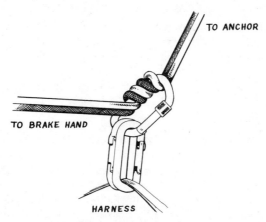

TO ANCHOR

TO BRAKE HAND

HARNESS

Fig. 9-8. Carabiner wrap brake system. Note that if the locking carabiner reverses, the wrap can unscrew the locking sleeve.

strands is typical. The principal hazard with this system is that the carabiner might flip around, allowing the wrapped rope to unlock the gate.

The figure-8 descender (Fig. 9-9) provides excellent friction control
but adds weight to the pack and is sometimes left at home or dropped
down the mountain. A climber who chooses to use one must be thoroughly familiar with the manufacturer's instructions and an alternative
system. The figure-8 is used by pushing a loop of the rappel rope through
the device's larger hole and over the end with the small hole. The small
hole is then clipped into the harness carabiners. It is vital that a locking
carabiner or two regular carabiners (Fig. 9-5) connect the figure-8 and the
harness. This device can, and has, twisted itself out of a single non-
locking carabiner. It should be noted that the figure-8 device warms by
friction during a rappel; reports of heat damage to ropes during high
speed rappels have been substantiated by tests.

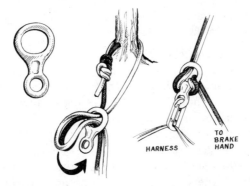

Fig. 9-9. Left, figure-8 descender; middle, figure-8 rope connection, and right, in
use.

Numerous other brake systems have been used. A simple one common
in Europe merely runs the rappel rope through a locking carabiner at the
harness, up over the climber's shoulder, and then down across the back to
the opposite, braking, hand.

RAPPEL ANCHORING

The primary requirement in setting up a rappel is finding or creating
an anchor that will not fail, ideally a thick tree with sound roots or a
large, solid rock horn around which a runner can be placed (Fig. 9-10).
Unfortunately, climbers are frequently forced to use less than ideal anchors—bushes, small trees, large boulders, fixed pitons or bolts on
established routes, and occasionally the climber's own expensive hardware. After multiple anchor points are located or placed, loops of sling
rope or webbing are used to extend each anchor to a single support point.

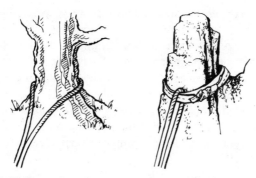

Fig. 9-10. Rappel anchors; adequately solid without a backup.

Parties often carry 20 or 30 feet of ⁹⁄₁₆-inch webbing or other sling material for this purpose.

Fixed rappel anchors on established descent routes deserve careful inspection, even when used very frequently. Most of these date from the era (before about 1973) when pitons and hammers were routinely carried and used. The shift to "clean" and usually hammerless climbing means the bolts and pitons used for rappel anchors today were placed years ago and have been weathering or rusting without replacement ever since. The day is approaching when parties will need to carry one hammer, a couple of pitons, and perhaps a small bolt kit so that everyone will not have to face a grim game of Russian rappel-anchor roulette. Organized efforts to improve fixed anchors in popular climbing areas deserve the support in money and time of all who enjoy these areas. Ropes simply placed around large trees on popular climbs dig grooves deeper and deeper in the trunks as many ropes are pulled through, eventually killing the tree.

Rappel anchors on snow and ice — bollards, pickets, flukes, planted ice axes, or ice screws — are described in Chapters 13, 14, and 15. Unlike anchors in rock, these melt out under pressure, thus parties of more than three or four may have to replace the anchors at least once before all members have descended.

Old webbing left by previous parties should be treated with great suspicion. A nylon rope pulled down through nylon webbing "scars" and weakens the webbing, and numerous parties may have repeated that process. Solar radiation and moisture weaken webbing further. Many old slings or an obviously very recent one are no guarantee of safety: as many as eight old webbing loops have been broken simultaneously in a rappel accident. Rodents have chewed through a sling left the day before. Wise practice and good citizenship are to replace the oldest loop of webbing with a new one of your own, carrying the old nylon out of the mountains.

Two or more anchors should be used if at all possible, and these must be rigged *independently* — that is, with the rappel rope supported in such a way that if all but one anchor were to fail completely, that one would hold the load (Fig. 9-11). Each anchor requires a separately tied loop of webbing, a practice which may create a shortage of material. Even so, sufficient material must be allowed for secure knotting of the slings. To prevent accidental cutting of the webbing, piton and bolt-hanger eyes should be padded, easily done by leaving one tag end of the sling long enough for the purpose. If the anchor sling must be placed around a sharp rock corner, judicious padding of sharp edges reduces chances of its being cut.

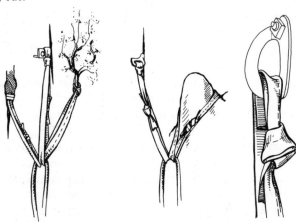

Fig. 9-11. Rappel sling use: two correct anchor set-ups for multiple but imperfect anchors. Note that each anchor point is independently rigged with a separate sling and each is supporting part of the load. *Right,* "tail" of a sling knot used to pad the eye of a bolt hanger.

There is a useful exception to the principle of multiple anchors: an unweighted backup can be set up to an independent anchor; everyone except the last person rappels with the security provided by the backup anchor, and the last person removes the still unweighted backup, confident that the main anchor which supported the rest of the party will be strong enough one last time (Fig. 9-12).

Descending rings are sometimes used to reduce rope wear and make retrieval easier. However, they are subject to damage and manufacturing defects, add an additional failure point to a single anchor, and violate the principle of independent anchors where only one ring is used with multiple anchors.

Rappels as long as half the rope length are made by threading a single rope through the anchor sling to the midpoint. Long rappels require two ropes: thread an end of one through the anchor and tie them together with a double fisherman's knot.

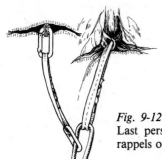

Fig. 9-12. Main anchor with unweighted backup anchor. Last person removes piton, runner, and carabiner, and rappels on main anchor only.

Beginning from the anchor sling, coil each half of the rope separately to form butterfly coils, one pair on each side of the anchor. The coils are each thrown down the pitch, one at a time: the half nearest the sling, then the rope end coil. The sequence is repeated with the other half of the rope. Throwing first the "center" and then the end reduces rope snags or tangling (Fig. 9-13).

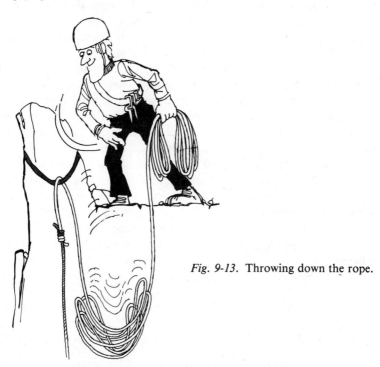

Fig. 9-13. Throwing down the rope.

Before anyone rappels from it the anchor should be tested by applying body weight (or as much as available space permits) to the rappel rope. When sufficient space is not available, the first person can carefully rappel down, on belay if a second rope is available, attach himself to the next anchor, and bounce on the rappel rope to definitely test the main anchor.

RAPPEL TECHNIQUE

Starting is usually the most nerve-racking part of a rappel. To obtain any degree of stability it is necessary for the legs to be nearly perpendicular to the slope. Thus, at the very top the rappeller must force himself to lean out; where this would be awkward or unstable, it may be possible to climb down several feet before leaning out and starting down. This also reduces strain on the anchor. With a brake system, the climber sits on the edge of the rappel ledge, and wiggles gently off, simultaneously turning inward to face the slope (Fig. 9-14). This technique is particularly useful when starting the rappel above an overhang.

A rappel should never be started with a wild leap into space; such acrobatics not only place a heavy load on the anchor but may leave the rappeller in a dangerously unstable position. Once started he moves smoothly down the slope, the rate of descent about that of a slow walk, without bouncing or placing other sudden strains on the anchor. Exhilarating, long, wide-swinging rappels followed by sudden braking can triple the load on the anchor and cause its abrupt and total failure.

The rappeller's body should be upright, nearly perpendicular to the slope, and facing partly sideways, about 45 degrees toward the braking hand. In this position a clear view down the rappel route may be obtained, allowing the rappeller to anticipate obstacles and slope angles, to avoid snagging the rope around brush or rock and avoid knocking off loose rocks. The knees should be flexed to allow comfortable, relaxed movement, the feet maintained apart for stability, and the braking-hand-side foot kept generally lower so irregularities may be "walked" over.

Occasionally a rappelling climber encounters an overhang, where the slope beneath is undercut for a distance. As long as the rope extends below to a point on the ground or ledge where the climber wishes to go, the rappel continues directly down the vertically hanging rope. Passing the edge above an overhang in mid-rappel, he may feel unstable; a technique similar to that shown in Fig. 9-14 (bottom) may be used to ease past the edge.

During such *free rappels*, climbers assume a sitting position, holding themselves upright with the guiding hand on the rope above. Uncontrollable spinning as twists in the rope unwind is a common experience.

RAPPEL SAFETY AND EFFICIENCY

Brake systems jammed with clothing, long hair, beards, and hard hat chinstraps create gruesome and very dangerous predicaments. Tuck

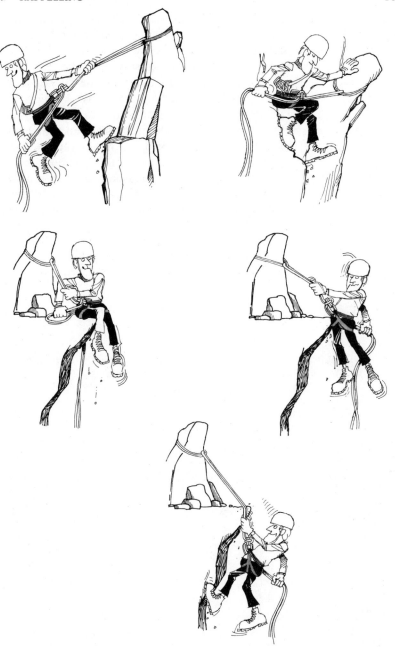

Fig. 9-14. Getting started on the rappel. *Top,* starting directly from high anchor, and climbing below a low anchor to start. *Bottom,* sitting down and squirming past overhang.

everything in, carry a knife in an available pocket, and watch the brake system to be certain it is clear. Should anything catch, instantly halt all downward progress until it can be pulled free or cut loose.

Of several *backup procedures* possible to safeguard the rappelling climber, each has its own precautions and limitations; their use depends on the particular situation. The individual must always be alert for potential problems regardless of the type of backup used.

1. A possible precaution is to tie a figure-8 loop or other bulky knot into each free end of the rappel rope. Surprisingly, people do rappel off the ends of ropes, and the knots can prevent this. Bulky enough knots might even save a climber who for some reason releases a braking hand, by preventing the rope ends from pulling through the brake system. However, the knots can also jam in an awkward location when the rope is thrown down.

2. A person at the bottom of the rappel can control the rappeller's speed, or stop him altogether, by pulling down on the rappel rope, thus increasing the friction in the brake system (Fig. 9-15). Rappels can be

Fig. 9-15. Free rappel halted by climber below pulling down on ends of rope.

safeguarded by the bottom person holding the rope loosely but ready to tighten it the moment the rappeller has difficulty. A sudden injury to anyone except the first person down can be controlled by this technique, which can be used routinely where there is no rockfall danger to the person below.

3. The rappeller may be belayed. He is then secure from even a total rappel-anchor failure provided a separate anchor is used for the belay. Belaying is recommended for all beginners, climbers with minor injuries, and for the first person down on a suspect anchor. However, this requires an additional rope. The last person cannot be protected by a belay. Setting up the belay and pulling up the rope for each person drastically increases a party's descent time.

4. Some climbers like the security of a prusik in place while rappelling, sliding the knot along as they descend. The loop is attached to the harness, and the knot is in place above the brake assembly (Fig. 9-16). This provides a backup for complete detachment or failure of the brake system. Care must be taken to keep the prusik from locking up unexpectedly; once under tension it may prove difficult to release. The loop must be kept short; too long and it can lock out of reach and have to be cut loose. Also, controlling the prusik knot requires the full-time use of the guiding hand, which is then unavailable for balance or protection. Climbers should be aware that the prusik knot can fail to set itself, particularly if the guiding hand fails to release its hold on the knot.

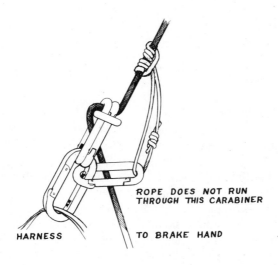

ROPE DOES NOT RUN
THROUGH THIS CARABINER

HARNESS   TO BRAKE HAND

Fig. 9-16. Prusik backup for carabiner brake rappel system.

Occasionally it may be necessary to stop partway down a rappel. With either the dulfersitz or brake systems, two or three wraps of the rope around the leg (plus the weight of the rope) generally provides enough friction to hold. When using a brake system, an alternative method is to pass the rope around the waist and tie two or three half-hitches around the rappel rope above the brake system. This can be released easily when the rappel is to be continued (Fig. 9-17).

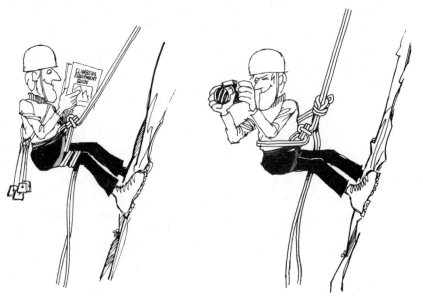

Fig. 9-17. Stopping in mid-rappel with rope wrapped around leg, and tied off around body.

On multi-rappel descents the first person down should carry enough hardware and sling material to anchor himself before freeing the rope for the others to descend. While they are rappelling, he establishes the next rappel anchor. If the slope is not entirely visible from the top or if there is a possibility he may end up hanging free and unable to pendulum-swing to the next rappel point, and thus be forced to retreat, the first person should carry easily accessible prusik slings. If such a retreat is at all likely, each strand of the rappel rope should be tied off separately at the anchor (for the first person's rappel only) to allow him to prusik on either of the single strands if necessary.

The following climbers should carry a runner and carabiners to quickly attach themselves to the new anchor and promptly disassemble their brake system so the next person, who should be all ready to go, can follow.

The bottoms of rappels are particularly exposed to rockfall. Many times they are in gulleys or other areas of unsound rock. Other people are directly up the fall line and those actually rappelling are particularly likely to accidentally dislodge rock. The rope rubbing against the rock is the worst offender of all. Climbers at the bottom must move out of the line of fire, to the side, if at all possible. Small, loose rocks at the starting point should be cleared from the edge.

ROPE RETRIEVAL

A final common problem is inability to retrieve the rappel rope due to a knot or end catching in a crack, behind a flake, against the edge of a ledge or due to excessive friction from the ropes sliding around each other or against the rock. This is at best frustrating, and when encountered during retreat in the face of a storm or nightfall, downright hazardous. If this occurs after the end being pulled up is out of reach of the climbers below, the party can face the grim choice of leaving the rope or having someone climb unroped to free it.

To avoid this situation, the first person down should always untangle the rappel ropes during descent and those following should make an effort to keep them clear. Twisted ropes are readily straightened by keeping the index finger of the braking hand between the two strands of rope. Before the last person comes down, one end of the rope should be pulled to make certain it can be retrieved easily. After test pulling, the last party member must be certain that if a knot joins two ropes it is free of the anchor and cliff edge, and while descending, tries to keep the rope out of places where it could jam. Once everyone is at the bottom, any safety knots in the rope ends must be untied before pulling down the rope. If two ropes were used, the party must pull on the correct one so that the knot is not pulled against the anchor. Ropes of different colors make it easier to distinguish which one to pull.

The rope usually pulls down fairly easily if the above procedures have been followed. A direct pull may not start it moving, but stepping to one side or the other or away from the slope may change the angle enough to permit it to slide. The rope should be pulled steadily, without jerks or stops, so the free end will not whip and wrap around anything.

When the rope has been pulled most of its length through the anchor sling, its weight usually provides enough "pull-down-force" to keep it coming. If friction prevents this, the steady pull usually frees the rope. The climber pulling the rope should warn others by calling "ROPE" loudly before the rope falls—a falling rope can deal a solid blow.

LOOK AFTER EACH OTHER
Rappelling is a technique in which there are certain mistakes that one must not make: once your partner is ready to go, check everything from the anchor points to whether the rope reaches the destination below. Pay particular attention to the brake system: is it set up backwards or upside down? Are the carabiner pair gates properly set up and locking carabiners securely closed? Once you are satisfied, wish him a safe trip.

 **PART THREE**

Rock Climbing

Plate 14. On Great Trango Tower, Himalaya. (Galen Rowell)

10 *

ROCK CLIMBING TECHNIQUE

CLIMBING IS A JOYOUS, instinctive activity; unless restrained, most children will scurry up trees, garden walls, building facades, and anything else steep and enticing. While society, in the form of parents, teachers, and the law, discourages these activities, some determined individuals persist and eventually find their way to the mountains. Those, on the other hand, who have submitted to social pressure and foresaken the steep and airy pathways should, and usually will, content themselves with hiking, and leave rock faces for those who are comfortable and happy there.

Rock climbing can be likened to climbing a ladder, although special techniques have been developed specifically for particular climbing situations. Techniques used by climbers may seem simple as explained within this chapter, but in actual practice may be difficult to do competently.

FUNDAMENTALS

Certain basic principles are prerequisite to essentially all forms of free rock climbing. Proven by experience, they provide the foundation to aggressive, safe, and successful climbing.

Attitude

To climb rock well, the climber must have the desire to do so. Rock climbing requires a strong commitment of mind and body. Making the necessary moves requires total concentration and complete confidence in one's capabilities. Confidence can best be attained by practicing with a top rope (belayed from above) to minimize possible injury in case of a fall, and to allow the climber to safely attempt harder and harder moves, eventually finding the limits of his ability.

Confidence goes hand in hand with physical conditioning. If hand, arm, or leg strength is not sufficient, it does not matter that the mind is willing. Conversely, physical ability alone will not move the climber if the mind is not willing.

Climbing with the Eyes

The distant view provides an insight into the character of climbing to be encountered, and presents the larger pattern of ridges with lower average inclination than the faces they divide; dihedrals, chimneys, cracks and ledge systems; lines of weakness inherent to the structure of rock, which are the routes the climber will follow. (For a detailed discussion on the formation and structure of rock, refer to Chapter 21, Mountain Geology.)

Throughout the approach the skilled routefinder repeatedly "climbs with the eyes," seeking continuous lines and evaluating the difficulties and hazards, noting the obvious difficulties or blank sections that may be encountered and the alternatives to avoid them. The joining together of these lines produces a route that will "go." For example, a bench may lead to a dihedral that is topped by a short chimney, then a ledge that leads to a crack system.

Generally, the eyes should climb the pitch first — look ahead! Study the general line to be followed, then look for specific holds. Alternative lines, holds, and resting spots should be noted before starting to climb.

Once on the pitch, visual examination of the terrain well ahead continues. Short-range views often revise original plans, showing that some holds are not as feasible as they look at a distance, but also showing new holds previously unnoticed. Climbing ahead with the eyes allows the better climber to flow gracefully, not only constantly revising the route, but planning in advance exactly how to use each hold.

Balance

Efficiency of movement and rhythm are intimately associated with a sense of balance. To climb in balance the climber stands erect with body weight directly over the feet and uses the hands only to maintain balance. The beginner's tendency to lean in and "hug the rock" gradually disappears as he learns, through practice, to stand erect, allowing his weight to be supported by his skeleton. As confidence increases, the climber discovers that the upright stance actually improves footing by allowing maximum friction to be developed between boot sole and rock. When climbing in balance, the eyes locate foot and handholds and determine how they are to be used: a foot is placed on the foothold and with hands aiding balance, body weight is shifted to that leg, and as the leg straightens the climber comes back into balance. In rock climbing the eyes are most important, since hand and footholds are not always conveniently positioned nor ideally designed to fit hand or foot.

While the beginning climber may regard a small flat ledge with suspicion, the more experienced climber may view the same ledge as a good hand or foothold and perhaps even a place to stand and relax. When a hand or foothold is suspect, he plans a series of moves to the next secure position, takes advantage of the suspect hold in what appears to be the most stable way, and moves smoothly and deliberately onto and off the hold or holds to the more secure position beyond.

Three-Point Suspension

Stability and security, especially on unsound rock, are promoted by maintaining three points of support at all times (that is, two feet and one hand, or one foot and two hands) while the remaining limb moves to the next hold. Using holds on either side of the direct line of advance helps provide a firmer base and greater mobility.

Controlled Motion

Controlled motion is climbing in balance, or in strenuous situations, moving with economy of effort to avoid undue fatigue. It is much more efficient to push the body upward with the legs than to pull it up by the arms. This is not to say that the arms are never used, but the more upright the stance and the greater reliance on the feet and legs, the longer the strength of the arms and hands will last. Keeping hands at about head height produces a good stance, helps conserve arm strength, and permits the climber to lean away from the rock to better view hand and footholds, a point extremely important in downclimbing steep rock.

The holds chosen should be as comfortably spaced as possible, without excessively high steps or long reaches. Intermediate holds, even small ones, should be used when available, but do not waste time looking for tiny intermediate holds when one big step or reach will do the job safely and efficiently. Jumping or lunging to reach a hold can have disastrous results if it is missed, or if it proves to be loose or illusory. Motion should be smooth, controlled and deliberate.

Whenever possible movement should be varied, spreading the work of raising the body among different sets of muscles, always trying to press downward rather than pull up. The climber should seek natural body positions, rather than cramped, awkward, or strained positions which promote fatigue.

CLIMBING TECHNIQUES

If a route has any appreciable length, it will undoubtedly require moves such as bridging, traversing, jamming, friction, counterforce, or a combination thereof.

Face climbing, because of its varied requirements is considered by many to be the epitome of the classic climb. Coupled with the demand for variety of techniques and skill is the intriguing puzzle of finding the combination of moves to make the route go.

Use of Holds

Handholds and footholds should be chosen for firmness, convenience, and size. If questionable they should be tested with a blow from the heel of hand, a kick of the foot, or a push or pull. Even if loose a hold may be secure enough to use, for example, in a downward direction, though it may fail if stressed outward or sideways. Use of knees should generally be avoided since knees are susceptible to injury and offer very little stability; nevertheless, even experienced climbers occasionally use a knee to avoid an especially high or awkward step. The main considerations are to avoid injury from pebbles and sharp crystals, and not to become trapped on the knees and unable to rise to the feet.

Footholds

Deft footwork in rock climbing as in all other active sports, is essential. Feet should be placed carefully (visually) on the holds in the desired position and left there, not moved or thrashed about in hopes of finding something better. With marginal footholds it is mandatory that once a foot is placed on a hold, it should not be moved or rotated; even a small change in position can cause the boot to slip off.

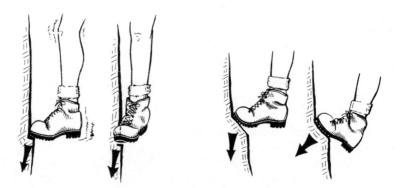

Fig. 10-1. Left, small foothold toeing in is tiring; edging is more secure. *Right,* sloping foothold; bending ankle increases surface contact area.

Toeing in on small footholds can be very tiring and places great strain on leg muscles. If wearing stiff boots turn the foot sideways to get the stronger inside edge of the boot and foot on the hold (Fig. 10-1). In very flexible boots or rock shoes the foot may have to point uphill with the boot sole "smeared" or "covering" the small hold. If muscles are under too much strain for too long a time the leg may begin to vibrate. "Sewing machine leg" can be very annoying at best and dangerous at worst; the best way to stop this vibrating is to change position, usually by moving on, lowering the heel, or straightening the leg.

Flexing the ankle allows the boot sole to be in contact with the rock and to be pushed down firmly, whether the hold be incut, flat, or outward sloping (Fig. 10-1). If handholds are adequate, additional security on slippery, steeply inclined, or extremely small footholds can be obtained by leaning away from the rock, thus creating an inward as well as downward pressure on the hold. Practice develops one's ability to lean out just enough to wedge the feet firmly on holds without unnecessarily tiring hands and arms.

Large footholds, called "buckets," are never scorned, but only as much of the foot as is necessary to stay in balance is placed thereon. Sticking the foot too far underneath a bulge can force the lower leg outwards, creating an out-of-balance stance, and thereby placing undue strain on hands and arms (Fig. 10-2).

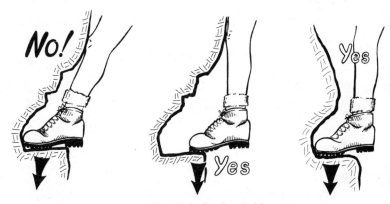

Fig. 10-2. Bucket hold.

Handholds

The cling hold, in its many variations, is the most commonly sought handhold; however, its overuse can lead to a "chin your way up the mountain" style of climbing and also to very fatigued hands and arms. A very useful variation is the "vertical cling" in which the climber grasps the edge of a crack, corner, or knob and leans slightly away from the hold while stepping upward. On small cling holds, the fingertips form to fit the

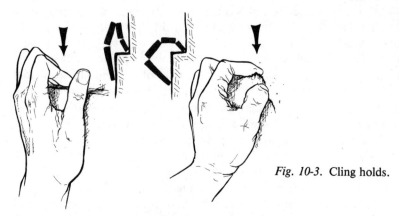

Fig. 10-3. Cling holds.

rock (Fig. 10-3). A larger hold, preferably sloping inward, becomes a true handhold for the entire hand. The best and most comfortable of all such holds are nicknamed "jug handles," or, when appearing at the end of a difficult lead, "Thank God holds" (Fig. 10-4).

Fig. 10-4. Jug handle hold.

Downpressure

When moving above a cling hold, the climber continues to use it as a downpressure hold by placing the fingertips, palm, heel, or outer edge of his hand on the hold and pushing down (Fig. 10-5). Downpressure holds may be used by themselves, or in combination with other holds. The heel of the hand may point in either direction, depending on which way the climber intends to move next. Once the arm has been extended and the elbow locked, the climber is in a position to balance one-handed long enough to move the other hand to a higher hold.

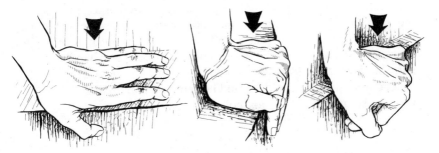

Fig. 10-5. Downpressure. *Left to right,* with palm of hand, heel of hand, side of hand.

Traversing

Often the route deviates from an upward line and traverses across the face. While traversing is no more difficult than moving in any other direction, attention to a few points may make the going easier.

Walking across a series of small holds, with the feet pointing in the direction of travel, offers good visibility of the route, but may force the body out of balance, thus increasing the hand strength required. If the rock is moderately steep and the ledge narrow, the feet should be shuffled along (Fig. 10-6). Stepping through should be considered only on low-angle rock, as it becomes very awkward to pass the inside foot through if the steepness of the rock interferes (Fig. 10-6). On steep rock the climber

Fig. 10-6. Traversing. *Left,* stepping through (awkward). *Right,* shuffling feet.

faces into the wall with toes pointing away from each other, thus placing the strength of the foot (big toe and ball) on the holds, bringing his body in closer to the rock for better balance, and allowing him to readily change direction (Fig. 10-7). In this position, when good handholds permit, the climber can lean back to better examine the route. Hop steps, to change feet on a small hold, should be kept to a minimum and done only with the security of good handholds.

Fig. 10-7. Traversing on small footholds on steep rock.

Hand Traverse

By utilizing a series of handholds, and with feet in friction against the rock, the climber can "hand over hand" across an otherwise blank section of rock (Fig. 10-8). Rare is the occasion that demands one or a series of

Fig. 10-8. Hand traverse, feet frictioning against wall.

hand traverse moves without support for the feet. If required to make a hand traverse, the climber uses his feet as much as possible, moves as rapidly as care will permit, and avoids prolonged hanging on a partly flexed arm.

Jamming

Crack climbing is less instinctive yet often more secure than maneuvers heretofore discussed. Some methods are obvious, as for example, using the edge of a crack as a cling hold, pulling downwards on a horizontal crack, or sideways against a vertical one (Fig. 10-9). The use of a crack as the sole means of crossing an otherwise "unclimbable" rock surface requires very specialized techniques performed with great skill.

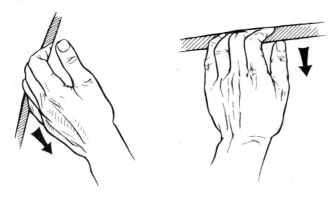

Fig. 10-9. Crack used as cling hold.

Less obvious but of great value is the technique of jamming. In theory, jamming is simply wedging fingers, hands, arms, feet, knees, legs, and/or any other portion of the body into cracks and lodging them securely enough to bear weight. The process may be summarized:
1. Insert a hand, foot, or other body part into a crack, preferably at a locally wider point.
2. Lock the body part by flexing or twisting it so that it pushes or "jams" against both sides of the crack and resists a downward pull.
3. Do the same with other body parts as required.
4. Raise the body, pushing with the legs as much as possible.
5. Repeat the sequence.

Each movement should be both deliberate and useful. Thrashing about, groping, and desperate pawing at the rock are useless and tiring. Before moving a hand or foot, look ahead, select a prospective place, then move the hand or foot to the new jam position and lock it in place.

Cracks come in all sizes, from too narrow to too wide:

1. Narrow cracks—up to 1½ inches—accept finger and toe tip jams; an occasional resting spot is welcome.
2. Medium cracks—1½ inches to 4 inches—require hand, fist, and foot jams.
3. Wide cracks—4 inches on up to, but not including, a size in which the whole body will fit. The so-called "off width crack," in which no part of the body fits well, is in this range (Fig. 10-10). Some cracks narrow towards their interiors, so the climber may be struggling awkwardly with a 5-inch "nasty" with the "outside" hand and foot, but jamming comfortably with the "inside" ones.
4. A crack wide enough to admit the entire body and wider is referred to as a chimney and requires bridging technique.

Fig. 10-10. Climber partly inside a wide crack.

Hand Jams

Fingers may be jammed in narrow cracks and small solution holes. After they are inserted as far as possible, a twisting or torquing action of the hand provides the necessary expansion to lock the fingers in place.

In very narrow vertical cracks the fingertips of the index and middle fingers are wedged as in Fig. 10-11a, with the thumb down and the wrist low.

In somewhat wider cracks (too large for fingertips, but too small for hands) all fingers may be jammed as far as possible (thumb down) and then torqued to lock (Fig. 10-11b). This same size crack will also accept a thumb lock. The thumb is placed in the crack vertically and then the index finger slides down onto the knuckle of the thumb to create the lock (Fig. 10-11c).

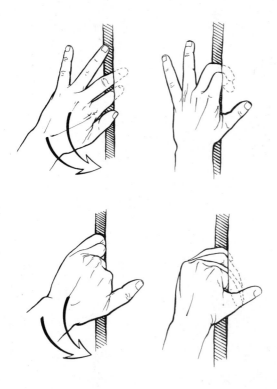

Fig. 10-11. Top: left, insert fingers, and *right,* twist hand to lock. *Middle: left,* insert fingers, and *right,* twist hand to lock. *Bottom:* insert thumb and fingers and lock by pulling fingers down against thumb.

As a crack widens, the entire hand can be inserted and pressure exerted between the back and the heel and fingertips. In an ideally sized crack expansion is provided by tucking the thumb across the palm, whereas somewhat larger cracks require that the hand be "cupped" to lock it in place (Fig. 10-12). Once again a twisting of the hand can improve the jam, and a placement just above a bottleneck will give maximum security.

With essentially vertical cracks the preferred hand jam is "thumbs up or out" (palms facing each other; Fig. 10-13a), allowing greater mobility of the arms. However, in diagonal cracks or because of oddities in the crack formation, it may be preferable to jam both hands "thumbs down or in" (palms facing away from each other) or to jam the upper hand "thumb down" and the lower hand "thumb up" (Fig. 10-13b).

The fist can be jammed in a variety of ways, with the thumb either tucked inside or on the outside to make the fist. Fists are best jammed on the same principle as placing artificial chockstones—inserted in a locally

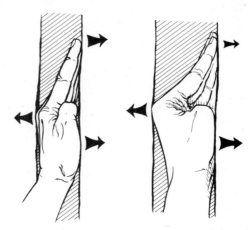

Fig. 10-12. Hand jams. *Left,* cupped hand with thumb tucked in. *Right,* thumb tucked across palm.

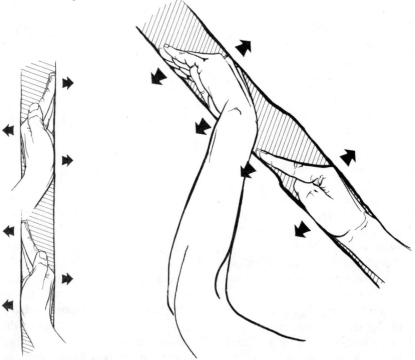

Fig. 10-13. Left, hand position in vertical crack. *Right,* hand positions in diagonal crack.

wider section of the crack and pulled downward to jam. Some expansion can be provided by flexing muscles in the fist and by pressing against the sides of the crack with the back of the thumb (Fig. 10-14). Changing the position of the fingers within the fist will make a slightly different size fist.

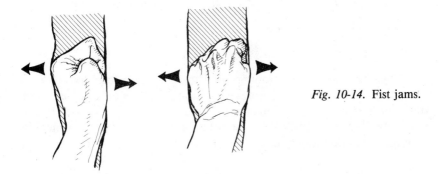

Fig. 10-14. Fist jams.

Foot Jams

In a corner the toe of the boot can be jammed using a technique best described as "smearing"—flexing the boot, with the heel at a lower level than the toe, and applying pressure down and in to wedge the toe in place (Fig. 10-15).

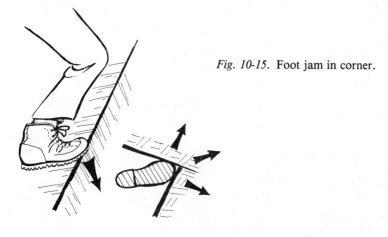

Fig. 10-15. Foot jam in corner.

The toe may be jammed in a crack either vertically or horizontally by inserting the boot with its sole parallel to the side walls and twisting to jam it. Since the twist on the ankle can become painful, this is not a good "resting" jam. Similarly the entire foot can be jammed, either vertically or horizontally (Fig. 10-16).

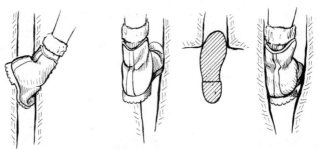

Fig. 10-16. Toe and foot jams.

The entire foot may be jammed end-to-end, either "heel-toe" or with the ankle flexed. If the crack is not wide enough to admit the full length of the foot, it may be jammed diagonally, with twisting force exerted by the ankle and leg (Fig. 10-17). Pressing the knee against the rock generally will improve the stability of the jam.

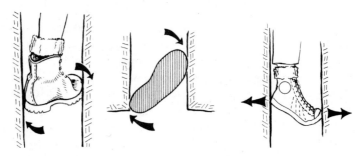

Fig. 10-17. Heel and toe jams.

Body Jams

Cracks too large for hands and feet to jam yet too small to admit the entire body must be climbed using jams of the arms, legs, hips, and shoulders. The same sequence is followed: insert small, expand to jam, move up. The arm lock uses the elbow pressed against one side of the crack, the heel of the hand pressed against the other side, with as much of the shoulder pressed into the crack as possible (Fig. 10-18). The outside arm may be placed across in front of the chest, pushing away from the body on the other side of the crack. A leg jam may be devised between the knee and heel/toe of the boot. Occasionally the leg and/or knee can be jammed without using the foot. The outside foot can sometimes be jammed, heel-toe; very often it just scrapes on the face, gaining purchase if footholds exist. The combinations and possibilities in climbing wide cracks are endless: each individual climber must experiment to find the techniques which work best.

Fig. 10-18. Arm locks in cracks.

Chimneying

The term chimney defines a size range of cracks between those which will barely admit the body ("squeeze chimney") to those so wide a climber's length will not span them. Whatever the width, the principle of climbing them is the same: the climber pushes outwards on both walls of the chimney (counterforce) to remain in place. To move, he relaxes the tension in one portion of his body, moves it up, reapplies tension, relaxes another portion and moves it up. Depending on width of the chimney and the climber, cross-pressure of the upper body is generally between back and hands, elbows and hands, or hand and hand. In the lower body the cross-pressure is most often between heel and toe or foot; knee, buttocks, and foot; buttocks and foot; or foot and foot. The combination that does the job is the one to use.

In a very narrow "squeeze chimney" the body is forced into a nearly vertical position and movement is so restricted that it is difficult to exert cross-pressure (Fig. 10-19). In the narrowest of such chimneys, sufficient cross-pressure can sometimes be created by merely inhaling deeply. Progress is by a shuffling, squirming action. If the chimney is deep enough, somewhat more rapid progress is possible by using a "diagonal inchworm" method: the lower body is shuffled up and to one side, then the upper body is shuffled until the body is again in a vertical position. The effort required to progress in a squeeze chimney is incredible. Sometimes the climber may make progress more easily by remaining on the outer edge or even outside the chimney and using face climbing techniques.

Somewhat wider chimneys, which the entire body can enter easily, are climbed by bridging (stemming) with the back, shoulders and feet

Fig. 10-19. Squeeze chimney.

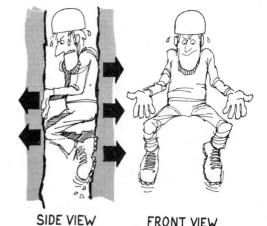

Fig. 10-20. Narrow chimney.

SIDE VIEW   FRONT VIEW

pushing against one wall, and the knees and hands (palms against the rock, fingers pointing down) against the other (Fig. 10-20). Whenever possible the hands should be kept low to create a wedge for the climber in the event the feet slip. To ascend, use either a one-thing-at-a-time squirming action, or a sequence of wedging the upper body while raising the feet and knees, then wedging them and moving the upper body up.

Probably the easiest and most secure chimney to climb is one about 3 feet wide. The arms and legs work alternately, as shown in Fig. 10-21, pushing against the opposite wall.

As chimneys become wider, the climber's position changes from facing across the chimney to facing in or out, with arms and legs pushing sideways (stemming) against the walls (Fig. 10-22). Progress is by arms and legs moving alternately or both legs then both arms. The final absurdity, a chimney that is too wide for the body to span in a vertical position, can sometimes be climbed with the body in a horizontal position. This type of chimney is rare, and the climber willing and able to climb it even more so.

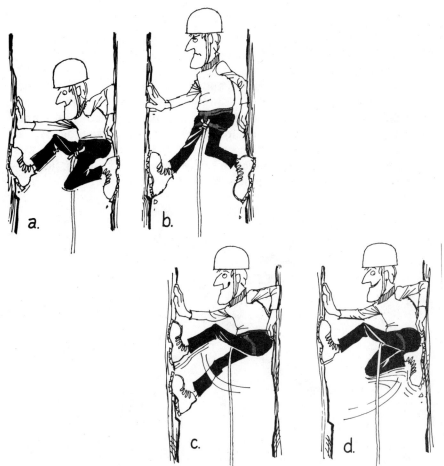

Fig. 10-21. Chimney climbing sequence.
a. Legs drawn up.
b. Legs straightened.

c. Left leg across.
d. Right leg back.
Repeat sequence.

Fig. 10-22. Wide chimney; use downpressure with hands.

Bridging

Bridging is, as the name implies, the spanning of a gap with the body, generally with one hand and foot on one side and the other hand and foot on the other side. Bridging techniques can be used wherever it is possible to push or pull on rock surfaces in opposition. This technique is very useful when climbing in a dihedral or in right-angle corners where there are small face holds on either wall. By bridging (spanning) across the corner opposition pressures can be applied allowing the climber to progress. Far from being of use only within corners, dihedrals, and chimneys, it is indeed common in face climbing to bridge between protrusions, indentations, cracks or any combination thereof (Fig. 10-23).

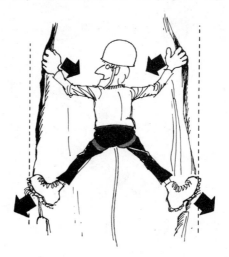

Fig. 10-23. Bridging on a face.

In a bridging situation it is not at all uncommon for the climber to be in a position of exposure, but the opposing force of the legs and arms working one against the other permits the maximum use of all available holds. Very often climbers, once the psychological disadvantage of exposure is overcome, find that getting out away from the rock is easier and safer as well as providing better visibility of the route ahead.

Counterforce

Very often a person can climb securely by using a combination of opposing forces. Some techniques involve only one or two points of support, others involve the entire body. As an example, a pinch grip on a flake or knob is an elementary form of counterforce (Fig. 10-24).

Counterforce holds are frequently used in conjunction with cracks. If the fingers can be inserted up to the knuckles in a small crack, the thumb

Fig. 10-24. Pinch hold.

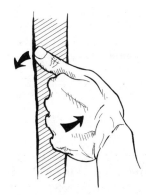

Fig. 10-25. Thumb and fingers in opposition.

can be pressed in opposition, on the opposite side (Fig. 10-25). With both hands in the crack the climber can generate enough outward force by "pulling apart" to stay on or move over the rock (Fig. 10-26). Closely spaced double cracks may be climbed with the same "pulling apart" action

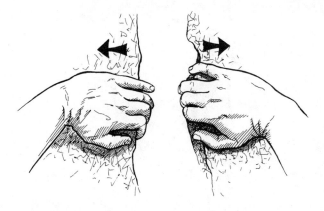

Fig. 10-26. Outward pressure.

Fig. 10-27. Climbing a ridge. *Left,* opposing forces with hands.

as the single crack, or by pressing inward with the hands. On a narrow ridge inward pressure with knees and hands gives maximum security (Fig. 10-27). Widely spaced double cracks may be climbed by a "pulling together" (Fig. 10-28), the climber leans out to force feet onto the rock and by shifting weight to one side or the other is able to move his hands, one at a time.

Fig. 10-28. Inward pressure using two cracks.

On steep rock widely spaced holds do not offer a great deal of stability and it is very possible that the body will rotate away from the rock as soon as a hand is released to reach for a new hold. To prevent this, keep the hands within vertical lines directly up from the feet (Fig. 10-29), and put as much weight as possible on the foot below the hand being moved.

Fig. 10-29. Relationship of hands to feet. *Left,* hands on vertical line outside of foothold; if one hand moves, climber swings like a gate. *Right,* movement of one hand will cause body to swing toward the rock.

Laybacking

Laybacking is the classic form of counterforce, the hands pulling and the legs pushing in opposition, with the climber moving in a series of shuffling movements (Fig. 10-30). A layback can be done where two rock faces meet with a crack in the corner, an "open book" where one side of a crack offsets the other and provides space for the feet, or along the edge of a flake.

Laybacking is so strenuous it is necessary to move rapidly, though delicately, keeping the arms extended as much as possible to put the strain on bones and ligaments rather than on tensed muscles. Feet are kept high enough to maintain friction on the rock, but not so high as to unnecessarily tire the arms. The closer hands and feet are together the more unstable the position becomes. In any one situation, only by getting out on the rock and trying can the climber determine the best position of the feet for maximum friction. Frequently the feet can be placed on small holds or a hand or foot jammed, allowing the climber to assume a more vertical, less tiring stance. In any case, the position should be adjusted to be as comfortable and relaxed as possible under the circumstances — remember, you are doing this for fun.

Fig. 10-30. Laybacking.

Fig. 10-31. Undercling.

Undercling

When the entire body is involved in counterforce climbing, good holds are vital for a strong push-pull or push-push combination. Undercling holds formed by solid flakes or undercut ledges provide good upward pulls for the hands while the body leans out, "pushing" the feet against the rock (Fig. 10-31). As an example, in a small recess or cave, one might stay in balance by pushing down with the feet on the floor and pushing up with the hands on the ceiling.

Combinations of these holds can be improvised: for example, an overhead flake can be pinched while the feet move higher, then it can be used for an undercling hold while the climber, with feet braced, leans out and moves to the next hold (Fig. 10-32).

Slab Climbing

Slab or friction climbing, balance climbing in its truest form, is done on downsloping footholds where surface undulations and roughness hold the foot by friction between boot sole and rock. For maximum surface friction, body weight must be directly over the ball of the foot. On low-angle slab, the climber finds it easy and comfortable to stand erect and walk, but on steep slab must use his hands either on minimal handholds or for friction.

Fig. 10-32. Sequence, *left to right:* using pinch hold, then undercling or layback, while reaching for cling hold.

In slab climbing, the eyes play an extremely important role, finding the small edge, rough spot, or change in angle necessary to provide maximum friction. On extremely difficult slab the friction footholds become so subtle the climber must actually use a hand to feel for the roughest surface on which to place the boot.

To maintain the body weight directly over the feet, the climber squats down until his hands, outstretched horizontally in front, touch the rock for stability (Fig. 10-33). As the angle of steepness increases, less squatting is required to reach the rock (Fig. 10-34). If necessary use the hands just touching the rock to maintain side-to-side balance while taking short steps to ensure keeping the weight over the feet.

Fig. 10-33. Low-angle slab.

Fig. 10-34. Steeper slab; body more upright, keeping weight over feet.

Slab climbing technique is basically the same regardless of the footgear used. Lug-soled mountain boots provide limited friction, adequate for general mountain climbing, but not for difficult slabs. Rock shoes, designed for maximum contact and friction, have smooth, medium-soft rubber soles that bend easily to conform to even minute irregularities on the rock surface.

Rock shoes are placed with the ball of the foot directly over the hold, whether it be an edge, depression, bump or rough crystals, the foot pointing uphill and with the heel slightly lower than the toe (Fig. 10-35). This foot position is maintained as the leg is straightened, bringing the climber's weight directly over the hold. It is necessary to apply weight to develop the frictional force caused by the shoe sole molding to the rock surface. If simply placed on a friction type hold without applying weight, the foot will tend to slip off.

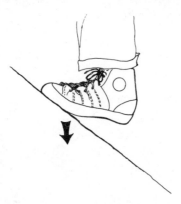

Fig. 10-35. Rock shoe properly placed — ball of foot over the hold.

A mountain boot generally will not flex enough to permit the ball of the foot to be placed directly over a friction type hold; therefore either edging or some other technique must be used. Upon encountering a difficult friction move or two, climbers have been known to take off their mountain boots and socks and make the necessary moves in bare feet, which will perform adequately, but not for long.

Manteling

To mantel is to use hand downpressure holds as a means of gaining a ledge or set of wide holds where there are no holds above, such as climbing onto a fireplace mantel, using only the mantel for support (Fig. 10-36). For the simplest mantels, the hands are placed about a foot apart, palms down and fingers of each hand pointing towards the other hand, on a chest-high flat ledge. The body is raised by straightening the arms (springing with the legs makes this easier). Supported on straight arms, the climber may then raise either foot to the ledge and stand up. If the ledge is above head height, he grasps the ledge, leans back a bit, and walks the feet up the face as far as practical. With a quick movement he changes from a cling hold to a downpressure hold, with elbows up, fingers of each hand pointing towards the other hand, usually one hand moving at a time. The climber then presses up, straightening the arms. The judicious use of any available footholds or even scrambling with the feet facilitates the move. Balanced on hands in mid-mantel, the climber may find that a bulge in the rock prevents standing up easily on the ledge; however, by manteling only partway the climber may be able to reach a handhold that was previously beyond reach.

To mantel on very small or sloping ledges or onto good ledges above sharply cut overhangs calls for much strength and gymnastic skill. Sharply undercut mantels are best maneuvered by a swinging technique, first hanging from the ledge, swinging under, then pulling up on the outward swing. Arm strength and a great deal of practice are necessary to become proficient in manteling.

Downclimbing

While downclimbing is in theory no more difficult than climbing up, it often seems so because the holds are not as visible as when climbing up. On easy and low-angle rock, the climber faces outward while descending, possibly using buttocks for support. As a general rule, hands should be kept low and ready to support the climber either by using downpressure or cling holds. As in climbing up, the weight should be over the feet and a balanced stance maintained; particular care and concentration must be exercised on friction slabs. As the angle of difficulty increases, it may become necessary to face sideways, leaning out where possible to see what

Fig. 10-36. Manteling sequence.

lies ahead. This position permits a view of the route, and allows good freedom of movement. When descending very steep or difficult rock, the climber must face in, moving as carefully as possible, occasionally leaning away from the rock to better see the holds (Fig. 10-37).

Good holds can be used only so far and then must be released, however reluctantly, lest the climber become so stretched out hanging onto a good hold that necessary hand and footholds cannot be seen or reached.

Fig. 10-37. Downclimbing. *Left,* easy—face out; *middle,* moderate—face sideways; *right,* difficult—face in.

Despite the seeming "unnaturalness" of downclimbing, it is a valuable technique well worth developing. Not always is it possible to set up rappels to get off the mountain or cliff, or there may be only a very short headwall to get over on the down route. Downclimbing is also invaluable for retreating when routefinding errors have led one astray.

PRACTICE AND CONDITIONING

The best practice for rock climbing is rock climbing. However, for many climbers the season is too short or the peaks too distant to attain top form. To gain maximum pleasure from rock climbing, most dedicated climbers keep in shape during the off season with a strong program of physical conditioning. Cross-country running is favored by most climbers for aerobic conditioning, and calisthenics that strengthen the heart, lungs, abdomen, legs, arms, and hands are primary; even squeezing a rubber ball is a useful exercise.

The key to proficient rock climbing is repetitive practice to the point of instinctive reaction, preferably in bouldering areas where top ropes can be used, and climbing short pitches that require good technique and force the climber to find the limit of his ability.

Plate 15. "Limestone Cowboy" (5.7), Rocky Mountains, B.C. (Patrick Morrow)

11 *

ROCK CLIMBING
PROTECTION

A PARTY SETTING OUT to do an alpine climb involving a few hundred feet of rock may require no equipment other than boots, suitable clothing, and other equipment discussed in Chapter 2. But if the rock is too difficult and exposed for unroped scrambling, they will rope up and belay. The basic procedure, introduced in Chapter 8, is simple: one climber, belayed by a second, leads up a pitch, sets up a belay, and belays the second climber up. The first climber then leads the next pitch or alternates (swings leads) with the second. The rest of the party generally follows the first rope team up the same route, usually in rope teams of two. If a lead climber falls and is not stopped by an obstruction, he will fall about twice the length of the rope between himself and the belayer (Fig. 11-1). But, since falls can occur near the end of a pitch as well as near the beginning, the total distance may be 300 feet or more. Since a 300-foot belayed fall can be just as deadly as an unroped fall to the base of the mountain, the leader places intermediate *points of protection* on the pitch by, for example, putting a runner around a tree and clipping the climbing rope into it with a carabiner. Then a fall would be only about twice the distance from the last point of protection (Fig. 11-1).

This chapter describes the equipment for and techniques of protected rock climbing. Ropes, carabiner, runners, and other equipment used in general mountaineering are discussed in other chapters. The items covered here are those basic to free rock climbing.

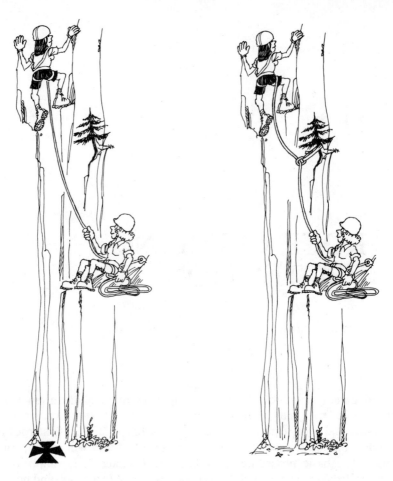

Fig. 11-1. Distance of leader falls. *Left,* unprotected lead; *right,* protected lead.

EQUIPMENT

The Tools

Artificial Chockstones

Although some protected rock climbs can be done with no more technical equipment than a rope, runners, and carabiners, most such climbs require the use of some type of device both for placing intermediate points of protection and for anchoring belays. The most common of such devices are artificial chockstones (chocks or nuts), pieces of metal of various shapes and sizes attached to loops of rope, webbing, or wire cable. A chock is placed or wedged into a crack, and a carabiner attached to the loop (Fig. 11-2).

Chocks have largely replaced pitons as the principal type of protection device: they are lighter and faster to insert and remove, do not scar the rock, can sometimes be placed where pitons cannot or would be of doubtful value, and do not require the use of a hammer. Many climbers carry

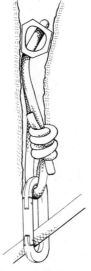

Fig. 11-2. Artificial chockstone used for intermediate protection point.

only chocks on most or all of their climbs. Pitons have not become obsolete, but they are generally regarded as special purpose items—sometimes left in place as "fixed pins" on popular routes, sometimes carried on alpine rock climbs when the climbers are not sure God has provided sufficient good chock placements, and sometimes used on direct aid routes (see Chapter 12, Pitoncraft and Direct Aid Climbing).

Chock Loops

The smallest chocks are wired with loops of wire cable attached by the manufacturer, and the largest must have a rope or webbing loop attached by the climber. Some intermediate sizes can be bought wired or unwired. The following points should be considered when there is a choice: wired chocks are easier to place and remove than chocks on rope or webbing loops, especially if the chock is epoxied to the loop; the wire acts as a handle to guide the chock in and out of place. Any advantage is that the wire will usually slip into a narrow constriction below the chock placement, where a rope loop might be blocked. A disadvantage of wired chocks is that they are more likely to be levered out by rope action (see Clipping In). The loop on a wired chock is generally stronger than a rope or webbing loop on the same size chock but is slightly heavier. As a general rule, chocks which do not allow the use of rope in diameters of 6 mm or larger should be wired.

Kernmantel-type rope is generally preferred to nylon webbing for chock loops, though the latter is sometimes used. If rope loops are used, follow the manufacturer's recommendations for the correct size. The loop should be tied with a double fisherman's knot and pulled tight by suspending one's full body weight from it. The climber should be aware of the fail strengths of the various sizes of rope and webbing and should also be aware that there is some reduction in strength of rope and webbing loops that must pass over edges on the chock.

The length of the loop on a wired chock is determined by the manu-facturer, but for rope loops it is a matter of the climber's preference. Although the majority of climbers prefer short loops (8 to 14 inches) for ease of carrying, some climbers prefer runner-sized loops on some of their chocks because these usually do not require an extra runner and carabiner when placed.

When buying chocks that require rope or webbing loops, be sure there are no burrs or nicks on any part of the chock that the loop touches, and avoid buying any chock on which the loop must pass over a sharp edge.

Chock Picks

A rope team will usually carry a chock pick for removing from cracks chocks that cannot be removed by hand. Some climbers prefer to have both members of a rope team carry picks, since the lead climber may need one to clean out cracks ("gardening"). A skewer-type tent stake makes a cheap and fairly effective pick, but the thought of the damage it could do in a fall induces many climbers to invest in a pick specially designed for the purpose by an equipment manufacturer. A shelf bracket with a hole drilled in the wide end is a good alternative.

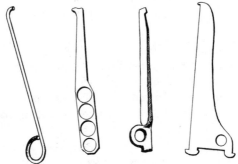

Fig. 11-3. Chock picks. *Left to right:* skewer type, tent stake, Leeper®, piton type, shelf bracket.

Rock Shoes

The great majority of alpine rock climbs are done with mountain boots. Occasionally, however, some part of a climb is difficult enough to make specialized rock climbing shoes desirable, or even essential.

Among the different types of rock shoes available, the main distinc-tion is between the light, flexible, smooth-soled type and those stiffer and heavier, with lug soles or other tread. The former allow greater sensitivity to the rock and are especially good on friction. The latter are good when climbing high-angle faces on small holds and on long direct aid routes where standing in aid slings for long periods is very painful in the flexible type.

When rock shoes are taken on an alpine climb they are usually carried in the pack and put on at the start of the roped rock climbing, or for the harder rock pitches. However, some of the stiffer soled, treaded shoes are reasonably comfortable for hiking and scrambling and can be used for the whole climb, eliminating the need for boots altogether, if the approach and return are fairly short and there is little or no snow travel. The smooth-soled type, on the other hand, are virtually impossible to hike in, and can even be somewhat painful while climbing.

Climbing Helmets

Helmets sold specifically for climbing by climbing equipment suppliers are recommended on all rock climbs. Since the helmet not only protects the head from rock fall, but also protects the head during climber falls, it should have a chinstrap which will prevent it from being lost during a fall. The use of a helmet is admittedly a nuisance, and has and always will be controversial. Helmets have, however, saved climbers' lives, and the lack of one, in many reported accidents, has without question resulted in a fatality.

Carrying Equipment

Most of a climber's hardware is carried on a hardware sling, worn over one shoulder. It is usually made of 2-inch flat webbing, sewn into a loop and then rolled and sewn into a rope-like shape over half to two-thirds of its length. Hardware slings can be bought at equipment stores or made at home.

The size of the hardware sling is important. If it is too short, it may be difficult and awkward for the climber to remove hardware from it. If it is too long, it will swing back and forth, creating balance problems and often making it difficult for the climber to see footholds. Not uncommon are instances of climbers stepping on chocks carried on an excessively long hardware sling when attempting to make a step up. The climber learning to lead would do well to use a runner for a hardware sling in order to experiment with different lengths before buying or making a sling.

There are different methods of *racking* hardware (carrying it on the hardware sling). Most commonly chocks are racked in ascending order of size from front to back, or with all wired chocks in ascending order of size in front of all unwired chocks also in ascending order of size. Carrying more than one chock per carabiner (Fig. 11-4) may mean less weight carried on the shoulder but can cause problems, especially with wired chocks, when the climber needs, say, the third chock down on a carabiner and can use only one hand to get it. The carabiners used to rack chocks are carried on the sling with the gates down and out (the gate side facing

Fig. 11-4. Racking hardware.

out with the opening end down), or up and in if carrying one chock per carabiner. Chocks on long slings are either worn around the neck, over the shoulder, or racked by doubling the loop over and clipping both ends into a racking carabiner. The *free* carabiners can be carried either in front or in back of the racking carabiners and are clipped to the sling either individually or in groups of two or three. Commercially made seat harnesses often have a built-in hardware loop that provides a much better place for the free carabiners and is also a good place to carry a chock pick, belay gloves, and belay and rappel devices. Some climbers even carry their chocks on the hardware loops, eliminating the need for a hardware sling, though this can result in chocks hanging too low and getting in the way of the feet.

Amount of Equipment

How many chocks, free carabiners, and runners should a rope team carry? Obviously there is no single answer to this, since the right amount of equipment depends on the climb and on the climbers' abilities, confidence, and personal styles. However, there are several considerations that should be weighed when putting together a rack for a climb.

If the climbers have good reason to believe that no pitch on the climb will need more than five chocks for protection, it may be tempting to carry only five chocks. That is wishful thinking. Chocks are used for anchoring belays as well as for protection. If two chocks are to be used at each end of a pitch to anchor the belays, one chock is left for protection. Further, nature is not always generous in providing cracks of the right size for the available chocks. If, toward the end of a pitch, the climber wants one more piece of protection, and his one remaining chock does not fit any available crack, he must either back down or finish the lead with no more protection. If a climber regularly uses more than two-thirds of the rack on a pitch, he is going too light and pushing his luck.

If the party has not done the climb before and does not have completely reliable information about it, they should be aware of the possibility that they might get off route and have to do harder and longer leads than expected, and should prepare accordingly.

While carrying a huge rack may eliminate the above problems, weight is a hazard that should always be taken seriously. The climber who takes a rack of 30 or more chocks on a moderate climb will likely have problems with balance and with making some of the hard moves, and will spend too much time fussing with equipment to have much fun.

While there is much variation in the optimum amount of equipment from climb to climb and from climber to climber, a few numbers might serve as useful suggestions for the novice. Probably the great majority of free rock climbs are done with racks of 10-20 chocks. As a minimum (apart from special cases where reliable information about chock requirements is available), they will range in size from those that will fit ¼-inch cracks to those that will fit 2-inch cracks, and the range is usually wider. Sometimes the chocks will be concentrated toward one end of the range if the climbers know that the climb takes mostly small, or mostly large, chocks. Ten to 15 free carabiners is a typical number, depending partly on the number of chocks per racking carabiner. Eight or 10 runners, including at least one double-length runner, is average, the actual number depending partly on the length of the chock loops.

Buying Chocks

The climber just learning to lead should not — unless on an unlimited budget — invest in a large rack of chocks. A small number, perhaps about eight, should do at the start, since the beginner will generally be doing modest leads, and on any harder leads will probably be able to combine the chocks with those of a partner. With increasing experience, a climber develops preference for types of chocks, establishes goals, and can then add chocks gradually as necessary.

The two most popular types of chocks are wedge-shaped and hexagonal-shaped chocks ("hexes"). Both are relatively easy to place and of proven value and versatility. A wedge-type chock will fit cracks of two different widths. A hex has three or four widths, depending on whether the hexagonal shape is regular or irregular. Many climbers use only a mixture of these two types. However, the beginner should get advice from as many experienced climbers as possible before buying anything, in order to learn something of the virtues and limitations of the various types. Once out of the beginner's stage, he would do well to keep up with new developments in chocks by reading climbing journals and experimenting with unfamiliar types of chocks as time and budget permit.

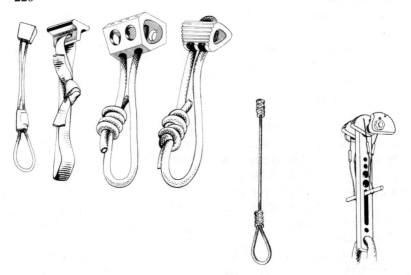

Fig. 11-5. Chocks. *Left to right, top:* wedge, Titon®, hex, camlock. *Bottom,* copperhead, Friend®.

PLACING PROTECTION AND ANCHORS

Since carabiners are used in virtually all protection placements, the novice should learn some general principles for their use: The gates should be either down and out (Fig. 11-6) or down and facing to whichever side minimizes the risk of the gate being forced open by a rock edge or nubbin during a fall. The rope should run from the climber through the carabiner without twists or kinks.

Fig. 11-6. Protection on trees: *left,* girth hitch; *right,* better method. Note: gates are down and out.

When using a runner, be sure the runner is not twisted before clipping the rope into the carabiner; otherwise, the carabiner may end up facing the wrong way.

Protecting on Trees

Trees and large bushes, when available, provide the most obvious points of attachment for protection. The most common way of attaching a runner to a tree is with a girth hitch. However, this method will magnify the stress on the runner in a fall. A method that decreases stress is to loop the runner around the tree and clip a carabiner into both ends (Fig. 11-6). The runner should usually be as low on the tree trunk as possible, although it may sometimes be desirable to put it higher up, or even on a branch, to avoid putting a sharp bend in the climbing rope or to provide a higher point of protection.

Obviously a tree used for protection should be strong enough to hold a fall, but unfortunately the climber has little more than common sense and intuition for guidance. Dead trees and trees whose exposed roots move when the tree is shaken should generally be avoided. Some species have shallow roots or brittle wood and should be used with caution; the climber unfamiliar with the types of trees in an area should check with local climbers.

Protecting on Rock Horns, Tunnels, and Chockstones

Rock horns often provide good placement. A runner is attached by placing it over the horn or by one of the methods used with trees. Sometimes, to prevent the action of the climbing rope from pulling the runner off, it can be attached with a slip knot and cinched up around the rock horn. When possible, avoid placing the runner where it will be pulled against a sharp edge of the rock in a fall. When that is unavoidable, padding with another runner or other soft material may be helpful.

The soundness of a rock horn is difficult to judge. Examine it carefully to see if it is an integral part of a much larger mass of rock. Look for cracks at the base. Test it by pushing and pulling, gently at first (a solid-looking rock horn may be a detached block just ready to fall), then with more force. Hit it with a hand or kick it and listen for a hollow sound, but bear in mind that this testing will not clearly show that the rock horn will hold against the extreme forces generated in a fall. When there is serious doubt about the soundness of a rock horn, look for another means of protection or consider continuing without protection. Many climbers follow the principle that a dubious rock horn is better than no protection at all, but clearly a rock horn that pulls loose in a fall may be worse than no protection as it follows the falling climber down the pitch.

Rock tunnels or columns (for example, formed by a point of contact between two large boulders) and natural chockstones can also be used for protection, in essentially the same way as rock horns, although they are less frequently encountered. The same general techniques are used to protect on tunnels and chockstones as on horns, and they should also be checked for soundness.

Using Fixed Pitons and Bolts

Bolts and fixed pins (pitons) are often found in popular rock climbing areas and are not uncommon on alpine rock climbs.

Bolts are most commonly used for belay anchors but also to provide protection on otherwise unprotectable stretches of rock (see Chapter 12 for bolt placement). The beginner will have no need to place bolts or leave fixed pins behind, but should know how to use them.

Bolts and fixed pins, when available and sound, generally provide the best and certainly the most convenient protection. Unfortunately, they are not always sound and should be checked. A piton that is only partially driven or whose eye is partially rusted out is questionable, and is best tied off with a runner (Fig. 11-7). Bolts can be checked by examining the rock around them for evidence of crumbling or cratering, and tested by clipping in and jerking. *Never* hammer on a bolt to test or "improve" it, since this will permanently weaken it.

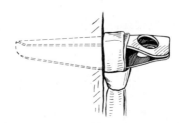

Fig. 11-7. Partially driven piton tied off.

When using a bolt or fixed pin for protection, it is advisable to clip in with a chain of two carabiners or a carabiner-runner-carabiner combination to reduce friction and rope drag (Fig. 11-8). Never use a chain of three or more carabiners because they can twist and detach themselves.

If the eye of a piton or a bolt hanger is bent over so that it is impossible to clip a carabiner into it, it may be possible to thread a runner through it. However, it should not be depended on to hold a hard fall as the runner could be cut.

Sometimes bolts are found without hangers. For that reason some climbers carry their own hangers plus a few ¼-inch and ⅜-inch nuts to fit the bolts. An alternative—especially useful when encountering bolts

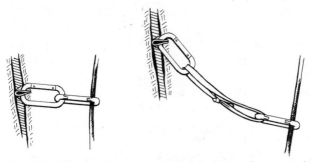

Fig. 11-8. Clipping into pitons; "chaining" to reduce rope drag.

that are too deformed to allow a nut to be screwed on—is to have available one or two smaller wedge-type wired chocks that have not been epoxied to the wire. Then to use a bolt without a hanger, slide the chock down the loop, fit the upper part of the loop over the bolt, snug the chock up, and clip into the chock loop with a carabiner-runner-carabiner combination (Fig. 11-9). But beware—such placements are very easily dislodged by rope action.

Fig. 11-9. Left, bolt with hanger in place. *Right,* wired chock on bolt without hanger.

Chockcraft

Basic Placements

The basic principle in placing chocks is deceptively simple: find a crack with a constriction at some point and place a chock of the appropriate size above the constriction; jerk down on the chock loop to set the chock (watch out for your knuckles!). However simple in theory, chockcraft is complex in practice, and much experience is required to develop an eye for good places to put chocks and an ability to place them skilfully.

The crack itself is the first thing to consider. When possible, avoid cracks that have crumbly or deteriorating rock inside. Many cracks that look good have a small loose flake on one side, often well disguised with grass and dirt. Some very tempting cracks are in fact formed by a detached flake against a large mass of rock. Even if the flake is large and seemingly solid, it may only have to move a fraction of an inch for the chock to extrude through, and the expansion force of a chock against the sides of a crack during a fall can be enormous.

When attempting to place a chock, always look for a likely constriction in the crack first, then select the chock to fit, rather than selecting a chock and looking for somewhere to put it. When a place is found, choose a chock that will have as much surface area as possible in contact with the rock; a chock with one side just resting on a small crystal is likely to be unsound. A chock that sticks partway out of the crack is usually poor protection (Fig. 11-10). If the crack is too shallow to get the chock all the way in, use a smaller chock if possible or find a deeper portion of the crack.

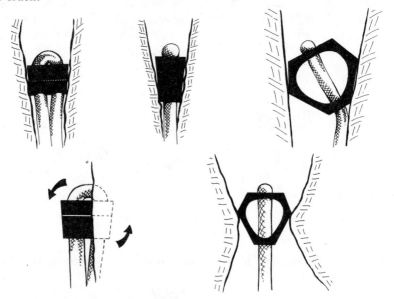

Fig. 11-10. Chock placements. *Top,* good; *bottom,* bad.

Outward-flaring cracks are a problem. A few types of chocks are specifically designed to fit in flaring cracks, as long as the angle of flare is not too great. Most chocks, however, if placed in a flaring crack will simply wobble on two corners. Occasionally a climber must make do with such a placement because there is nothing better to be found—and then climbs very, very, carefully until another placement can be made.

Parallel-sided cracks are another problem. Some chocks are so designed that they can be placed in a camming position in such cracks (Fig. 11-11). When so placed they can be weighted by hanging spare hardware from them to keep them from dropping out. Chocks of various sizes can also be "stacked" in many ingenious ways, but one method only will be described here. If two wedge-shaped chocks are placed in contact, one upside-down, their outer surfaces will be approximately parallel. If the pair barely fits into a parallel-sided crack, they are set firmly and the rope clipped into the one placed right-side up. The upper chock should be clipped to the lower one in some way to keep it from being lost if the placement should drop out.

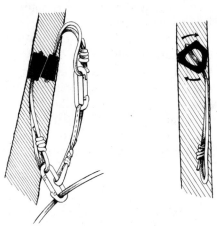

Fig. 11-11. Left, stacked chocks. *Right,* hex chock crammed in parallel-sided crack.

Horizontal cracks can sometimes take simple placements if the interior of the crack is wider than the lips at some point. If not, a camming placement or stacked chocks may hold. In either case, however, if the chock is on a rope loop and the loop must run over a sharp lower lip, as often happens, it cannot be depended on to hold a hard fall, for the loop may be cut (Fig. 11-12).

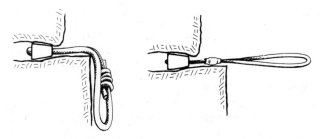

Fig. 11-12. Left, poor; rope loop could be cut over sharp lower lip. *Right,* wired chock better.

When placing a chock with a rope loop, the side of the loop with the knot should face out when there is a choice, in order to ensure that at least one-half of the loop fits into the crack. When the loop will not fit into the crack at all, a wired chock is usually a better choice.

One type of "chock" placement that can be used when there is nothing else available involves jamming the knot of a runner into a crack. Such placements, however, are of doubtful value.

Once a chock is placed, the climber can either clip the climbing rope into it directly or extend the chock loop with a runner (see Clipping In). If the loop of a wired chock is to be extended, never attach the runner directly to the loop, as it would probably be cut in a fall; use a carabiner-runner-carabiner combination (Fig. 11-13). When extending a rope chock loop with a runner, there is a choice of attaching the runner directly to the loop or using a carabiner-runner-carabiner combination: the extra carabiner provides another pivot point to reduce the chance that rope action will pull the chock out, and makes it easier for the second to "clean" the placement, but it also uses up carabiners faster, provides an additional possible failure point, and is slightly more difficult to place.

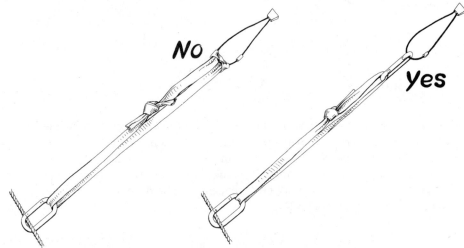

Fig. 11-13. Attaching runner to wired chock. *Left*, bad; *right,* good.

Opposing Chocks

Occasionally a climber finds a crack in which a chock can be dropped behind a constriction in such a way that it will hold against an outward pull, or even an upward pull. Most chock placements, however, will hold only a downward pull. Although the novice might consider this no disadvantage — since a falling climber can be depended on to fall downward, not upward or sideways — there are several situations in which a chock placement must be capable of holding an upward or sideways pull. When the climbing route changes direction at or above a placement, the resulting bend in the rope may simply pull the chock up and out of the crack. Also, in some cases a fall taken on a higher chock will put a force in an up and out direction on the lowest chock (see Clipping In for more discussion of these problems). Further, belay anchoring systems, which must often be set up with chocks, usually require at least one anchor designed to hold an upward pull to keep the belayer from being pulled sharply upward by a leader fall. Finally, many horizontal cracks cannot take simple placements, so if a placement is to hold, the force somehow must be sideways, to pull the chock, or chocks, into the constriction. The standard way of dealing with such situations, when multi-directional placements are not provided by trees, pitons, or whatever, is to place a pair of opposed chocks.

It is essential that the novice climber learn at least one generally usable method of placing opposed chocks before setting out to lead. The simplest method is to pass one chock loop (or a runner attached to it) through a carabiner attached to the other chock loop and clip the climbing rope in (Fig. 11-14). This often works well in horizontal cracks if the chocks can be set firmly, but is not very reliable in vertical cracks, since the bottom chock will drop out if it cannot be firmly set. Furthermore, in a fall, the force on the upper chock loop is double the force on the lower loop. A more generally reliable method is to hold the chocks together under tension by tying a runner to the carabiners on the chock loops with clove hitches and cinching up one side of the runner (Fig. 11-15). The climbing rope can then be clipped into the slack side of the runner. It should not, however, be clipped into the upper chock loop directly with an

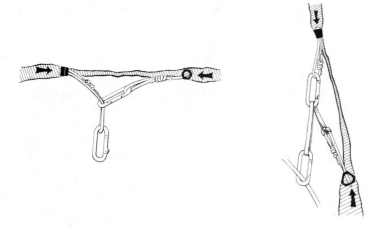

Fig. 11-14. Opposed chocks. *Left,* horizontal crack; *right,* vertical crack.

Fig. 11-15. Opposed chocks held in place by tension.

independent carabiner, since an upward pull can cause the carabiner to ride up and pull out the upper chock.

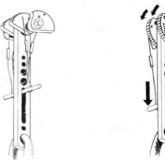

Fig. 11-16. Friends®. *Left,* expanded. *Right,* crossbar pulled, ready to insert in crack.

Friends®

A new type of chock, called a "Friend®," requires some special discussion. The Friend®, a sophisticated, spring-activated camming device (Fig. 11-16), is the latest, but perhaps not the last, in a series of devices developed to provide reliable placements in cracks where ordinary chocks are difficult or impossible to place, such as parallel-sided cracks, flaring cracks, and cracks under roofs. A Friend® can usually be placed quickly and has made it possible to do some extremely difficult pitches that are otherwise virtually impossible to protect. On more modest climbs, they can be very convenient, saving time and effort in places where protection is needed and ordinary chocks would be tricky and time-consuming to place.

A Friend® seems easy to place: hold like a hypodermic syringe, pull the cross-bar back, place in a crack and release the bar (Fig. 11-16). But there are some pitfalls of which the climber should be aware.

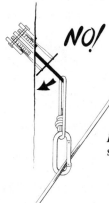

Fig. 11-17. This Friend® will let you down. The shaft should be placed more nearly vertical.

If the bar must be pulled all the way back to get it into a crack, it may be impossible to remove. Use a smaller one or another type of chock.

Do not put the Friend® any deeper into the crack than it has to be for a good placement; if placed too deeply, it may be impossible to reach the cross-bar to remove it.

When placed behind flakes or in deep cracks, a Friend® has been known to "walk up" into the crack, out of reach, as a result of rope action. A Friend® should usually be extended with a runner in such placements.

A Friend® should always be placed so that in a fall the direction of pull is parallel to the shaft, or it can rotate and pull out (Fig. 11-17).

A Friend® should never be placed where the shaft would be forced against an edge in a fall (for example, in a horizontal crack with the shaft resting on the lower lip) as it would snap off.

Although a Friend® is extremely versatile and can therefore usually reduce the total number of chocks required for a climb, occasionally a more conventional chock in the same size range may be easier to place. When carrying them it is usually a good idea to carry at least a couple of other kinds of chocks in the same size range.

LEADING AND FOLLOWING

Planning the Route

In popular rock climb areas for which guidebooks are available, routefinding is seldom a problem: if a line of fixed pins or bolts does not make the route obvious, the guidebook will generally describe it in some detail. In alpine rock climbing, routefinding is usually more difficult. Sometimes no guidebook description is available, and even if one is, it may be very sketchy, saying no more, for example, than that the route ascends the NE Buttress for several hundred feet of moderate climbing. For that reason, the party must be prepared to do some planning and routefinding.

Planning should begin as soon as the party can see the buttress, face, ridge, or whatever they intend to climb. Look for major features that generally indicate weaknesses in the mountain's defenses that the line might follow: crack systems, dihedrals, chimneys, areas of broken rock. Note areas of small trees or bushes that could indicate belay ledges. Note deceptively tempting lines that lead up to broad roofs or blank walls — these may not be visible from near the start of the climb and the unobservant party may be led to climb five pitches up such a line only to back down, or wait to be rescued. Using such observations, develop some general but flexible plan for the climbing line, keeping in mind likely looking alternatives at various points. Once at the start of the first pitch, routefinding and planning continue, with an eye to picking out more local features. The general principles are the same: look for natural weaknesses, form a tentative plan for the pitch, including, if possible, the belay spot and perhaps a place for the first piece of protection, and note alternatives in case the planned line should lead to a blank wall. Be prepared also to "look around the corner" for easier alternatives that might not have been visible from below. When faced with a choice between pitches of differing difficulty, try to look at the following pitch; better to climb two moderate pitches than to do an easy pitch and then be faced with one that may exceed the party's ability. Throughout the climb, remember to note retreat possibilities in case the climb must be aborted, as well as possible descent routes if there is no established descent route known to the party.

Selecting a Placement

A climber moving up from the belay, or from the last intermediate point of protection, will reach a point beyond which it would be preferable not to continue without added protection. If the rock provides a place for protection at that point, the first thing to do is find as secure and comfortable a stance as possible; it may take several minutes to put in a good placement, during which time the climber would probably slip off an insecure hold, or become dangerously tired in an uncomfortable or awkward position. In some cases, it may not be possible to find a suitable stance, and then a choice must be made among three unpleasant possibilities: downclimb and look for a lower placement (or downclimb to the belay and ask a partner to lead the pitch), hang on desperately and hope to get in a placement before arms or legs give out, or continue to the next available placement point. To a large extent, this problem can be avoided by looking ahead, anticipating such situations and placing protection before it is needed. But it cannot be completely eliminated, and one must be as prepared for it as possible: do not panic, make the decision quickly, and stick with it. Surprisingly often, the correct decision is to continue without protection to the next possible placement.

When the climber has found a secure, comfortable stance and is faced with two or more usable cracks, of different sizes, what rules should be followed in deciding which one to use? It is tempting to always place the largest possible chock, but this is a bad practice, since the placement using the largest chock may not be the soundest. Equally important is the fact that sometimes it is necessary to conserve chocks in a certain size range. If it appears likely that the rest of the pitch will require a significant number of large chocks, it may be best to place a smaller chock where there is a choice. But remember that usually a larger chock will hold a harder fall, which sometimes dictates using a larger chock even when one would prefer to conserve large chocks. A final consideration is ease of retrieval. A placement that would be difficult, or perhaps impossible, for the second to remove should be avoided in favor of one that allows easier retrieval, so long as safety is not reduced.

Clipping In

Once having placed a chock or other protection, the climber must decide whether to clip the rope into it directly or extend it with a runner. If the placements do not follow a straight line and the rope is clipped in directly, it will zig-zag through them, causing severe rope drag. Rope drag is at best an annoyance and at worst can cause the climber to fall. Extending some or all of the placements will often straighten the line enough to eliminate the problem of rope drag (Fig. 11-18).

If a piece of protection is placed under a roof and the line goes over the roof, the placement must be extended far enough to allow the rope to clear the roof without a bend (Fig. 11-19). Otherwise, not only will there be rope drag, but if a fall occurs higher up and the load is taken on a placement above the roof, the rope could be cut by the edge of the roof.

When some or all of the protection is chock placements, and if the rope zig-zags through the placements, it can pull the chocks up and out. A chock placement can also be pulled out if the rope bends through it and a fall is taken on a higher placement: the rope will go taut and the direction of the force on the lower chock will bisect the angle made by the rope, possibly causing the chock to be pulled out (Fig. 11-20). If the

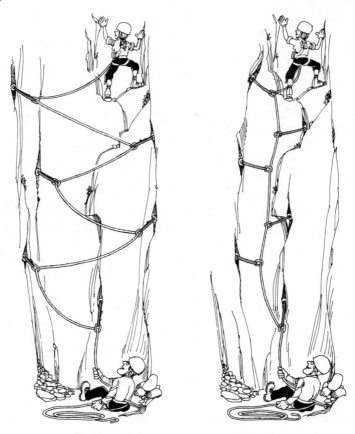

Fig. 11-18. Left, bad; zig-zag line creates rope drag and can cause chocks to pull out. *Right,* better.

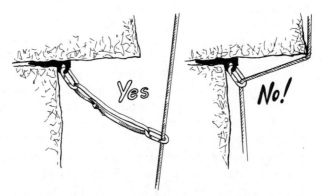

Fig. 11-19. Placements under roofs. *Left,* good. *Right,* bad; bends cause rope drag and rope could be cut by rock edge during a fall.

chock pulls out, the next chock up may pull out as well. The result may be that the line of chocks will "zipper" out from the bottom up, leaving the climber with, at most, the chock he fell on.

Fig. 11-20. "Zippering"; force on bottom chock is up and out.

Extending chock placements can often eliminate the problem of chocks being pulled out in either of the above two ways. Another solution is to place chocks in opposition at changes of direction of the climbing line. Although this uses up chocks faster, and does not eliminate rope drag, the alternative method — extending the placement — has the disadvantage of increasing the length of a fall. If a placement is extended 3 feet and the climber falls from above the placement, the extension increases the fall by 6 feet. If a double or triple runner would be required to avoid the risk of pulling out the chock, the value of the placement is drastically reduced. In such cases, it is often better to place chocks in opposition if it seems likely that the resulting rope drag will be tolerable.

If the line is straight, or nearly so, it may be possible to clip in directly to most or all of the placements. But even with a straight line only a small amount of rope action may be enough to pull out a wired chock. Another problem is that as the climber moves past a chock after clipping in directly, the rope may bend sharply through the carabiner to the tie-in point at his waist, pulling the chock up and out (Fig. 11-21). Consequently, the climber should consider extending some of the placements or placing some chocks in opposition even when the line is straight.

Fig. 11-21. Non-extended chock pulled up and out as climber moves past.

Despite the obvious importance of not allowing chocks to be pulled out, the climber should not be led by the considerations discussed above to mechanically extend or place opposed chocks on every placement. When it is not necessary, it wastes time, equipment, and sometimes strength, and an extension lengthens any potential fall on that placement. Each placement should be considered individually.

Moving Past a Chock

A climber who has clipped into a chock is likely to turn full attention to making the next move, happily oblivious to the chock sneaking out of its placement. The carabiner can get caught between the rope and the climber's hip, pulling the runner and chock loop up; or a knee or foot may catch the runner or chock loop with the same result. The climber must use care in moving past a chock, rather than giving exclusive attention to the next move.

Retrieving a Placement

Frequently a chock is used only to protect one hard move, beyond which is easy ground or perhaps a bombproof piece of protection, rendering the chock of no further value. In such cases, the climber may be able to retrieve the chock by simply reaching down and pulling it out.

Obviously, this should be done only when it can be done safely (for example, after clipping into the next solid placement). And it should be done only when there is something to gain, when the chock could cause rope drag or when it might be needed higher up on the pitch, and only when it is not needed to protect the second.

Frequency of Protection

The universal fears of falling and being hurt lead many climbers, especially novices, to place protection before almost every move, depleting their hardware racks when there is still a long way to go to the end of the pitch, and costing valuable time on a long climb. A less obvious argument against over-protecting is that the climber who routinely stops every few feet to fuss with hardware is missing one of the great attractions of rock climbing, the exhilaration of moving smoothly and continuously up the rock. It is almost as easy — at least for some — to succumb to the opposite temptation and put in much less protection than one feels comfortable with, either to show off or to avoid being thought weak or timid. Weigh the possibility of a long fall leading to serious, perhaps permanent, injury against the temporary psychological lift of being admired for daring.

A climber who is aware that it is possible to overprotect and is also not inclined to show off still has the problem of deciding where and how often to place protection, given personal abilities, the character of the rock, and the time and equipment available. The closest thing to a reasonable general rule is to place protection where one would feel uncomfortable without it, keeping in mind the temptations mentioned. But how comfortable one feels without protection at some point is not always based on a rational assessment of the danger: a climber who feels comfortable making a difficult move 6 feet above the last piece of protection may be risking a nasty fall onto a sharp rock horn, and a climber on low-angle friction slab with no projections to hit if he falls, may be terrified at running out 20 feet beyond a piece of protection, even though he may only be risking minor injuries.

A fall will always be somewhat more than double the length of rope from the last point of protection, because there is always some slack as well as stretch in the rope. Further, if the belayer gives a dynamic belay, intentionally or not, the length of the fall may be significantly increased.

A very important, but frequently neglected, consideration that should affect the frequency of protection is the quality of the placements. If most of the available placements on a pitch are poor or questionable, a relatively large number of them will increase the likelihood that at least one will hold should a fall occur.

A final, somewhat technical point concerns the *fall factor*, the ratio of the length of a fall (excluding rope stretch) to the total length of rope between climber and belayer. Thus, if the climber places a piece of protection 60 feet out and takes a fall 20 feet beyond it, he will fall 40 feet, with 80 feet of rope out, for a fall factor of 40/80, or 1/2. The fall factor, rather than the length of the fall, is the major determinant of the force on the climber's body and on the placement that holds the fall: the higher the fall factor, the greater the force. Therefore, it is often possible to place protection somewhat less frequently toward the end of a pitch than nearer the beginning, without increasing the risk that the force of a fall would cause a placement to fail.

Protecting Traverses

Inexperienced leaders often protect themselves carefully on a hard traverse but fail to place protection for the second after completing the difficult portion. This forces the second to climb the same difficult section without the same protection the leader placed for himself, and can result in a wild pendulum across the face (Fig. 11-22).

Traversing situations call for some foresight. If a pitch continues up after a traverse, the climber should try to avoid putting in protection at or near the end of the traverse, unless doing so seriously increases the risk to himself, in order to shorten the second's pendulum if he falls. A possible alternative on such a pitch is to belay the second with an extra rope.

Hauling Packs

Occasionally it may be necessary or advisable to climb without a pack for part or all of a pitch, either because the weight of the pack would make the pitch too difficult or because the line goes up a squeeze chimney.

In such cases, the climber may haul the pack up part or all of a pitch by trailing a second rope tied to the pack. At the end of the pitch he sets up a belay, hauls the pack up hand-over-hand and unties it, and throws the end of the rope down again to haul up his partner's pack. If a second rope is not available, he may, after setting up a belay and having his partner untie temporarily, pull the rope up through the protection, and throw down the free end. If the difficulty is short and the rope long enough, it may be possible to tie in to the climbing rope some distance from the end, tie the pack into the end, leave it on a ledge, climb up the hard section to a secure spot, and haul the pack up. Other methods, and variations on these, may occur to the innovative or the desperate. In many cases, ice axes are hauled separately to reduce the chance of the packs getting stuck.

Any equipment being hauled must be attached securely to the rope. For example, ice axes should not be attached by merely dropping the shaft through a loop or a carabiner at the end of the rope.

Since there are serious disadvantages involved, the climber should think twice before hauling a pack just because climbing without it would make the pitch more enjoyable. First, it uses up valuable time, especially

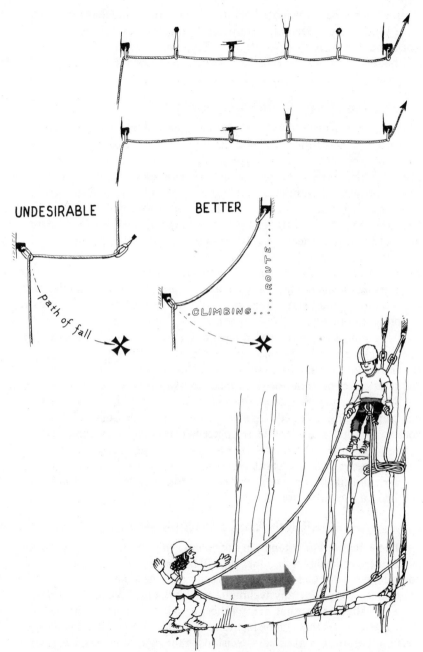

Fig. 11-22. Traversing. Top, traverse protected before and after hard move midway. Middle, shortening the second's pendulum fall. Bottom, using extra rope to belay second.

if, as often happens, the pack gets stuck and requires much ingenuity and extra time to free. Second, hauling even a light pack can be very hard work and can leave the climber with dangerously reduced arm strength for the rest of the climb. Finally, if there is any loose rock in the path of the packs, hauling will usually launch it.

Following a Pitch

The novice who follows and cleans a pitch will, more often than not, arrive at the top festooned with runners, chocks, and carabiners still attached to each other and in no discernible order. While providing comic relief for the rest of the party, inefficiency and sloppiness can create serious problems: equipment may be dropped and lost; chocks and carabiners hanging down near feet will make for awkward climbing and can lead to serious falls on traverses; and untangling and transfer of equipment at the top of the pitch can consume a lot of time.

However, with a little thought, even a novice can follow a pitch efficiently. A few suggestions may be helpful:

Start preparing to climb as soon as the lead climber is off belay. After getting out of the belay setup, break down the anchor system, staying clipped into one anchor until on belay.

Put on the pack *before* anything else, except perhaps a hardware sling. After racking all chocks and carabiners on a hardware sling or runner worn over one shoulder and then putting all other runners over the other shoulder, give the area one last look to make sure nothing is left.

When cleaning the pitch, use some method that minimizes the risk of equipment being dropped. One way is to clean, when possible, from the rock to the rope. For example, if a placement consists of chock-carabiner-runner-carabiner, first remove the chock from the crack, unclip it and rack it, then remove the carabiner from the runner and rack it, then the runner, and finally the carabiner on the rope. Thus, if the follower is careless, at most one item will be dropped.

PERSONAL RESPONSIBILITY

There has been no attempt in this chapter to provide definitive descriptions of the "correct" techniques that all competent rock climbers use nor to state a set of rules that can be easily and mechanically followed to guarantee safety. For any technique used by some competent climbers, there are alternatives that many other, equally competent climbers use. And a set of rules that can be memorized to guarantee safety is equally an illusion. One must make many decisions in the light of incomplete knowledge, with no clear rule to follow, and—when the decision has to be made in the middle of a pitch—without the luxury of being able to consult one's favorite expert, even if that expert is on the other end of the rope.

While it is not the business of any climber to tell other climbers what risks are reasonable and what excessive, no climber wants to take avoidable risks simply out of ignorance. But the control of risks, to whatever level of risk one finds acceptable, is not a matter of memorizing points of technique and rules. It is a matter of understanding the reasons underlying the techniques one has mastered, being constantly aware of everything in the climbing environment that can affect choices, and making decisions as thoughtfully as time will allow. The climber who has mastered but not understood some set of techniques and who mechanically follows some set of rules supposedly designed to guarantee safety has ceased to think and has become a danger to himself and his fellow climbers.

Plate 16. Direct route on Reed Pinnacle, Yosemite. (Galen Rowell)

12 *

PITONCRAFT AND DIRECT AID CLIMBING

THE HIGH STANDARDS OF free climbing developed in recent years have reduced the use of direct aid climbing technique, in which the climber literally hangs from the devices he installs. Direct aid techniques are, however, still necessary for sections of climbs where the difficulty exceeds most climbers' current free climbing limits, or when weather conditions have made a normally free section impossible. Additionally, direct aid occasionally provides a free climber a safe way out of trouble or back on route.

This chapter deals with the craft of piton placement and removal, and with direct aid climbing techniques, in which piton use is more extensive today than in any other phase of climbing. In direct aid climbing pitons have not been as rapidly replaced by chocks as in free climbing.

PITONCRAFT

Climbing, using chocks only for all artificial protection or anchors, as discussed in Chapter 11, is called clean climbing. Use of pitons might be termed "dirty" due to the crack damage caused by their repeated placement and removal. Pitons are viewed by some as tools out of the past, yet pitons were used—not without controversy about the ethics of their use—in the 1930s, and have served as the primary artificial protection or anchoring devices for 40 years. Today, although pitons are still available in climbing shops, many climbers own only one or two, and have never carried pitons nor piton hammer on a climb. Further, the number of currently active climbers who are proficient in placing pitons is dwindling rapidly, thus leaving an accomplished few to teach others the craft.

Chocks have rapidly replaced pitons for free climbing, due to the ease of placement as well as the desire among climbers to preserve the original character of the rock. Crack damage from repeated piton placement and removal can and has permanently lowered the difficulty of some popular climbing routes. What were once very thin cracks on often-climbed routes are now enlarged by piton scars—scars that accept chock placements in most cases, or fingers, and in a few cases, a whole hand. Many former aid climbs are now done free due to the altering of the rock by pitons.

Pitons continue to have a place in climbing, particularly in direct aid climbing and occasionally in alpine climbing. Further, the average climber will find old fixed pins remaining on existing routes throughout the world. The knowledge of piton placement is needed in order to judge the degree of security that a rusty old antique may be expected to provide when encountered on a climb. No fixed piton should be trusted completely. If possible, always back it up with a chock or another piton.

In remote alpine climbing when the combination of very thin cracks and the need for protection or anchors is encountered, a thin blade piton and piton hammer may be necessities. A piton is also a better multi-directional anchor and provides more security in a horizontal crack than can normally be expected of a chock.

The following discussion of piton hammers, pitons, and their placement and removal covers the basic information needed by most climbers. Anyone planning to use pitons on a climb would do well to experiment with their placement and removal and test their holding ability, preferably by locating a climber with experience in their use to arrange some instruction. There are many tricks to both placement and removal which are beyond the scope of this chapter but are well worth the expenditure of a day's time and an aching arm.

Piton Hammers

Piton hammers, essential for driving and removing pitons and occasionally removing chocks, receive a lot of hard use and should be of good quality. A 20- to 22-ounce hammer (Fig. 12-1) is recommended for piton placement.

One end of the hammer head should have a good-sized flat striking surface for driving pitons; the other end should taper to a pick. A short blunt pick enables the user to direct blows very precisely to a small area—useful for example, when removing a piton from an awkward placement. A longer thinner pick can be used to clear moss and dirt from cracks or to pry chocks out. If the pick is slightly hooked or has two or three notches, it can be used to pry out pitons as well as chocks and is preferred by some climbers who use both chocks and pitons. Battering and prying cause hammer heads to loosen if not securely fastened, so when selecting a

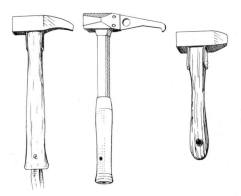

Fig. 12-1. Piton hammers. *Left to right:* Chouinard, Mjollnir, and mediocre.

hammer check it closely to make certain the head is fastened tightly and in such a manner that it will survive hard use.

Grip, shaft size, and balance are matters of personal preference. A longer shaft delivers more force to the hammer blow and more leverage when prying; however, it may be awkward and certainly adds weight. The shaft may be wood, fiberglass, or metal, and there seems little reason to advocate one material over another. All handles, regardless of the material used, should be protected by tape.

The hammer must be attached to the climber to prevent loss. Most climbers use a sling made from lightweight nylon cord or webbing. Check the sling from time to time to be certain it has not been cut or abraded. The sling must be long enough to enable the hammer to be used at arm's length.

The hammer may be carried in a pants pocket or stuck through a harness loop provided for that purpose on some harnesses, but neither arrangement is very satisfactory and a hammer holster is recommended (Fig. 12-2). Before buying a holster, make sure the hammer fits, can be easily removed, and is held firmly enough not to accidentally fall out. A spare hammer is recommended for long aid climbs in case one is dropped or broken. Many climbs have ended abruptly with the loss of a hammer.

Pitons

Pitons may be crudely described as metal spikes which are pounded into cracks in the rock as intermediate points of protection, for belay anchors, or as a means of aiding ascent. The blade is the part driven into the rock and the eye is the point of attachment for the carabiner (Fig. 12-3).

Until 1960 most pitons were made of soft iron or other ductile metal which would bend to fit the cracks into which they were driven. Holding

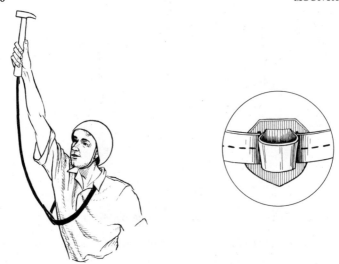

Fig. 12-2. Hammer sling correctly sized and hammer holster for use on harness or belt.

Fig. 12-3. Pitons with parts named. The size of an angle piton is measured forward of the eye toward the tip.

power rarely exceeded 1000 pounds and quality control in manufacture was poor.

Soft iron pitons, originally good for one or two placements only, now have been relegated mainly to use as fixed pitons on popular routes and as expendable anchors, having been replaced for nearly all purposes by the newer, stronger, and more durable chrome-molybdenum alloy pitons. Chrome-moly "pins" depend on stiffness for holding power when driven; their blades bend very little, but are gripped along their length by protrusions within the crack (Fig. 12-4). Without doubt, chrome-moly pitons are the safest and strongest on virtually every kind of rock.

Fig. 12-4. Piton placements.

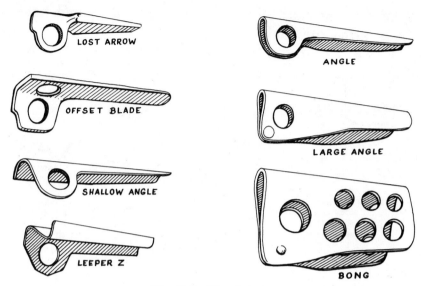

Fig. 12-5. Piton types.

Pitons may be divided into two general types: (1) blades, whose holding power results from their being wedged into tightly fitting cracks, and (2) angles, whose holding power is derived from both wedging and blade compression (Fig. 12-5).

Blade pitons are described in terms of both length and thickness, from long to short and from "knifeblades" through thick. Between the medium blades and the small angle pitons, the Leeper Z®-shaped pitons and "shallow angle" pitons are preferred by some over extra thick blades and wedges because they are lighter and because their shapes give greater holding power, particularly in shallow cracks.

Angle pitons are made in sizes from ½ to 1½ inches. Larger-sized angles (from 2 to 6 inches), usually made of aluminum, are called "bongs." Angle pitons and bong placements are shown in Fig. 12-6.

Basically the use of pitons is simple: locate a crack, drive in a piton that fits, test the placement manually, clip in, and climb. The last person up removes the pitons. Since the pull on a piton is almost always downward, horizontal cracks are preferred over vertical ones. The piton should be driven in a locally wider portion of the crack, particularly if the crack is vertical, to reduce the likelihood of failure due to shifting or rotation under load (Fig. 12-7). If possible, the eye should point in the direction of pull (Fig. 12-8).

First, look at the crack to select the best place to drive the piton. Try to visualize the particular piton on your rack which will fit the crack; if

Angle pitons must be placed with both edges and back
bearing on the rock.

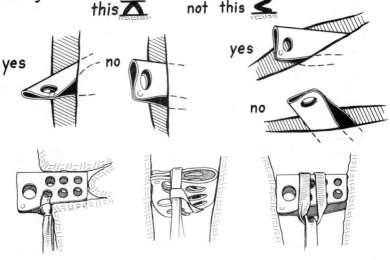

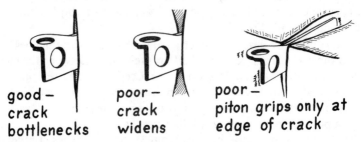

Fig. 12-6. Top, angle piton placement; bottom, bongs, left to right: tied off
through lightening holes, sling around entire bong, and bong used as chockstone.

Fig. 12-7. Piton placements.

one seems to fit, drive and use it, and if not, try a piton of another size.
Selecting a piton and then trying to find a crack to fit it may result in
accepting less than the best placement and wasting a lot of time.

Before driving, insert the piton finger-tight at one-half to two-thirds
of its length; knifeblades and offset blades to one-third their length.
Drive it with the hammer until only the eye protrudes. Soundness of
placement may be gauged by feel and sound; it should feel as though the
piton were being driven against increasingly firm resistance and the pitch
of the sound should rise with successive blows of the hammer. Inspect
each piton to make sure that as much of the blade as possible is in contact
with solid rock — a piton placed between two protrusions in the crack

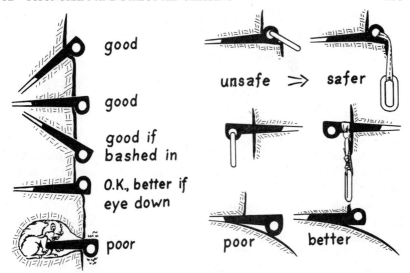

Fig. 12-8. Piton placements.

could easily rotate and pull out. Pitons driven in vertical cracks must be tested by tapping lightly on the head in a downward direction. Similar testing of pitons driven in horizontal or diagonal cracks is perhaps less essential but strongly recommended. If the piton shifts or displays other signs of potential failure it will be necessary to try elsewhere; use a longer or thicker piton in the same place, or resort to some of the tactics described below, especially stacking or nesting.

Pitons placed too solidly or awkwardly for easy removal should be left as "fixed pins." Pins found in place should not be bashed or subjected to thoughtless hammering, especially if made of soft iron, but tested by tapping lightly and redriven firmly if loose. Sooner or later the best-equipped climber will reach a spot where nothing fits or where those pitons that can be driven fail to inspire confidence. In such situations the following tactics are basic; refinements are limited only by the climber's ingenuity. If there is any basic rule, it is "use whatever works."

Occasionally, a piton cannot be driven fully, that is, all the way to the eye. There are two possible reasons: (1) the piton has "bottomed out," that is, the crack depth does not permit the piton to go farther, or (2) the piton thickness is slightly too large for the crack. If "bottoming out" is the cause, the placement is rarely secure and a different placement should be used, perhaps in the same position with a shorter piton. In the second case and if the piton is solid, it may be tied off with "hero loops" or runners, using the slip knot, girth hitch, or clove hitch (Fig. 7-14 and 12-9). "Hero loops," short loops of ½- or ⁹⁄₁₆-inch webbing, are used for tie-off.

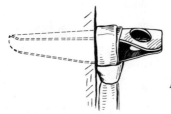

Fig. 12-9. Partially driven piton tied off.

The carabiner should be clipped to the hero loop, not into the eye of the piton. A second hero loop may be tied to the eye of the piton and attached to the load-bearing loop or runner to avoid losing the piton if it pulls out.

If the available pitons on the rack do not fit the crack, two or three pitons may be driven together (Fig. 12-10). Blades are "nested," one on top of the other; angles are "stacked," again, one on top of the other. Under the general guideline of "whatever works," any combination may be used; however, some combinations are extremely difficult to remove. The main effort should be directed toward obtaining the most solid and stable placement possible, but remember that the holding power of such combinations is limited; therefore their primary use is in aid climbing. If the crack is wide and shallow, a combination of pitons may be stacked or nested and then tied off. When combining two pitons, drive them as a single piton, and really bash them in. If using three or more, drive the

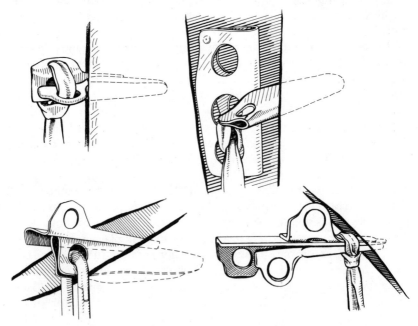

Fig. 12-10. Examples of stacking and nesting.

final piton between others which have been inserted by hand.

Angle pitons of 2 inches or larger may be used as artificial chockstones. Runners can be tied through the lightening holes of partially driven large angle pitons. However, the best method of tying off large angles is to tie the runner around the entire piton, as is frequently done with bongs even in ideal placements.

Because of blade taper the surfaces of a piton exert extremely large forces on the sides of a crack during and after the driving process. These forces can cause the crack to widen, particularly behind a flake, which may dangerously loosen other pitons in the same crack; although solid when placed, these may not hold in a fall — in fact the lower ones may be dropping out below as the leader progresses. Always be aware of where and what you are climbing: the seemingly most solid of piton cracks may be expanding as you move upward.

Piton Removal

Piton removal is facilitated by avoiding awkward and inaccessible placements, such as off-set corners. Generally, hammering the most solidly driven piton back and forth along the long axis of the crack will work it out. Blades should be driven in one direction until they stop moving, hit hard two or three more times in the same direction, and then driven back in the other direction. After being driven hard first one way, then the other, they can be driven back and forth more easily, and finally tapped lightly back to the center position for removal by hand. With angles, less piton movement is needed — just enough to create a "removal groove." Bongs are most easily removed by reaching inside the crack and driving them out.

An old steel carabiner and runner may be used to apply outward pressure while hammering on a stubborn piton or to jerk a loosened piton free (Fig. 12-11); an aluminum carabiner will likely be broken if used for this purpose. A slightly drooped or notched pick on the hammer can aid in prying pins from tight placements, but take care not to break the hammer handle off.

Fixed Pitons

In the past many soft iron pitons have been left where originally placed. These pitons bend to conform to the crack when driven and thus are sometimes almost impossible to remove, often being broken during the attempt.

Fixed pins found in the mountains may be in bad condition. The eye may be broken or badly rusted; the pin itself may be rusting within the crack and the pin may be so loose that it can be extracted with the fingers. All fixed pins should be examined as closely as possible and then used with suspicion.

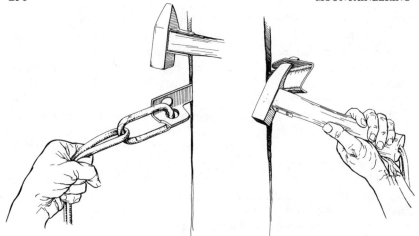

Fig. 12-11. Piton removal. Use of cleaner-biner, and hammer used to pry.

NUTS AND BOLTS

As mentioned earlier, chocks (nuts) are used for aid climbing; their placement is described in Chapter 11. Chocks have considerable advantage where driving a piton could expand the crack.

Due to the length of the chock loops, the elevation gained with each placement may be 6 to 12 inches less than when using pitons. Friends® are particularly valuable tools for the aid climber, since they are quick to place in cracks under roofs, saving much energy and being perhaps more secure than pitons in this situation. The climber desiring to use Friends® for aid may wish to use tubular webbing with two loops (Fig. 12-12); the longer loop is used for protection placements on free climbs, while the short loop is used for aid placements. Friends® have sufficiently high forces against the crack sides even with only body weight hanging from

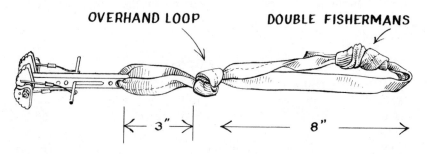

OVERHAND LOOP   DOUBLE FISHERMANS

← 3" →   ←——— 8" ———→

Fig. 12-12. Friend® with webbing loops; small loop for aid climbing and large loop for protection placements.

them, to occasionally cause a crack to expand—with the potential of pulling out. This is particularly true of the smallest Friend®, which has a narrower expansion range of about ⅞ to 1⅛ inches.

Bolts

Bolts are often encountered on aid routes where cracks for chocks or pitons do not exist. Their placement requires drilling a hole in the rock deeper than the length of the bolt. The hanger (for carabiner attachment) and nut are placed on the bolt, the bolt inserted and then driven into the hole (Fig. 12-13).

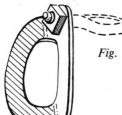

Fig. 12-13. Bolt, with hanger and nut in place.

On climbs, bolts may be found with or without hangers. In areas where hangers customarily are removed by the second, climbers must carry both hangers and nuts of ¼- and ⅜-inch sizes to fit the bolts. In some areas the common practice is to leave hangers and nuts on the bolts.

Bolts are generally at least as safe as fixed pitons. Inspect the rock around the bolt for evidence of crumbling or cratering and test it by clipping in and jerking, but *NEVER* hammer a bolt found in place to test or "improve" it; repeated hammering, in fact, loosens bolts which would otherwise be reliable.

Bolts will be found as belay anchors in many climbing areas. Two ¼-inch bolts for such a purpose are inadequate. Three should be a minimum, and preferably one should be ⅜-inch. Belay bolts should be spaced 8 to 12 inches apart, either in a horizontal line or in an L-shaped pattern.

AID CLIMBING

Direct aid climbing is defined in the United States as the use of anything other than the rock's natural features for support or rest while climbing. Aid techniques vary from the leader's use of the second's shoulder—or head—for a foothold, the impromptu grab of a runner on an otherwise free pitch, or the continuous use of etriers (discussed later) with the many types of rock climbing hardware.

At one time, aid climbing was literally tension climbing: the leader was held in position by tension from the belayer while placing the next piton. The climber, hanging one-handed from a piton, would pull up slack rope, clip the rope to the next higher piton and haul himself up with help from a pull on the rope by the belayer.

Slings or stirrups which offered the leader a place to stand were the next innovation. Frequently of ¼-inch manila rope, they served adequately but were terribly uncomfortable when used with soft shoes. Sometimes rope ladders with metal steps were used for comfort, but these jammed in cracks and were awkward to carry. Since the end of World War II, chiefly as the result of pioneering efforts in Yosemite Valley, revolutionary changes took place, elevating aid climbing techniques to a high level.

Single Moves on Aid

Likely the purest of free climbers has at some time held onto a runner hanging from a protection point in order to rest. Likely also the hold was released after resting and upward motion continued using only the natural features of the rock. Unfortunately, not all climbers have the necessary ability, willingness to accept a potential fall, or the strength necessary to surmount all obstacles at a single bound. The use of that runner for a handhold until the next rock handhold is reached would be a single move on aid. Many climbers use similar aid moves occasionally when they are either technically, mentally, or physically unable to continue otherwise.

Fig. 12-14. Runner from chock for single aid move.

A single aid move on a free route is technically unethical, although hardly an unpardonable sin, and permits the novice climber to negotiate and enjoy a route which might otherwise be beyond his ability. A short climber, faced with an impossibly long reach may place a protection point (chock or piton) at head level or above and utilize a runner hanging from it as a hand or foothold (Fig. 12-14). Stepping directly on a piton or bolt may also be preferable to a potential fall. A climber who has strayed off route onto more difficult climbing than prepared for may use one or several aid moves to regain the route and/or move to easier terrain. One caution: a finger through a piton or bolt hanger eye for a handhold becomes a messy amputation in a fall.

The single aid moves described are typical for the leader. The second on the rope rarely needs to resort to them; he simply requests tension from the belayer above, grasps the rope with one or both hands, and pulls up over a difficult move or two. A follower can also use prusik slings to pass a nasty move or two, but must warn the belayer to hold the tension on the rope.

Direct Aid Equipment

Although aid climbing requires all the items used in free climbing as well as some specialized tools described below, the main difference between the equipment needed in free climbing and aid climbing is quantity; because hardware is so much more closely spaced on aid pitches, more of everything, especially carabiners, is essential.

Stirrups, now generally called etriers (Fig. 12-15), are short webbing ladders used as the principal means of ascending in aid climbing. On routes involving only occasional moves on aid or in remote areas where weight and bulk in the pack are critical, etriers may be improvised from runners or tied from ¼- to ⁹⁄₁₆-inch webbing; however, for the extended use on any route where aid climbing predominates, the preferred practice is to tie them from 1-inch flat webbing.

Twelve to 20 feet of webbing are required for each etrier, depending on the climber's height and the number of steps desired. A guide to sizing is described in Fig. 12-15. In general, etriers should be long enough to permit the climber to easily step from the top step of one to the bottom step of another which is connected to an aid anchor placed at arm's reach. The number of steps in each etrier — usually three, four, or five — is a matter of individual preference. Whatever the method used for tying etriers, that illustrated or any other, the top step is always positioned so that when the climber is standing in it, the piton or chock to which it is clipped is about midway between waist and knees. This permits standing in the top step nearly all the time when placing the next anchor. The pair of etriers should have identical step spacing.

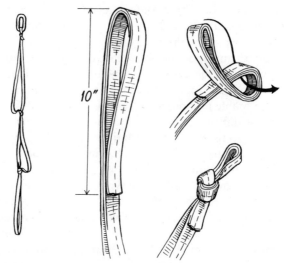

Fig. 12-15. Etriers. Completed etrier and tying sequence using the Frost knot. The amount of webbing needed to make this etrier is twice the finished length plus 10 inches for each step plus 8 inches extra for Frost knot. A 60-inch etrier with three steps takes 158 inches.

After the etriers have been tied and tightened, a carabiner is clipped into the carabiner loop of each etrier and left there to be moved with it from placement to placement. On less than vertical aid climbs, a short loop sub-aider can be clipped into this "etrier carabiner" to provide an extra high step for the climber. Aid climbing may be done with two etriers; however, current practice is to use a pair of etriers on each etrier carabiner. The etrier pairs are made from different colored webbing for ease of identification.

In addition to chocks (discussed in Chapter 11), and pitons (covered at the beginning of this chapter), there are some specialized tools which may be employed on extended aid routes.

Mechanical ascenders are substitutes for the prusik knot which facilitate cleaning and hauling on aid routes (Fig. 12-16a).

RURP (Realized Ultimate Reality Pitons), hatchet-shaped pitons about the size of postage stamps, are designed to chop their way into extremely thin, shallow cracks (Fig. 12-16b).

Cliffhangers, or skyhooks, can be hooked over tiny nubbins, ledges, or flakes (Fig. 12-16c).

Bashies/copperheads are soft aluminum blocks or copper devices which are bashed into shallow grooves or placed in piton holes (Fig. 12-16d).

A belay seat is a small fabric seat sling in which to sit when there is no

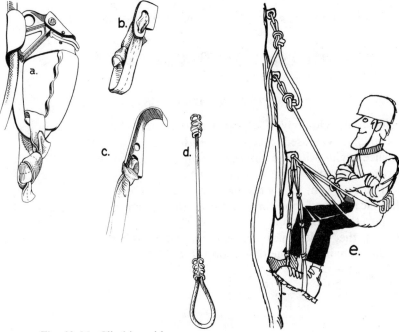

Fig. 12-16. Climbing aids.
a. Ascenders
b. RURP   d. Copperhead
c. Skyhooks   e. Belay seat in use

handy ledge from which to belay (Fig. 12-16e). This is unnecessary when using a "sit" type climbing harness.

A "daisy chain" or "cow's tail" is made of 1-inch tubular webbing tied in a series of loops, each approximately 3 inches long; the overall length of the daisy chain should equal the climber's maximum reach when one end is connected to his climbing harness (Fig. 12-17).

Direct Aid Technique

Leading

Yosemite direct aid technique originally used two etriers, each with a carabiner for connection. Current practice favors two pairs of etriers (total of four) with one carabiner to connect each pair. The four-etrier method is presented here as the primary one currently used for long aid climbs. The two-etrier method may be desirable for short aid sections and is described in Supplementary Reading (Appendix 3) as well as in the previous edition of this book.

In the following sequence of aid climbing it is assumed that pitons are

OVERHAND LOOPS   DOUBLE FISHERMANS KNOT

Fig. 12-17. Daisy chain.

being used exclusively. The same basic sequence is followed, regardless of the anchor type used, except a tie-off loop is used with pitons. This sequence begins with the climber standing in the top steps of the pair of etriers suspended from one anchor and ready to place the next anchor.

1. Place a piton, finally testing with a downward tap.
2. Place a tie-off loop through the piton eye and clip a "free carabiner" into the tie-off loops.
3. Clip the "etrier carabiner" on which there is a pair of etriers and a daisy chain, into the tie-off loop (Fig. 12-18).

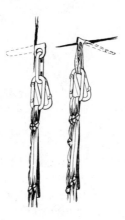

Fig. 12-18. Etrier connection. *Right,* with webbing tie-off loop. *Left,* with carabiner connection to piton.

4. Place a foot in one etrier and transfer weight to the foot gradually. If the piton placement seems secure, test with a slight hop in the etrier to load the placement. If the security of the placement is questionable, ease weight onto the etrier, taking care not to bounce or overload the placement while moving up and making the next placement. Move the other foot into the second etrier.
5. Clip the free end of the daisy chain into the harness, then remove the other daisy chain from the previous placement at the harness end.

Fig. 12-19. Resting on foot (for clarity the daisy chain from the placement to the harness is not shown).

6. While standing in the etriers remove the etrier carabiner from the previous placement and connect it to a convenient place on the harness (Fig. 12-19).
7. Move up in the etrier foot loops until the placement is approximately at waist level and connect the climbing rope in the "free carabiner."
8. Shorten the daisy chain connection, leaving about 6 inches of slack, and relax.
9. Repeat the procedure starting with the next placement.

The current use of the ⁹⁄₁₆-inch webbing tie-off loops on pitons is a relatively new concept which eliminates use of one carabiner per placement (Fig. 12-18). The many tie-off loops used should be checked carefully before every climb, and should be replaced if cut or damaged, or if they have sustained a fall.

Climbing an aid pitch using a 150-foot rope may involve 30 to 50 placements; this means 30 to 50 tie-off loops if pitons only are used, 30 to 50 free carabiners, some runners to extend placements as necessary, and 30 to 50 pitons or chocks. More than the minimum number of chocks will be necessary to ensure needed sizes are available. The weight of all this equipment builds character and perhaps explains why more and more climbs are now done free.

The novice on his first direct aid climb is frequently dismayed by the seeming insecurity of the stance in etriers; however, the climber should stand or climb in etriers the same way as on the footholds they replace — that is, legs should lift the body from step to step with hands used mainly for balance, not as a means of hauling up the climber's weight. The toes of the boots press firmly against the rock face for additional stability.

There are two ways by which the climber can free both hands, or rest on a steep aid pitch, without calling on the belayer for tension. The quickest way is to tuck one foot under the buttocks and sit on it (Fig. 12-19). With hands free the climber can fuss with hardware, take pictures or simply rest.

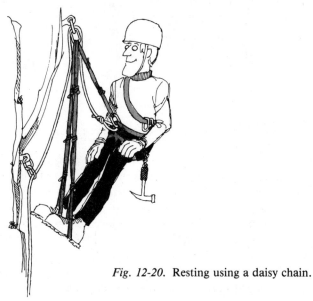

Fig. 12-20. Resting using a daisy chain.

The other method uses the daisy chain (Fig. 12-20). The daisy chain length is adjusted at the harness end to provide the proper distance to simply allow the climber to sit in the seat harness to rest. This position also allows free use of the hands.

Some aid climbs follow cracks behind relatively thin flakes or behind large semi-detached blocks. The danger in such situations is that the pressure created by the hardware placement and/or the leader's weight may expand the crack, allowing the pitons or chocks below to drop out, or may pry the rock off the mountain, dropping rock, leader, hardware, and all into the belayer's lap. (Chocks are less likely than pitons to cause such a crack to expand.) If successive pitons are placed in the same crack

Fig. 12-21. Daisy chain used to free hands while reaching above bulge to place next anchor.

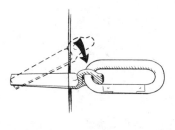

Fig. 12-22. Piton placed at angle to direction of pull; before and after pull.

and crack expansion is likely, the free etrier should be clipped to the highest piton as soon as it has been driven sufficiently to hold the weight of the climber, who then shifts weight gradually onto the etrier, hoping it will hold in case the piton below fails. The piton is driven farther after the move has been made; driving it at an angle to the direction of pull may permit it to rotate slightly and relocate itself rather than pulling completely out under load (Fig. 12-22).

When leading on aid, as in free climbing, it is desirable to keep the rope in as straight a line as possible to minimize friction. Each placement can be extended with runners as described in Chapter 11. Minimizing rope friction due to the many, many placements on an aid pitch is extremely important.

Following (Seconding) and Cleaning

Once the leader has established the new belay it is the follower's turn to climb. Not only must the second climb to the next belay position, but he must "clean" the pitch, that is, remove all the pitons, chocks, carabiners and runners left by the leader.

The sequence for following on etriers is similar to that of leading except the second (follower) should unclip the rope from each piton before clipping in the etrier carabiner. Standing in etriers, the follower may be unable to reach the piton below to remove it. In this case, he either clips two etriers together or uses one or two runners to lengthen the etriers. When the climbing is predominantly direct aid, and on long climbs where a heavy pack must be hauled, it is generally faster and more efficient for the second to climb the rope, rather than the rock, using mechanical ascenders (Fig. 12-23). Then the climbing rope can be tied to an anchor by the leader, rather than being used to belay, thus freeing the leader to haul the pack up using a second rope which is normally dragged behind while climbing.

Fig. 12-23. Climber jumaring.

A widely used brand of mechanical ascenders (Jumars) has lent its name to the process (jumaring). After the leader has secured the climbing rope to two or three bombproof anchors, the second connects his jumars to the rope. One etrier is connected to each jumar. Additionally, a daisy chain or runner is connected from each jumar to the harness. Since the second has no need to move from one etrier loop to another and since it is desirable that his feet do not come out of the loops, they should be secured to the feet with one of the methods shown in Fig. 12-24.

The second remains tied to the end of the climbing rope and moves up as if prusiking, moving one jumar at a time. As each piton or chock placement is reached, it is often necessary to remove one jumar from the rope, replace it on the rope above the piton/chock, then transfer weight to this etrier to provide slack in the rope for unclipping the climbing rope.

To prevent loss of hardware in case it is dislodged unexpectedly in cleaning, some climbers prefer to connect a runner between harness and piton/carabiner combination before attempting removal.

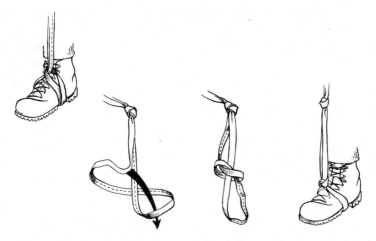

Fig. 12-24. Top, girth hitch around boot. *Bottom,* slip knot adjusted to snug up on boot.

In theory using ascenders is as safe as using prusik knots or climbing with an overhead belay. Most, if not all, accidents which have occurred involving their use can be attributed to human error. To be sure, doing everything correctly will not ensure immortality; however, it does significantly lessen the chances of being killed through procedural error. To summarize:

1. The anchors must be absolutely bombproof, inasmuch as the minimum load they are called upon to hold is that of two people and a heavy pack.
2. The harness of the second should be tied to both ascenders and the end of the rope; thus, three points of security exist. Additional assurance can be gained after moving up some distance by tying a figure-8 loop in the rope below the jumars and clipping it to the harness. By replacing the figure-8 loop with a new one every 20 feet or so, the length of a possible fall, should both ascenders fail, is limited. Remember to untie the previous knot each time. If a figure-8 loop in the rope is used, it is preferable that it be connected to the climber's harness using a runner with a carabiner for attachment at each end. The second, collecting hardware as he goes and using ascenders with etriers, is faced with a maze of hardware, ropes, etriers, and runners. He must NOT disconnect the wrong thing. The added big figure-8 knot, if connected directly to the harness, adds to the confusion.
3. When attaching the jumar to the rope, the safety trigger must be fully closed or the jumar may pop off the rope. If the trigger is closed, the jumar should not come off a rope of 7 mm or greater diameter. Failure of this nature occurs most often on diagonal ascents.

4. When following complicated traversing or overhanging pitches, it may be safer, faster, and easier for the second to climb the pitch belayed. Protected by an overhead belay furnished by the leader, the second may stand in etriers, or, on occasion, take tension while removing the hardware in relative security.
5. As a precaution, always carry two loops of 7- or 8-mm rope which can be used for prusiks.
6. When jumaring be aware of sharp rock edges which the rope above may be touching. The bouncing due to rope stretch can cause fraying of the outer sheath of kernmantle ropes and even rope core damage. Minimize rapid jerky movements.

Sack Hauling

On long technical ascents a party must carry many pounds of food, bivouac gear, and water, in addition to climbing equipment. Normally, one does not joyously contemplate leading steep, difficult rock under a heavy pack, so other means must be found to transport gear. Early "big wall" climbers either hauled loads hand-over-hand or prusiked with packs hanging from their waistloops. During the early 1960s the following technique was devised for hauling on long and difficult climbs. It has the great advantage over earlier methods of employing leg power and body weight rather than weaker, more easily fatigued arms. An additional benefit is the cheery diversion it provides the leader while the second jumars and cleans the pitch.

The leader climbs with two ropes — the climbing rope and a separate hauling line simply dragged behind, and each climber carries a pair of jumars. After anchoring the climbing rope so the second can ascend and clean the pitch, the leader attaches one jumar upside-down, to an anchor, and weights it with the hardware rack. A pulley is attached to the same anchor, above the jumar, and after all slack is pulled up, the hauling line is inserted in the jumar and pulley as shown in Fig. 12-25. The second jumar, with an etrier attached, is clipped to the hauling line, right-side up. To raise the pack, the leader simply pushes down with one leg to raise the haul line, then moves the jumar back up the rope and repeats the sequence. The upside-down jumar acts as a ratchet to prevent the haul sack from sliding back down between pulls. A plastic bottle or tape over the knot at the haul sack will prevent rope wear and possible breakage, thus saving the lunch for when it is needed.

In cases of difficult hauls the pulley jumar can be attached to the climber's harness rather than use the foot loop, enabling the climber to push down and away from the rock with both feet. This method is used by some climbers all the time in the belief that it is less strenuous than the one-leg technique.

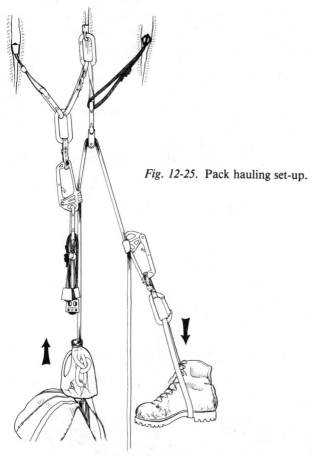

Fig. 12-25. Pack hauling set-up.

The efficiency of this technique is reduced if the rock is of low angle or very broken up, and it may be necessary for the second to help the pack over overhangs or other obstructions. On traverses, it is wise to have a very light (7-8 mm) third rope which the second may use to lower the bag across and prevent damage to its contents.

Traversing

Pendulums and Tension Traverses

Pendulums and tension traverses offer means of reaching cracks, ledges, or other features off to one side of the original climbing route which are otherwise inaccessible except by bolting. Tension traverses are generally used for short distances and on low-angle rocks: the climber leans sideways against the rope and "walks" across, using friction and the few holds that may be available. The belayer pays the rope out slowly and smoothly as needed while maintaining tension.

To pendulum, the climber moves above the area to be crossed, places a secure anchor, connects the climbing rope to the anchor, then climbs or is lowered down an appropriate distance to permit a swing or pendulum to the desired ledge or new crack. If the climber is lowered from the anchor by the belayer, take care not to lower him too far. Lowering a little farther if the pendulum is too short is easy, but raising him back again may be impossible. With the belayer holding tension, the climber, supported by the rope, runs or swings across to the objective (Fig. 12-26). In long pendulums, repeated swings may occasionally be required to build momentum until the objective can be grasped. The belayer can be relieved of the strain by a jumar on the rope which is attached directly to the anchor.

Fig. 12-26. Leader performing traverse to ledge. Note: runner and descending ring are not retrievable.

After completing the pendulum, the leader, if continuing up a pitch, will climb above the pendulum anchor, or as high as safely possible, before clipping into further protection, in order to reduce rope drag and shorten the length of a possible fall for the second.

If the pendulum pitch ends below the pendulum anchor, after the leader has established a belay, the second climbs only to the point where the leader started the pendulum, then with tension from the belayer, performs a pendulum in the same manner (Fig. 12-27). Care must be taken to ensure the rope does not rub against the rock during the pendulum swing, particularly if multiple swings are necessary; the rope can be dangerously abraded. The anchor and either a runner or carabiner are left behind when the rope is pulled through before the climb is resumed.

Always be certain the pendulum anchor is bombproof; it is best to use at least two anchors.

Fig. 12-27. Follower about to perform pendulum traverse. Note that the piton and carabiner will not be retrievable.

Tyrolean Traverses

Tyrolean traverses have been made to less accessible pinnacles by lassoing them, anchoring the near end of the rope securely, and prusiking or sliding on carabiners across the intervening space. With the advent of modern techniques and climbing philosophy, Tyrolean traverses have sunk to an insignificant role in the climber's repertoire, though they continue to be of importance to rescuers, expedition climbers, and others needing to move people and equipment efficiently across rivers, gorges, crevasses, and similar obstacles (Fig. 12-28).

TO CONCLUDE

To the beginner on his first aid pitch, direct aid climbing may seem the perfect illustration of the saying "anything which can possibly go wrong will." Climbers soon learn to organize equipment carefully and to follow the same sequence of movements every time. They cultivate the ability to select the correct size piton or chock with a minimum of trial and error. With practice they learn to place hardware securely enough to be safe without mashing it in so hard that time is wasted removing it, learn to place anchors as far apart as practical without wasting time and effort stretching for "that extra inch." Especially while learning, each movement should be thought out and performed carefully and deliberately. Experience develops the necessary efficiency of movement which enables the proficient aid climber to move steadily, smoothly, and confidently.

PART FOUR   *

Snow and Ice Climbing

Plate 17. Southeast arete of Piz Bernina, Italian/Swiss Alps. (John Cleare)

13 *

BASIC SNOW TRAVEL

THE VERY THOUGHT of snow makes many mountaineers rejoice at the contemplation of marvelous vistas and easy travel; others cringe at the thought of barren, cold, wet terrain. While the latter group may sometimes be more nearly accurate, mountain travelers who restrict their excursions to snow-free landscapes miss easy travel along veritable snow-paved highways through some of the most magnificent scenes the mountains have to offer.

In many ways hiking and climbing on snow is more complex and more variable than on rock or bare trail because the medium itself is so variable. Not only are the outward form and texture important, as with rock, but so also are the aging and packing through which the snow has gone, the firmness of the crust, and the solidity of the underlying snow. Unless the temperature is too high, the delicate crystals of new snow fall as classic powder snow, often greater than 90 per cent air. After such snow reaches a certain minimum depth, travel over or through it without special equipment is virtually impossible, or at best good only for building character, and the mountain traveler typically resorts to skiis or snowshoes. Consolidation of the newly fallen snow takes place rather rapidly, however. Coarser, more rounded crystals form on the surface, becoming the well-known corn snow of spring. Skiis or snowshoes may be quite necessary on this type of surface, too, but more often than not travel without special equipment will be possible. By summer, consolidation is nearly complete, although the surface may vary from rock hardness to deep slush within any one day (see Chapter 22, The Cycle of Snow, for more detail).

This chapter and those which follow do not discuss specialized forms of snow travel by skiis or snowshoes. For more information consult the specialized texts listed in Appendix 3, Supplementary Reading.

THE ICE AXE

The ice axe is one of the most important pieces of mountaineering equipment a climber owns. Without it, safe alpine travel is restricted to snow-free trails and easy scrambles. But once proficient in its use the climber can venture onto virtually all forms of snow and ice, enjoying a greater variety of mountain landscapes during more seasons of the year.

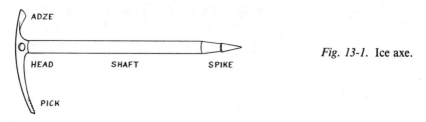

Fig. 13-1. Ice axe.

Uses of the Axe

The modern ice axe, while an inherently simple tool, has a variety of uses. Not only does the axe assist in travel over snow, glaciers, and pure ice but it has a myriad of other uses described in Chapter 6, Wilderness Travel. Despite all these added advantages, the primary use of the axe is in snow and ice travel, to provide the necessary balance and/or anchoring support to prevent a fall, and to stop a fall should one occur. These two vitally important yet somewhat distinct functions are discussed in more detail in Chapter 14, Snow Climbing.

Parts of the Axe: Form and Function

Head: Pick and Adze

Ice axe heads are usually constructed of steel, and sometimes of aluminum. Aluminum-headed axes are lighter and are adequate for basic snow travel, but tend not to retain their edges on hard snow or ice. Steel-headed axes, while heavier, are markedly stronger and are the only kind suitable for more advanced snow and ice climbing.

While straight picks were once commonplace, mountaineering research has led to the widespread adoption of curved or drooped picks. This design provides better hooking action in snow or ice, thus causing the axe to dig in faster during self-arrest. A moderate hooking angle of 65–70 degrees (Fig. 13-2) is appropriate for general mountaineering uses. If technical ice climbing is anticipated a hooking angle of 55–60 degrees is better as it coincides with the arc followed by the axe head when it is

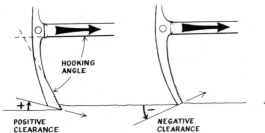

Fig. 13-2. Ice axe clearance.

planted during a steep wall ice climb. The climber must be aware that the modern ice axe with a drooped pick may dig in so quickly in the snow during self-arrest that it may be wrested from the climber's grip.

For an ice axe to be effective in anchoring and self-arrest on hard snow the pick must be able to bite its way into the surface. Picks with negative or neutral clearance (Fig. 13-2) tend to skate or drag on hard icy surfaces and do not penetrate reliably into these surfaces during self-arrest. Axes having picks with positive clearance tend to pull into the surface when pressure is applied, and thus are the preferred design.

Teeth on the axe pick are valuable, although older axes without teeth may still be in use. Deep teeth provide additional gripping power for hard snow and ice anchoring. Axes with teeth extending 1 or more inches shaftward from the tip of the pick are quite acceptable, but some extend all the way to the shaft for additional anchoring support on technical ice climbs. Axes without teeth may be modified manually to add them, provided the width of the pick is great enough so that strength is not appreciably reduced. Modification should be done with a file, not a grinding wheel, so as not to change the temper of the metal and reduce its strength.

The adze of the axe is used primarily for stepchopping on hard snow or ice. Another important but passive function of the adze is to serve as a platform for the palm of the hand when the axe is held in the self-belay grasp during snow climbing. Adzes may be flat or curved, straight-edged or scalloped, straight-out or drooped. Experience has shown that a flat, straight-edged, non-drooped adze with sharp corners is functionally most effective.

Shaft

Until about 1970 nearly all ice axe shafts were made of wood. Dense, straight-grained hickory was considered to be best because it combined high strength with light weight. Ash was common during the 1960s but as its use increased so did reports of shaft breakage. Today, metal (aluminum and titanium) shafts are most common, although glass or carbon-filament reinforced plastic are available.

The strength of the shaft is most important to boot-axe belays where, in general, the stronger the shaft the more reliable the belay. Natural wood shafts vary widely in strength, but ash is the weakest. Good hickory shafts are surprisingly strong, although variability in natural materials makes it difficult to know exactly which are "good" shafts. While wood shafts do dampen vibrations and offer a warmer grip, metal is the surest way to guarantee a high-strength axe shaft.

Spike

The spike, one of the key elements in the balance and self-belay functions of the axe, must be kept sharp. While the axe does have demonstrated value for balance on rocky trails or talus slopes, be wary of dulling the spike, reducing its effectiveness in snow, glacier and ice climbing. The spike on axes with metal shafts is generally crimped, riveted, or epoxied to the shaft. The preferred spike design is flat in the same plane as the pick of the axe.

Ice Axe Length

The length of the ice axe shaft has been subject to the interpretation of every age, from the 1½-meter (5-foot) alpenstocks of the alpine pioneers to the 65- to 75-cm length in current use. Axes of 40 cm (16 inches) are now available for technical ice climbing.

Depending on its use the optimal length of the axe may be determined more by the angle of the slope being climbed than by the height of the climber. An axe ideal as a cane on a flat trail may be too long to be easily plunged into a moderately steep snow slope when performing a self-belay or setting an anchor. Long axes (above 80 cm) were more common during the past two decades and do have value for crevasse probing and anchoring in deep loose snow. Short axes (60 cm or less) are specialists' ice climbing tools (Chapter 15, Ice Climbing), excellent for swinging axe placements on steep slopes but difficult for self-arrest. Research and experience have shown that moderate length ice axes (65 to 75 cm) are best for the range of alpine situations the average mountaineer encounters.

Wrist Loop

The wrist loop is the variable length piece of perlon or webbing which can be used to attach the ice axe to the climber when necessary. Debate continues in mountaineering circles on the length and uses of the wrist loop. Some mountaineers point to the very real value of the loop on crevassed glaciers or long steep slopes where losing an ice axe could be dangerous, to both the loser and companions below. In addition, the loop is useful in mixed climbing (where any combination of snow, ice and rock are encountered) to allow the ice axe to hang freely during a climbing move or two on the rock. Alternatively, some mountaineers point to the danger of a flailing axe, still attached, causing more injury to the climber during a fall than the fall itself. The awkwardness and potential danger of switching the loop at every corner during the switchback phase of a snow climb is also a drawback to use of the loop.

A similar debate has raged regarding the length of the loop: some mountaineers claim that the traditional short wrist loop attached to the axe with a glide ring (Fig. 13-3) is adequate for basic snow and glacier travel. It is easy to use and is often readily available pre-attached to the ice axe when purchased. Some climbers feel that during a fall an ice axe attached to the wrist by a short loop may be more readily controlled. Others argue conversely that the proximity of the flailing axe may create more danger than one attached to an extended loop or wrist leash. The short loop cannot be used to reduce arm fatigue during stepchopping or ice climbing so readily as the longer loop. In addition, the glide ring stop on the axe shaft lessens the strength of the shaft and may interfere with driving it in during self-belay and crevasse probing.

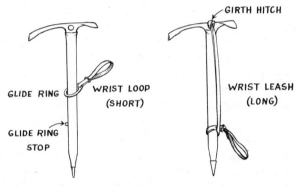

Fig. 13-3. Ice axe loops. *Left,* short loop with glide ring; *right,* wrist leash attached through carabiner hole.

Climbers who cite such disadvantages of short wrist loops prefer one about as long as the axe itself, attached to it through the carabiner hole (Fig. 13-3). It should be long enough so that the axe shaft can be grasped near the spike through the loop when the loop is held taut from the head of the axe. This length allows for the optimal transfer of force to the wrist area, reducing arm fatigue during stepchopping and ice climbing. In addition, the wrist leash allows the axe to be used by the climber as a separate anchoring point, with the loop providing the line of attachment to the climber's harness. For convenience while traveling over non-technical terrain, the wrist leash may be shortened by wrapping it around the axe shaft to minimize dangling. Some ice axes are now sold without a loop of any kind, but a wrist leash may be easily constructed of 5- or

6-mm perlon, or ½-inch flat webbing. Shorter length loops are adequate for basic snow and glacier travel, but the wrist leash is preferred if any but the most basic of snow travel is anticipated.

Fig. 13-4. Carrying the ice axe.

Carrying an Ice Axe

On approach trails, in scrambling, rock climbing, or other situations where the axe is not needed, it is best affixed to the pack by an ice axe loop. It is wise to cover at least the pick with a rubber or leather guard, since packs have a tendency to bump into people while on a trail, at a rest stop, or even while driving to the trailhead. If the axe is in proper condition, i.e. *sharp*, it is even more important to use safety guards.

On non-technical terrain the preferred way to carry an axe is with the shaft parallel to the ground, the spike forward and the pick down (Fig. 13-4) to minimize damage to a companion who inadvertently bumps or falls against it from the rear. When travel alternates between snow and steep brushy or rocky terrain, requiring periodic use of both hands, the axe may be carried by simply sliding it diagonally between the straps of the pack and the back, spike down and pick out, well seated and clear of the neck (Fig. 13-5). This works well for short stretches as the axe can be placed and retrieved quickly, but remember to remove it from this position before removing the pack; a loose ice axe is often a lost ice axe.

While the ice axe carry described above is generally preferred for temporary storage, two other options are available to the climber wearing a seat harness. First, a carabiner may be used to clip the axe, through the carabiner hole, directly to the harness or hardware rack. While an axe so attached is quite secure, removing it is usually a two-handed operation, and two free hands may be a rare luxury on mixed climbs. An alternative

Fig. 13-5. Temporary storage of ice axe.

is a standard holster affixed to the harness for quick storage and recovery of the axe as needed. When making a climbing move be careful not to force the axe back through the holster — and bounding off down the slope.

Care of the Axe

Metal-shafted axes require almost no special care or treatment; wooden shafts need protection. Boiled linseed oil or a 50/50 mixture of linseed oil and turpentine should be rubbed into the wood and allowed to soak into the end grain around the spike. To protect the interface between the metal spike and the lower portion of the wooden shaft from rock, ice, and crampon damage, wrap the junction with adhesive tape.

Inspect the shaft of the axe, especially if wooden, regularly before each use. A deep dent or gouge in a wood shaft may weaken it to the point of failure under load, but do not confuse major gouges with the minor nicks and scratches which accumulate over time. Any hole in the axe shaft is a point of potential failure.

Clean any mud or dirt off the axe after each use and remove any rust which may accumulate on steel portions. Wooden-shafted axes should either be hung by the heads or laid flat to prevent bowing of the shaft. Check the pick, adze and spike regularly. When sharpening is needed, use a small hand file, since heat from a grinding wheel may change the temper and strength of the metal.

CRAMPONS

Although today's lug-soled boots are very satisfactory for trail walking, rock and general snow climbing, without alteration they are less useful on frozen snow and steeper slopes. Early climbers wore nailed boots which took slippery snow and ice in stride, but still often relied on wearisome stepcutting to progress upslope. In 1908, however, a radical development occurred: creation of the first 10-point crampon. While many alpinists of the day thought these crampons took "unsporting advantage" of the peaks, they proved to be the one climbing aid which could relieve the tremendous stepcutting burden on many climbs and open up a vast array of new snow and ice faces to climbing.

Crampon Design

A few basic crampon design characteristics have resulted from the experience and research of the past several decades. Most crampons are fashioned from chrome-molybdenum steel, an extremely strong alloy, which requires less metal, resulting in a lighter crampon. The early standard 10-point crampon has been eclipsed in form by the addition of two forward-slanting points to create the 12-point crampon. First produced in the 1930s, these 12-point models eliminate such stepchopping and allow "front-pointing" up steep snow and ice slopes (Chapter 15, Ice Climbing). Ten-point crampons are still in use, but the 12-point models have been enthusiastically adopted by virtually all climbers.

One may also encounter special purpose four-point instep crampons designed for quick attachment to and removal from the boot; light in weight, these may prove useful for short sections of ice encountered unexpectedly on a trail, but they are totally inadequate for general-purpose mountaineering.

Another major design choice is between rigid and hinged crampons. Rigid crampons are specialized tools for technical ice climbing. In most climbing situations, hinged crampons have proven to be perfectly adequate and reliable, especially if only a modest amount of front-pointing is anticipated.

Proper crampon fit is essential. When purchasing crampons try them on with the boots on which they will be worn. Attachment prongs at the sides and rear should fit the boot snugly without significant "bending to fit." Adjustable crampons allow for variability in instep and heel width, and a wide range of lengths. When the boot is lifted from the floor the prongs should hold the crampon to the boot without being strapped on (Fig. 13-6). When fitted properly, about two-thirds of the length of the front points of 12-point crampons should protrude beyond the toe of the boot. If planning to use them on more than one pair of boots, check for fit on both pairs.

Attaching Crampons

Special care must be taken to ensure that crampons, once strapped to the boots, remain there until the climber is ready to take them off. The security of the crampon attachment relates both to the way in which it is strapped to the boot and to the nature of the strapping material. A buckle harness of neoprene-coated nylon is best since it is strong, does not absorb water, or stretch, and can be easily transferred from one pair of

Fig. 13-6. Crampon properly fitted, and typical adjustable crampon.

crampons to another. Leather straps are less expensive but stretch when wet and will eventually rot or break. Cotton webbing is least desirable, since it readily accumulates snow and may sometimes freeze directly to the buckle. In emergency situations, nylon cord will work.

When strapping on crampons the buckles should be positioned on the outward side of the boots to minimize the chance of "catching a buckle" while walking. The most common strapping system involves two independent straps, one connecting the front four attachment rings over the instep of the boot, and the other wrapping around the ankle from the two rear attachment rings (see Fig. 13-7). To minimize the possibility of the front straps loosening, thread the strap *from the outside in* through each attachment hole, and then give the strap an extra twist.

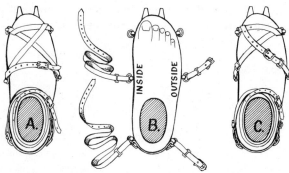

Fig. 13-7. Crampon attachment. *Left,* two-strap, attached; *middle,* four-strap; *right,* four-strap, attached.

A second popular strapping system involves four independent straps per crampon: two small short straps with buckles on one side, and two longer straps to wrap around the boot (see Fig. 13-7). This system is usually faster to use.

All beginning mountaineers are well advised to become thoroughly familiar with their crampons and straps before going on their first climb. Verify the fit, including the position of the front points (about two-thirds of the length protruding) at home. Practice the strapping system in the comfort of a living room as crampons are often put on in the dark by feel, sometimes by flashlight, and very often with cold, numbed fingers. The best method is simply to lay each crampon down with all rings and straps outward, place the boot on the crampon, and tighten the straps.

Crampon Maintenance

Crampon maintenance demands close attention. As with ice axes, keep crampon points sharp, best done with a hand file since a grinding wheel may overheat the metal and destroy the temper necessary for strength.

Many snow and ice routes involve short, unavoidable sections of rock. While crampons should take such punishment without disintegrating, extended use of this nature will dull and splay the points. All mountaineers should check the sharpness of their crampons before each climb. Check also for parallel alignment of the points, since splayed points easily lead to slashed legs. Seriously misaligned points should not be hammered but rather should be straightened by an experienced metal worker to retain the strength of the crampon. Crampon straps should also be checked before each use for abrasion and rotting and, on adjustable crampons, all nuts and bolts should be checked for tightness.

Wrapping the bottom of the crampon with plastic tape or a layer of coat nylon cloth minimizes problems of snow "balling up" when traveling through soft, sticky snow. Particularly where slushy snow overlays a hard ice base, this balling of snow can be quite dangerous; wrapped crampons are safer.

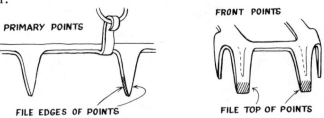

Fig. 13-8. Sharpening crampons.

Crampons can be *dangerous*. When they are worn, every step must be taken with care to avoid snagging trousers, gashing legs, and stepping on ropes. The annals of mountaineering are filled with tales of injuries resulting from improper crampon usage. When carrying crampons on or in a pack, cover the points to prevent injury during a fall or to another party member who may bump into the pack. Spider-like rubber crampon-point protecters are the most common solution, although surgical tubing may be cut into short sections to accomplish the same end.

WANDS

Wands used for marking routes on snow and glaciers are usually made at home of 3- to 4-foot long green-stained bamboo sticks from a garden supply store, where they are sold as plant supports. To convert them to wands simply add some sort of "flag" to one end of each stick. Plastic route-marking tape or coated nylon, being durable and water repellent, are the most satisfactory flag materials. A secure and permanent attachment of the flag to the wand (Fig. 13-9) is important since open snow slopes and glaciers can be remarkably windy.

Wand length is a matter of choice. However, wands shorter than 30 inches provide very little usable height for good visibility in most snow conditions, and those longer than 4 feet are a problem to carry. The longer wands are advisable for winter use when the snow is usually softer and the wands must be pushed in farther for stability and where fresh snowfall may bury them even deeper.

The use of wands in marking routes is described in Chapter 16, Glacier Travel.

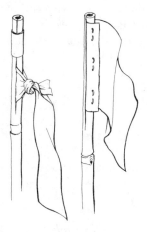

Fig. 13-9. Wand construction.

TRAVELING ON SNOW

While certain aspects of snow conditions, equipment and technique may be learned from mountaineering texts, there is no substitute for direct immersion in the subject. The mountaineer soon learns that, with good conditions, travel on snow is often far easier and more relaxing than on a standard mountain trail—no hopping over boulders, watching out for sticks and logs on the trail, or constant adjusting to minor changes in the ground gradient.

Pacing on Snow: The Rest Step

On long snow slopes a frustrating sensation that no progress at all is being made erodes the sense of adventure. Looking ahead at miles of distance or thousands of feet of elevation to cover often tempts beginners to adopt a "dash and gasp" pace of snow travel, trying to rush the objective. Halts for recuperation become more frequent as time marches on and they begin to wonder how and why they ever became involved in such insanity. The only sure way to get to the top is to find a suitable pace that can be maintained, and maintain it. The solution is the "rest step," undoubtedly one of the most important techniques of a snow climber. It is used whenever energy expenditure is so great that either legs or lungs need an interval of recuperation between steps. The rest takes place after one foot is swung forward for the next step. Body weight is supported on the rear leg while the unweighted forward leg muscles are relaxed. The leg supporting the weight should be straight and locked at the knee so that bone, not muscle, can do the work. The pace is slow, since for every step there is a pause. Breathing must be synchronized with the sequence. For example: inhale as rear foot advances to a new position; exhale as the unweighted advanced leg rests, the body supported on the rear leg; repeat. When the air is thin it is the lungs that need a pause. At high elevations climbers must make a conscious effort to breathe deeply and frequently. At lower altitude it is leg muscles that need extra time to accumulate energy.

An important element of the rest step is mental composure. When the summit seems to remain constantly distant for hours on end, the mountaineer must trust the rest step to slowly but steadily chew up the miles. Snow is a perfect medium for this process since for long stretches conditions may not change, but nonetheless one must be alert to potential hazards as they occur.

Stepkicking

Depending on the steepness and hardness of the surface, the mountaineer needs a variety of techniques to travel over snow. Basic to any snow travel is the concept of stepkicking — creating a path of steps in the snow to provide the best possible footing for the party with the least expenditure of energy (more advanced snow climbing techniques will be covered in Chapters 14 and 15). Steps are made by swinging the leg into the snow surface, with the weight of the leg and its momentum providing most of the force with a minimum of muscular effort. In soft and moderately soft snow swinging kicks will be enough to make adequate steps. The harder the snow, the more muscular effort will be required. In general, it is easiest for the rest of the party to follow in good balance if steps are spaced evenly and rather close together. The spacing may also have to be closer together than the stepkicker needs, since those following may have shorter legs. The rest of the party members use the same leg-swing as the first climber, improving the steps as they climb. The foot must be kicked into the step; simply walking on the existing platform does not set the boot securely in position. In compact snow the kick should be somewhat low, the toe driving in and deepening the step. In very soft snow it is usually easier to bring the boot down from above, shearing off a layer of snow which strengthens the step. A basic principle of all snow travel is that parties travel single file when ascending, letting one climber at a time do the hardest work. The physical exertion of the lead climber on snow is greater than that of any other member of the party. In addition, he must be mentally alert to safeguard those behind and to choose the best route. The lead should therefore be changed regularly so that no one climber remains in front until exhausted.

ROUTEFINDING ON SNOW

It has long been known that snow and ice-covered landscapes provide easy avenues. On the Alaska tundra, for instance, very little travel can take place except during winter, for at other times the landscape is a hopeless mire of brush and mush. In the mountainous areas of the Pacific Northwest many routes involving heavy brush, logging debris, or long talus slopes are only practicable when covered with several feet of snow. Such otherwise interminable slopes are transformed into veritable highways when covered by consolidated snow, and for this reason many a peak is best bagged in the spring. During the same season snow bridges often provide quick passage over rushing streams, although the climber must beware of those undermined by moving water or melted to the point of collapse. As spring merges into summer and obstacles emerge, the route along a valley floor or up a slope may be quite erratic, taking advantage of every remaining snow patch for the few yards or steps of easy traveling it provides.

In general, the wise mountaineer planning a route involving any snow travel begins with observations of snow and weather conditions of the previous several months. A prolonged thaw in late winter, for instance, followed by a cold snowy spring may indicate a need for caution; weeks or months later the thaw's thick crust may hold a heavy load of spring snow ready to avalanche. Alternatively, a winter with little snow and a sunny but cold spring may transform a gully which as a rule has good stepkicking snow in May into one with rock-hard consolidated snow. Nevertheless, since much of the change in the snow surface takes place rather quickly, the weather and temperature immediately preceding and during the ascent are of greatest importance.

Snow is considered excellent if the climber can stand on or near the surface, only fair if he sinks to his calves; when immersion is knee-deep or greater it is good only for building character. Crusts on the snow have a major influence on route selection in winter and spring. Differential consolidation is equally important: south and west slopes, bearing the full heat of afternoon sun, consolidate earlier in the season and quicker after storms, offering hard surfaces when east and north slopes are still soft and unstable. Similarly, dirty snow absorbs more heat than clean; slopes darkened by rocks, dust, or uprooted vegetation usually provide relatively solid footing.

The principles that apply in large apply also to smaller features. The walking on one side of a ridge or gully, or even on one side of a clump of trees or a large boulder, is often more solid than the other. When the going is very bad it is well to detour toward any surface with a different appearance and possibly better support. Sometimes unstable and stable crust may be only a foot or so apart, and deep slush only a step from hard ice.

Location of the best and easiest route varies from day to day and hour to hour. In cloudy weather snow conditions are unlikely to change significantly around the clock, but a clear cold night after a hot day suggests an early start to take full advantage of the strong crusts on open slopes. As the sun rises higher, the search shifts for shadows where remnants of crust linger. Late on a hot afternoon all crusts deteriorate and the deep shade of trees and steep cliffs offer the best slopes of a bad lot.

Early season snowcover is scattered with pitfalls. As soon as snow falls on a hillside it begins a slow protracted settling called "creep," moving away from logs, trees and rocks, forming a fissure below or next to each. Since new snow usually camouflages these holes, or "moats," wise mountaineers probe or avoid likely spots and step wide off logs or rocks.

Later in the season the moat below a large rock or cliff may no longer be camouflaged, but may be as wide, as deep, and as difficult to cross as a glacial crevasse. Differential melting both initiates and emphasizes fissures; snow adjacent to objects such as logs, brush, or rocks is likely to be hollow or undercut. When the temperature of the ground is at or above freezing, extensive melting occurs at the ground/snow interface. The route should follow either solid snow or solid ground, avoiding margins; when they must be crossed, cat-like steps avert wrenched ankles and broken legs.

As the months progress into summer, walking conditions become so nearly uniform that the major difference is between the hard surfaces of early morning and the morasses of hot afternoons. The Cascades of Washington State, by July in an average year, present summer snow conditions. By August—again on the average—consolidation is so complete that snow conditions do not change significantly with time of day. However, new vexations develop: suncups may grow into *nieve penitentes* (described in Chapter 22, The Cycle of Snow) through which travel is a relentless, exhausting grind. Moreover, consolidation is not an unmixed blessing, for on the hard slopes of autumn every foot of the route may require crampons or stepchopping, and the climber remembers fondly the yielding surfaces of spring in which mere swings of the boot made such superb steps.

Snow Couloirs

Whether on a glacier or snaking upward toward a rock precipice, snow and ice gullies are often the key to passage, having a lesser overall angle from bottom to top than the cliffs they breach. Deeply shaded gullies are more often lined with ice than snow, especially late in the season. Even in spring, however, when all open slopes hold deep slush the couloirs are likely to be hard snow or ice from freezing or avalanche-scouring.

Safe passage through a mountain couloir is usually dependent upon the time of day. The inviting aspect of a couloir in morning, contrasted with the forbidding menace of its enclosing cliffs, frequently proves in afternoon to have been a crocodile smile. Gullies are the garbage chutes of mountains and, however quiet they may be during night, with the sun they begin to transport toward sea level such rubbish as avalanching snow, rocks loosened by frost-wedging, and ice blocks weakened by melting. The climber strives to be out of the couloir before the sun arrives, which means an early start to accomplish a round trip, an alternative route for the descent, or a bivouac. Most, but not all, of the debris comes down the center; but even when keeping to the sides it is well to cock a sharp ear for suspicious sounds coming from above and to have one member of the team watching for quiet slides and silent missiles.

In steep couloirs avalanches often erode a system of deeply incised ruts that usually are either avoided or crossed with all possible haste. However, early in the year rut floors offer the soundest snow available and in cold weather may be quite safe—particularly for a fast descent.

Couloirs can become increasingly nasty the higher they are ascended, presenting such nuisances as extreme steepness, verglas, moats, rubble strewn loosely over smooth rock slabs, and cornices. Many lead into traps or cul-de-sacs, the gentle angle at the bottom compensated for by culmination in a frosty chimney. This rule is by no means invariable though — when the couloir heads at a col it can well afford to offer a lower average angle than the face.

Despite negative aspects, many snow and ice routes follow gullies. Generally the techniques are simple cramponing and stepkicking but crevasses, moats, and suncups, or blocks of fallen rock and ice, make rockclimbing techniques useful. Some of these irregularities are welcome for the sake of their belay potential.

When the bed of the gully is uncompromisingly steep, moat-crawling along the side of the gully is often more secure. Moats can sometimes be rather deep, requiring bridging between the snow and the rock wall; they also tend to be of irregular width, occasionally presenting alternately a tight squeeze and a gap too wide to bridge. During the morning ascent cramponing or stepcutting may be faster; in afternoon a nervewracking descent on steep ice is hardly tempting compared to descending a moat with its lessened exposure and increased protection from rockfall.

Ridges

Routes along or near the crests of ridges have the advantage of freedom from rockfall and avalanche hazards, but the disadvantage of exposure to the full brunt of wind and weather.

In regions of moderate to heavy snowfall, ridges often prove to be the only wise choice when an ascent is at all lengthy. Routefinding is generally less critical than on other portions of a mountain and safe retreat is usually open. Ridge routes are less sensitive than others to the time-of-day factor; they are ordinarily not threatened by avalanches and falling debris resulting from afternoon sunlight and warming. The most significant hazard facing a snow traveler choosing a ridge route, however, is the cornice.

Cornices

The shape of the ridge crest determines the extent of cornice-building. Often a ridge that slopes on one side and breaks into an abrupt cliff on the other develops gigantic cornices, whereas a knife-edge ridge or one gentle on both sides has only a tiny cornice, if any at all. When the physical features are right for cornice-building, wind direction decides their exact location (Fig. 13-10), and since storm winds have definite patterns in any given mountain range, most cornices in the same area face in the same direction. In the mountains of Washington State, for example, most

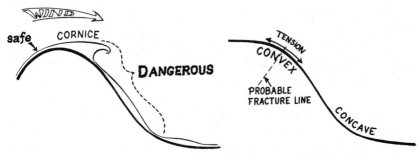

Fig. 13-10. Cornice.

storms blow from the southwest and the majority of cornices therefore overhang on the north and east. Since these same exposures were steepened by past glaciation the ridges are ideally shaped for the purpose. It must be remembered that temporary or local wind deflection can contradict the general pattern. In rare instances cornices are even built one atop the other, facing in opposite directions, the lower one partially destroyed and hidden by later formations.

Approaching from Windward

From windward a cornice gives little indication of its presence, appearing as a smooth slope that runs out to meet the sky. Observation of surrounding ridges tells a great deal about the probable frequency, location, and size of cornices in the immediate area, not only on the high divides but on subsidiary ridges, knolls, and boulders. Fracture lines from partial collapse are sometimes visible, either as deep cracks or as slight indentations.

Not every snowy ridge conceals a cornice, but great care must be exercised in finding out whether any particular one does or not. If at all possible a safe vantage point should be found — a rock promontory or tree jutting through the crest — from which the lee side of the ridge is clearly visible. Otherwise the belayed leader approches the ridge at right angles, probing with his axe and testing with his weight. Only when the extent of the overhang has been clearly established should other members of the party join him.

To ensure a sufficient margin of safety the party must follow a course along a corniced crest well behind the probable fracture line, which is sometimes difficult to determine, since the line of fracture may extend 30 feet or more back from the lip of the cornice. Moreover, though rocks or trees projecting from the snow suggest safety, if they are the tops of buttresses, the ridge joining them may curve far back into bays supporting wide cornices. Many a party has looked back along a ridge and shuddered at the sight of its tracks poised over a chasm.

Approaching from Leeward

From leeward a cornice is readily apparent, resembling a wave frozen in the act of breaking. At close range the overhang is an awesome spectacle, but if the weather is cold enough the climber may forge ahead without fear, trusting the cornice to be a strongly engineered structure. It is even possible, and often necessary, to force a direct passage while crossing a pass or seeking a summit route on the far side of the ridge. A late-season cornice that is almost completely broken down need cause little concern, but earlier in the year the route of approach should be chosen with care, keeping as much as possible among trees or along crests of spurs, away from the line of fall. It is easiest to penetrate an overhang where a rock spur leads toward the summit or where a partial collapse has occurred.

Cutting through a healthy cornice is a task only to be undertaken if the structure is judged strong and solid. First the leader must bring up his second so that he will be belayed close to the problem at hand. The point of least overhang is attacked, with the belayer positioned beyond danger. The leader cuts straight uphill, undermining as little of the mass as possible, preferably standing to one side of the path he is cutting. Once he has surmounted the crest his immediate task is to install a sound belay behind the fracture zone before attempting to bring up his companions.

Descending on Snow

The route down is sometimes quite different from the route up. By afternoon the upward path may be so subject to avalanching that a steep or circuitous way down on rock is best. Snow terrain suitable for uphill climbing is often poor for descending, such as icy surfaces that make for good cramponing but poor glissading. Route variations may range from going down a different side of the mountain, which may be hazardous if the terrain is unfamiliar, to moving a few feet from icy shadow onto sun-softened slopes. Snow in good condition is almost the ideal medium for losing altitude rapidly, yielding comfortably under the foot without the jolting shocks that the body must absorb on rock. Far from increasing the risk, within reasonable limits speed and elan make the footing more secure. While the actual techniques of downclimbing snow are discussed in Chapter 14, suffice to say here that snow descents are highly favored.

Avalanches

Snow avalanches occur by the thousands every winter and spring in mountainous country and are a major concern when routefinding on snow. Although these avalanches generate tremendous forces and are a serious threat to a mountaineer, knowledge of their characteristics can help one avoid being caught and to survive if buried. Experts do not fully understand all the causes of these complex phenomena, nor can avalanche conditions be predicted with certainty. However, the guidelines given here and in Chapter 22, The Cycle of Snow, will aid the alpine traveler in developing judgment about the presence and degree of avalanche danger, and developing safe routefinding habits.

Avalanche Conditions

A high percentage (about 80) of all avalanches occur during and shortly after storms; snow falling at the rate of 1 inch per hour, or more, or snowfall accumulating to a depth of a foot or more, increases avalanche danger rapidly. Storms starting with low temperature and dry snow, followed by rising temperatures, are even more likely to cause avalanches, because the dry snow at the lower level forms a poor bond and

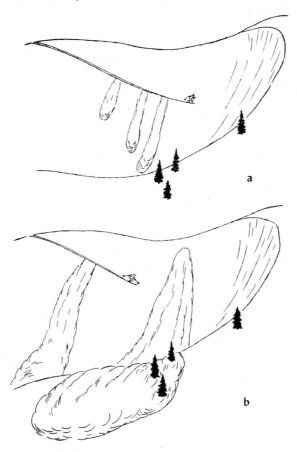

Fig. 13-11. Instability in loose snow. *Top,* minor surface instability. *Bottom,* highly unstable — large quantities of snow involved.

has insufficient strength to support the heavier snow deposited later in the storm. Rainstorms or spring weather with warm winds and cloudy nights can warm the snowcover; the resulting water may percolate and cause wet snow avalanches. Many other factors — temperature, wind, and even the shape of the snow crystals — can also affect or create avalanche conditions. Rapid changes in temperature and wind — particularly if sustained at 15 miles per hour and over — cause adjustments in the snowpack and affect its stability. Small snow crystals — needles and pellets — result in more dangerous conditions than the usual star-shaped forms.

Location can be as important a factor as internal conditions: snow on north-facing slopes is more likely to slide in midwinter, while south-facing slopes are dangerous in spring and on sunny days. Because wind-deposited snows add depth and create hard, hollow-sounding wind slabs,

Fig. 13-12. Instability in slabs. *Top,* minor instability; *bottom,* grave instability.

leeward slopes are more dangerous than windward slopes, which generally have better-compacted snow of lesser depth.

New avalanches in an area indicate dangerous conditions. Little sunballs or cartwheels roll spontaneously down a slope during the warming of loose snow and frequently indicate deep instability. A slope actively sunballing, or streaked with tracks, may be dangerous. Spontaneous surface slides can also occur on fundamentally sound slopes, the degree of danger depending on the depth of snow involved. Surface slides which start from the climbers' tracks cause alarm unnecessarily unless they tend to deepen, involving lower snow layers. If any one of these symptoms of instability are encountered and the route leads onto slopes that have had even greater exposure to the sun or are steeper than those being negotiated, the need for increased caution is apparent.

Testing a slope by throwing rocks onto it is too localized to be of much value, but allows at least some rough conjectures; if a rock can start even a small avalanche, a person can do much better. Indeed, short of mortar bombardment the best test is the climber himself. A well-belayed person can find out a good deal by deliberate attempts to avalanche a suspected slope; the belay must obviously be so placed that it cannot be involved if the attempt is successful. These tests should not be performed if there are parties in the potential avalanche path. It must also be kept in mind that danger can vary within the slope: only a few feet away from a point proven safe, increasing steepness or greater exposure to sun or some unknown local condition may be just enough to trigger a slide.

Recognizing Avalanche Terrain

According to the classic law of avalanches there is least danger on ridges, more on the valley floor, and most on inclined slopes. Even when the entire alpine world is shuddering from the roar of sliding snow the ridges may be safe, though perhaps presenting serrate profiles or cornices that cancel their usefulness. A valley floor is the catchment basin for avalanches. In narrow-floored canyons the danger is obvious, but often equally great on a broad plain surrounded by mountains; there are recorded instances of avalanches sweeping over the flat for more than a mile, and even climbing the opposite side of a valley. Large avalanches are most common on slopes of 30 to 45 degrees but may occur on slopes ranging from 25 to 60 degrees (Fig. 13-13). Above 60 degrees smaller avalanches may sluff frequently during or just afer a storm, but the slope is generally too steep to accumulate large quantities of snow.

Slides rarely start in dense forest or closely spaced rock projections on slopes, but such obstructions are little protection when a large avalanche comes from above, witness borne by the shattered trees in avalanche fans and the wide swaths cut through old timber. Downslanting brush and

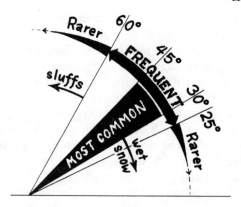

Fig. 13-13. Avalanche probability as a function of slope angle.

small trees tell plainly their slope is so frequently swept that timber has no chance to grow.

Avanlanches usually follow existing channels. Gullies are many times more dangerous than adjacent slopes, their existence proclaiming them as natural chutes. Furthermore, a slide on any one slope within a gully's drainage system can sweep the entire main channel, and by undercutting every tributary on its descent may either pick up bigger loads or leave the tributaries poised and ready to discharge their loads at the slightest disturbance.

The climber should glance upward frequently along the way and avoid routes exposed to cornices, snow perched precariously on rock ledges, or masses of icicles. Their collapse could cause a fall which, even if it did not immediately overwhelm the party, might disturb an otherwise stable slope.

Passage through Danger

Since passage through dangerous terrain is sometimes necessary, there remains to be considered how the hazards can be minimized for a party forced to cross a questionable slope. Although avalanches have been conside.ed thus far as a menace sweeping down on the climber from above, relatively few victims are claimed by such slides. Most avalanches that involve a climber are triggered by the climber himself, posing the twofold problem of attempting not to disturb a slope, and if unsuccessful in this, of minimizing the consequences.

Whenever possible the party should stay above the avalanche danger. If a ridge route is not feasible and sidehills must be crossed, a doubtful traverse is taken high, at the very top of the slope, leaving most of the dangerous snow below the party. It should be remembered that snow is tautly stretched over protuberances and firmly compressed in hollows—

convex slopes are thus more prone to avalanche than concave ones (Fig. 13-14). For instance, the outer lip of a hillside bench may be perfectly sound while the steep slopes below it are weak with tension. Short slopes may be as dangerous as long ones.

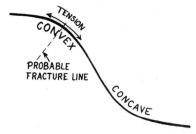

Fig. 13-14. Convex and concave slopes.

When the route lies up a questionable slope, general stepkicking practice is modified from switchbacking, which undercuts snow, to a path straight up the fall line. Only one person moves at a time, the others watching from safe places, ready to call out if a slide starts or to effect a rescue if needed. If the slope is very narrow a firmly anchored belayer can safeguard each climber, the belay rope acting in the same manner as an avalanche cord in the event the climber is caught in a severe avalanche. Although he should make a determined effort to stop the avalanched climber, a belayer should not tie into the rope directly, for once a climber has been engulfed in a wet, heavy avalanche the belayer might as well try to snub an express train, and risks being snatched into the slide too.

Before venturing onto a suspected slope each person should put on warm clothing and mittens. All equipment should be loose and free to be thrown away, not only so it will not drag the victim down, but also because loose articles provide clues to the location of a buried person. The rucksack may be carried in the hands, ready to throw away or to clutch in front of the face to gain breathing space. During winter mountaineering where many of the slopes traveled are of dubious stability each person should trail from his waist about 100 feet of brightly colored avalanche cord, or carry an approved electronic signaling device.

Avalanche beacons are by far the most effective means available for locating a buried avalanche victim quickly, and are highly recommended for skiers and climbers entering remote areas, especially during times of high avalanche danger. Several makes are available, all expensive (but less than the cost of a rope — or a life). The beacon is a small, battery-operated receiver and transmitter. Each member of the party carries one turned on and set to transmit almost inaudible high-frequency beeps. If a party member is buried, all the others switch to receive mode and start searching. The closer they come to the transmitting beacon the louder the signal will become.

The crossing is made gingerly on foot, only one person at a time, with long smooth strides, taking care not to cut a trench across the slope, such as is efficiently done by skiis. Persons following the leader step carefully in the same footprints. The party is silent, the better to hear the start of an avalanche and sound the alarm.

Trying to outrun an avalanche is futile; dash for the side of the slope or at least for a rock or tree to cling to. As a last resort, throw aside all equipment, jam your axe deeply into the underlying snow, and hang on. If carried away, fight to keep on the surface, swimming on your back with head uphill, flailing arms and legs. If buried, inhale deeply before the snow stops to expand your ribs and raise arms and hands over your face to make a breathing space.

Dry, powdery snow poses slight danger of quick suffocation, containing trapped air and being loose enough to allow respiration. In heavy, wet snow suffocation due to chest compression is probable, even if a person's face is above the surface. A cubic foot of wet snow weighs as much as 55 pounds; packed solidly after the slide stops, it holds the climber like a vise, compressing ribs and preventing respiration. Thus the trapped climber must obtain breathing room while in motion. Rescue must come quickly, for wet snow contains little air, and breath will soon glaze and seal the surface around his face. Once the avalanche stops and struggling appears futile, the victim must conserve energy and oxygen by waiting quietly for help, listening for the sound of rescuers, shouting only when there is some chance of being heard.

The techniques of avalanche rescue are covered in Chapter 20. However, a hasty search can be immediately initiated by the rest of the party provided that they carefully observe: first, the point on the slope where the victim was caught; second, the point where he disappeared; and third, where the point of disappearance on the moving surface of the avalanche stops, noting these with respect to fixed objects nearby — trees or rocks.

Avalanches are not to be trifled with. Any safe alternative route, however much longer, more tiring, and difficult, is preferable to one in doubt. When no safe route of ascent can be found the only sensible procedure is to turn back. If, on the return, descent is cut off by imminent avalanching, the party should sit down and wait for late afternoon or evening cold to stabilize the slopes. After shadows cover the snow, time must be allowed for it to freeze and consolidate, since freezing itself sometimes starts a slide. During periods of general danger all travel should be in the morning or evening — or even at night.

Plate 18. Makalu looms over Sherpani Col on Hongu-Barun, Nepal. (John Cleare)

Plate 19. Reaching summit plateau of Mt. McKinley, Mt. Foraker behind.
(Patrick Morrow)

14 *

SNOW CLIMBING

THE CLIMBING CLASSICS of this era are technical rock and ice ascents in which improvements in equipment and technique have expanded concepts of what can be achieved to limits early mountaineers would have considered sheer madness. Snow climbing, in contrast, has changed relatively little since the development of crampons some 70 years ago. But lack of technical change does not alter the fact that snow climbing skills are an essential part of mountaineering competence. As in the past, the security of the snow climber rests primarily on physical strength, a positive mental attitude, and good technique — not on equipment.

As climbing media, snow and ice blend together, and any definitions that distinguish between them must be arbitrary. However, for climbers two critical features distinguish snow from ice. First, many forms of snow allow stepkicking, though often crampons are useful, biting into the firm snow or ice beneath the step; ice, except at very low angles, requires crampons for secure footing. Second, even the hardest snow, though climbed with crampons and ice climbing technique, does not allow protection as reliable as that available to the ice climber (see Chapter 15, Ice Climbing).

CLIMBING TECHNIQUES

Snow climbing skills include a variety of techniques for ascending, traversing, and descending, among which are stepkicking, cramponing, and stepchopping. Assuming the climber has these skills, the primary factors in determining the technique used on a given section of snow will be how hard and/or steep it is.

Ascending

Stepkicking is the basic skill of snow climbing, and is all that is needed when the snow is soft enough for the climber to feel secure in kicked steps without assistance from crampons or chopped steps. The main concern is making adequate steps with the least expenditure of energy. The most efficient kick is a swing of the leg in which its own weight and momentum provide the needed impact, with as little muscular effort as possible. In soft snow these swinging kicks will be sufficient, but the harder the snow, the more muscular effort will be required.

Steps that are kicked level, or tilted slightly into the slope provide more security. The smaller the steps, the more important it is that they slope inward.

On harder snow, stepkicking will result in less secure steps. What constitutes a secure step will vary with the climber's skill, experience, and strength, and with such factors as pack weight, altitude, wind, and fatigue. The average climber will probably need steps deep enough to take the ball of the foot when going straight up and at least half of the boot on a diagonal ascent.

In stepkicking how the feet are placed and the way the ice axe is used are determined by the angle of the slope and the direction of travel. In the following discussion estimates of the slope angle for which a technique is appropriate are necessarily arbitrary. Low to moderately angled slopes (up to 30–35 degrees) are climbed with the axe in the cane position, i.e., held in one hand by the head and used as a point of balance, and steps are

Fig. 14-1. Axe in cane position, steps kicked straight in.

kicked straight in (Fig. 14-1). As the slope steepens the climber can continue to walk normally, kicking steps straight into the slope and taking a line directly up the slope. At steeper angles (over 45 degrees) more security can be obtained by placing the axe in the stake position (Fig. 14-2): the axe shaft is placed above the climber and held at the head with both hands, or with one hand on the head and one on the shaft, and rammed in as far as it will go. This is particularly useful on steeper, soft snow. Holding the axe as shown in Fig. 14-3 and placing it above and at a right angle to the climber is effective on steeper, harder snow covered with a soft layer; the pick reaches the harder base while the shaft gets some purchase in the softer surface snow.

Fig. 14-2. Axe in stake position.

Fig. 14-3. Axe technique for steep, hard snow.

When ascending diagonally on moderate slopes, the climber places the axe above and ahead (Fig. 14-4), kicks his feet in, pointed in the direction of travel, and moves two steps before repositioning the ice axe. The first step places the climber in an out-of-balance position; the second step returns him to the in-balance position. The climber, moving diagonally up a slope is in-balance when his inside foot (foot closest to the slope) is forward and above his outside foot. The climber is in an out-of-balance position after moving the outside foot up and forward of the inside foot. As a rule, the steeper the slope the lower the diagonal line followed.

Fig. 14-4. Ascending diagonally.

Following a diagonal line of ascent may require, at some point, a change in direction, done in the following sequence (Fig. 14-5): first, when standing in the in-balance position, the climber places the axe as close to directly above as the stance allows, then moves his downhill foot into the out-of-balance position, both hands grasping the head of the axe. Then, holding onto the axe with both hands he moves back into a position facing uphill with splayed feet, and finally turns in the new direction of travel into the in-balance position, holding the axe in the uphill hand.

Fig. 14-5. Performing a turn on diagonal ascent.

As using the axe in the cane position becomes awkward on slopes over 40–45 degrees, it can then be used in the cross-body position (Fig. 14-6): the axe is held perpendicular to the slope, one hand on the head, which points in the direction of movement, the other gripping the shaft just above the spike. Most of the weight placed on the axe should bear on the shaft; the hand on the head merely stabilizes the axe. The feet are moved in the same sequence as shown in Fig. 14-4. If the splayed-foot position feels unstable when changing direction at these steeper angles, the steps can be kicked more straight into the slope.

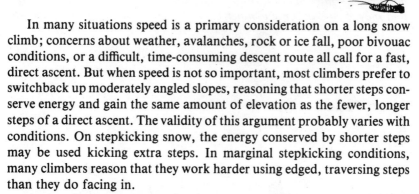

Fig. 14-6. Using the axe in cross-body position.

In many situations speed is a primary consideration on a long snow climb; concerns about weather, avalanches, rock or ice fall, poor bivouac conditions, or a difficult, time-consuming descent route all call for a fast, direct ascent. But when speed is not so important, most climbers prefer to switchback up moderately angled slopes, reasoning that shorter steps conserve energy and gain the same amount of elevation as the fewer, longer steps of a direct ascent. The validity of this argument probably varies with conditions. On stepkicking snow, the energy conserved by shorter steps may be used kicking extra steps. In marginal stepkicking conditions, many climbers reason that they work harder using edged, traversing steps than they do facing in.

As the climber encounters harder snow, marginal steps can be kicked or chopped, then used like face holds on rock. Crampons provide added security under these conditions. Snow so hard that it is not practical or possible to kick adequate steps, i.e., steps in which the climber feels secure, requires crampons and/or stepcutting (see Chapter 15, Ice Climbing).

Traversing

On soft, low to moderately angled snow, traverses are accomplished by sidehill-gouging (see Chapter 6, Wilderness Travel). On harder snow and/or steeper angles this can be exciting; under these conditions most climbers prefer to face into the slope, kicking the toe of the boot into the slope. If possible the route should avoid long, horizontal traverses, which are less efficient than a diagonal line of ascent.

Descending

The ability to descend moderate to steep snow efficiently and confidently is one mark of the skillful snow climber. Many otherwise competent and aggressive climbers blanch at the prospect of going down a steep snow gully. Besides the superb view of the exposure, there is the disadvantage that on the steepest snow the axe must be placed low to move down, leaving the climber without a handhold above as when ascending.

Plunge-Stepping

On descents, just as on ascents, the choice of technique is determined primarily by the snow's hardness and its angle. On soft snow, the climber usually faces downhill and simply walks down. As the snow hardens and the angle steepens, the climber plunge steps, that is, faces outward, steps bravely out from the slope, and lands stiff-legged on his heel (Fig. 14-7). *It is essential to stay erect over the feet and land with the leg vertical; leaning back into the slope results in a glancing blow and less secure steps, and may even dump the climber into an unpremediated sitting glissade.*

Fig. 14-7. Plunge-stepping.

Aggressive strides create the deepest steps, but discretion is needed on very soft snow; it is possible to imbed the lower leg in the snow and then travel past it, fracturing a leg or injuring a knee. When plunge-stepping on lower-angled and softer snow the climber holds the axe in one hand, using the self-arrest grasp described later in this chapter. Holding the axe ahead and to the side of his body to remain erect over his feet, he spreads and moves his arms to maintain balance just as on a footlog. Some climbers hold the axe in both hands in the self-arrest position, but this allows less movement of the arms to maintain balance. At some point, on harder or steeper snow, this style of plunge-stepping will not feel secure and it will be necessary to plant the axe as low as possible in a self-belay (as discussed later in this chapter) and then move the feet (Fig. 14-8). Plunge-stepping can be secure with steps that hold only the heel of the boot, but most climbers do not trust steps more shallow than that.

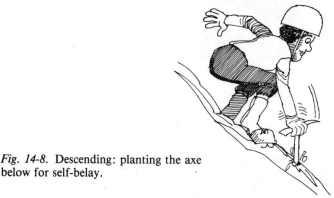

Fig. 14-8. Descending: planting the axe below for self-belay.

On the hardest and steepest snow, or whenever the climber feels insecure walking down or plunge-stepping, it is best to face in and back down, taking the longest possible steps, and holding the axe in the cane, stake, or self-arrest position, as appropriate for the slope's angle and hardness.

Glissading

For those who master it, glissading can be the fastest, easiest, and certainly the most exhilarating way to descend many snow slopes. Here again, the hardness of the snow is the primary determinant of the technique used, with steepness and safety of runout, in the event of a fall, important considerations also.

The sitting glissade (Fig. 14-9) is the easiest to learn and works on soft snow where glissading on the feet is impossible. The climber simply sits in the snow and slides, holding the axe in self-arrest position. Any tendency of the body to pivot head-downwards may be thwarted by running the spike of the axe, rudder-fashion, along the surface of the snow, to one side of the body.

On soft snow, it may be helpful to stretch out the legs, spreading body weight over a greater area, in order to start sliding and to maintain momentum. Lifting the knees and placing the feet flat on the surface of the snow reduces speed. On snow that is crusted or firmly consolidated, pitted with icy ruts or small suncups, or dotted with occasional rocks or

Fig. 14-9. Sitting glissade.

shrubs, stability and control are greater, a better view of the slope obtained, and damage to the anatomy minimized by sitting in the standard sitting glissade position, i.e., fairly erect with boot soles planing along the surface.

In the sitting glissade position, speed is decreased by dragging the spike and applying increasing pressure on it. After momentum has been checked by the spike, the heels are dug in for the final stop — but not while going along at a high speed rate or the result is likely to be a somersault. Emergency stops at high speed are made by self-arrest.

Turns are almost impossible in a sitting glissade: the spike, dragged as a rudder and assisted by body contortions, can effect a change in direction of a few degrees at most. Obstructions in the slope are best avoided with a right-angled pattern of straight-down slides and straight-across traverses rather than trying to steer past them at high speeds.

Skills and conditions permitting, the *standing glissade* is preferred, allowing the climber to see farther ahead than the other glissading positions, and thus giving the best chance of spotting hazards in time to stop or steer around them; it allows the most effective steering, including diagonal lines of descent, and avoids wet and abraded clothing. Its only drawback, and it is a major one, is the difficulty of learning it. Skiers or those with an aptitude for that sport often pick it up with relative ease, but others find it a frustrating skill to master. It also is difficult to get the needed practice unless one is willing to trudge uphill repeatedly to have another try at it. The standing glissade is best done on a firm base with a softer layer on top. At lower angles, and with a safe runout, harder slopes can be maneuvered and very low-angled slopes can be skated, if firm enough. As snow softens, steeper slopes are needed to maintain speed.

Correct standing glissade technique is very similar to downhill skiing. The position is a semi-crouch over the feet with bent knees and outspread arms (Fig. 14-10). The feet can be together or spread, as needed, for

Fig. 14-10. Standing glissade.

stability, with one foot advanced slightly to further improve stability and prevent nosedives. Speed is increased by bringing the feet closer together and leaning farther forward over the feet. Slowing down and stopping are accomplished by standing up and digging in the heels, by turning the feet sideways and edging, by crouching and dragging the axe spike as described below for the crouching glissade, or by performing a turn similar to skiing: rotate the shoulders, upper body, and knees in the direction of the turn and roll the knees and ankles in the same direction to rock the feet onto boot edges. Transition areas, where the snow texture changes, are tricky: if softer, slower snow is encountered, the head will outdistance the feet (advance one foot for stability); if suddenly confronted with harder, faster snow or ice below the surface, the climber who does not lean well forward finds himself suddenly viewing the sky. *On slopes near the margin of his abilities, the climber must keep speed under strict control by regular braking and by traversing.*

The *crouching glissade* is done much like the standing glissade, except the climber holds the axe in the self-arrest grasp, to one side of the body, sits back and drags the spike in the snow (Fig. 14-11). Speeds are slower

Fig. 14-11. Crouching glissade.

than in a standing glissade, a benefit where one's skills or the condition of the slope make lower speeds desirable. With three points of contact, the crouching glissade is more stable and takes less skill than the standing glissade; however, turning is more difficult, as is controlling speed with edging.

As in much of mountaineering, efficiency results from a smooth blend of several techniques. In particular, climbers lacking finesse in the standing glissade often use a combination — breaking into a plunge step to control speed, stepping off in a new direction rather than making a ski-style turn, and skating to maintain momentum as the slope angle lessens.

Glissading can be hazardous and certain precautions must be taken. *Glissade only when there is a safe runout* — a runout is not in itself a sound guarantee if the slope is so long and steep that an out-of-control body could be injured before reaching it. Unless a *view of the entire run* can be obtained beforehand, the first person down must exercise extreme caution and stop frequently to study what lies ahead. The major risk in glissading is a loss of control at such high speed that self-arrest is not possible, particularly likely on the best glissading slopes — firm snow. *The glissader must maintain control of his speed.*

Adjust equipment before beginning the descent, and stow crampons and other hardware within the rucksack. *Never attempt to glissade while wearing crampons*: it is too easy to catch a point in the snow. Put on mittens: snow is so cold and abrasive it can chill and flay the hands until they lose control of the axe.

Sometimes in soft snow, the glissader may initiate movement of a surface mass of snow which continues down the slope taking along the glissader-turned-passenger. These are in reality small avalanches, termed avalanche cushions. The climber's problem is to judge if this cushion will turn into a major avalanche or if it is simply surface snow movement which is safe to ride. If the moving snow layer is more than a few inches deep, attempting to self-arrest is meaningless since the pick of the axe cannot penetrate to the non-moving layer below. Sometimes the ice axe spike can be driven through the moving snow layer and into the non-moving snow to slow the climber but it is unlikely to stop him. Unless very certain that riding the cushion is safe and that speed can be controlled, the climber had best get off, usually accomplished by rolling sideways a few feet out of the path of moving snow and performing self-arrest to stop.

SECURITY ON SNOW

The snow climber's first concern is to prevent a slip from becoming a slide down the slope. The technique for this purpose is termed *self-belay*. Once a real slide on snow occurs, *self-arrest* is the most reliable means of stopping, although the effectiveness of self-arrest varies greatly with snow conditions and the climber's proficiency. Under most conditions of snow and terrain these two techniques permit the climb to progress rapidly and in reasonable safety. Experienced snow climbers know the limitations of both from practice, and during the climb recognize conditions where more security is needed. They may climb roped together, since two or three team members using self-arrest simultaneously will likely be more effective than one alone. Anchored hip belays or boot-axe belays are usually reserved for short sections where the greatest possible security is required.

Self-Belay

The term *self-belay*, as used in this chapter, involves placing the ice axe shaft in the snow prior to a fall to prevent a simple slip or stumble from becoming a slide down the slope. The axe shaft is placed while the feet are secure, and moved only when both feet have advanced and are again in the most secure position possible. Used in this manner, on ascent, descent, or traverse, the ice axe is available as a backup handhold during the time when a fall is most likely to occur, i.e., when the feet are moving. To be a reliable self-belay the shaft must be placed deeply enough and in firm enough snow to hold the full weight of the climber if necessary. The less secure the climber feels, the more important it is to set the axe as a self-belay.

The key to successful self-belay when a fall occurs is to *hang on to the axe at the snow surface*. If the axe shaft is not completely into the snow, hold it at the snow surface with one hand, while keeping the other hand on the head to minimize the risk of levering it out (Fig. 14-12). Like any skill, this takes practice, best done on hard snow slopes with a safe runout.

Fig. 14-12. Stopping a slip with self-belay.

For a self-belay to be of any use, the climber must have confidence that should a fall occur, the axe will hold while he replants his feet in the snow. If the climber is not certain the axe placement will hold body weight, it is time to make a critical decision: back off, rope up and belay, or climb on, recognizing the risks that are being taken.

The handhold on the axe for self-belay differs from that of self-arrest, both shown in Fig. 14-13. The best axe penetration, particularly on hard snow, is obtained by holding the axe by the adze with the pick pointed forward, so that the force of the thrust is distributed over the adze. A secure self-belay can certainly be done with the axe held in the self-arrest grasp, but on hard snow, with the adze pointed forward and hand gripping the pick, considerable force is concentrated on the palm. That, in turn, tends to discourage maximum effort to plant the axe, the key to successful self-belay.

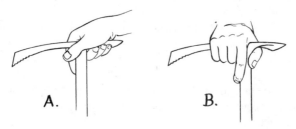

A.   B.

Fig. 14-13. Left, self-belay grasp. *Right,* self-arrest grasp.

Self-Arrest

In self-arrest the climber uses an ice axe to stop his slide down the slope when a self-belay fails, when he falls without the support of a self-belay, or during glacier travel when a rope team member falls into a crevasse. Self-arrest is an unroped climber's only chance to stop his slide, and for that reason, is the single most important snow climbing skill to be learned. A climber's life and the lives of rope team members may well depend on self-arrest skills. Every climber must be proficient and reliable at self-arrest, from all positions, practiced on increasingly steep and hard snow with a safe runout to determine individual limits.

Self-Arrest Position (Fig. 14-14c)

1. One hand on head of axe with thumb under adze and fingers over pick — self-arrest grasp; the other hand on the shaft just above the spike; both hands grip firmly.
2. Pick is pressed into the slope just above the shoulder so that the adze is near the angle formed by neck and shoulder; shaft crosses chest diag-

Fig. 14-14. Self-arrest.

onally, held firmly close to the opposite hip. A short axe is held in the same position, although the spike will not reach the opposite hip.

3. Chest and shoulder pressed strongly on shaft; spine arched slightly away from the snow surface. This arch of the back is critical: it places the bulk of the climber's weight on the axe head and on the toes (or knees), the points which dig into the snow to effect the arrest. This arch is best accomplished by concentrating on pulling up on the end of the shaft, which is more difficult to do with a shorter axe. That pull starts the arch and rolls weight toward the shoulder by the axe head. Note: the arch can be carried to excess by those unwilling to get chest and face down into the snow.

4. Legs stiff and spread apart, toes digging in (*if wearing crampons, keep the toes off the surface until almost stopped*).

5. *Hang onto the axe!*

The firm grip on the head of the axe holds the pick close to the shoulder and neck. The other hand must be near the *end* of the shaft lest the hand act as a pivot around which the spike can swing into the thigh, inflicting a nasty wound.

Particularly in soft snow the stiff, outspread legs with digging toes increase drag and add stability. During arrest on hard snow or ice while wearing crampons, the feet *must* be held up away from the slope until speed is reduced, so that crampon points do not catch and flip the climber backwards. The knees help to stabilize the sliding climber but do not stop him on hard snow or ice, especially if he happens to be wearing slippery wind pants.

Good self-arrest form may be aesthetically satisfying, but, in practice, *instantaneous application may be absolutely critical.* A sloppy but fast arrest may be all that is needed to stop. Excessive concern for good form that results in a slower application may allow the climber to accelerate to a speed that even perfect form will not check. *The emphasis is on driving in the pick as hard and as quickly as possible.*

Fig. 14-15. Wrong way to do self-arrest — do not roll toward spike.

Arrest from Different Positions

The first step in all self-arrests is to grasp the axe in both hands in the self-arrest position. The next is to get the body oriented for a self-arrest, i.e., head uphill, face down. The simplest self-arrest is the one in which the climber has already fallen that way. Falls which leave the climber with head uphill and face up generally are not much more difficult; he need only roll onto his stomach *toward the head of the axe* (Fig. 14-14). If the axe head is on the right shoulder, he rolls to the right; rolling left might jam the spike into the slope before the pick, wrenching the axe from his grasp (Fig. 14-15).

Arrests from head-first falls are more difficult: the problem is getting the feet swung downhill, to bring the climber around with head uphill and ready to go into self-arrest (Fig. 14-16). The climber falling with head downhill and face down reaches downhill and *off to the side on which the axe head lies* and places the axe in position to serve as a pivot point around which the legs swing downhill. Placing the axe off to the side on which the head lies is critical, for this swings most of the axe out of the slide path; to place it on the other side would require bringing the head of the axe across the slide path, with the risk of sliding over it and injuring the chest and face.

Fig. 14-16. Self-arrest from face down, head downhill fall.

When the climber has fallen with head downhill and face up he first places the axe off to *the side on which the head lies* (Fig. 14-17), then twists and rolls toward it. Here too the axe, placed to the side, serves as a pivot point around which the legs are swung downhill.

Two points about the head downhill self-arrests must be stressed. One, it is essential to get upper body weight on the axe head to effect the arrest. This may be particularly difficult to do from the face up position; the climber must remember to twist and roll toward the axe head. Merely planting it to the side may not get sufficient pick penetration. Two, once the axe head is planted the climber should consciously swing his legs around it and pointing downhill.

Arrest Variations

In loose snow of winter and early spring the pick may not reach compact snow and the usual self-arrest may be useless. The falling climber being nearly submerged, the most effective braking instruments are feet, knees, and elbows, all widely spread and deeply pressed into the snow. The greatest drag potential of the axe in this situation lies not in the pick but in the shaft — thrust vertically into the slope or dragged in the self-arrest position. Pivots are usually unnecessary, the fall often being stopped while the climber is still head down. Under any snow conditions, *the speed with which the arrest position* is attained is the key to success. In soft snow the reflexive speed of ramming in pick and toes brings a quick stop. On hard snow a quick stab at the slope with the pick or spike — or even boot heels — may stop a fall before it gets started. On the other hand acceleration is so terrific that the first instant of fall is often the whole story. Once underway on hard snow the climber commonly rockets into the air and crashes back to the unyielding surface with stunning impact, completely losing uphill-downhill orientation.

Arrest on extremely hard snow is very difficult if not impossible, but should always be applied whether or not a belay is also set up. Occasionally in the first instant of fall the pick lodges in a crevice or behind a hump and effects a stop even on a very steep slope. As mentioned before, crampons must be managed with extreme care during self-arrest.

Limits of the Arrest

The arrest stops a fall by friction of axe and body against the snow. When the slope is too steep or slippery — "too fast" — even the most skillful technique may not stop the slide. Moreover, even successful arrests require at least a little time, during which the climber slides some distance. Therefore *the effectiveness of the self-arrest is limited by the climber's speed of reaction and the steepness and length of the slope.* Also, though a climber may be confident that under a particular set of conditions he

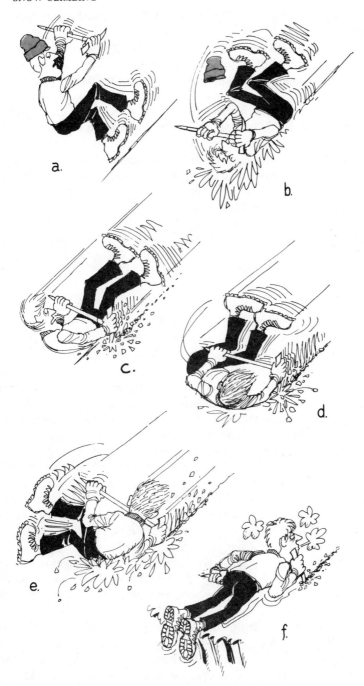

Fig. 14-17. Self-arrest from headfirst fall on back.

can stop within 100 feet, faith in the arrest is misplaced if the slope terminates in a cliff 75 feet below.

Although strength obviously is a factor in self-arrest, learned expertise is more significant than simple muscular strength. Self-arrest is a complex skill that requires practice, particularly arrests from head-downhill falls.

Should a climber find that all initial efforts at self-arrest are unsuccessful, he must *FIGHT IT!* Softer snow or a lower angle farther down the slope may allow self-arrest there. Even if they do not stop the climber, efforts at self-arrest may slow the slide and prevent injuries from rolling, tumbling, and bouncing, and will tend to keep the climber sliding feet first, the preferred position for hitting rocks, trees, and other obstacles. If the sliding climber is roped to one or more partners, decelerating the slide increases the chances that their self-arrests or belays will hold.

Climbers must at all times be aware of their arrest limits. If a slope seems too fast or too short, or if the party is not sure of its collective strength and skill, they continue with anchored belays.

The Uses of Self-Belay and Self-Arrest

Self-belay is a preventative measure, while self-arrest is a recovery measure. If not for the difference in grasp on the ice axe for these two techniques, perhaps no confusion would exist. Some climbers, who learned self-arrest as the primary security technique on snow, fear emphasis on self-belay means diminished emphasis on self-arrest skills, but in fact, the purpose of these two techniques is distinctly different, and both should be learned equally well. Once learned correctly, it is likely that where the axe can be planted securely, self-belay is all that will be needed—preventing the fall. The climber should be alert to changes in snow conditions which even with the axe driven as deep as reasonably possible into the snow make the axe placement insecure in holding a slip. When this occurs, it is perhaps best to change to the self-arrest grasp— ready just in case. Another concern comes to mind, however. If the axe shaft will not hold, will a self-arrest be effective?

To rely exclusively on self-arrest sacrifices the advantages of prevention by self-belay, and leaves the climber sprawled on the snow, vulnerable to a slide in which he may accelerate beyond his or anyone's self-arrest limits.

The climber must learn to quickly change the hand from self-belay grasp to self-arrest grasp. If a self-belay fails, he should first grasp the axe just above the spike, then change the hand to the self-arrest grasp and perform an arrest. This requires practice. Beginners and those lacking the necessary practice or confidence in their ability to perform this extra step in self-arrest are advised to self-belay holding the axe head in the self-arrest grasp.

Roped Climbing Teams

Anyone who climbs snow routes should have a clear concept of the appropriate uses of the rope, particularly when rope teams climb without anchored belays. Roped, unbelayed travel is typical on low- and moderately angled glaciers, where the primary risk is a fall into a crevasse, the theory being that team arrest will provide adequate protection in the event of such a fall. If proper glacier travel precautions (see Chapter 16, Glacier Travel) are adhered to, experience shows traveling roped to be a safe practice, when supplemented by anchored belays—e.g., a boot-axe belay —at points of particular risk.

The security of roped and unbelayed travel becomes more uncertain on steeper glaciers, on steep snow faces and ridges because of the limits of team arrest. On steep and hard snow one member of a rope team may be unable to hold the load of a partner who slides down the slope or plummets into a crevasse. At that point the rope converts an individual fall into a team fall.

Logically, there would appear to be two alternatives open to a group committed to a snow climb steep or hard enough to make team arrest unreliable: to climb unroped, which would be foolhardy on a glacier, and although possibly justifiable on a snow face or ridge, contrary to the conservative approach to climbing advocated in this book and practiced by most climbers. The other option would be to belay the entire climb, which is impractical on any major snow route. Most of these cannot be completed in one day, belaying all the way, and even if the party is willing to bivouac, so slow a pace is likely to leave a party exposed to excessive risk from rock and ice fall, avalanches, storms, and frayed tempers.

In practice, long snow routes are climbed roped and mostly unbelayed, with belays on steeper or harder sections, when climbers are tired or injured, and sometimes, when objective hazards threaten the party. The security of the party, when traveling unbelayed, rests on the skills of each of the individual climbers. *They must not fall.* If they do, they must stop themselves immediately with a self-belay or a self-arrest.

When a falling climber fails to self-belay or self-arrest the other team member(s) must react quickly. If the falling climber is below his rope partner(s) and the partner(s) are warned, they should rely on self-belay. Carrying a few feet of coils in the hand can be a great help here: dropped, they allow the climbers trying to hold the fall an extra moment to get into position by slamming their axes in and bracing themselves, allowing their legs and the dynamic quality of the rope to absorb the force of the fall. If unwarned or if the self-belay fails, they resort to team self-arrest. Note: carrying coils on a glacier is not recommended; extra rope simply increases the distance the victim falls into the crevasse.

Two important rope management techniques may increase the chances of a self-belay or self-arrest working by reducing the load placed on it. One is climbing on a doubled rope. A climbing pair could be 60–75 feet apart, adequate for safe glacier travel yet reducing the sliding distance and load if one partner should fall while above the other. A second technique is to climb in separate parallel tracks, the theory being that a fall by one partner will result in loading the rope to the side of and below his partner while the falling climber pendulums below. Also, the friction of the rope penduluming across the snow may help absorb some of the force of the fall. Although this may be impractical on ascents where kicking two separate sets of steps would be a waste of time and energy, it could be used on ascents of harder snow and should be considered for any descent.

Finally, another way of reducing risks is in the order of roping up. As a rule, the weakest, least skilled and experienced climber should be last on the rope while ascending and the first on the rope while descending. This puts the climber most likely to fall in the position where a fall will be of the least serious kind, i.e., below the other climbers and coming quickly onto a tight rope. However, it also means the weakest, least experienced climber may be the team's last hope if one of the supposedly better climbers falls above and takes a long slide, the worst fall possible.

Snow Belays

Several belay techniques are available to the snow climber. Far and away the most secure is the anchored *sitting hip belay* in which the climber first stamps or chops a seat in the snow, then stamps in or chops platforms so that both feet are braced against them with outstretched, stiffened legs, and settles into a standard sitting hip belay (Chapter 8, Belaying), insulated from the snow with a pack, ensolite pad, or some other material.

The sitting hip belay, backed up with an anchor, can be very secure on hard snow or deep, heavy, wet snow. Its disadvantage is the time and energy required to make the stance, which in hard snow will probably have to be chopped out with the axe, precluding its use except for occasional belayed sections.

Also useful on snow is the *boot-axe belay* (Fig. 14-18). Though less secure than an anchored sitting hip belay, the boot-axe belay is much faster to set up and can be used when a team is moving together and belaying is required. The technique should be practiced until a sweep and

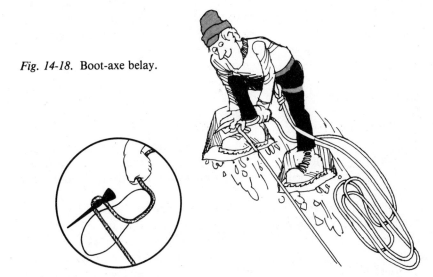

Fig. 14-18. Boot-axe belay.

jab of the ice axe set up the stance within a couple of seconds, the axe providing an anchor to the slope and the boot a brace for the axe, and both giving a friction surface over which the run of rope is controlled. The elements of the stance are as follows:

1. A firm platform is stamped out in the snow, large enough for the axe and uphill boot.
2. The ice axe shaft is jammed into the snow at the rear of the platform as deeply as possible, tilted slightly uphill against an anticipated fall.
3. The pick is perpendicular to the fall line, thus applying the broadest dimension of the shaft against the force of a fall.
4. The belayer stands below the axe, facing at approximately a right angle to the fall line and toward the side on which the climber's route lies.
5. The uphill boot is stamped into the slope against the downhill side of the shaft at a right angle to the fall line, thus bracing the shaft against downhill pull.
6. The downhill boot is in a firmly compacted step sufficiently below the uphill boot so that the leg is straight, stiffly bracing the belayer.
7. The uphill hand is on the axe head in arrest grasp, bracing the shaft against downhill and lateral stress.
8. From below, the rope crosses the toe of the boot, preventing the rope from trenching into the snow.
9. The rope bends around the uphill side of the shaft, then down across the instep of the bracing boot, and is controlled by the downhill hand

(the braking hand); apply braking through greater friction, by bringing the rope uphill around the heel, forming an "S" bend.

The boot-axe belay should be dynamic (see Chapter 8, Belaying): too abrupt a stop can shear the axe out or pop it upward out of the snow. Wooden axe shafts have broken under the stress of this technique.

Taking up rope requires much dexterity of the belayer: the uphill hand must guard the axe, take up rope, and in case of complete failure, grab the axe head in arrest grasp. The downhill — that is, the braking hand — as with all belays, must never leave the rope. Every climber should be equally adept at installing the boot-axe belay with either foot uphill, since above all it is essential that the belayer face his climber's fall line; if the climber falls behind the belay, the rope unwraps from the axe and there is no belay.

Although the effectiveness of the boot-axe belay has been questioned in some quarters, it has proven to be a useful technique provided its limitations are understood, and more important, provided it is thoroughly practiced, both by setting it up and testing to find those limitations.

Standing belay stances consisting of slots for the feet and lower legs require less stamping or chopping than sitting stances. They are, however, far less secure because the belayer tends to be toppled out of them under the force of the fall. They can be arranged so that the climber faces into the slope, out from the slope, or sideways. Facing into the slope is the poorest choice because the belayer is completely wrapped by the rope if his partner falls below him. Further, it is difficult to pay out rope for the smooth, dynamic belay often required in snow climbing.

Facing out is better because it gives a less complete wrap around the belayer. It also allows him to watch the fall, an important factor in timing and regulating a dynamic belay. It shares a major weakness with the facing-in stance: there is no bracing against toppling downhill. In both stances, the belayer should lean into the slope, against the pull downhill. Standing belays *must* be backed up with an anchor.

The most reliable standing belays are ones in which the belayer faces sideways, as in the boot-axe belay stance (Fig. 14-19). The downhill leg should be straight, locked at the knee and braced in a slot. The uphill leg should be on a line with the downhill leg and the direction of the fall. *The downhill hand should be the braking hand* to allow best control for a gradual dynamic belay.

Another useful snow belay is the standing carabiner-ice axe belay (Fig. 14-20). This is as secure as a boot-axe belay and provides easier rope handling. As shown in the figure, the straight bracing leg guards the ice axe. The force of a fall will pull the belayer more firmly into the stance. The length of the short sling should be adjusted so that the carabiner is

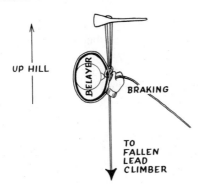

Fig. 14-19. Anchored standing belay on snow, belayer facing sideways.

completely exposed at the edge of the boot for best stability. If wearing crampons, be careful not to pierce the sling with a crampon point.

Whatever the method used, the belay must be set up close to the difficulties, and if the leader is belayed, the belay stance must be to one side of the fall line. On diagonal ascents the belay should be outside the turning point, and on direct ascents, to one side or the other of the line of ascent. When climbing a ridge, it may not always be possible to predict a fall line and plan a belay in advance, and in case of a teammate's slip the best course of action may be to jump off the opposite side.

Fig. 14-20. Standing carabiner-ice axe belay.

Anchors

Anchors, which are as critical in snow belays as in any other, include pickets, snow flukes, and other deadmen anchors, and bollards.

Pickets, aluminum stakes that come in lengths from 18 to 36 inches, have been made in several styles, including round and oval tubes and angled and T-section stakes. In use, they are driven into the snow or buried. They can be used singly, but are far more reliable if used in pairs, with one backing up the other. Pickets are awkward to carry and provide relatively little security for their weight, because of their narrow cross-section. They are seldom used today and have been replaced by the *snow fluke* or *deadman anchor.*

A deadman anchor consists of any object buried in the snow. The most common deadman anchors, often called snow flukes, are commercially produced aluminum plates with nylon webbing or metal cables attached (Fig. 14-21). For maximum strength and reliability these should be tipped back 45 degrees from the angle of pull. A slot is cut in the snow so that the cable or webbing pulls straight and loads the anchor without riding up over the snow. In theory, when placed in this manner, the deadman will serve as a dynamic anchor, traveling deeper into the snow when loaded. In practice, they may behave in more complicated ways: if tipped too far forward or back, or if the load is to the side rather than straight out, they may pull out. If the plate or the cable travels down into the snow and hits a harder layer, the deadman can be deflected and may pull out. Snow flukes are available with bent faces, flanged sides, or fixed cables—features intended to make them maintain the correct orientation while traveling through the snow and to make them self-correct if deflected.

Although the deadman anchor/snow fluke has increased the security of snow anchor systems, their performance is unpredictable. They are

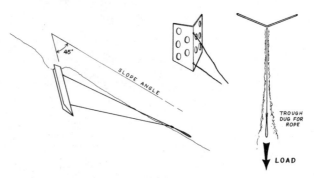

Fig. 14-21. Top, snow anchor. *Left,* side view of placement. *Right,* cable trough and correct direction for loading.

most reliable on hard, homogeneous snow, i.e., typical summer snow, and also tend to hold well in deep, heavy moist snow. They are least reliable under typical winter conditions, i.e., snow with layers of varying density where they may deflect off harder layers, and in dry, unconsolidated snow. Deadman anchor/snow flukes come in various sizes, their holding ability generally increasing with size.

The construction of *snow bollards* as anchors is an essential skill. The only reliable anchor in soft snow, and possibly the most reliable anchor in all kinds of snow, a bollard should be crescent-shaped with extended arms and a lip to keep the rope or webbing in place (Fig. 14-22). They can be chopped in hard snow or stamped in soft snow, but the softer the snow the larger and deeper they must be—up to 10 feet across and 18 inches deep. Webbing is preferable to rope around the bollard because it distributes the load over more surface area, as does padding with packs, clothing, etc.—particularly advisable on soft snow. When the rope or webbing is placed, do not pull on one end to adjust it—this may saw into the bollard. A bollard can also be used as an anchor for one or perhaps two rappels, then replaced with a new one.

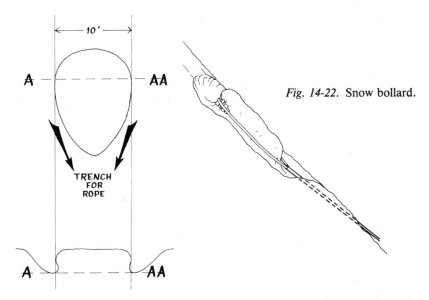

Fig. 14-22. Snow bollard.

The security of any snow anchor can be increased by combining it with others to back it up. This practice is strongly recommended, particularly in soft snow: the first anchor, while failing, may absorb enough of the force of the fall to allow the backup anchor to hold. As a rule, when combining snow anchors, either space them several feet apart, if they lie in the fall line, or place the backups out of the fall line (snow flukes should always be in line). In either case, if the primary anchor fails and weakens the snow around it, the area around the backup anchor may not be affected.

Unlike rock climbing protection, the snow belay stance should not be arranged so the initial shock load from the fall is transferred directly to the anchor. Rather, the stance should be planned'so that the shock load is taken on the belayer's body and dissipated as much as possible by a dynamic belay and the dynamic qualities of the rope, which the climbers devoutly hope will be sufficient to contain the fall. If they are not, the belayer will ultimately be yanked out of his stance, but the anchor will then be loaded with less than the initial force, and this is more likely to hold.

FINAL THOUGHTS

On rock or ice technical difficulties make climbers painfully aware of their limited skills and experience. On snow, however, it is far easier to blunder into climbing conditions at or beyond one's limits without clearly recognizing it: the snow slope gradually steepens or hardens, the day passes along, the party tires and gradually climbs into trouble.

The level of protection available to snow climbers dictates a conservative approach, at least early in their climbing careers. The same shaky protection that makes belays questionable makes retreat difficult and dangerous. Snow climbers cannot simply rappel off when the situation is beyond their ability. A descent down a long, steep, hard snow slope will generally be more tiring and hazardous than the climb up it.

Snow climbers prepare themselves before taking on big climbs, maintaining their skills — climbing, belaying, self-belay, and self-arrest — through regular practice and climbing. They get in condition. They learn about weather and avalanches. They learn about the mountains and routes they propose to climb.

Finally, snow climbing conditions are, above all else, a product of the season. Beginning snow climbers should start in the late spring and early summer, the most likely time for good, easy stepkicking. As the season moves on into late summer and fall, and hard snow prevails, cramponing skills are needed and self-belay and self-arrest become less reliable. Finally, in winter, snow conditions are the least predictable, and avalanches are a routine threat. These factors, plus the short days and erratic, often severe weather, make winter climbing a specialty for those with considerable experience in spring and summer snow climbing.

Plate 20. Northern flanks of Nuptse dwarf climbers in Western Cwm of Everest.
(John Cleare)

Plate 21. Bugaboo Glacier icefall, Purcell Range, B.C. (John Cleare)

15 *

ICE CLIMBING

THE WORLD of the ice climber is made up of all the forms in which ice exists, from lacy crystals to clear glass. In the high mountains, frozen precipitation acted upon by pressure, heat, and time becomes *alpine ice*, as found in glaciers, ice fields, and couloirs. Whenever or wherever water freezes, *water ice* forms, creating a thin rime over rock or the challenge of a frozen waterfall. Water ice is usually harder, steeper, and more brittle than alpine ice, but at high altitudes and low temperatures, alpine ice and water ice may be indistinguishable.

Although rock comes in various forms, it is relatively stable. Yesterday's crack and slab problem will likely be there next year; this morning's exhilarating ice route may be only wet rock by afternoon. The ice climber needs not only a knowledge of basic climbing techniques, but must gain experience to anticipate ever-changing conditions.

Different ice climbing techniques are used depending on the steepness of the slope. Flat ice can be walked on fairly easily, especially if there are rocks embedded in the ice, as on a bare glacier. As the slope steepens, an ice axe can be used to chop steps. Over long sections, this is tiring, and crampons are strapped on. The "flat-footing" French technique is admirably suited to walking on ever-steepening ice up to a limit, but on the steepest slopes, the German technique of front-pointing is more appropriate. Security is a function of skillful foot work as well as from the use of hand tools and ice screws, physical conditioning, skill, and judgment.

The vocabulary of steepness is vague at best, but the following table gives a rough guide to the terms used in this chapter:

gentle—up to 30 degrees   extremely steep—60 degrees and over
moderate—30 to 45 degrees   vertical—80 to 90 degrees
steep—45 to 60 degrees   overhanging—over 90 degrees

CLOTHING AND RELATED EQUIPMENT

Ice, by its very nature, is generally found in rather harsh conditions. The thermometer may "bottom-out," the wind may howl, and if nothing else, the climbing medium itself is below freezing. So, before putting on crampons and reaching for ice tools, the ice climber needs to dress accordingly.

As with all climbing clothing, ice climbing garb should be a blend of comfort and function—loose fitting enough to give the freedom of movement required, but with pant legs and gaiters snug enough not to catch a crampon point. On ice, an article of clothing dropped is usually an article of clothing lost; wrist loops on mittens and gloves are particularly important. Foot-to-knee insulated gaiters and boots that fit well—snug in the heel and instep, with room for toes to wiggle—will help keep all-important feet dry and warm.

Forcefully chopping steps or placing tools displaces ice, causing fracture lines. It may also cause the ice to shatter dramatically, and thus ice climbing areas often have large, sharp hunks flying and falling in the vicinity of climbers. Both helmet and goggles are strongly recommended: even a small piece of ice can easily damage an eye.

Crampons come in great variety, but finding an "all-around" pair for ice is relatively easy. They should have medium-length points, and must have front-points. Properly fitted hinged crampons are extremely versatile. They work well with most types of climbing boots, and are less expensive than rigid-frame crampons, but vibrate slightly more than rigid-frame crampons when kicked into hard water ice.

Frozen-waterfall specialists prefer rigid-frame crampons. Although most types of crampons should be worn with full-shank rigid boots to prevent over-stressing the metal crampon frame, some newer crampon models, such as the LAS Foot-Fangs®, are strong enough to be worn with boots having less than full shanks.

Crampons need to be sharp: the harder the ice, the sharper the crampon. Points should be checked prior to each climb and sharpened if they are at all blunted.

TRAVEL ON ICE

Walking on Ice

Ice climbing is balance climbing, moved from one *position-of-balance* to the next (weight of the body over the feet, inside foot above and in front of the outside foot). In the technique of self-belay (Chapter 14), the axe is moved only when the body and feet are in balance, and the feet are moved only when the axe is in position to support a possible slip. The exception to this generalization is when climbing extremely steep, vertical, or overhanging ice: the body can never be in balance without support from the hand tools.

Without hand tools, ice climbing is similar to rock climbing, using fist jams, pinch grips, mantle moves, and other rock techniques. With a hand tool, handholds and steps can be chopped to aid progress.

Stepcutting on Ice

The earliest method of ascending steep ice was to simply cut steps in the ice and walk up them. The development of crampons has reduced the need for stepcutting, but has not eliminated it. An ice section may be encountered unexpectedly by a group without crampons, or the problem may be short and the time to put crampons on and off would cause unwarranted delay. There might be a broken crampon in the party and a lot of ice between them and home, or they might be caught on steep exposed ice with an inexperienced or injured member. Even with crampons, a slight cut from the axe can create more secure footing.

Whichever type of steps are used, the basic principle of moving the axe only when in a position-of-balance applies. A climber chops steps while in balance, then places the axe for security while moving. Very often this results in a sequence of cutting, and moving, two steps at a time.

There are two basic types of steps, *zig-zag diagonal steps* and *pigeonhole steps* (Fig. 15-1). On gentle and moderate slopes, diagonal steps are used: a single line of steps for gentle and a double parallel line on moderate slopes where balance is more of a problem. Pigeonhole steps are made straight up on steeper slopes.

When making diagonal steps on relatively soft ice, such as summer serac ice, the climber stands in the position-of-balance with the axe in his outside hand and swings it from the shoulder, cutting with the adze and letting the weight of the axe do the work. (On harder ice, this takes muscle, and two hands may be necessary.) Successive swings are used to slice ice out of the step. The swings cut away from the body, starting at

Fig. 15-1. Stepchopping—ascending. *Left,* diagonal steps; *right,* pigeonhole steps.

the heel-end of the new step and working toward the toe. The adze scoops out ice chunks, from the step, and the adze and pick finish it. On hard ice which fractures easily, the pick is used horizontally to define the bottom line so that the vertical chops do not destroy the hard-earned foothold. An outward jerk on the axe just as the pick penetrates the ice will cause the pick to chop out the ice instead of sticking in it. The step should slope slightly inward to help keep the boot from slipping out. On gentle slopes, it may be sufficient if it holds only a small part of the boot. On steeper slopes, it should be able to contain the whole boot.

When changing direction, chop a hold large enough for both feet to create a secure position for turning and switching hands on the ice axe. On steeper sections, small fingerholds can be cut to aid balance while stepchopping. The stepchopper needs to take into account the various lengths of legs in the party. One climber may be able to reach 5 feet and maintain balance, but the legs of another climber may be a wee bit shorter. Steps should be spaced accordingly.

Pigeonhole steps, for direct ascent of steep ice, are placed about shoulder-width apart and within easy stepping distance of each other. Since each hole functions as both a hand and foothold, they should be large enough to hold the front half of the boot and have a small lip which functions as a handhold. Once the step is cut, small chops with the adze create the lip easily.

The easiest way to descend ice on chopped steps is by ladder steps (Fig. 15-2) which can be cut one at a time or two at a time in exactly the same way as an individual zig-zag diagonal step. To cut two steps at a time, the climber starts in a position-of-balance: the two new steps will be position-of-balance steps also, cut directly below the existing steps. When both steps are ready, the climber steps down with the outside (lower) foot and then the inside (higher) foot. To cut one step at a time, the climber starts in a position-of-balance. The first step is cut for the outside (lower) foot. The foot is moved down into the step. The next step is cut for the inside (higher) foot, which is moved down into it. The steps form a vertical ladder down the ice slope.

Fig. 15-2. Stepcutting — descending. Ladder steps.

Since most stepcutting is done on a slippery medium and often in exposed areas, the stepcutter will usually need to be belayed. The fatigue caused by much stepcutting makes balance more difficult, as does the movement required when chopping steps. A wrist leash on the ice axe is a necessity at this time, not only to support the hard-working hand, but to prevent loss of the axe if it is dropped.

As with most ice climbing techniques, practice in chopping steps before time of need is essential. Whether it is by design or accident that the party finds itself without crampons and confronted by slopes of ice, stepcutting practice will never be wasted.

Cramponing

Modern crampon technique has evolved from two complementary techniques, "flat-footing," or French technique, developed by French climbers and "front-pointing," or German technique, developed by German and Austrian climbers. When the two are used under appropriate circumstances, they enable the climber to move efficiently and with minimum fatigue over the variations in the icy terrain. Generally, flat-footing is used on lower-angled slopes and where point penetration is easy; front-pointing is most common on slopes steeper than 45 degrees and on very hard ice. In practice, most climbers blend them into what has been referred to as American technique. In any technique, the most important element is confident use of the crampons. Practice on gentle and moderate slopes helps develop skill, confidence, and the aggressive approach needed at steeper angles.

The skilled ice climber, whether flat-footing or front-pointing, displays the same deliberate movement as the skilled rock climber on a difficult slab. The crampon points must be carefully and deliberately placed on the ice, the weight transferred from one foot to the other smoothly and decisively. Essential to skillful cramponing is boldness — exposure must be disregarded and concentration focused solely on the climbing.

Boldness is not blind bravado. It is not a blend of the beginner's naive faith in the equipment added to the discovery, while attempting a severe ice climb, that the techniques read about seem to work pretty well — so far. Instead, it is confidence and skill — born of time and enthusiasm, nurtured in many practice sessions on glacial seracs and on ice bulges in frozen gullies, and matured by ascents of gradually increasing length and difficulty.

FRENCH TECHNIQUE
(PIED À PLAT — "FLAT-FOOTING")

Once learned, French technique is the easiest and most efficient method of climbing gentle to steep ice and hard snow. Only the basic tools — crampons and ice axe — are needed.

Since French climbers both developed and perfected the flat-footing technique, their terminology is commonly used by ice climbers. Terms using "pied" refer to the feet, while terms using "piolet" refer to the ice axe. For example, pied à plat means "flat-footing."

The chart below outlines the various foot/axe placements for ascent and includes arbitrary estimates of the slope for which they are appropriate, although technique and slope combinations will, in practice, vary with the skill of the climber. The French terms for each are included, since anyone planning to pursue the topics of snow and ice climbing should be familiar with them.

Feet (Pied)	Axe (Piolet)	Slope
marching (marche)	cane (canne)	gentle 0–15 degrees
duck walk (en canard)	cane (canne)	gentle 15–30 degrees
flat (à plat)	cane (canne)	moderate 30–40 degrees
flat (à plat)	cross-body (ramasse)	moderate 35–50 degrees
flat (à plat)	anchor (ancre)	steep 45–65 degrees +

Good French technique depends not only on the balance and rhythm of the climber, but also on ability to use the tools properly. Correct ice axe placement must be learned; only practice will give the ice climber the knowledge and confidence that a placement will hold.

The ice should be studied for a probable axe placement. A slight depression above and slightly to the side is a good possibility. Ice is more compact in depressions than in bulges, and will hold the pick of the axe more securely. The axe is swung naturally, from the shoulder. The pick displaces ice as it penetrates, causing fracture lines to radiate outward through the ice. If the pick were placed in a bulge of ice, the fractures in the ice would cause the bulge to shatter or to break off en masse, called "dinner plating." Opaque ice has more air trapped in it than clear ice, is softer and less brittle, and will usually hold a good placement.

If the climber aims carefully, the first swing should result in a satisfying solid "thunk" — the sound and feel of a well-placed ice axe. It is only through experience on many climbs with a wide variety of ice types that the subtleties of ice and axe placements can be learned.

Ascending

Walking on gentle slopes with crampons requires little more technique than walking anywhere else. The feet are kept slightly farther apart than normal to avoid snagging a crampon point on clothing or on a crampon strap on the other foot. All 10 points under the foot are stamped firmly into the ice (pied marche — "marching"). The ice axe is used as a cane with the pick forward and the palm on top of the adze (piolet canne — "ice axe cane") in the self-belay grip. As the slope steepens slightly, pointing the toes directly uphill becomes awkward, and they turn outward, duck fashion (en canard — "as a duck") (Fig. 15-3). The axe is still used as a cane (piolet canne).

When the increasing angle of the slope causes too much ankle strain, it becomes necessary to turn sideways to the slope and ascend diagonally (Fig. 15-4), which allows a more relaxed, comfortable step. As a rule, the steeper the slope, the lower the angle of the line followed. The ice axe is kept in the uphill hand in the cane position (piolet canne). Even though the ascent is diagonal, the feet are still placed flat (pied à plat), with all 10 crampon points stamped into the ice; trying to edge on crampons will

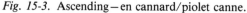

Fig. 15-3. Ascending—en cannard/piolet canne.

Fig. 15-4. Flat-footing. Diagonal ascent, cane position.

cause them to come out of the ice. Start with the feet pointed in the direction of travel. As the slope steepens, the feet must rotate downward to keep them flat on the ice; on the steepest slopes they may be pointing downhill.

The ascent is done in a two-step sequence, from a position-of-balance, out-of-balance, and then back to a position-of-balance. From the in-balance position, the downhill (outside) foot is brought in front of and above the uphill (inside) foot into the out-of-balance position. The downhill leg crosses over the knee of the uphill leg, because if the cross is made at the ankle, stability is compromised and the next step will be difficult to make. To return to the in-balance position, the lower (inside) foot is brought up behind and placed in front of the outside foot. Body weight should be over the crampons and not leaning into the slope, since this can cause crampon points to be twisted out of the ice. Natural irregularities and lower-angled spots in the slope can be used to ease strain on ankles and make upward progress easier.

The ice axe is kept in the uphill hand in the flat-foot/cane technique. When the climber is in the in-balance position, the axe should be at or near the hip, then planted in front at approximately arm's length, far enough ahead and uphill so that it will not need to be moved until the next in-balance position has been reached.

Following a diagonal line of ascent may require, at some point, a change of direction. From the in-balance position, the axe is placed as directly above as the stance will allow. The downhill (outside) foot is moved into the out-of-balance position, about the same height as the other foot and pointing slightly uphill. The downhill hand is placed on the head of the axe. The axe is held with both hands, giving security to the turn. As the body turns into the slope, the inside foot is moved to point in the new direction and slightly uphill. The climber is now facing into the slope, holding onto the axe with both hands, and standing with feet splayed outward. Return to the in-balance position is completed by bringing the foot which is pointing in the previous direction above and in front of the other foot. The downhill hand releases the axe. The climber is now in-balance, facing the new direction, and holding the ice axe in the uphill hand.

As the slope changes from gentle to moderate, the use of the axe in the cane position becomes awkward and greater security is gained by holding the axe in the cross-body position (piolet ramasse) (Fig. 15-5). The inside hand grips the shaft just above the spike; the outside hand is on the head with the pick pointing forward (the self-belay grasp). The spike is driven into the slope about waist high, with the shaft perpendicular to the slope and approximately horizontal across the climber's waist. Most of the weight placed on the axe should be at the hand on the shaft. The hand on the head stabilizes the axe and is a reminder not to lean into the slope. The feet are kept flat and moved in the two-step out-of-balance, into-balance sequence, the axe replanted at each in-balance position. A full-length ice

Fig. 15-5. Flat-footing. Diagonal ascent, cross-body axe position.

axe is needed to keep the body out instead of leaning into the ice when using this technique; even experienced ice climbers have difficulty doing French technique correctly with a shorter axe.

Changes of direction with the axe in cross-body position (Fig. 15-6) are made in the same sequence as that described for flat-foot/cane technique. If the splayed-foot position feels unstable at these angles, the change of direction can be done on front-point placements.

Fig. 15-6. Changing direction. Flat-footing, diagonal ascent, cross-body axe position.

When the angle of ice steepens, and more security than the cross-body technique (piolet ramasse) provides is desirable, the axe is planted in the anchor position (piolet ancre) (Fig. 15-7): with the outside hand just above the spike, the axe is swung so that the pick is anchored in the ice in front of and above the climber's head with the shaft parallel to the slope. The inside hand reaches up and grasps the axe head in the self-arrest position. By pulling down on the anchored axe, the climber steps up to a new in-balance position. A gentle and constant outward pull must be kept on the shaft to set the teeth and keep the axe locked into the ice. The axe is removed by pushing the shaft toward the ice and lifting the pick up and out of the ice. To keep the feet flat at these angles, the body must lean farther away from the slope, with knees and ankles flexed.

If possible, the feet should be moved by crossing over in the two-step out-of-balance, into-balance sequence. However, at the steepest angles, they are shuffled. Since the toes are pointing almost straight downhill, the shuffling movement results in a backward climb up the slope. The axe should be removed and planted from the in-balance position, with the foot on the axe side at least slightly higher than the other foot, allowing

Fig. 15-7. Flat-footing. Axe in anchor position.

the upper body to rotate and make a smooth, strong swing. Keep those feet flat!

When using the flat-foot/anchor technique, direction can be changed as described for the flat-foot/cane technique, or by changing the axe to the other hand and placing it on the other side.

French technique puts great demand on both leg muscles and balance. A helpful position, called pied assis, can be used to rest tired muscles or for a more secure position when replanting the ice axe (Fig. 15-8). From the in-balance position, the outside (lower) foot is moved up and under-

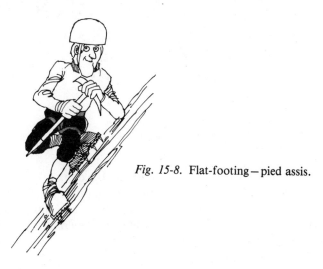

Fig. 15-8. Flat-footing — pied assis.

neath the buttocks, with toes pointing straight down. Sitting down on that foot is not only a balanced position, but a relatively comfortable one.

The invaluable flat-foot/cross-body and flat-foot/cane techniques can be sufficient for most major alpine routes, which, whatever their reputations, rarely exceed 40 to 50 degrees. The flat-foot/anchor technique, most often used for short, steep sections, marks the upper limit of French technique.

Descending

Gently sloping ice is descended by facing directly downward and bending the knees slightly (pied marche). All 10 bottom crampon points must be planted positively and firmly into the ice. The axe is used in the cane position (piolet canne). As the angle steepens, the toes are splayed out duck fashion. The knees are bent more and spread apart (en canard) with body weight over the feet so that the crampon points will bite securely into the ice (Fig. 15-9). The thigh muscles will do the bulk of the work, a fact which an out-of-shape climber will immediately and unhappily discover. For greater security, the axe is planted perpendicular to the slope (piolet ramasse; Fig. 15-9, right).

Fig. 15-9. Flat-footing—descending duck walk. *Left*, axe in cane position; *right*, axe in cross-body position.

When descending slightly steeper ice, the duck walk should bring the body closer to the ice. The axe, used in a support position (piolet appui) (Fig. 15-10), is held near the middle of the shaft and placed beside the climber with the pick uphill and the spike downhill. Both pick tip and spike should be resting on the ice.

Fig. 15-10. Flat-footing—descending duck walk. Axe in support position.

Fig. 15-11. Flat-footing—descending. Axe in bannister position.

As the slope steepens and positive support is needed, the axe is used in the bannister position (piolet rampe) (Fig. 15-11). The axe is swung and planted as far below the climber as possible. As the climber crampons down, his hand slides down the shaft toward the head. A slight outward pull is maintained on the shaft to keep the pick locked in the ice. When the axe head is behind the climber, the shaft is pushed toward the ice to release the pick, and the axe is replanted.

When the slope becomes too steep to descend facing outward, the climber faces sideways and descends diagonally (Fig. 15-12). Footwork changes from the duck walk (en canard) to the same flat-foot technique which was used to ascend diagonally. The axe is used in the anchor position (piolet ancre): with the outside arm, the climber swings the axe out in front and plants the pick in the ice, then flat-foots diagonally down below the axe. The shaft rotates as the climber passes below it.

Fig. 15-12. Descending, axe in anchor position.

Many climbers, on their first encounter with flat-foot crampon techniques, find them awkward and needlessly complicated, particularly the ones used on steeper slopes. Once mastered, however, these techniques provide great security because they so admirably achieve the objective of keeping the climber in balance over the feet, with maximum penetration of all 10 vertical crampon points. Only those climbers apparently equipped by nature with ball-bearing ankles have no difficulty keeping their feet flat; to the rest this is a considerable problem, and some may find it necessary to adapt techniques to fit their own physical capability. As a rule, as ankle flexibility reaches its limits, the strain can be eased by pointing the toes downward so that the flex needed to keep the feet flat comes from the more normal forward flex in the ankle and from the knees, which are bent away from the slope and spread well apart. Boots which are flexible at the ankle help. For long bouts of flat-foot cramponing, unlacing the upper boot may permit more ankle flex.

FRONT – POINTING (GERMAN TECHNIQUE)

Developed by the Germans and Austrians for climbing the harder snow and ice of the eastern Alps, front-pointing can take an experienced ice climber up the steepest and most difficult ice slopes. Using this technique, even average climbers can quickly overcome sections which, if attempted by French technique, would require the utmost in skill or would be simply impossible.

Front-pointing, in contrast to the choreography of flat-footing, is straight-forward and uncomplicated – much like stepkicking straight up a snow slope. Instead of kicking the boot into the snow, the climber ascends by kicking the front points into the ice and stepping directly up on them.

Just as in French technique, good front-pointing technique is rhythmic and balanced climbing, with the weight of the body over the crampons. Efficiency of movement is essential, whether placing front points or hand tools, or moving in any direction on the ice. Energy consumed by needless flailing during the climb means that much less energy higher on the climb, where it is most needed.

Crampon Technique

Except in extremely hard ice, a firm deliberate kick is usually enough to make sharp points bite. Too rigorous or repeated kicking wastes precious energy and may shatter the ice, making a secure placement more difficult. When the points are planted, foot movement should be avoided because it can cause the points to rotate out of the ice.

Front-pointing uses not only the two forward points of each crampon, but also the two vertical points immediately behind them. These four points, when properly placed, provide a platform on which to stand. The best placement is gained when the foot is straight into the slope (Fig. 15-13). Splayed feet tend to rotate the outside front points out of the ice.

Fig. 15-13. Front-pointing.

Leveling the heels pushes the first set of vertical points into the ice, while raising the heels removes these stabilizing vertical points, tends to lever the front points out of the ice, and flexes muscles in the calves, which fatigue easily. Heels feel lower than they actually are; if the climber thinks "heels down," the feet will probably be in the correct horizontal position. This is especially important when coming over the top of steep ice onto a gentler slope, where the natural tendency is to raise the heels, relax concentration, and hurry; this must be avoided in order to keep the points from shearing out of the ice.

Full-shank stiff-soled boots make front-pointing easiest. Three-quarter shank boots can be used but require more muscular effort. Wearing soft-soled boots while front-pointing puts severe strain on crampons, and on calf, foot and leg muscles, which must work harder to place and keep crampons in secure placements (Fig. 15-14). .

Unlike flat-foot technique, which requires considerable practice to perfect, most people pick up front-pointing quickly because it feels natural and secure. Unfortunately, this encourages climbers to use it excessively on moderately angled slopes where flat-foot technique would be just as secure and more efficient. The efficiency of flat-foot technique makes it valuable for long alpine routes; most of the stress is placed on the thigh muscles, where most people have more strength than in their calves. Once mastered, flat-footing is far less tiring on a long climb than front-pointing and even climbers who strongly prefer front-pointing would benefit from alternating the techniques to give calf muscles a rest.

Fig. 15-14. Front-pointing with soft-soled boots.

Fig. 15-15. 3-o'clock position.

A technique called the 3 o'clock position (pied troisème) (Fig. 15-15) is really front-pointing with one foot while flat-footing with the other: the climber looks for irregular flatter spots, nooks and crannies in the ice, and takes advantage of them, placing his foot flat in one of these spots to rest the calf muscle of that leg. The axe is used in whatever technique is appropriate to the slope and conditions. The 3 o'clock position is a fast and powerful technique used on a direct line of ascent, allowing the climber to distribute the effort of climbing across more muscle groups by alternating techniques with each leg. The practice of combining flat-foot technique and front-point technique, whether alternating legs or switching techniques for a period of time, is referred to as the "American technique."

Certain surface conditions on steep slopes, where either flat-foot or front-point technique would be appropriate, make one preferable to the other. On frozen snow, snow with an ice crust, or on soft or rotten ice, flat-footing is more secure because it gets more points into the mountain. The soft snow over ice or hard snow, front-pointing or the 3 o'clock position allows the climber to blast through the surface layer to get points into the firmer layer underneath. Front-pointing is the only technique for the average climber to use on really hard ice for all but very gentle slopes, and when altitude, fatigue, wind, or fear make it unwise or impossible to flat-foot with finesse, the climber resorts to front-pointing or 3 o'clock technique.

Axe Technique

Unless holes in the ice or solid ice columns are available for handholds, as on frozen waterfalls, steeper slopes are easier to front-point with assistance from an ice axe. Even though front-pointing was developed first by the Germans and Austrians, French terms have come to be used for the various ice axe techniques which are used while front-pointing. The chart below outlines the foot/axe placements for front-pointing and includes arbitrary estimate of the slope for which they are appropriate.

Feet (Pied)	Axe (Piolet)	Slope
front-pointing	low dagger (panne)	steep 45 to 55 degrees
or	high dagger (poignard)	steep 50 to 60 degrees
3 o'clock (pied	anchor (ancre)	steep 45 to 60 degrees
troisième)	traction (traction)	extremely steep, 60 degrees+ vertical, overhanging

It is often necessary to surmount a short, relatively steep section of ice which may be best overcome by a few quick front-pointing moves. The simplest axe technique for this situation is the low dagger position (piolet panne) (Fig. 15-16): the axe is held by the adze in the self-belay grip, the pick pushed into the ice about waist high to give the necessary assistance to balance. The dagger position tends to push the climber back away from the slope and out over the feet, the correct front-pointing position.

Fig. 15-16. Front-pointing with axe in low dagger position.

If the slope is a bit too steep to insert the axe at waist level, the axe is moved to a position above the shoulder, the high dagger position (Fig. 15-17). The pick is inserted dagger-style, but the head is now held in the self-arrest grasp. High dagger technique (piolet poignard) is used in relatively soft ice or hard snow where the pick will penetrate easily.

Fig. 15-17. Front-pointing; high dagger position.

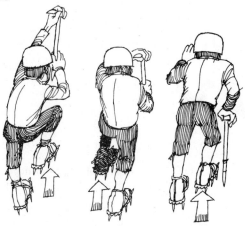

Fig. 15-18. Front-pointing; anchor position.

When confronted by harder ice or a steeper slope, the climber abandons the high dagger position (piolet poignard) for the anchor position (piolet ancre), used when flat-footing (Fig. 15-18). While standing on front points, the climber holds the axe near the ferrule and swings the pick in as high as possible. When front-pointing up, he grasps the shaft higher and higher until the adze is held in the anchor position, and front-points until the adze is about waist high and the adze is held in the low dagger position (piolet panne). At this point, he replants the axe.

The axe technique usually associated with steeper sections and hard ice is called piolet traction (Fig. 15-19): the axe is held near the ferrule and placed high. The slope is ascended by pulling down on the planted axe and front-pointing upward.

On very hard ice, or on extremely steep sections, balancing on front points while replanting the axe may be difficult and it becomes necessary to use a second ice tool so there will always be three points of support as

Fig. 15-19. Front-pointing; traction with single axe.

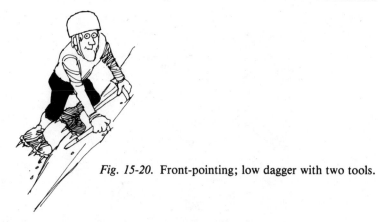

Fig. 15-20. Front-pointing; low dagger with two tools.

when rock climbing. On ice, if one point of support fails, the other two must be sufficient to hold the climber until the third point can be replaced. The legs carry most of the weight, but the arms must assist.

Most ice axe techniques involve only one hand; thus the climber may use two axes, one in each hand. The anchor technique (piolet ancre), however, requires two hands on a single axe. When two tools are used, the same technique may be used for both hands such as the low dagger (piolet panne) (Fig. 15-20) or different techniques can be used for each hand. In serac ice, piolet poignard and piolet traction work well together (Fig. 15-21).

Fig. 15-21. Front-pointing: left tool, traction; right tool, high dagger.

Fig. 15-22. Front-pointing; traction with two tools.

The most frequently used double-axe technique is piolet traction, in which the climber pulls down on both tools (Fig. 15-22). The feet are about shoulder width apart and level with each other, a stable position which adds to the comfort of the climb. The climber plants the first tool, then the second tool, and steps up on the front points to a new level position. As the cycle is repeated, concentration should be on hand tool and front-point placements. As in rock climbing, rhythm is as important as balance.

Various hand tools have been developed specifically for double-axe techniques (Fig. 15-23). Actually greatly modified ice axes, they are shorter than a full length ice axe, enabling the climber to place the pick with greater accuracy. Because of design, each type is best placed with a specific technique.

A curved pick tool such as on MSR Sumner® "shortie" (55 cm) requires a more natural swing, much like a 70-cm ice axe. A sharply angled tool, as the MacInnis-Peck Terrordactyl®, requires a sharp downward flick at the end of a short swing. A tubular-nosed tool, such as the Lowe Hummingbird®, works best with a short arc swing. For any ice tool, the aim is for accuracy and a solid placement—the first time. One or two swings saved at the bottom of a climb mean that much more energy at the top of a tiring pitch.

For extremely steep or vertical ice, wrist leashes on ice tools are an energy-saving necessity (Fig. 15-24). The loop should be large enough for the hand to fit through easily and should help hold the hand in position

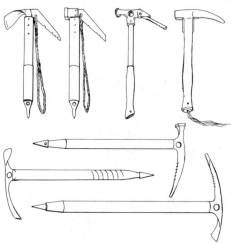

Fig. 15-23. Ice tools. *Top, left to right:* Terrordactyl®, Terrordactyl® hammer, Hummingbird®, and Alpine Hammer®. *Bottom, top to bottom:* North Wall Hammer®, Sumner®, and Chouinard®.

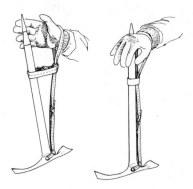

Fig. 15-24. Wrist leash for ice tools. *Right,* tape to hold wrist leash.

on the axe (for ice climbing or stepchopping, this position is just above the ferrule). The loop should be attached or held next to the shaft just above the correct hand position. This will keep the hand and shaft together whether the fingers are locked around the shaft or not.

By using a wrist leash it is possible to hang from an ice tool without maintaining a forearm-killing grip. The arm is straight, the hand and arm are relaxed, and the weight of the body is on the skeleton. Some type of rough tape, such as tennis tape, on the shaft of the tool will make the grip more secure, again saving energy. Tape is, however, not recommended on a full-length ice axe since it inhibits good penetration of the shaft during self-belay on snow.

Vertical and Overhanging Ice

Vertical or overhanging ice presents special problems and challenges. Although with modern techniques and tools and good physical conditioning, bold climbers can ascend vertical sections and slight overhangs, others may need to resort to direct aid. Severe overhangs as found on seracs and bergschrunds may yield only to artificial aid techniques.

On vertical ice, the body cannot balance on front points alone without support from arms and hand tool placements. Foot technique is either front-pointing or the 3 o'clock position (pied troisième). The double-axe technique used is traction (piolet traction). On vertical ice, the hand tool placements are made as high as possible and off to the side a bit to protect the head of the climber from dislodged hunks of ice or an unexpectedly dislodged tool.

From the back the climber's body resembles an "X" against the ice wall (Fig. 15-25), feet level with each other, heels slightly down and the arms straight. The hands pull outward slightly on the tools to keep the tool teeth set in the ice and apply inward pressure on the crampon points (this can be likened to a slight layback move on rock). The feet move up to new level positions then the ice tools are, one at a time, reset higher.

Fig. 15-25. Front-pointing steep ice. *Left,* "X" body position; *right,* moving up.

The *monkey hang* is a sequence for passing ice bulges or small over-hangs (Fig. 15-26). Starting from the "X" body position the feet walk up the ice, but without raising the body. The climber loosens but does not re-move one hand tool and rises to a standing or nearly standing position by pushing with the feet and pulling on the two hand tools, and in one con-tinuous motion smoothly removes and replants the previously loosened tool higher. The muscles of arm and hand relax, hanging from the re-planted tool. The second tool is loosened and replanted higher. The climber has returned to the "X" position ready to repeat the sequence.

Another technique for vertical or slightly overhanging ice uses hand tools and aid slings or etriers attached to the two hand tools and to the front of the climber's seat harness. Alternately placing the hammers, the climber "walks" in etriers up the ice (Fig 15-27). A third hammer is used as a protection point.

Fig. 15-26. Monkey hang.

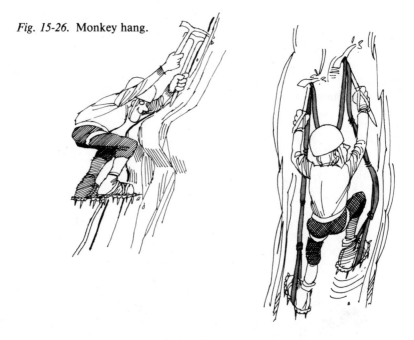

Fig. 15-27. Vertical to overhanging ice — etrier method.

When a slope becomes too severe for a climber to surmount by the techniques described, he resorts to artificial aid, exactly as on rock except ice screws or ice pitons are used rather than rock hardware. While ice screws may be amply secure when first placed, body weight causes pressure melting of the ice next to the screw, possibly allowing them to be pulled directly out of the ice. The rate that melting and loosening occurs depends on the temperature and the extent of direct solar radiation. Accordingly, aid climbers on ice must not dally, but move steadily from one placement to the next. Bouts of aid on ice are generally shorter than on rock so less total equipment is required; the two-etrier method is more common than that using four etriers.

Traversing Extremely Steep Ice

The principles for traversing are much the same as for ascending steep ice, but because the direction of travel is to the side instead of straight up, it is more difficult to keep one foot perpendicular to the ice while replacing the front points of the other foot. If the heel rotates, the front points will also rotate and come out of the ice. Hand tools also tend to rotate easier if the direction of travel is sideways.

Starting from a secure position, feet level with front points and hand tools planted, the climber places the leading tool to the side out at about 45 degrees from the body and lower than for ascending (Fig. 15-28). If the tool is placed too far to the side, the climber may pendulum while trying to replant the trailing tool. Once the leading tool is planted, he can either shuffle on front points or cross one foot over. Most climbers prefer the shuffle; it is less awkward and feels more secure. He then moves the trailing tool closer to his body. In good ice, the trailing tool can often be securely planted in a placement made by the leading tool. This is especially true when leading with the tubular Hummingbird® and following with the Terrordactyl®. The small hole left by the Hummingbird® makes an excellent starting hole for the larger nose of the Terrordactyl®.

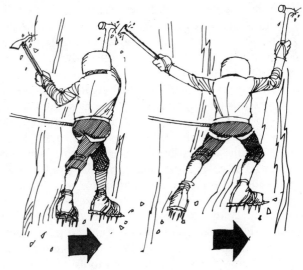

Fig. 15-28. Traversing steep ice.

Descending Extremely Steep Ice

Although front-point and hand tool techniques are generally the same for descending as for ascending, as on rock, downclimbing is more difficult than ascending. It is more awkward to place front points while stepping down than when stepping up. There is a tendency to step too low, causing the heel to rise, and the front points either do not penetrate or shear out immediately. It is also more awkward to place a hand tool because the tool must be placed closer to the head, which means that the swing will be done with a bent arm. Lack of visibility (the body obscures the view of the route) is another factor. Descending on a slight diagonal will alleviate the problem. Since rappels are possible, or an "easier way down" may exist, descents are not often front-pointed. However, during an ascent a climber may decide to descend, rest, and/or try a different line. Practice in descending will increase confidence and skill in front-point techniques.

Hand Tools for Extremely Steep Ice

Hand tools can be mixed or matched, from the large selection available (Fig. 15-23); the choice depends upon the climber's preferences, strength, ability, monetary resources, and the type of climb under consideration. Part of the fun of ice climbing is experimenting with and learning to use the various tools.

The primary function of the pick is to penetrate the ice, hold against a pull along the shaft, and then to release easily when its grip is no longer needed. The holding and releasing characteristics of a pick are determined both by its geometry and by its teeth: as a general rule, the steeper the droop and the more, sharper and deeper the teeth, the better the pick will hold; the smoother the pick, the easier it is to remove. A heavy tool cuts and penetrates best, particularly if the weight is concentrated in its head. The sharpness of the cutting edges of the pick, adze, and spike is crucial for climbing hard ice. The sharper and thinner the edge, the better it works, but the more vulnerable it becomes to the rock that every axe hits. Given these parameters, variation in design is to be expected.

Each tool has its strengths and limitations. A climber with exceptionally strong hands and forearms and a high level of skill may take advantage of the extra reach of two full-length ice axes with drooped picks. These give an advantage of reach that the shorter tools do not have, but their length and weight make them more difficult to place than shorter tools. For this reason, most climbers prefer a full-length axe partnered with a shorter hand tool, or two shorter hand tools.

The Sumner® "shortie" and Chouinard's North Wall Hammer®, both

55 cm in length, are examples of ice hand tools which are most like regular ice axes. The picks are curved more than a regular ice axe to hold better in ice, and the shorter length is easier to swing on steep angles. The Sumner® has an adze for stepcutting or clearing away rotten ice for placement of protection. Instead of an adze, the North Wall Hammer® has a hammer for placing protection. The Sumner® is a relatively light tool which works beautifully in serac and relatively soft water ice. When weight is added to the head (as with some lead sheet and tape) it has good penetration in hard water ice. It can be removed easily by lifting straight up on it. The North Wall Hammer® has a relatively heavy head which penetrates and holds well in soft to very hard ice, but it can be difficult to remove.

The Alpine Hammer® is an example of a multipurpose rock and ice tool. The curved, toothed pick penetrates well into soft and moderately hard ice. It is light and easy to handle, but can be difficult to remove. Sideways twists can fracture the pick.

The thinness and sharpness of the tubular-nosed tools, e.g., the Hummingbird®, have made them popular for use in hard water ice. The harder the ice the better this tool works. The thin tube shatters the ice less than a conventional blade pick does, often giving a secure placement with a single swing. It is moderately easy to remove by twisting sideways while holding the head; up-and-down levering motions can fracture the nose. If the climb will involve ice with sand or rocks close to the surface, the Hummingbird® should be left at home. Even one rock can dent the sharp, tubular nose, making it useless for ice work until it is resharpened or replaced.

The Terrordactyl® has a sharply down-angled pick which penetrates extremely well in soft to very hard ice and removes fairly easily with an up and down levering motion. Again, avoid sideways twistings of the pick.

One tool with an adze and one with a hammer is a versatile combination: the adze is used for chopping and scraping the ice, whether for steps, belay positions, or ice bollards, and the hammer can be used for placing protection.

For a long and difficult climb some climbers recommend taking a third tool for an anchor at belay points or to place protection. More important, it prevents a climber finding himself with only one usable hand tool, the other being broken or lost. Some hand tools now have easily replaceable picks. A spare pick is light in weight and takes little room in a pack. Two holsters (or a double-sized holster) on the seat harness make it possible to carry one or two hand tools conveniently and easily when not in use, yet allow for easy removal of a tool when it is needed. Many holsters appear to have been designed for small rock tools, and removal of an ice tool from such a holster can be difficult. When selecting a holster for an ice tool, check for ease of removal.

PROTECTION ON ICE

Today's ice climbers have available anchors offering a security undreamed of by earlier generations of mountaineers. However, there is some sacrifice of safety in the time and energy required to place protection. The common result is fewer protection points in a rope length on ice than a leader would place in a rock pitch of the same length.

Ice slopes and gulleys are areas especially threatened by the objective hazards of rockfall and icefall. Speed and avoiding points of concentrated danger are a climbing party's best defenses. Where an ice slope has little exposure or where hand tool placements are secure enough to catch any slip of the feet, a party will often climb unroped for faster progress as long as there is no threat from hidden crevasses.

Ropes

The UIAA-approved single rope is the one most often used in ice climbing, preferably a 45-meter (150-foot) length. Water-repellent ropes are worth considering when selecting a climbing rope for use on ice: since they do not soak up water as do regular perlon ropes, they do not become inflexible frozen cables which may refuse to run through carabiners, leaving the attached climbers in a difficult situation. The cost is higher for a water-repellent rope and its advantages may be worth the added expense; however, experience indicates the water-repellency quality will not last the usable life span of the rope.

Natural Protection

Although natural protection is seldom present on alpine ice, it is often found on frozen waterfalls, where runners can be placed around ice columns. Very often the natural protection found will not be ice, but rock alongside the waterfall or protruding through the ice. The experienced climber learns to take advantage of the situation.

Ice Bollard

The ability to make a good ice bollard should be in every ice climber's repertoire for it can be one of his most useful anchors (Fig. 15-29). Although more commonly a rappelling anchor, an ice bollard can be used as a belaying anchor, and properly made and tied together, two bollards—one cut for an upward pull and another for a downward pull—are a strong, multi-directional anchor. The strength of a bollard, whether made in snow or ice, is proportional to its size and to the hardness of the snow and ice. If made of hard, solid ice, a bollard can be stronger than the rope.

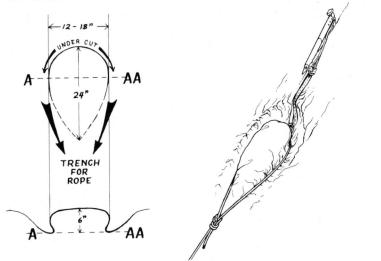

Fig. 15-29. Ice bollard. *Right,* ice tool for backup anchor.

A completed ice bollard is teardrop shaped when viewed from above, and horn shaped when viewed from the side. To construct an ice bollard, only an ice axe and good, solid ice are needed. The ice should be uniform, without cracks or holes. First the outline of the bollard is carefully cut with the pick of the axe. In hard ice, 30 to 45 cm (12 to 18 inches) are needed for the diameter. The trench around the bollard is made by working outward from the outline using both the pick and the adze. This trench should be at least 15 cm (6 inches) deep. The sides and top half of the bollard must be undercut to form a horn to prevent the rope from "popping" off over the top of the bollard. This is the most critical part of the process, since a heavy-handed blow with the axe can cause serious fracture lines or crack off a large part of the bollard. (The use of the ice bollard as a rappel anchor is discussed in Chapter 9.)

Ice Screws and Ice Pitons

The first ice pitons were extra long, blade-type rock pitons with holes, notches, or bulges to increase their grip on ice. After World War II, climbers experimented with new designs, T- or X-shaped or circular in cross-section, with greater shaft areas to decrease the load-per-square-inch on the ice, and holes to help the shaft freeze into the slope.

When ice screws first appeared in the early 1960s, enthusiasts claimed they would revolutionize climbing, bringing security to the ice slopes where previously the only rule was "the leader must not fall, and nobody else, either." Critics, however, scoffed that the screws were not much superior to the older ice pitons. This proved particularly true of the older, lightweight, relatively weak "coat hanger" ice screw, which is rarely used today. Ice screws were improved during the late 1960s and 1970s and today are considered reliable leader protection (Fig. 15-30).

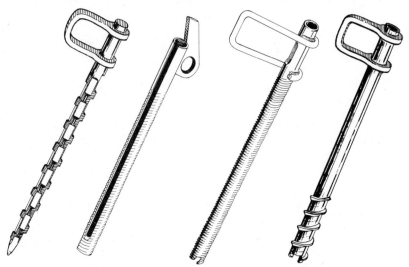

Fig. 15-30. Ice screw/piton types. *Left to right,* Warthog, Snarg, MSR, Salewa.

The tubular, hollow-core ice screw is the strongest and most reliable design and should be used whenever possible. It works well in temperatures of both winter and summer climbing, and it is relatively easy to place and remove from the ice. It minimizes fracturing of the ice by allowing the displaced ice to work itself out through the core of the screw. After the ice screw is removed from the ice, the ice inside the core must be removed immediately, or it may freeze inside, and an ice screw with a solid ice core will refuse to penetrate the ice. Some ice screws, such as Chouinard's tubular and the MSR are cylindrical tubes with slightly conical interiors which permit easier ice removal. The ice core, if frozen to the interior, can be pushed out by a length of stiff wire.

Lowe Alpine Systems (LAS) has developed a hollow-tubed, pound-in ice screw with small threads which drives in rapidly with light blows even in hard ice, and can be removed relatively easily, either by levering it out with an axe pick or by screwing it out. A slit in the side allows for easy ice removal. It works best in hard ice, but may be unreliable in temperatures above freezing.

Developed as an attempt to make an easy-to-place and easy-to-remove screw, the solid screws are driven in like a piton and screwed out. They can offer good protection in water ice at temperatures below freezing, but are less effective in other forms and at higher temperatures. Melt-out is sometimes rapid because of limited thread displacement and, under load, they tend to shear through the ice as do coat hanger screws.

One example of this type of screw is the "Wart Hog," which has good holding power, and is reliable in temperatures both below and above freezing. Since it is solid and displaces ice upon entry, it is placed with many light blows. As it is hammered in, the screw will rotate a bit in a clockwise direction. The Wart Hog should not be used unless it can be hammered in all the way. It is not as strong as a tubular screw and can break if either tied-off or clipped into while only partway into the ice. One of its main disadvantages is that it can be difficult to remove and may need to be chopped out, an exasperating waste of energy.

A location for a good ice screw placement is the same as for a good tool placement. Natural depressions, in which few of the fracture lines caused by the insertion of the screw will travel to the surface, are among the better choices. On bulges, the effect is just the opposite: before placing the ice screw, any surface layer of soft snow or rotten ice should be scraped off with the adze until a hard and trustworthy layer is reached. A small starting hole punched out with the pick or spike of a hand tool facilitates a good grip for the starting threads or teeth of the screw. This hole must be made gently with light taps to avoid fracturing the ice. The screw is placed firmly in the ice of the starting hole and angled uphill 45 to 60 degrees against the anticipated direction of pull (Fig. 15-31). If the ice is extremely rotten, a large horizontal step is made in the ice with a hand tool and the screw is placed vertically at the back of the step. Once in the

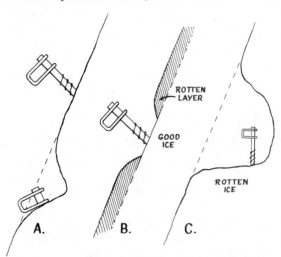

Fig. 15-31. Ice screw placements. a. Placements in solid ice surface. b. Placements with soft or rotten surface layer. c. Placement in rotten ice.

starting hole and angled correctly, the screw is pressed firmly and twisted into the ice at the same time. On hard ice, a few light taps may be necessary to make the threads catch. A screw with sharp cutting teeth can sometimes be placed by hand, but if it becomes difficult to turn by hand, the job can be finished with a lever through the screw's eye (Fig. 15-32); the pick of a hand tool or another ice screw is useful for this.

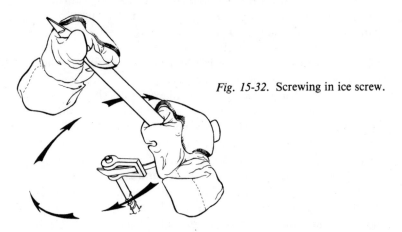

Fig. 15-32. Screwing in ice screw.

The screw should be twisted in all the way to the eye, tight and solid, and a carabiner clipped into the eye. As in rock climbing, the carabiner should open down with the gate out. To slow melt-out in soft summer ice or when the sun is shining on the snow, ice can be packed around the head. If the screw cannot be put in all the way (rock under ice is an effective screw stopper), it will need to be tied off, preferably with ⁹⁄₁₆-inch tubular webbing, tied in a slip knot around the screw as close to the surface as possible.

Fractured ice weakens the placement, rendering the ice screw useless. When this occurs, the screw should be removed and another placement tried 1 or 2 feet away. One protection point placed too close to another will cause fracture lines to the other, thus weakening both points. In good solid ice, 2 feet is usually enough separation, but on rotten ice, more may be needed. Some glacier ice will fracture and shatter at the surface, but by continuing to install the screw and gently chopping out the shattered ice with sideways strokes of the pick, the climber may obtain a deep, secure placement.

Climbing extremely steep ice can be fatiguing, both physically and mentally, especially for the leader, who must put in the protection and stay on the slope at the same time, and must have the energy and strength to complete the pitch and set up a good anchor system at the top. Unless the ice is rotten, only one screw is placed at a protection point. If the ice is hard and solid, or the slope not extremely steep, only one or two protection points will be placed on the pitch. On a moderate to steep slope, it may help to chop a step to stand in while placing the ice screw. On extremely steep ice, the energy consumed by chopping the step can be better used for climbing. Saving energy is safety; the screw should be placed and the climb continued.

Placing an effective ice screw usually requires two hands — a bit tricky on extremely steep, exposed ice. One way to ease the situation is to slip one arm through the wrist loop of a solidly planted hand tool (Fig. 15-33). Another method often used is to have a piece of webbing, the "daisy chain" used in aid rock climbing, on the front of the seat harness. This webbing can be attached to the wrist loop of the same solidly planted hand tool.

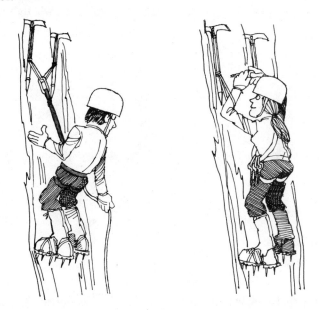

Fig. 15-33. Left, support from hand tools; preparing to place protection. *Right,* placing ice screw.

Climbers also devise some slightly unconventional protection points. On frozen waterfalls or on high alpine routes, where large ice columns form only an inch or two apart, an ice screw tied off with webbing can be inserted behind these ice columns and turned sideways to form a type of deadman. Sometimes a solid sheet of ice will be separated from the underlying rock by an inch or two, making a vertical slit that can be enlarged enough to insert a screw tied off with webbing; again the screw is turned sideways to function as a deadman. Two holes can be punched in the ice sheet, and a runner threaded through them. On mixed rock and ice climbs, rock equipment, such as chocks, can be wedged into ice holes.

Boot-Ice Screw Belay

A method of belaying that can be used on flat or gentle ice slopes is the boot-ice screw belay (Fig. 15-34). A tubular ice screw is placed securely in the ice, a carabiner is attached to the eye, and the belay rope is clipped through the carabiner. The uphill cramponed boot is placed on top of the ice screw so that the middle inside crampon point (the fourth counting from the front) goes through the carabiner. The belay end of the rope goes up through the carabiner, over the instep, and around the ankle. The belayer can control the amount of drag either by the amount of wrap on the boot ankle or by adjusting the amount of space between the carabiner and the side of the boot. If a fall occurs, the rope is slowly tightened low against the ankle with the uphill hand.

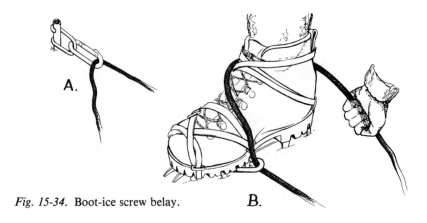

A.

B.

Fig. 15-34. Boot-ice screw belay.

Belay Set-up

Although following the general principles developed in Chapter 8, belay set-ups on ice require special consideration detailed in the example below, which although describing an intermediate belay position, may also apply to the initial belay point.

When near the end of a pitch, the leader looks for a lessening of angle or a slight depression to stand on. He places a hand tool off to the side for temporary protection, and chops a step large enough to comfortably hold both feet splayed out sideways. The first screw is placed about waist to chest level and in front of the climber, which positions him in line with the primary anchor. The leader ties into this with a clove hitch or figure-8 knot. The hand tool can be replanted so that it is above and to the side of the first screw and can then be attached to the screw by its wrist leash or a runner, providing backup for the anchor. The "off belay" message can be given to the second so that one anchor below can be removed to save time. A second screw is placed on the other side and 60 to 100 cm (2 to 3 feet) higher than the first. The climbing rope from the first screw is tied into this second screw with a clove hitch. There should be little or no slack between the two screws (Fig. 15-35). An extra carabiner is placed on the second screw, and the belay rope is then clipped into this carabiner (Fig. 15-36). When the second climbs up, exchanges gear with the previous leader, and leads out, the second screw in the anchor system becomes the first point of protection for the new leader. It also serves to remind the leader to stay to the side of the belayer, instead of leaving the belayer to gaze at 24 sharp crampon points directly overhead. Since the belayer is not hanging from the anchors, pressure melt-out should not be a problem. However, the belayer should be conscious of the anchors and replace any that do not seem secure.

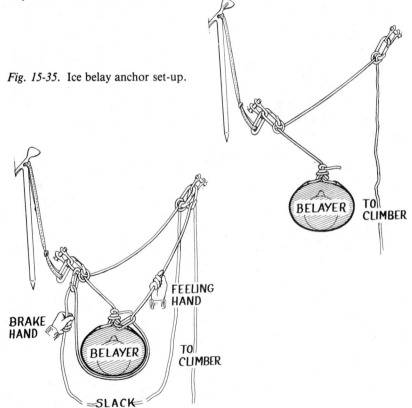

Fig. 15-35. Ice belay anchor set-up.

Fig. 15-36. Ice belay set-up for an iced-up rope.

This anchor arrangement works well for either a hip belay or a mechanical belay device. If the hip belay is used, the belay rope on the feeling hand side should be passed through a carabiner on the front of the seat harness to prevent the rope from riding up into the armpits of the belayer. This belay system is similar to the "semi-hanging hip belay" described in Chapter 8.

At temperatures around freezing, the rope can become ice-coated or cable-stiff. Not only would it quickly jam in a mechanical belay device, it would be extremely difficult to hold in a standard hip belay. When this happens, a secure system can be set up as shown in Fig. 15-36. Using the semi-hanging hip belay as previously described, a second carabiner is put on the first ice screw. The climbing rope now goes from the climber, through the carabiner on the second screw, around the back of the belayer, through a carabiner on the first screw, and folds back into the braking hand of the belayer. This system is effective even when the climbing rope is stiff and heavily iced.

"Running Protection"

Due to changing nature of ice from hour to hour and the possibility of rapidly deteriorating weather, some multi-pitch ice climbs can become extremely hazardous as the day progresses. On such climbs, speed is safety, but progress is slow if each and every pitch is belayed. In order to move faster, it may be necessary for the members of a rope team to move simultaneously to avoid being on the climb when rockfall, avalanches, or thunderstorms threaten. This does not mean solo climbing: the leader places protection and the second removes it so that they will have at least two points of protection remaining between them. Even when using running protection, the climbing team may occasionally set up a belay stance to exchange gear, swap leads, or give tired muscles a short rest.

This technique sacrifices much of the safety of belaying in order to gain a degree of safety from speed. The decision to use it requires fine judgment, based on extensive experience.

Plate 22. Khumbu Icefall below southwest shoulder of Mt. Everest. (John Cleare)

16 *

GLACIER TRAVEL

IF IT WERE NOT for crevasses, a separate consideration of glacier travel would seem superfluous, since nearly all the required techniques are treated in other chapters. However, crevasses do create special problems for travel in glacier-clad mountains — ask the climber who has fallen into one.

Most insidious of its kind is the hidden crevasse, its distinction being that the more harmless the outward appearance, the greater the threat. The most casual observer takes protective measures in the face of obvious chasms; the really hazardous holes are those that show on the surface as mere cracks or are completely invisible. It is easy to move from a snowfield onto a snowcovered glacier without recognizing the need for added protection. Also, even after much experience, a climber who has traveled under a lucky star may imagine himself able to negotiate glaciers without special precaution, confidently depending on his wisdom to predict when and where he will come upon a crevasse; an alarming percentage of such gifted seers, however, eventually lose either their second sight or their luck.

TRAVEL AMONG CREVASSES

Safe travel among crevasses does not have to be entirely a matter of luck, but can be achieved by a knowledgeable and properly equipped climbing party. The degree of safety is dependent on the particular environment, experience, judgment, physical conditioning, and party strength, and is enhanced by appropriate climbing technique and equipment.

The Rope

The first rule of traveling glaciers is to *rope up*. Whether stepping onto a known glacier or onto a snowfield of unknown status, whether or not crevasses are visible, whether or not crevasses ever have been reported as existing there in the past, the rule with but one exception is: *rope up*—the exception being the occasion in which avalanches present a greater hazard than crevasses. Even though a fortunate climber makes hundreds of climbs during a score of seasons and never once steps into a crevasse, if he is as wise as he is lucky he has kept up the premiums on his climbing insurance by wearing a rope during all of these climbs, realizing that too frequently a climber's first unroped fall into a crevasse is his last.

The mere act of roping up does not in itself provide any magical security on a glacier (or anywhere else, for that matter). It is the proper *use* of the rope, along with the other glacier climbing tools, that minimizes the consequences of a fall into a crevasse. For all glacier travel (minor exceptions to be noted later) the rope is to be fully extended between climbers, with only enough slack to keep the rope leader from having to tow his companions up the mountain.

On moderate climbs the preferred number on a rope team for glacier travel is three climbers on a rope 120 to 150 feet long. If the number of climbers in a party make rope teams of two appropriate (for example a party of seven would divide best into one rope team of three and two rope teams of two), it is convenient to rope up with the rope doubled, leaving the climbers only one-half rope length apart. In this case, the rope leader takes the ends, tied into the harness separately, and the second climber ties into the doubled middle of the rope. The prusik slings of both climbers should be on the same strand; presuming that the rope leader has a higher probability of taking a fall into a crevasse, the other rope strand may be freed and made available for the rescue. With but two on a rope a crevasse must be arrested by a single axe; more than three on a rope so shortens intervals between climbers that if one drops in a hole another is often dragged down before he has time to take any action. Due to the difficulty of crevasse rescue, *two rope teams are the recommended minimum for glacier travel*, since a single team may be pinned down in arrest position, its members unable to free themselves to begin rescue. Even if able to do so, a single rope team may be insufficient to effect rescue, and in any event extra equipment and manpower expedite matters, many times having proven the margin between failure and success. If, however, the rope teams do not travel close enough together to render immediate assistance to one another, the advantage is lost.

On glaciers where belaying is required, rope teams of two are more practical than three: the climbers usually tie in to each end of the rope and proceed, using the belay techniques described in the chapters on snow and ice climbing.

Since the main hazard of glacier travel is falling into a crevasse, and hanging from a waistloop results in constriction of the diaphragm and eventual suffocation, most modern climbers use a seat harness of some kind, either homemade of nylon tubular webbing (see Chapter 7), or one of the available commercially made climbing harnesses, with the rope tied in using one of the knots described in Chapter 7 for this purpose.

Prusik slings are attached to the rope and a chest sling and carabiner should be worn. Mechanical ascenders, if used, need not be attached to the rope before need, but must be readily accessible after a fall into a crevasse.

Rope team order on glaciers is sometimes slightly different from that described in Chapter 8. Usually the first person should be the one most experienced in detecting and avoiding crevasses, but when they are thoroughly masked, an alternative policy is for the lightest member of the party to lead, followed by the climber most skillful at belays and arrests.

The basic aim of glacier travelers is to complete their trip without falling into crevasses. Should they fail in this, however, it is even more fundamental that members of a team must never fall into the same crevasse. Consequently, whenever possible, the team *crosses the visible or suspected crevasse at right angles*. When the route precludes such a course, echelon formation is used (Fig. 16-1), somewhat awkward but good insurance that if one climber plunges into the depths his companions will not immediately join him; at the worst they will topple into neighboring chasms, a sufficiently unhappy situation, but better than everyone landing in the same hole.

An alarmingly common error is for the party to cluster close together at rest stops. A number of alpine tragedies have resulted from this convivial instinct when a chosen rendezvous proved to be the bridge over an unseen crevasse, strong enough to support one or two climbers at most. If areas of indisputable safety cannot be found, the rope must be kept extended during rests just as during travel. A party establishing camp on a snowcovered glacier similarly remains roped for a long period, stomping and probing the surface thoroughly before according any trust to the site.

During extended periods of glacier living, skis and snowshoes are often of inestimable value. Climbers equipped with such footgear distribute their weight more widely then when clumping along on boots, and by placing less strain on bridges, fall into fewer crevasses. Neither skis nor snowshoes can be considered substitutes for the rope, but in semi-arctic ranges or winter mountaineering they may be needed for easy travel, and if available give considerable insurance against falling in a crevasse as a bonus.

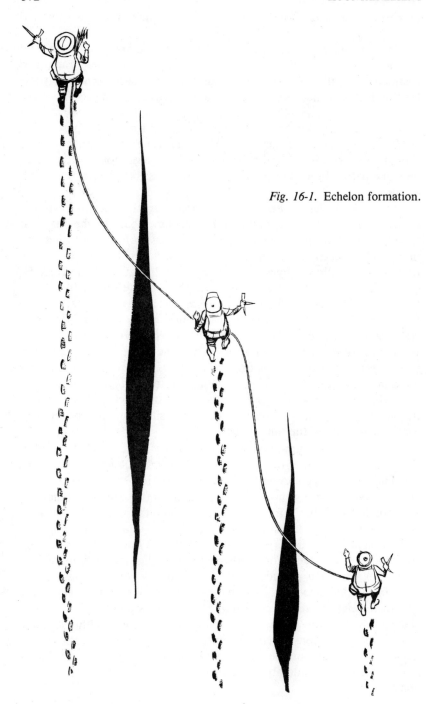

Fig. 16-1. Echelon formation.

Ice Axe and Crampons

Glaciers being rivers of snow and ice, a climber's ice axe and crampons are as important tools as his rope; their use is fully discussed in Chapters 13, 14, and 15.

Much glacier travel is on snow in which steps can be kicked as required, or the surface is of such a consistency and grade that lug-soled boots grip well enough to render crampons unnecessary. With harder snow and/or a steeper slope (say to greater than 30 degrees) crampons come into use, as they do for surfaces wholly of ice. Surface variations from snow to bare ice, and intervals of steepness, force a choice between cutting occasional steps for assistance and security or wearing crampons continuously. Most glacier climbers will wear crampons.

Many glacier climbs start before dawn, and the colder, harder snow often makes crampon wearing advisable. Conversely, the mid-day descent of the same route, through sun-softened snow, calls for removal of the crampons to avoid the danger of falls caused by balls of soft sticky snow between the points.

Wands

The description and construction of wands is covered in Chapter 13, but since they are primarily a glacier travel tool, their use is described here. Wands can be valuable aids in marking the true end of a partially exposed crevasse, identifying turns and in general, marking the climbing route for the return. Even on glacier climbs where the descent route is intended to be different from the ascent route, a party should consider the use of wands on the ascent, and weigh the possibility of retreat, particularly one caused by bad weather, against the loss of a bundle of route-marking wands.

Wand spacing on straightforward sections of a route is a function of party size and leader's judgment of weather prospects for the duration of the climb. If visibility is poor or shows a probability of deteriorating, wand spacing as close as the total party length, when roped and moving in single file, may be appropriate. For a "typical"climbing party (if there is such a thing) of three ropes of three people each, this would be a spacing of between 80 and 110 yards. A route so marked can be descended in zero visibility conditions by "feeling" the way from wand to wand. When the *last* person in the party reaches a wand, the word is passed forward, and if the leader does not have the next wand at hand, in sight, underfoot or whatever, the party immediately stops until the leader locates it. This procedure is repeated for each interval. As an assist for this sort of exercise, it is helpful, when placing wands, to angle them back along the route, so that they become pointers. This somewhat reduces height, and visibility of the wand, but can be compensated for by using longer wands. If less severe conditions are experienced than those described above, spacing between wands can be more generous; however, when wanding a route, remember that the search for the wands will be downhill on the return, so try not to place them in hollows, or on the down side of ridges. A turn, or a significant feature of the route such as the pinched-out end of a partially exposed crevasse, is often marked with a pair of wands, as is the uphill side of a bridge across a crevasse.

Clothing

Despite sometimes sweltering conditions on glacier surfaces, the iciness of crevasse interiors must be taken into account. Trousers, at least, should be of wool for travel on a crevassed glacier, and warm wool upper garments (shirts or sweaters) should be worn, or carried. It might be possible, while hanging in a crevasse, to struggle into a wool shirt, but putting on a pair of trousers under these conditions is an exercise best left to the imagination.

Crevasses

Except when photography is the object of the trip the best route is one that completely avoids all crevasses if possible. Simple and self-evident as such strategy seems, determining such a route may be difficult. Although scale cannot be accurately estimated from far away, the "distant view" is important. As one approaches a glacier, the long angle from the valley frequently tells more about the surface than the foreshortened perspective from the surface itself. A downward or cross-valley view is even more valuable. From a distance the route may be quite obvious, while once among icefalls and crevasse fields, finding a route that "goes" may be a matter of blind luck. Often it is worthwhile to make a quick pencil sketch of significant features of the route, as an aid to memory, and to mark the relative positions of major crevasses and other barriers.

Although valuable, the distant view does not reveal all. Often a crevasse which from far away appears a mere crack turns out to be many feet wide. However, if one crevasse can be seen from several miles away, odds are that on close approach it will prove to be merely the largest of a cluster. Finally, even if the climbers have a near view of the terrain to be traveled and can see every tiny break in the surface, hidden crevasses must always be suspected.

Some familiarity with the mechanics of glacier motion and the development of crevasses is helpful to the glacier traveler. Fig. 16-2 and 16-3 sketch aerial and cross-section views of a "typical" glacier, with features important to climbers identified. A living glacier, even one which at any given time may have a retreating snout, is sliding downhill off the

Fig. 16-2. Glacial features.

Ice Features

A. Moat
B. Bergschrund
C. Firn line
D. Crescentric crevasses
E. Nunatak
F. En echelon crevasses
G. Marginal crevasses
H. Terminus or snout
I. Braided outwash stream

Moraine Features

1. Lateral moraine
2. Medial moraine
3. Terminal moraine
4. Outwash plain (and ground
    moraine)
5. Erratic
6. Old terminal moraine
7. Old lateral moraine

mountain under the influence of gravity and the weight of accumulating snow and ice on its upper regions (accumulation zone). It is this glacier movement which generates crevasses, in combination with the friction of the ice mass against its bed and modified by obstructions, changes in direction, and steepness. These crevasses may be hidden or visible, mere cracks or huge, few or many in any particular area—but they are there.

It is a moot point among mountaineers whether to climb glaciers early in the season when last winter's snow bridges many crevasses, or to climb late in the season when most crevasses are open. Current practice seems to favor early season climbs following routes which (if possible) traverse areas of lesser incidence of crevasses. Understanding what controls crevasse formation is helpful in planning such a route.

Crescentric crevasses (Fig. 16-2) develop wherever the ice increases its rate of flow, commonly where the glacier bed steepens. The change in angle may be so small it is not evident on the surface and is only indicated by belts of crevasses forming long arcs concave downvalley, at right angles to the direction of flow.

If the incline is very steep, an *icefall* forms (Fig. 16-3), the surface broken into a profusion of crevasses extending every which way, with large ice towers or *seracs*. Below a sharp declivity there may be no crevasses, since the glacier is slowing down after its plunge, but sometimes pressure from the cataract above buckles the surface into *pressure ridges,* with attendant crevasses. In a steep icefall a considerable portion of the downward advance is by avalanches, a hazard that influences routes both through a fall or anywhere underneath one.

Lateral marginal crevasses (Fig. 16-2) are opened by the faster motion of a glacier's center relative to its sides, where friction along the valley walls has a restraining effect. Lateral crevasses invariably trend upvalley. The characteristic of both crescentric and lateral fractures to angle upstream toward the glacier center is frequently useful in guessing the

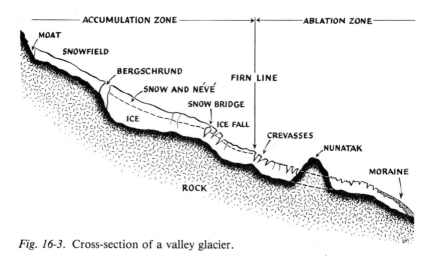

Fig. 16-3. Cross-section of a valley glacier.

hidden extension from a single surface hole. Crevassing, however, is not so simply methodical, for minor surface stresses produce random fractures which follow no pattern whatsoever. Protuberances of rock through the ice, *nunataks* (Fig. 16-2 and 16-3) usually have a halo of crevasses and thus are best avoided, but if the rock does not quite reach the surface, the crevasse pattern may completely baffle the routefinder. The only general rule applicable to crevasse location is that they can occur anywhere and anyhow on a glacier.

Crevasses are most hazardous to the climber in the zone of accumulation, where they are frequently bridged by snow. New snow may completely fill the depths, or with the assistance of a cornice-building wind, may arch over inner emptiness. The entire structure may melt away or collapse of its own weight during the summer, leaving an obvious pit. Often glacier motion widens the crevasse and by stretching the bridge cracks it open; the climber who assumes the visible thin fissure represents the entire width of the chasm can be unpleasantly surprised.

At the glacier's upper limit is a giant crevasse, the *bergschrund* (Fig. 16-2 and 16-3), formed where the moving part of the glacier breaks away from the ice cap. Sometimes the bergschrund is the final problem of the ascent, with the summit only a short stroll above. If the glacier is diminishing, the surface lowers, leaving a steep arcuate precipice above, which may be capped by hanging glaciers with still more menacing crevasses and bergschrunds. Above the highest bergschrund there is often perched a snowfield separated from the rock face by a *moat* (Fig. 16-2 and 16-3) formed partially by melting and partially by creep, thus being similar in origin to a bergschrund and frequently every bit as difficult to cross.

Detecting Crevasses

While traversing a glacier, the climber should continually search the route ahead for indications of hidden holes. Suspicion increases in areas likely to be crevassed, such as the sides of the glacier, around nunataks, and icefalls, and at any sharp bends or drops. Memory or photos may be useful, for on many glaciers crevasse patterns change little from year to year. A thin snowcover which masks crevasses without bridging them is particularly hazardous, and extreme caution is mandatory in late spring, after snowfalls, and near exposed ice. Once one crevasse is discovered the climber does well to keep in mind that crevasses usually form in parallel belts, and usually have hidden extensions.

When a crevasse is suspected, the climber seeks visual clues, all of which stem from the natural inclination of snow arching over emptiness to *sag* under the pull of gravity, creating a shallow trough with a linear form that distinguishes it from suncups, which tend to be circular. A sag smoothed over by a continuing succession of storms gives no surface indication of its existence, but any interval of good weather allows gravity to do its work; the sag may then give itself away by a slight difference in sheen, texture, or color. Snow in the trough may have a flat white look and a fine texture from being newer than the old névé, but may be dirtier from collecting windblown particles of dust, or may have the chalky appearance typical of a windslab, since the trough presents the wind with a lee slope. Proper light helps in spotting sags. In the dull illumination of fog and in the glare of midday sun details are blurred. With moderate light from a low angle, such as in early morning or late afternoon, differences in snow textures are distinctly revealed and shadows outline the characteristic linear form of the sag.

Very commonly there is not the slightest clue to the location, size, and direction of crevasses, and the party must *probe* the surface with ice axes. Continuous probing is scarcely practical through a large suspected area but it is advisable at points of maximum probability; that is, on the lips and at the ends of open crevasses, across all sags and dubious bridges.

The axehead is held firmly in the arrest grasp and attached to the climber by the wristloop. The shaft is thrust into the surface well *in advance of the climber's weight, with a smooth sensitive motion*, the angle as *nearly vertical* as convenient, since otherwise the climber is merely skimming the surface rather than penetrating the underlayers. If resistance to the thrust is uniform it has been established that the snow is solid at least to the depth of the shaft. If resistance abruptly lessens, probably a hole has been found, and further thrusts are made to establish its extent. The value of probing depends largely on the climber's sensitivity to changes in resistance and his skill in interpreting the meaning of such changes. The shaft may seem suddenly to plunge into space when actually it has merely broken through a buried crust into a softer stratum. In the structure of the axe, a smooth line from spike to shaft is essential for accuracy: a blunt-pointed spike or a jutting ferrule may give a false reading. The length of the shaft remains a limiting factor, since obviously all one can find out is whether a bridge is as thick as the shaft is long. In heavily crevassed areas, where the holes are smoothly surfaced with recently fallen snow, a shovel is a valuable addition to the leader's equipment. With it he can dig through the roof of a crevasse discovered by probing and visually determine its width, length, and direction.

NEGOTIATING A ROUTE

End Run

If a crevasse pinches out anywhere within reasonable distance the end run (Fig. 16-4) is preferred over other tactical maneuvers, even though it

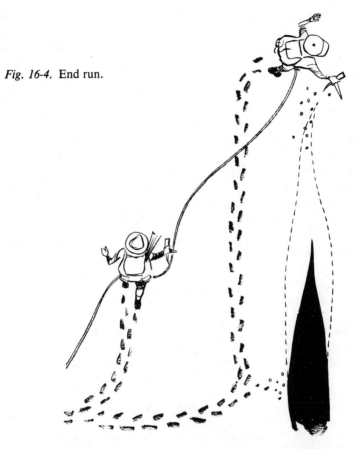

Fig. 16-4. End run.

may involve traveling half a mile to gain a dozen feet of forward progress; the time taken to walk around is generally much less than necessary
to force a direct crossing. Important to remember in an end run is the almost invariably hidden extension of a visible crevasse. Climbers frequently err by aiming at the visible end; unless the true, or subsurface,
end has been clearly seen during the approach it is wise to make a very
wide swing around the corner. In late summer the visible end is often the
true end of a crevasse, but early in the season even the tiniest surface
crack may be a chink in the roof of an immense cold cavern.

Bridges

When end runs are impractical because of the distance involved or because the ends of the crevasses are adjacent to other crevasses, the party
looks for bridges. One variety consists of remnant snowcover sagging
over an inner vacuity. Another kind is less a bridge than an isthmus be-

tween two crevasses with a foundation that extends downward into the body of the glacier.

Ideally any bridge should be closely and completely examined before use. A side view may give a stamp of such unqualified approval that the party can stride across in perfect confidence. If overhanging snow obscures dimensions the leader must explore at closer range, probing the depth and smashing at the sides, walking delicately all the while and equally ready for an arrest or a sudden drop. The second gives a belay, anchored by the third team member, who is also prepared to start rescue if the leader falls (Fig. 16-5).

A bridge excessively narrow for walking or apparently quite weak may be crossed by straddling, or even slithering on the stomach, thereby lowering the center of gravity and distributing weight over a broader area. When the bridge is extremely dubious but still the only feasible route, much care, and secure belays for all members of the climbing party, are required. Middle climbers on ropes of three should be belayed from both front and rear. All should walk with light feet and take care to step exactly in the established tracks without the slightest deviation.

Bridges vary in strength with changes in temperature. In the cold of winter or early morning the thinnest and airiest of arches can have incredible structural stength; when crystals melt in the afternoon sun even the grandest bridge may suddenly collapse of its own weight. Each must be tested with care, being neither abandoned nor trusted until its worth is

Fig. 16-5. Crossing bridged crevasse.

Fig. 16-6. Crossing sunken bridge.

determined. Moreover, dependability in the morning does not mean that testing can be omitted in the afternoon.

Jumping

Narrow cracks can be stepped across, but increased width requires jumping, often faster than an end run and sometimes the only possible passage. Crevasse jumping, however, is one of the alpine techniques dramatized far out of proportion to its importance, although distinction must be made between the routine hops of fact and the long desperate leaps customary in novels and movies.

Care must be taken to find the precise edge of the crevasse, which often overhangs. The jumper holds his axe in the arrest position in case he falls short and must claw for purchase on the far side. The belayer leaves slack in the rope exceeding the width of the crevasse: at best harsh words may result if the jumper makes a splendid effort but while still in forward flight is suddenly snapped backward by a taut rope.

A running jump can carry somewhat farther than a standing one, but not so far as usually expected. With full gear it is difficult to get up much momentum, particularly since the dashing climber is likely to plunge deep into the snow, or perhaps even through the overhanging lip of the crevasse — an inglorious conclusion to a thrilling beginning. If the jump is so long that a run is required, the approach is first carefully packed. Before takeoff the lead man leaves his rucksack and other encumbrances with

Fig. 16-7. Jumping a crevasse.

companions, rolls down shirt sleeves and puts on mittens, checks his waist knot and prusik slings. In point of fact, running jumps are not often practical: most are made from a standing start or with but two or three lead-up steps. Unlike the heroes of fiction the ordinary real-life mountaineer finds more than adequate challenge in leaps of 3 or 4 feet on a flat surface; if he falters in midflight he at least has a fighting chance to claw over the lip with axe and feet. A jump is obviously much less dangerous once one climber is across, for then the belay is on the landing side and if the second man falls short he has assistance from the rope in scrambling out of the hole.

Downhill jumping, such as from the overhanging wall of a berg-schrund, is a different matter entirely. With momentum from a descending run a climber may perhaps clear prodigious horizontal distances. Such leaps, however, are made only in desperation. Danger can be minimized by a proper landing position, with the feet slightly apart for balance, knees relaxed to absorb shock, axe held ready for arrest, and the belayer alert. Still, the landing platform is an unknown quantity that may be so weak the climber plunges through into the crevasse, or so hard he breaks both legs. Moreover, the choice between jumping and slower methods of passage usually is made late in the day when weary climbers are likely to forget the brittleness of bones, the forces generated by a falling body, and the world record for the broad jump.

CREVASSE RESCUE

Thus far this chapter has concentrated on avoiding crevasses. However, because of the probability of encountering completely hidden crevasses, and of falling into an open crevasse because a snow bridge collapses or for other reason, avoidance may not be possible, and thus anyone setting foot on a glacier should be practiced in the techniques of crevasse rescue.

In many cases, a speedy spread eagle by the unfortunate climber, and a tight rope applied by the other team members, will prevent excessive penetration into a hidden crevasse, and he can crawl or be pulled to (relative) safety. When a climber is well and truly in a crevasse, there are five proven rescue techniques, discussed below.

Main force is a simple, often-ignored technique, requiring only that an adequate number of pullers be available at the site of the fall. Thus this technique is most applicable to climbing parties of several rope teams, where good glacier climbing practice has kept the party together. Most simply stated, this rescue method entails an adequate number of climbers taking hold of the rope to the fallen climber and pulling him out. No co-operative action is required from the victim and so this method is applicable to the rescue of an injured or unconscious person.

Z-pulley is a method of providing mechanical advantage to the system for hauling out a fallen climber, and allows a smaller labor force to accomplish a rescue than that required for main force. Like main force, the Z-pulley method requires no effort from the victim. Two rope teams should be adequate for a Z-pulley rescue, which is described in detail later in this chapter.

Single-pulley is another method of applying mechanical advantage to the crevasse rescue problem. Although Z-pulley has a greater theoretical mechanical advantage, single-pulley has the practical advantage that, once in place, the haul-out is more simply performed and faster than a Z-pulley. However, the single-pulley method usually requires an additional rope (besides the one from which the fallen climber hangs) and always requires a conscious, co-operating victim. The method is described below.

Prusiking, described in detail in Chapter 7, is a method by which a climber who has fallen into a crevasse may climb out. A self-help rescue method which does not require a large number of rescuers, it is, however, possible only for a conscious, relatively uninjured victim.

Bilgeri, another technique applicable to crevasse rescue, is useful to a small party or isolated rope team. Like prusiking, bilgeri requires positive action from the victim.

Preparation

A successful crevasse rescue, by any method, depends on advance planning and proper "gearing up" of each member of the climbing party. As an automatic part of roping up for the glacier, each climber should attach prusik slings to the rope, with the foot loops put down through the climbing harness waistband and tucked away, usually in the trouser side pockets on the appropriate side. A middleman should attach one prusik to his rope in front and one behind, since in a fall he may be caught by either end. If mechanical ascenders are used, they may be attached to the rope as described for prusik slings or carried in an easily accessible location. In addition to prusik slings (or ascenders), each climber should have a rescue pulley, several carabiners, and nylon or perlon runners easily available for setting up a pulley system. A chest sling and carabiner, to aid in prusiking, are worn by many climbers—a recommended practice. As part of the preparation for a possible crevasse rescue, each climber clothes himself adequately. Shorts and a sweat band is a uniform which ensures zero survival time in the depths of a crevasse.

Since any member of a glacier climbing party may fall into a crevasse, *every* member should be practiced in the techniques of crevasse rescue *before* setting foot on a glacier.

First Moves

If a climber falls into a crevasse, the first and most important action of the other member(s) of the rope team is to drop into and hold the most solid possible self-arrest position. Once the fallen climber is stopped, the actual rescue can begin. Unless an adequate number of other climbers is available right at the site, to immediately haul out the victim by main force, the first rescue action is for the victim's rope partners to stabilize the rope and free themselves to begin or assist the extraction process.

Assuming a three-man rope team with one endman in a crevasse, the following actions are taken:

1. The middleman and remaining endman plan and prepare for the middleman to take over the whole load of the fallen climber.
2. The endman gradually transfers the load to the middleman, staying ready to take up his share again should the middleman prove unable to hold it alone.
3. Once free of the load, the endman moves up to a position on the rope between the middleman and the victim, but closer to the middleman (the victim may have fallen through the middle of a wide, but roofed crevasse), on solid snow (probe quickly). The endman plants his ice axe shaft solidly in the snow (this is no place for shorty ice axes), next to the tight rope, with the head at right angles to the line of the rope and with the top of the shaft angled back, away from the crevasse (see Fig. 16-8).

   The endman then attaches a sling to the tight climbing rope with a prusik knot and to the shaft of the axe, snugging the knot to the rope and extending the sling out from the axe.

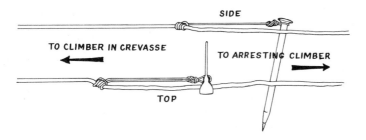

Fig. 16-8. Anchoring climber in crevasse.

4. The endman guards the prusik knot and the planted ice axe while the middleman gradually transfers the load to this anchor. The middleman stays ready to resume the load if the anchored ice axe/prusik combination appears insecure.

5. Once the rope to the victim is secured to the anchored ice axe, the middleman assumes guardianship of that anchor, giving his ice axe to the endman and freeing the endman to advance *cautiously,* probing with the ice axe to the edge of the crevasse, or hole, to check on the victim.

6. In addition to guarding the anchor, the middleman should maintain a boot-axe belay on the endman during his reconnaissance.

7. The endman establishes communications with the victim, if possible, determining his consciousness, condition, extent of any injuries, ability to help in rescue, etc.

8. Unless necessary to restore breathing or circulation, or to relieve significant discomfort, the fallen climber should wait until the rope has been stabilized and anchored before taking any self-help action which would jerk or swing the rope.

9. The fallen climber should pull himself upright, clipping the rope into the chest sling carabiner, if one is worn. The prusik sling foot loops are put over the boots (this can be an experience when wearing crampons and a heavy pack) and the knots are slid up the rope, through the chest sling carabiner, until the weight can be taken on the prusik slings and off the harness.

Speed, with caution, is important to the well-being of the victim. The preparatory actions described above, once understood and practiced, are considerably faster to do than to describe.

The Rescue

The preparatory phase completed, the rest of the rescue can be accomplished by the most appropriate of the methods detailed below. All participants should be aware of the high probability of other crevasses in the area and never move about unroped. If several rope teams are involved in the rescue, a work area should be probed and if crevasses are discovered, they should be marked with wands and avoided. Any rescuer who must approach, or work, near the crevasse edge should be belayed. Whatever rescue method is used, an ice axe should be placed under the rope to the victim at the edge of the crevasse to prevent further trenching of the rope into the snow, and the axe anchored so as not to be lost.

Main force rescue is accomplished by two or three rope teams of climbers laying hands on the rope to the fallen climber and pulling him out by hauling in unison, hand over hand or walking backwards. In this rescue method, as in the other haul-out methods (Z-pulley, single-pulley) the victim should remember to keep his hands clear of the rope as he comes out over the edge of the crevasse.

Fig. 16-9. Z-pulley system. For clarity of illustration no anchors for the climbers are shown. All should be connected to anchors.

The *Z-pulley system* is set up using the rope to the fallen climber, as shown in Fig. 16-9. Thus, the middleman of the rope team with the fallen climber must unrope to facilitate the rope's passage through the pulley system. His position is guarding the anchoring ice axe and he will also guide and reset the anchoring prusik knot during the pulley operation. Being unroped, he should not leave this position and unless the slope is uncommonly level he should hook up to the anchor with a security sling.

To set up the Z-pulley system, the climbing rope is laid out in a "Z" pattern, one apex of which is snapped into a pulley located at the main anchor. A short sling, fastened with a prusik knot to the climbing rope near the crevasse edge, is connected to a pulley to the other apex. As the rope is hauled in, the floating pulley on the short sling moves upward toward the main anchor pulley. Now the rope is anchored with the safety sling attached to the main anchor while the pullers slide the sling attaching the floating pulley down for a new grip. Too long a pull at one setting must not be attempted — if the two pulleys touch, the "Z" will snap out of the rope and the mechanical advantage will suddenly be lost, with a corresponding increase in effort required. Mechanical advantage is regained as soon as the pulleys move apart again. For greatest efficiency the main anchor should be well back from the crevasse, and all ropes should pull as nearly parallel as possible to the loaded rope. A long lift with each setting of the safety prusik knots speeds the operation.

Sometimes the terrain is cramped and a pull in the opposite direction may be necessary, toward the edge of the crevasse. Theoretically the same mechanical advantage with reversed pull can be obtained, with a system similar to the one illustrated, by rigging another pulley from an additional anchor located near the main anchor. In practice the added friction reduces the overall system's mechanical advantage somewhat. There is also great risk of pulling out the additional anchor, which must therefore be well guarded if this system is used.

An unconscious or seriously injured victim cannot assist in his rescue, but one who is able can participate by prusiking while the rescue team is working. Each foot prusiked is a foot less that needs to be gained by the pulley haul.

The *single-pulley system*, shown in Fig. 16-10, can be a very useful rescue technique where the rope from which the victim hangs has become deeply trenched into the snow, either from the original fall or because an ice axe was not placed under it at the lip of the crevasse. A single-pulley rescue is usually performed with an extra rope. However, if the victim is not in too far, the free portion of the climbing rope (that portion not being used to anchor the victim) may be used.

Presuming the availability of an extra rope (the climbing rope of the rescue team), the procedure is as follows: the rescue team frees enough rope to drop a doubled loop to the victim. A rescue pulley is attached with a carabiner to the loop of the double portion of the rescue rope. The doubled rope with the pulley and carabiner is lowered to the victim over an ice axe placed at the lip of the crevasse. The victim clips the carabiner into his seat harness. After attaching the pulley and determining which

Fig. 16-10. Single-pulley system. Pulley is attached to seat harness of climber being raised. Note: more than one person would normally be required to effect the rescue.

side will be the "up moving" rope, the victim clips the "up moving" rope into his chest carabiner to reduce the tendency to topple over backwards.

While the rope with the pulley and carabiner is being lowered to the victim, other members of the rescue team should be anchoring one end of the rescue rope. When the victim is clipped into the pulley, the rescue team pulls on the other end of the loop rope as directed. Simultaneously the climbing rope is raised and passed through the safety prusik sling to eliminate the possibility of suddenly dropping the victim into the crevasse again should the pulley system fail. The victim, having tucked away all loose ends of clothing and equipment, assists, if not hanging free, by scrambling up the wall on all fours, using hands and feet to gain any possible purchase.

After the victim's weight has been taken off his climbing rope, but before he has been hauled up to the edge of the crevasse, the climbing rope should be freed from its trench in the snow to prevent its interfering with the final haul-out.

Prusiking as the sole rescue method can be a slower, more difficult process under actual climbing conditions than when practiced in a clean-edged crevasse, on a level section of glacier under sunny skies. However, if other rope team members cannot free themselves, and if assistance from other climbers is unobtainable, the self-rescue method of prusiking may be the only way out. Techniques are as described in Chapter 7 with the added problem of wet or icy rope and slings and the difficulty of working the prusik knots over the crevasse lip.

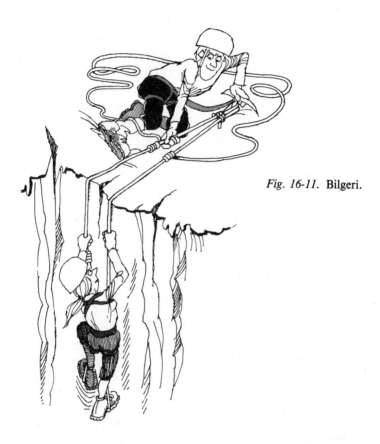

Fig. 16-11. Bilgeri.

Bilgeri (Fig. 16-11), a rescue technique from earlier climbing generations, may be useful in a modified form in some crevasse rescue situations. A rope team of three with one fallen into a crevasse, and without assistance from other rope teams, *may* find it easier to self-rescue with the bilgeri method than by prusiking out. Like prusiking, bilgeri requires both hands and feet, making it practicable only for uninjured, or slightly injured, climbers. Also, if laid goldline rope is involved, its low-load stretch renders bilgeri ineffective if the fallen climber is at all deep in the crevasse.

After the fall has been arrested, the load must be transferred to the middleman as described previously in "First Moves." The endman anchors the fallen climber, unties the rope from his harness, ties a loop in the rope end large enough for a foot loop, and lowers it to the fallen climber. The rope with the loop is secured to the anchor with a second prusik sling as shown in Fig. 16-11. The fallen climber places one foot in the rope loop and the other foot in one prusik sling, then simply unweights (lifts) one foot, the right for example, calls "Right," the rescuer above pulls in slack in that rope and resets the prusik to the anchor. The fallen climber steps on the right sling and lifts his left foot, calling "Left." The upper climber then pulls in the slack on that side, sliding the prusik sling out to hold the rope tight. The above sequence of right and left is repeated until the fallen climber is extricated. This method has an advantage over prusik, or the pulley systems, when the crevasse lip is surmounted: since the rope being pulled is unweighted, there is less tendency for the prusik knot to hang up on the lip.

The foregoing discussions have not addressed considerations of crevasse rescues from steep slopes, or falls through the middle of wide-roofed crevasses, or alternatives to rescue back out the way the victim entered, or crevasse lip problems. All are real-world situations to which the following comments apply.

If a fall into a crevasse has occurred from a steep slope above the crevasse, overall security of both the rescuers and the victim may be increased if the operation can be moved to the slope below the crevasse. The practicality of such a move is enhanced if rescuers are already available below the crevasse.

A fall through the middle of a roofed, wide crevasse presents added problems for both the victim and rescuers. The victim may be hanging free, without a stabilizing wall to support him and rescue efforts may dislodge quantities of snow and/or ice to fall on him. The rescuers, to establish communication with the victim and prepare for the rescue, will be moving onto an area of proven weakness and must take particular care not to add to the roster of victims. Additionally, the climbing rope to the victim will usually be more or less deeply trenched into the snow. Probably the best rescue procedure for such situations is to not waste time trying to establish separate communication holes or sending down other climbers to assist (presuming the victim is conscious), but rather to stabilize the lip of the hole as quickly as possible with an ice axe under the rope at the lip and to conduct an expeditious haul-out by whatever of the previously described methods seems most applicable. If the particular situation finds the victim raised up under a considerable overhang (or the snow roof), one he cannot surmount, then consideration should be given to a judicious enlarging of the hole by a well-belayed rescuer, with as much as possible of the removed snowcover being scraped or thrown *away* from the hole to minimize what falls on the victim.

Every crevasse fall may not be best resolved by the classic rescue methods of hauling out the victim. The crevasse and surrounding features should be surveyed to determine if ledges exist to which the victim may be lowered or swung, or if the crevasse bottoms out or opens up on the glacier. A crevasse fall victim may well be able to walk out the end or stem/climb a snow ramp to the surface. If a ledge, or the crevasse bottom is available for the lowering, it should be utilized, since the victim's wait and preparation for rescue will be more comfortable than either hanging in his harness or standing in slings. Additionally, the climbing rope to the victim will be unloaded and easier to prepare for rescue. However, even though the victim is on a ledge, or the crevasse "bottom," the rope to him must continue to be anchored and guarded.

With all rescue methods great difficulty can be encountered in bringing the victim the final few feet to the surface. The climbing rope tends to cut into the crevasse edge in stopping the fall: unless buffered with an ice axe the rope saws deeper still during the rescue and may utterly vanish into a deep groove, freezing there so that no amount of effort can budge it. A person thus stalled is in serious trouble.

One solution is to tunnel down along the rope, taking care not to drop debris on the victim. Failing that, rescuers can drop a spare rope to which the victim shifts his weight while the other is freed. Usually the rope can be peeled back out of the slot once it is unweighted. If that fails, it may be necessary to *carefully* chop away the adjacent snow.

If spare line is not available the stuck rope must be salvaged. In the prusik method a person usually, by the time he reaches the buried section of rope, is trailing enough slack to reach his rescuers. He ties in again to his climbing rope near his prusiks and then unties his original waist knot and sends up the end on a retrieving line. With this anchored he can retie his foot slings on the free rope and resume ascent.

Even when the rope has not gouged deeply into the lip there is always the problem of prusiking the last few feet: when the knots bear against the wall, the final stretch must be surmounted by a scramble or a hard upper haul. It is much easier for the climber to scramble over the lip when he remembers to *unclip his chest sling* from his prusik slings and/or climbing rope. In a pulley rescue the last bit over the lip may similarly require brute strength, though usually by the time the imbedded portion of the rope is reached enough slack has been hauled in for free ends to be lowered.

If the rope has gouged into the lip so deeply that the victim is pulled into the wall rather than over the edge, a sling can be attached to the rope behind the lip to use as a step to get up over the edge.

Icefalls

A glacier climb may include icefalls in the best (or only) route to the summit, and while they may appear forbidding, their broken-up condition may offer relatively easy going to the astute routefinder. Good routefinding through the confused jumble can often reduce an apparently steep wall to a series of no more than 40- to 50-degree pitches.

The advisability of an icefall route depends on the stability of the icefall in question; fresh debris, or the lack of it, may indicate what can be expected. Icefalls are often protected from avalanches by the broken nature of the terrain, but it is most important to be aware of any snow or ice masses poised above. Routefinding can be tricky, with progress suddenly and abruptly halted by an enormous crevasse or a blank wall. Once in the icefall, the climbers' view may be restricted to the array of seracs and crevasses in the immediate vicinity. For this reason, the party should get a distant look before entering the icefall, and where practical select in advance each portion of the route and each avenue of escape, taking special pains to memorize salient landmarks, particularly those adjacent to unstable areas that must be climbed as rapidly as possible and at the optimum time of day. Appearance or disappearance of the sun can cause thawing or freezing, and in both cases, avalanches. Exits or refuges, such as cleavers, should be noted for use in case of need, and on warm days or with a southern exposure, the risk of seracs becoming unglued and crashing down on the party will preclude climbing some icefall routes altogether.

While working out an interesting icefall route, and perhaps alternating ordinary glacier travel with belayed ice climbing techniques, a climbing party should never forget that the icefall is part of a glacier, with hidden crevasses an ever-present hazard.

Rockfall Hazard on Glaciated Peaks

Any mountain terrain is more or less subject to rockfall, but the erosional effect of glaciers make glaciated peaks particularly susceptible. Most glaciers which are used as climbing routes have ground themselves into softer sections of the mountain, leaving somewhat harder ridges, cleavers, walls or aretes towering overhead as prime sources of rockfall. When the glaciated peak of interest is volcanic in origin the potential for frequent and dangerous rockfall is increased because of the usually rotten, unstable nature of volcanic rock.

Rockfall upon the unlucky glacier traveler may be induced by factors as unpredictable as earthquake or random chance; however, there are relationships between rockfall and time of day, time of year, daily temperature change, etc., which allow a knowledgeable climbing party to minimize the hazard.

Given a normal winter accumulation of snow and ice, an early season climb is less subject to rockfall than one later in the summer because of the cementing effect of the remaining snowcover. Whatever the season, early on and early off is a good practice for glacier climbs. Higher elevation nighttime temperatures, even in midsummer, are often cold enough to freeze loose rock in place and prevent most rockfall, but direct sunshine, as a warming agent, incites rockfall by progressively melting ever deeper areas of binding ice, and converting it to lubricating liquid. The two daily periods of greatest hazard are morning, when the sun melts the previous night's ice bonds, and evening, when cooling temperatures refreeze the meltwater which in expanding may break loose rocks to fall on the glacier below.

In the northern hemisphere, more hours per day of relative freedom from rockfall can usually be found on northern exposures. Southern and eastern slopes are affected earliest by the sun and thus should be climbed earliest.

Hard hats are recommended for any glacier climb through areas of known or potential rockfall.

 PART FIVE

Safe Climbing

Plate 23. Cornice on Himalchuli, Tibetan border peaks of Sringi Himal behind.
(John Cleare)

17 *

CLIMBING SAFETY

As MOUNTAINEERING IS among the most rewarding of sports, so too it can be among the most demanding. The dangers, like the rewards, are found on both physical and psychological levels; disregard or ignorance of any of these hazards may cause the loss not only of the pleasurable benefits, but even of life. This book would be incomplete if it did not outline how to recognize and avoid the hazards and how to realize the ultimate goal of returning safely from the mountains.

From the very outset all climbers should realize that the burden of safety and accident prevention rests with the individual. Through skill, knowledge, suspicion, and caution, the probability of having an accident can be reduced almost to nil.

ELEMENTS OF DANGER:
THE STATISTICAL PICTURE

Sooner or later in their careers, climbers encounter situations of potential accident, and it is well for them to be forewarned of the most common factors which contribute to mountain accidents, and to reflect upon the basic sources of mountaineering hazards.

Since 1947 the American Alpine Club has published annual descriptions and analyses of climbing accidents in North America. These are available in booklet form and demand close study by every mountaineer. During the decade 1951-60, 345 accidents were recorded in the United States, 122 of which were fatal; between 1961-70, 756 accidents were listed from the United States and Canada, with 209 people killed. For the eight years, 1971-1978, so far reported in the decade of this publication, the corresponding numbers have again increased, to 1038 accidents with 348 fatalities. Only true climbing accidents are included in these totals, as distinguished from those which merely occur in mountain regions. Moreover, the tally shows only those accidents voluntarily reported. Numerous others, even fatalities, occur each year which are never publicized beyond the immediate vicinity. Furthermore, these recorded tragedies are but a fraction of the total world loss; in Europe and in Japan, where large numbers of people regularly engage in mountaineering, the toll is many times greater than in North America.

The statistics published in these annual reports roughly indicate the elements of danger in the sport of climbing, and they show the basic patterns which recur again and again. The most common causes of the accidents reported were (1) fall or slip on rock; (2) slip on snow and ice, and (3) falling rock or other object. The most common contributing causes were (1) climbing unroped, (2) exceeding abilities (inexperienced), and (3) inadequate equipment.

Although every accident is a little different from every other, many of the contributing factors are surprisingly common, and most of the varied causes involve human frailties. Failure of rappels, ropes, pitons, and knots due to improper use is frequent. Injuries from failure of half-learned techniques in exposed situations are common. Mistakes in judgment are as varied as the personalities of the people who make them.

Study of statistics and evaluations of accidents enable mountaineers to make use of the unfortunate experience of others to evaluate their own actions. As climbers absorb the experience of others they begin to realize that the maxims of the Climbing Code (Chapter 1) are not arbitrary, but have been forged from actual misfortune. They develop a sound judgment and an attitude which limits danger to a sane proportion of the endeavor. They understand the demands and accept the responsibilities and thus become mountaineers.

CLIMBING HAZARDS

The hazards of mountaineering fall into two basic divisions, and an understanding of the dual nature of the problem is essential for the development of a safe attitude. Perhaps the most easily recognized are the objective or physical hazards inherent in the very structure of the mountains and their environment. No less important, but far harder to evaluate are the subjective hazards which arise from the complexity of the all-too-human climber.

Objective Hazards: The Physical Dangers

Natural Processes

The objective hazards include all the natural processes which exist or operate inevitably, whether or not man is involved. Darkness, storms, lightning, cold, precipitation, altitude, avalanches, rockfall, "acts of God" —all such impersonal factors fall into this category.

Mountains are turbulent places, full of swift violence, where humans are dwarfed by comparison. Climbers who cultivate the dynamic view of the mountain will be amazed at the persistence of the continuous destructive forces but never surprised by the rapidity with which conditions can change. The snow that loosens all day and slides in late afternoon, the little midday cloud that unleashes lightning by 3 o'clock — these are things mountaineers cannot control and therefore must learn to recognize and avoid. They are awed by the part natural forces play—and wisely arrange to be elsewhere while the game is on.

To avoid destruction climbers first learn *how to recognize* the impending signs of these hazards and second, *how to avoid* them. If they have learned their lessons from other chapters of this book they know there are places on a mountain where the surface disintegration proceeds more slowly, with long intervals between avalanche or rock slide. They recognize the possibility of rockfall and wear hard hats to reduce their vulnerability. They tread lightly to avoid knocking down loose rocks on climbing companions, and realize that with alertness and mental resolution they can avoid essentially all such man-caused rockfall. They know where hidden crevasses might exist, they rope up and choose routes which minimize the possibility of falling into one, and they are prepared to extricate themselves or companions in event of snowbridge collapse. They have learned to recognize avalanche-prone slopes and what to do in case of being caught in an avalanche. With experience, they develop the keenness of their observations and the astuteness of their judgment to choose the right route at the right time to avoid being caught by what are generally called accidents.

Among the objective hazards confronting climbers, the route- and terrain-type hazards are perhaps more evident—simply because of their physical presence—than the weather-type hazards: cold, wind, rain, snow, storm, lightning, fog, white-out, sun, and darkness. Consideration should be given by climbers to each of these potential hazards although they generally are not catastrophic unless the climbers are unprepared. However, weather-induced hazards are deserving of the serious attention of every mountaineer, namely, avalanches, hypothermia and lightning.

Hypothermia

Of the many objective hazards that lurk in the wilderness perhaps the most insidious and least understood is hypothermia — the lowering of the body's inner core temperature by cold, wetness, wind, and fatigue. Cold need not be extreme — deaths have occurred at temperatures well above freezing. Wetness could be caused by rain, melting snow, immersion, or even perspiration. Wind vastly increases the chilling effect of cold and wetness (see wind chill chart, Chapter 2), and fatigue lessens the victims' ability to protect themselves.

Understanding the effects of cold on the body aids in understanding the genesis of hypothermia. The first response to exposure to cold is constriction of the blood vessels of the skin and, later, of the subcutaneous tissue. The effect is to decrease the amount of heat transported by blood to the skin, consequently lowering skin temperature. The cool shell of skin now acts as an insulating layer for the deeper core areas of the body; skin temperatures may drop nearly as low as that of the surrounding environment, while the body's core temperature remains unchanged at its normal 99°. However, a drop to 50°F always numbs the skin so that ultimately all sense of touch and pain is lost, rendering the hands, for example, almost useless in performing fine or coordinated movements. Shivering begins shortly after the initial constriction of surface blood vessels and may continue for several hours if exposure to cold is continued. Although it produces considerable heat, shivering consumes a great deal of energy, and if intense and prolonged can result in exhaustion. Inevitably, if this heat loss continues, the body's inner core temperature begins to fall below 99°. As this occurs, body functions are impaired, the victim loses coordination and eventually consciousness. If the situation is not quickly remedied, he dies.

The insidious nature of hypothermia is its absence of warning to the victim, and the fact that as its severity increases, chilling reaches his brain, thus depriving him of the judgment and reasoning power to recognize his own condition. Without recognition of symptoms by a companion, and treatment, this vicious cycle leads to stupor, collapse, and death.

Details on the prevention and treatment of hypothermia as given in Chapter 19 should be assimilated by everyone who ventures into the mountain environment.

Lightning

Though not one of the principal perils of mountaineering, lightning has caused a number of serious — and mostly avoidable — accidents. The very nature of their sport places climbers on or near the most frequent targets: peaks and ridges help produce the vertical updrafts and raincloud conditions which generate lightning; the prominences serve to trigger the strokes. Climbers therefore should understand the basic mechanisms involved and fix in their minds the fundamentals of evasive action.

For all practical purposes the hazards are three: (1) a direct strike, (2) ground currents, and (3) induced currents in the immediate vicinity of a strike.

Electrical potential builds up in a cloud in somewhat the same manner one's body picks up an electrical charge on a dry day. Air is normally a very poor conductor (good insulator) of electricity; trees, rock, or earth are better conductors, more so when wet; the human body is still better;

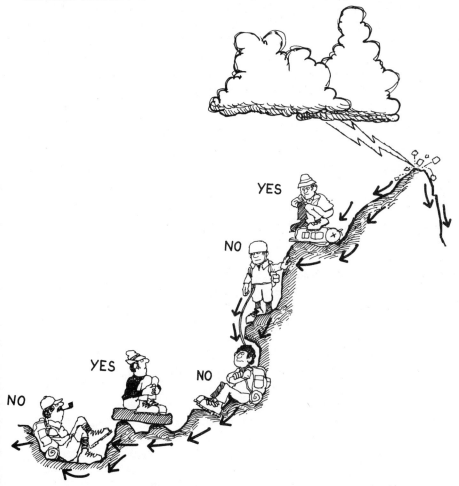

Fig. 17-1. Body positions and location in an electrical storm indicating relative safety from ground currents. (Arrows show probable paths of ground currents.)

and most metals are best of all. Lightning seeks the path of least total resistance between the cloud and earth — the shortest possible line through the air. Ordinarily the closest ground point is directly below the cloud, but a summit off to one side can be closer and become the bull's-eye.

Air ceases to be a good insulator when subjected to a sufficiently high electrical pressure; it *ionizes* and thereupon loses its insulating quality and becomes a conductor. The ionizing breakdown around a conducting projection often gives off a crackling noise (notorious in the Alps as the "buzzing of the bees") caused by small sparks. The distinctive odor of ozone is usually noted. A bluish glow or *corona* (St. Elmo's Fire) may be seen. If a person's head is the projection, the hair (if any) crackles and stands on end. Corona discharges have often been observed when the nearest cloud seemed too far away to be at all relevant. The sound or sight of corona does not necessarily indicate danger, but lacking more precise indication should be regarded as a warning, especially when thunderclouds are nearby. Additionally, any atmospheric activity symptomatic of commotion should stir suspicion. A sudden rush of cold air perhaps announces a strong cold front with possible lightning. A cloudburst of enormous raindrops or monster snowflakes or huge hailstones almost certainly means a cumulonimbus is overhead.

Lightning is, of course, electricity, which is a stream of electrons. When the more than 100 billion billion electrons in an average bolt strike a peak or a tree they do not just lie there in a puddle, but immediately spread out in all directions. In the process considerable damage can result. Two factors determine the extent of human injury; the quantity of current, and the part of the body affected.

The worst threat is the passage of electricity *through* the body in a way which impairs some vital function such as heart, brain, or breathing action. A current from one hand to the other through the heart and lungs, or from head to foot through virtually all organs, is most dangerous, even if relatively small; one can survive a larger current from one foot to the other through the legs.

Climbers face other potential hazards: large currents can cause deep burns at points of entry and exit; a mild shock may momentarily startle them or set off muscular spasms, or they may move about in semi-consciousness, and in either case may fall off a cliff.

First thought should be given to avoiding areas which might be hit. The governing rule is to seek a location with nearby projections or masses which are somewhat closer than one's own head to any clouds which may drift by. In a forest the safest shelter is amid the shorter trees. The middle of a ridge is preferable to the ends; avoid shoulders.

An electrical discharge at a strike point instantly radiates outward and downward, with the intensity of the flow, and consequently the danger to climbers, decreasing rapidly as the distance from the strike increases. On firm rock, especially when wet, the major path in most cases is along the surface. Lichen patches, cracks, or soil may hold moisture and thus provide easy paths. High-voltage currents tend to jump across short gaps, as in a spark plug, rather than take a longer path around.

Current flows because of a voltage difference between two points along its path. A person bridging two such points with some part of his body presents a second, and probably better path for the current, some portion of which is therefore diverted through his body. The wider the span the greater is the voltage difference and the greater the flow through the body.

With this background, several precepts can be listed:

1. Avoid moist areas, including crevices and gullies.
2. Span as small a distance (occupy as little area) as possible. Keep the feet close together; keep the hands off the ground.
3. Sit, crouch, or stand on insulating objects if possible – a coiled rope or a sleeping bag, preferably dry.
4. Stay out of small depressions; choose instead a narrow slight rise. A small detached rock on a scree slope is excellent.
5. Stay away from overhangs and out of small caves. Large caves are very good if one keeps clear of the walls and entrance. However, a cave might well be the lower terminus of a drainage crevice, and in such case should be avoided.
6. When on a ledge, crouch at the outer edge, at least 4 feet from the rock wall if possible. If there is danger of falling off in event of a shock, tie in *crosswise* to the prospective flow of current. Make the tie short and avoid placing rope under the armpits.
7. Rappelling when lightning is imminent should be avoided, but may be a valid calculated risk if it is the quickest way to escape a danger zone. Dry synthetic rope presents the minimum hazard.
8. Contrary to popular belief, metal objects do not attract lightning as such. However, in the immediate vicinity of a strike, metals in contact with one's person may augment the hazard from *induced currents*, the nature and mechanism of which lie beyond the limits of the present discussion. Induced currents usually are quite small, but when added to ground currents may mean the difference between life and death. Thus, it is best to set aside all metals, but to keep them close by (don't worry about articles buried in the pack). A metal pack frame might well be positioned to provide a more attractive path for ground currents beside and past one's body. At distances greater than 100 feet from a possible strike there is no need to divest oneself of metal objects.

The Subjective Hazard: The Climber

Climbers cannot control the physical nature and the *objective hazards* of the mountains, nor can they completely control the psychological factors which make up the *subjective hazards*. Looking back on an accident one always finds both objective and subjective causes — neither alone is sufficient. The destructive forces daily at work on the mountain are inconsequential unless a human being is in their way at the crucial time. The subjective and controllable factors seldom in themselves cause death, but they do sometimes set the climber on a collision course with one of the objective hazards. It is the combination which is dangerous. A slope may be ripening to an avalanche tomorrow — a climber, ignorant of snow structure, may trigger it today. A rock, slowly weakening by natural processes, may be preparing to fall next week — the weight of a careless climber may pull it loose today. This subjective factor, which brings a particular climber to a given danger point at just the perilous time, is nearly always at the root of a climbing accident.

A climber seeking to control the danger will ask which factors of the subjective hazard can be controlled. There are subjective elements in every phase of a climb: the party management, the choice of route, companions, equipment, and techniques, the effort spent in acquiring skill and knowledge, the preconditioning, even to a great extent a basic philosophy of approach to mountaineering. If all these elements have been given thoughtful attention the potential physical danger may never strike.

Of all the psychological hazards the most deadly is *ignorance*: inexperience, climbing beyond one's abilities, unpreparedness, lack of necessary equipment, lack of confidence because of fear or apprehension, poor judgment; second is its partner, *overconfidence*. The perils of ignorance can be avoided by study and experience; the background of mountaineering knowledge which a climber should have is the scope of this book. However, even the educated and experienced climber can be guilty of overconfidence.

Persons with show-off tendencies may be driven by ego to climb beyond their abilities with no margin of safety for the unexpected. A more subtle form of overconfidence arises from familiarity with a given climb: people have been killed because a strong and experienced leader thought he could repeat with novices a climb he had made before with experts. Group overconfidence — the fallacious belief that there is safety in numbers — is an insidious danger, one which is the task of leadership to control. Another attitude, not peculiar to climbers but common to nearly every individual, is the feeling of dwelling under an umbrella provided by his own special providence, that accidents happen only to the other fellow.

An additional aspect of overconfidence is the generally recognized fact that an individual's ability does, through elusive psychological and physiological factors, vary from time to time. Every experienced mountaineer can remember days when his climbing lacked the usual "feel" and when he had difficulty with pitches well below his normal standard. If a false pride prods him into persisting on a difficult climb during one of his off days, danger can develop. The prudent climber learns to recognize bodily limitations such as inadequate conditioning, overexertion, fatigue, muscular cramps, altitude sickness, dehydration, and incipient blisters, and his temporarily lowered ability, and reacts to them promptly to prevent their becoming a contributing cause or aggravation of an accident, perhaps choosing an easier objective, with no loss of enjoyment.

A great part of climbing safety lies in climbing competence. The fearful follower, the brash exhibitionist, the rigid traditionalist all find themselves in situations where their techniques institute the very slips they are trying to avoid or protect against. A lifetime commitment to the better method, an eagerness to consider, a willingness to study, to adopt, to practice and to perfect the skills of the sport is not to be traded for any other factor in safety.

Subjective dangers are present on every climb. Their control lies in awareness of all the varied factors which influence judgment and decision-making in the mountains. A climber who gains this perspective is never content to fumble or gamble his way up or down a mountain.

Cumulative Factors

Although many accidents occur like "a bolt out of the blue," others, in retrospect, can be seen to have developed, step by inexorable step—following a sort of remorseless logic—until they culminate in the final tragedy.

A typical example might begin with the climber who oversleeps and, in the rush to make up lost time, leaves home without his ice axe. On the climb the surface of the snow is soft enough to lure him onward, although his companions must belay him. The party dozes on the summit, extending the stay there by another half-hour; descent begins three hours later than planned. Perhaps the return proceeds without mishap, but a fall, a sudden storm, and the party is without the time, daylight, and equipment it needs to ensure the survival of all its members.

Occasionally these potential accidents can be recognized while developing, but not always. An alert leader can turn back his minimally equipped party in the face of obviously worsening weather, but there are those days which seem to start wrong and get worse, and on such days—and everyone, climber or not, has them—it might be well to temper valor with discretion and select more modest objectives or simply go for a nice walk in the woods.

A CLIMBING CODE

A Climbing Code was proposed early in this text as a guide to the safe, and hopefully successful, completion of the climbing venture undertaken. Application of these guidelines will limit the consequences of a large number of unexpected developments. Although the brief statements given may appear to the sophomore to be too inflexible for his operations and only truly applicable to the freshman, the principles in this list reflect the ongoing decisions of seniors and graduates as they enjoy their chosen sport. The elements of the Code are worth repeating with a brief explanation of the reasons behind them.

A climbing party of three is the minimum, unless adequate prearranged support is available. On glaciers, two rope teams are recommended. Party size as stated here is generally the minimum required to handle an accident situation. The numbers suggested may at times help one to retreat from an overambitious step, but the real issue is having someone present to initiate rescue and first aid, and to go out for more extensive help. There are also a far from negligible number of these situations where early response is the key to success, and even prearranged support may be too late. Immediate help may be the only help that counts.

Rope up on all exposed places and for all glacier travel. No sensible person falls in an open crevasse intentionally. It is the "hidden" crevasse — so called because it may well be impossible for even the expert to detect — that causes the trouble. Crevasse rescue is infinitely easier with the victim already tied in, still alive, and still near the surface. Exposure speaks of the consequences, rather than the likelihood, of a misstep. Obviously there are exposed places where one may stand or sit without serious hazard, but in the ongoing action of climbing, the shift of attention, the change of mood, the chance of loose footing or "acts of God" may readily escalate exposure to fatality. An early habit of roping up in exposed spots may give one a long enough career to develop the judgment for variations.

Anchor all belays. It is possible to locate a belay stance in which the belayer could not possibly be pulled out should his partner fall; however, the difficulty is knowing for certain such a likely stance is really "bombproof." The direction and magnitude of the force which the belayer must hold are not easily determined, and this fact, combined with the possible need to tie off a fallen climber, dictates setting up and attachment to a substantial anchor. Finally, as in the discussion of roping up, a well established habit based on the broad experience of the climbing community reduces the likelihood of wrong choices in either tense or over-relaxed situations.

Keep the party together, and obey the leader or majority rule. Keeping the party together concentrates party strength, maintains communication among party members, and reduces the number of locations where these may be needed. Admittedly some parties are large enough to be divided into self-sufficient subgroups, but this should be done only if each subgroup has adequate strength for its goals and adequate and defined leadership. It is too easy to divide once and to drift into splinter groups without the above constraints. Certain high altitude tragedies have highlighted this phenomenon. The full acceptance of leadership or majority rule not only makes for a more relaxed trip, it greatly reduces any trend toward party disintegration.

Never climb beyond your ability and knowledge. Trying moves beyond present ability or at the boundary of knowledge is a step in a climber's learning and growth, but this process should generally take place in a practice situation — a low-level traverse, an upper belay — rather than in mid-climb. Any such move must have extra protection, adequate not only to prevent injury in case of a slip but also to permit return of the fallen climber to the route.

Never let judgment be overruled by desire when choosing the route or turning back. Desire is a very useful element in the climbing venture, reducing weariness to a minor annoyance and calling forth true best efforts. If not constrained it also leads to a crawling approach to catastrophe: just another half hour, just around that next corner, that rock just might hold. Of course the turnaround time should be reconsidered during the day as the current strength or weakness of the party is assessed, as observations of the weather replace predictions, as the travel surface and route detail are at hand. But the decision to change must involve the same calm evaluation that went into the original choice, not wishful thinking induced by nearness of the goal.

Carry at all times the clothing, food, and equipment necessary. Almost any trip stretched to day's end can turn into an enforced bivouac, changing the whole nature of the activity. Protective equipment, whether technical or survival, is of no use at home, and cannot often be compensated for by nerve or skill.

Leave the trip schedule with a responsible person. A trip schedule indicating intended route and expected time of return can greatly reduce both cost and delay in any search and rescue operation. Need of such assistance may not be anticipated, but the vagaries of life should not be disregarded with so cheap a safety feature. The schedule generally needs only limited detail, permitting the freedom of on-sight choice, although major changes require evaluation for their impact on this protection. Finally the "responsible person" recognizes the imprecision of time predictions, and the climbers recognize their responsibility to check in on return.

Follow the precepts of sound mountaineering as set forth in textbooks of recognized merit. Too often news reports of mountaineering successes, failures, or accidents, or magazine articles of exciting adventure contain misquotes, partial quotes, or emotional opinion of authors not active in the sport. And fictional portrayals of climbs and climbers in novels, TV, and movies are usually just that—fictional.

Behave at all times in a manner that will not reflect unfavorably upon mountaineering. Constraints follow rapidly upon the heels of misuse.

THE SAFE ATTITUDE: A BASIS FOR CONTROL

To this point the endeavor has been to analyze the dual nature of climbing danger, and to emphasize some of the knowledge fundamental to a safe attitude on the part of the climber, an attitude which permits no more than a reasonable proportion of danger on any climb.

The development of a safe mountaineering attitude proceeds along three lines:

First, each climber must be instilled from the very beginning with a respectful attitude toward mountains, a realization of the basic relationship between their hazards and his limitations.

Second, each person must develop the climbing skill and knowledge of specialized techniques and equipment which supplement his natural abilities.

Third, each must encounter—preferably vicariously—the actual situations which teach him the distinction between safety and danger and enable him to evaluate his margin of safety at all times.

The development of all three lines is parallel: with increasing knowledge and practice of technique comes experience in practical mountaineering situations as well as an intellectual investigation of the fundamentals of the sport. Progress is made when the climber comprehends the reasons for a Climbing Code and resolves to follow its rules. Further study and experience bring understanding of the danger inherent in both the mountain and the climber himself. Using this knowledge the mountaineer can evaluate any climbing situation and is equipped to recognize the fundamental causes—the seeds—from which an accident can grow.

By the time he has understood this much about climbing danger, the mountaineer will have some definite ideas on the kind of climbing he wants to do and how he wants to do it. These ideas make up his attitude toward the sport, in which a paramount element is his consideration of safety.

Of first importance is an attitude of continual suspicion. There is always something in the complex situation that he could have overlooked. Ever alert, he thinks his way up a mountain, analyzing and evaluating, basing decisions on sound reasoning, continually probing for hidden peril and planning ahead to meet it, above all forever suspecting there is something undetected just beyond the limits of his awareness.

As a corollary to his suspicion, every climber must be thoroughly familiar with both the preventive and the corrective safety technique. The safe climber is ready to deal with danger should it develop. High on a glacier far above timberline he asks himself, "Could I survive here if something unforeseen should happen, if we were unable to descend on schedule and were forced to remain all night?" Study of first aid and rescue technique, plus adequate equipment for emergency, should enable him to either answer "Yes" or prompt him to descend and return another day when conditions are more in his favor.

One element of the safe attitude is a generality which applies to every hazard ever encountered in the mountains, and that is always to minimize the time of exposure to danger. Often a calculated risk cannot be avoided, such as when retreating from the peak in a sudden storm. Whatever the reason for taking the risk, it is no more than common sense to better the odds of survival by moving through the danger area as quickly as is consistent with safe travel.

"Margin of safety" is a concept often discussed by climbers, and the individual's evaluation of this margin most fully embodies his attitude toward climbing danger. No one can predict infallibly the boundary of safety, the exact demarcation between routine travel and catastrophe, and the wise mountaineer allows for this uncertainty by keeping the margin of safety as a cushion between himself and peril. The margin is not an absolute thing; it changes character continually to meet changing conditions, but ideally it affords a constant degree of protection for the climber.

Since safety rests upon a number of factors, whenever a weakness appears in one respect the margin must be maintained by adding strength somewhere else. For example, ignorance of the precise breaking strength of rock, or the exact friction between boots and wet vegetation, leads the climber to add the rope. When the moving team might be unable to catch a fall, he adds a belay and anchor. In doubtful weather he carries extra clothing, food, even bivouac gear, and marks the route carefully. Knowing that rappels sometimes fail, he uses the technique with caution and belays the rappeller. If a member of the team is weak or inexperienced, a balance of strength is maintained by the addition of another strong companion—or by choosing a less difficult objective. The list can be elaborated endlessly, but the principle is always the same: the weakness of one safety factor is countered by the strengthening of others.

Such are some of the elements of mountain safety. Only the innocent ignorants are content to set forth blindly on a haphazard struggling journey. The well-trained climbing party proceeds safely into the mountains, skillfully directed by responsible leadership that has planned carefully for every reasonable eventuality. At the same time, each member of the team is prepared to co-operate, if need be subordinating his own will; the group responsibility found among mountain climbers is seldom matched in any other human endeavor.

Setting a proper margin of safety and controlling climbing danger— the supreme test of a climber's attitude—depends on his knowledge and his judgement. And out of his understanding of the dangers and responsibilities grows a deeper appreciation of the rewards of mountaineering.

Plate 24. Rappelling into ice cave on Mt. Stanley, Ruwenzori Range, Uganda.
(John Cleare)

Plate 25. Sun rising above Chamlang, Nepal Himalaya. (John Cleare)

18 *

LEADERSHIP AND THE CLIMBING PARTY

The Group

IN MOST AREAS of life, man works in groups to achieve goals more effectively, whether the goals are social or individual. In mountaineering, people climb in groups because they have found that with the help of others they can climb more safely, more successfully, more enjoyably.

On expeditions to remote areas and in climbing organizations or classes, even the most rugged individualist who wishes to participate subordinates his whims of the moment to the needs of the group so that both individual and party success will be achieved. In this way the individual makes a unique personal contribution to the group, but does so within the framework of the group, and thus the climbing party becomes more than the sum of its members. The individual members feel more confident — more aggressive in ascent and more enduring under stress — when they know they are part of a group. On the other hand, the group cannot exist apart from its members. It is created and sustained by their will; the members have a group only as long as they will to be together, to work together and to sustain each other.

Many climbers, however, tend to be strongly and aggressively individualistic and show little inclination to submerge themselves in a group just for the sake of doing so. Moreover, many of the more experienced climbers tend to prefer small parties of close friends held together by a mutual desire to achieve a specific goal. Even in such groups, there is always a leader — a person who is usually first to verbalize the thought on everyone's mind, one who assumes the initiative more often than the others, the individual who most frequently seems to be in the right place at the right time to coax, cajole, and prod companions.

While the group must have unity, it must also have direction, and this involves two aspects: steering and propelling. The group must steer in one direction and, at the same time, be propelled in that direction, too. This is the aim of leadership.

The Leader

The leader is responsible for the safety of the party and the success of the trip. Knowledge, experience, and climbing skill help meet these responsibilities, but of far greater importance is the ability to deal with others, to be sensitive to their attitudes, physical requirements and limitations, to inspire and encourage them and to guide them in the exercise of their own initiative so that their efforts contribute to the achievement of the team goal. Effective leaders possess various blends of personality traits and acquired skills which enable them to motivate, guide, and inspire others seemingly without conscious effort.

The essential attributes can be acquired through a planned program of experiences supplemented by study and discussion. Generally the "people" skills and attitudes developed in previous leadership situations will be the foundation. To this the potential mountaineering leader must add the specialized skills and knowledge of climbing. The effort necessary to acquire, blend, and apply these attributes effectively varies widely with individuals. No one is born with all the necessary attributes fully operative; they must be developed.

Character and intelligence may best summarize the variety of personality traits which must be properly blended in an individual to enable effective leadership. There is no single optimum combination but all effective leaders must possess, among other traits, sufficient amounts of self-discipline, integrity, decisiveness, objectivity, and adaptability. Above all, every leader must consciously accept the basic responsibility, the certain knowledge that the party will look to him for stability and guidance in a crisis — and be prepared accordingly.

Although experience is important, it is not the most important quality. The members of a party look instinctively to the person who inspires the most confidence. This may not be the climber with 20 years of experience if those years were spent in compulsive climbing motivated by egoism or thrill-seeking. Rather, it might be the person with only 2 years experience who also has a lifetime accumulation of common sense and good judgment. Physical strength and agility are desirable but not necessary, since the leader may even be the rearguard and not lead a single pitch of the climb; what matters is the party's willingness to follow the leader's judgments and decisions. However, the leader must be in adequate physical condition for the climb; a tired leader becomes less effective as fatigue increases.

As party size and trip length increase, so do the complexities of leadership. On a weekend climb by two close friends, it may be feasible for one person to plan the menu, buy the food, furnish the transportation, do the route research and even supply most of the technical climbing equipment; when longer trips and larger groups are involved, this is impractical and probably impossible for one person. The leader cannot do everything, nor is that desirable; rather duties should be delegated to others whenever possible. Delegation of duties and responsibilities relieves the leader of detail work, establishes an overview of the entire trip, ensures that all tasks are performed, and builds morale by involving the individual members in the climb.

In a large group or in one in which the members are not well acquainted, the leader should appoint an assistant who, if need arises, can assume the role of leader. Next, one person might be assigned the task of planning the meals, another the job of arranging transportation, and a third that of coordinating equipment.

On a climb with others of less experience, the leader may also have to become a teacher and share knowledge and experience. Techniques may have to be taught and, when possible, time allotted for the "student" to practice these techniques. Inexperienced leaders need—and should be provided—the opportunity to gain experience in all phases of climbing leadership; indeed, helping others learn to lead is the acme of leadership, requiring patience, empathy, and generosity.

While actually climbing, leaders are always thinking ahead, anticipating the problems that may arise and planning their solutions. In camp, they think of the climb; on the ascent, of the descent; in success, of retreat. They watch the horizon for that little cloud no bigger than a man's hand, note symptoms of weariness in companions and assess what strength can be counted on in crisis, and plan for bivouacs or alternative routes of descent. If their party is ascending a face, they study the ridges on either side; if climbing a ridge, they study the faces on each side. Verbalizing problems and soliciting optional solutions both relieves the leader's isolation and keeps the party alert, because any one of them may suddenly become leader. Everywhere on trips, leaders mentally cross bridges before reaching them; and more—they borrow trouble: what to do if a rucksack were lost here, if a belay stance failed to materialize, if a slope were to avalanche? Above all, leaders must continually question assumptions, realizing that things go wrong primarily because of bad assumptions. By keeping these things in mind, by being alert and thinking ahead, every leader is, to that extent, master of what happens on any particular climb and will, to that extent, increase in ability to lead in the future in any place or situation.

However, the most common, and the most vexing, problems of leadership are not the major disasters leaders fear and for which they have prudently prepared themselves, but rather, the little exasperating mishaps which arise at the most inopportune moments — a lagging, footsore member of the party who is breaking in new boots on the job, or (more serious), a party member too ill or fatigued to continue the climb but able to descend or stop and wait for the party's return.

There is no set of systematic answers for such trying situations and there is no way or relieving the leader of responsibility for dealing with them. The only proper recommendation can be to follow the safest, most conservative course. In practice, the leader must use good judgment in evaluating the factors pertinent to reaching a decision, and then must make the decision firmly and unequivocally. An effective leader recognizes the potential for serious consequences inherent in many seemingly trivial problems.

Any mountaineering trip involves a rich spectrum of choices and makes continual demands on the will. A route must be found, equipment selected, dangers evaluated, the tired body must be inspired with the will to move. Without leadership, even a strong party may wander aimlessly, sit paralyzed with indecision, or lie abed while only the sun climbs. With good leadership, even a relatively weak party may expect to achieve its goals.

The Party and Its Strength

A party is strong or weak in relation to its goals and several things may make it so: the mountaineering proficiency of the members, the size of the group, and the party's morale. Morale is the most difficult to analyze; in general, a party has good morale when it has good leadership, good "followship," and good luck.

Mountaineering proficiency involves many things, chiefly climbing ability, experience, and good physical condition. A strong party would consist of several experienced, well-equipped climbers in good physical condition, each agile on rock, and each able to handle rope and ice axe with ingrained reflexes. What constitutes a weak party is not so easy to define. In some cases, a party is strong enough if it has only two strong climbers in addition to many weak climbers. In other situations, a group of 10 strong climbers and one ineffective climber is too weak a party. The individual might merely be clumsy, slow or inexperienced, and yet jeopardize the entire party. A party with no experienced members is a weak party in any situation.

In small parties, rope teams are usually formed by tacit agreement among the climbers. In larger parties or in groups where the climbers are relative strangers, the leader may assign climbers to rope teams, basing these assignments on experience, speed, and personality. Each team should have enough strength to rotate the lead, distributing the work of stepkicking and trail building, and allowing less proficient climbers to expand their fund of experience.

At all times, the leader should know who and where the most competent climbers are so that their abilities can be directed toward the most critical needs of the party. One may need to assign a patient, reliable friend as rearguard to encourage slow or weak members, or may need to send a team ahead to scout or prepare a portion of the route. If the leader is at or near the head of the party, an assistant should probably be near its rear to ensure continuity of control in the event the leader's entire team becomes involved in an accident.

Deciding the most appropriate size of a climbing party requires consideration of many factors. Ideally, the minimum size of a party is the number of people who can handle an accident situation adequately. Traditionally, a minimum party of three has been standard: if one climber is hurt, the second can stay with the victim while the third goes for help. Variations from the basic unit of three depend on the particular situation. On difficult terrain or in adverse weather, when it would be dangerous for one person to go alone for help, four is the safe minimum. On the other hand, if there is a support party nearby, a rope of two may elect to climb alone. On a glacier climb, four to six people are needed where a speedy crevasse rescue may be necessary. A climb in a remote area where there is no support for hundreds of miles must be planned for complete self-sufficiency and, therefore, becomes an expedition of relatively large numbers.

A party gains in strength if it has a support team of climbers nearby or if there is another climbing party in the area. The latter case often proves to be a parody of safe mountaineering, because the other party might itself be exhausted or need rescue. To be useful, a support party must be willing and able to do rescue work and ready, moreover, to initiate rescue automatically at a prearranged time. In cases where there would ordinarily be no support in the area, the climbing party should arrange in advance to have support available somehow, as near to the area as possible, leaving its plans and time schedule with a responsible person who will dispatch help if the climbers do not return when due.

A mistake to be avoided is the belief that a larger party is a safer party. A larger party can start bigger avalanches and kick down more loose rock. It can retard itself in many ways, both in camping and climbing. No matter how well organized and led, the largeness of the group tends to breed overconfidence and carelessness, even among good climbers. The large parties of 40 to 60 are now a thing of the past; a party of 12 to 15 is presently considered to be the maximum number which can impose itself on a wilderness environment without serious damage to the ecosystems, and even this is too many for some areas.

The Trip

Some climbers like to make adventure their objective and strike out into the wilderness deliberately ignoring "cookbook" information, thus enjoying the challenge of a pioneer ascent on even the most heavily traveled peaks. Most parties, however, aim at a more definite objective and, to attain it, the leader first gathers all the information available concerning the best approaches, the best campsites, the location of the various climbing routes and their difficulty.

After the party has chosen its objective, plans have to be made for food, transportation, and equipment. Each member should be fully informed of these plans well in advance of the day of departure.

Time is one of the most important considerations in planning any climb. The party will be safe and successful according to how it uses its time. Other factors, such as proficiency, size, and morale, contribute to the party's strength in many ways, but the most important of these is the way they enable the party to use its time.

A time schedule should be drawn up. Good scheduling requires thorough consideration of many factors and will usually swing the balance from failure to success. In addition to estimating time requirements for the climb itself, the trip planners allow some extra time for minor mishaps, inadvertent bivouacs and the like, before leaving the trip schedule with the support-dispatcher. The extra margin of time gives an extra margin of confidence, for the party can afford to climb more conservatively than if hurrying to meet a deadline.

Consider, for example a party camped at 5000 feet below an 8000-foot summit. The leader determines that ascending to 7000 feet will be straightforward and will take 2 hours. The next 500 feet is steep ice and may take 1½ hours. The final 200 feet of rock and 300 feet of scrambling will take 3 hours. The ascent will, therefore, total 6½ hours from camp to summit. Descending the rock by rappel will take 1 hour; descending the ice will take as long as the ascent, 1½ hours. The long glissade down the bottom slope should require only ½ hour. Hence, the total descent will require 3 hours, and the total climb 9½ hours. On this particular day darkness comes at, say, 8:30. The party wants an hour on the summit and 2 hours of daylight left after return to camp, and 2 additional hours must be allowed as a margin of safety. Thus, the starting time from camp in the morning is — despite the moan of the indolent and the cry of the dissenter—6 o'clock. A similar projection of estimated times along high-ways, trails, and through the brush will fix the necessary departure time from home in order to reach high camp at a decent hour.

The accumulated experience of the party affects its time use directly. An expert routefinder can choose a route with little wasted time. Like-wise, the experienced leader can evaluate situations and make good deci-sions faster than the less experienced person. Experience adequate for easy trips may be inadequate for harder ones; but, in general, an ex-perienced leader has not only an accumulated store of knowledge to draw on, but also the very habit of decision-making, so that lack of experience with the details is compensated for by confidence and shrewdness in on-the-spot decision-making. The more experienced the leader, the less unfamiliar situations will cause uncertainty and hesitation.

The climbing ability and physical stamina of the party also affect its time use. If the climb is difficult, all members of the party must be suitably experienced and capable. If the climb is a pre-dawn to after-dark tour, the members must have the endurance to maintain a steady pace for the whole time *plus* reserves of strength for coping with the unforeseen.

On the trail or on the peak, many problems can be avoided by setting and maintaining a good pace. This is not to say that the pace must be fast or slow (relative terms—what is fast for one party might be slow for another and what is fast on one terrain might be slow elsewhere), but that it must be suited to the group and its objective. A small party generally moves faster than a large one and can be more casual in setting its pace; however, a larger party must be kept moving steadily because a greater number of people devour time and tend to exert a braking action on themselves.

Most long climbs involve camping for one or more nights. Camps should be located with the time factor in mind. The higher the camp, the greater the time available next day for the climb (or the later the party can sleep). On the other hand, the scenic camp high on a peak is attained at the cost of a long, pack-laden trudge up from the valley floor.

An extremely important responsibility of leadership is that of keeping the party together or, at the very least, in strong enough units to deal with an emergency. In small parties of equally proficient climbers, little effort is needed to achieve this and when one member or one team lags, the others usually realize a problem has arisen and slow their pace. In larger parties, the leader and assistants must work together to avoid having their group splinter into a number of independently wandering fragments. This sort of situation most often arises within organized club outings and climbing courses; leaders of these groups may need to exert considerable control to keep the lead rope from charging ahead and losing contact with the last team.

Although it is hard enough to keep the party together on the ascent, it becomes even more difficult on the descent, and the leader, who is normally the last person off the mountain, must have crystal-clear plans and instructions laid out and issued regarding rendezvous points for regrouping in the event of separation. Glissading has played a major role in the breaking up of many parties on the descent, particularly those with limited experience: the first glissaders frequently come to the bottom of the run and take off down the mountain long before the last ones can overtake them. To prevent this, the leader should require a rendezvous of the entire party reasonably near the end of the glissade.

The climber who leads the descent must keep the party under control and not moving so fast as to cause a separation of the group, thereby dramatically weakening it and creating the substantial additional burden of trying to locate the missing member or members while still endeavoring to maintain sufficient strength to complete the descent. A party which stays together can use its strength for the attainment of its original objective and to return to camp.

The Margin of Safety

In all planning and in all decisions, the leader must think in terms of the margin of safety — the reserve of time, energy, and equipment a party has maintained for handling unexpected trouble. Even with the most detailed planning and maximum alertness, there is always the unexpected; precautions should be taken to ensure the ability to deal with it.

The party must be prepared, with surplus food, clothing for colder weather than is anticipated, more rappel slings and chocks than needed, an abundance of extra flashlight batteries and bulbs. To emphasize a point already discussed, the leader plans for a reasonable margin of daylight in setting the starting time. The leader also takes the precaution of roping the party before it is absolutely necessary, rather than waiting untl the very fine line between class 3 and 4 climbing has been crossed. In making decisions regarding turning back or bivouacking, or in failing to make them, if the leader does not make ample allowance for turning back, the bivouac is sure to follow. If the party is caught by darkness, however, the leader insists that they bivouac while still on easy ground rather than climb until hung up or completely exhausted.

The more experienced a climber, the more he realizes the margin of safety is a good half of the enjoyment. The student need not be experienced, however, to realize that the more efficient the leadership, the more smoothly the climbing party functions as a group and the wider the margin of safety.

Becoming a Leader

There are still two important problems to be considered: how a person can learn to lead and what basic guidelines exist for making leadership decisions.

Becoming a good leader is a do-it-yourself project, requiring desire and initiative. The best way to become a good leader is to lead and to watch others lead, to organize informal private trips with friends on short, familiar climbs and gradually move on to more ambitious projects. If possible, the trainee should climb with more experienced leaders and observe how they plan and how they work with their teams. Potential leaders should seek assistant-leader positions with these experienced climbers and become involved in the planning and decision-making process. Finally, throughout their careers effective leaders at all levels take time to assess their own performance: did they do as well as they could have? what went right? why? what went wrong? why? how could things have been improved?

The Climbing Code, discussed in Chapters 1 and 17, is the soundest set of guidelines yet advanced for making decisions, general principles which retain their validity under a wide variety of circumstances. As the sole basis for decisions, it may cost the novice leader some summits, at first, but it is unlikely to cost a life. Later, as experience and insight into the complexities of leadership are gained, the leader may modify and adapt the individual rules of the Climbing Code to specific situations; however, it is unlikely that the leader will ever depart radically from it because it is based on a common sense approach to safe mountaineering.

The challenges of leadership bring about its pleasures as well as its burdens. As awesome as the responsibilities appear initially, the exercise of competent leadership can become surprisingly easy when one has fully accepted these responsibilities, has prepared for the task, and can use common sense in adjusting to rapidly changing situations.

Plate 26. Pinnacle on Mt. Hale, Sierra Nevada. (Jeff Campbell and Galen Rowell)

19 *

FIRST AID

THIS CHAPTER IS NO SUBSTITUTE FOR
CURRENT FIRST AID TRAINING

WHEN ACCIDENTS OCCUR away from civilization, a doctor's services are seldom immediately available, and it is therefore the responsibility of all who venture into the mountains to possess a working knowledge of how to examine and properly care for disabled persons until professional services can be obtained. To this end it is highly recommended that ALL wilderness travelers be trained in current first aid procedures taught in a standard first aid and personal safety course, preferably a mountaineering-oriented first aid course of recognized merit, for only with supervised classroom and practical experience will an individual be prepared to handle an emergency situation efficiently and with confidence. Further, emergency care practices and procedures are continually changing and being improved; periodic refresher courses are recommended.

There are numerous conditions which can affect a party member, thereby incapacitating not only the victim, but the entire party as well. This chapter does not attempt to cover every possibility, but only to *summarize* the more common problems, with emphasis on life-threatening emergencies, and major injuries which if not treated properly could result in permanent or long-range impairment. It should also be noted that this chapter focuses on *first* aid—that given in the absence of professional medical help.

Procedures for dealing with life-threatening emergencies are presented in the order of their importance: pulmonary resuscitation, cardiopulmonary resuscitation, and control of hemorrhage and shock.

GENERAL PROCEDURES
FOR ACCIDENT RESPONSE

Turbulent emotions after an accident frequently confuse those involved. Therefore, knowing exactly what to do and when to do it are extremely important. It is well to memorize an optimum sequence of actions, and to carry an action checklist in the first aid kit. Then, when accident occurs, a dependable formula is available.

1. *Take charge of the situation.* Keep cool. Don't panic. Hasty actions, though well meant, may be fatal.

2. *Approach the victim safely.* Do not approach from directly above if there is a possibility of rock or snow slide.

3. *Perform urgently needed first aid and emergency rescue.* Immediate pulmonary resuscitation, cardiopulmonary resuscitation, and control of hemorrhage can be vital since time is of the utmost importance in avoiding certain death. If the victim is injured in an area of high potential snow or rock avalanche or extreme lightning danger, evacuate quickly to a safe location, but do not cause further injury.

4. *Treat for shock.* Always suspect and treat for shock after an accident. Do not move the victim until the extent of his injuries has been ascertained. Keep the victim as comfortable as possible. Reassure him (Tender Loving Care).

5. *Check for other injuries.* Examine gently and observe for shock, wounds, fractures, dislocations, contusions (bruises), or other irregularities.

6. *Plan what to do.* Preferably the most experienced person should direct the first aid. While this person makes a careful examination of the victim, assistants should gather first aid kits and assemble necessary supplies. After the immediate treatment, decide if the victim can be evacuated under his own power. If there is any doubt, assume he cannot. Then decide if the party has sufficient manpower for evacuation or if further aid should be summoned.

7. *Carry out the indicated plan.* If unable to evacuate the victim, make preparations for bivouacking in the area. If possible, transport the victim to timberline or a sheltered area such as a crevasse. Above all, however, ALWAYS THINK AND ACT IN TERMS OF THE VICTIM. When sending for help, be sure at least two of the stronger members are sent with all the information necessary to effect a rescue. This includes not only information on the victim's condition but the condition of the remainder of the party as well. If possible, complete an accident report of the type shown in Chapter 20 at the scene before leaving. If the party has sufficient strength, manpower, and expertise to evacuate, the procedures of Chapter 20 should be followed.

PULMONARY RESUSCITATION

In mountaineering, the stoppage of breathing from causes other than death results most frequently from crushing chest injuries, electrocution by lightning, drowning, or drug abuse.

Resuscitation is best carried out by the mouth-to-mouth method. The victim is placed on his back with head tilted backward by pressure with one hand on the forehead and the other beneath the victim's neck or lifting the chin. The first aider takes a deep breath, opens his mouth wide and places it tightly over the victim's mouth, at the same time pinching the nostrils shut with the fingers. The first aider gives four quick full breaths into the victim's mouth (any obstruction is readily apparent at this time and should be corrected), then removes his mouth and looks for chest movements associated with the breathing process. At the same time, the first aider listens and feels for the exchange of air at the patient's mouth and nose. After the initial four quick breaths, a single breath is given 12 times per minute for adults and 20 times per minute for children. Note that a child's lungs are smaller than an adult's, and therefore shallower breaths or even very light puffs are required, depending on the size of the child.

In cases of drug abuse or electrocution by lightning, artificial respiration may have to be performed for a long period of time, perhaps an hour or more, before the victim can resume independent respiration.

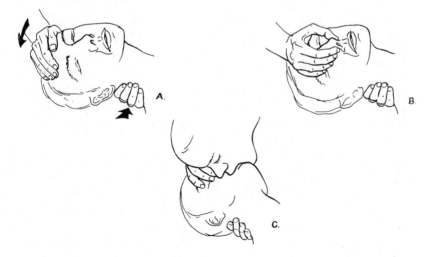

Fig. 19-1. Mouth-to-mouth resuscitation.
a.   Tilt head back.
b.   Pinch off nostrils; take deep breath.
c.   Make airtight seal to mouth and give four quick full breaths.

CARDIOPULMONARY RESUSCITATION (CPR)

Artificial respiration is of value only if breathing alone will revive the victim; it is of no use if the victim's heart has stopped, since without circulation, oxygen cannot be carried to the vital organs. In this case, heart action must be replaced by external chest compression, which combined with artificial respiration, is called cardiopulmonary resuscitation or CPR. Its use, however, can be quite hazardous. Whereas a victim's weak breathing may be assisted by mouth-to-mouth artificial respiration, if his heart is pumping, even weakly, he will NOT benefit from attempts to assist his heart by compression.

To be successful, closed-chest cardiopulmonary resuscitation depends on thorough and careful training. It is doubtful that one will be able to achieve artificial circulation of oxygenated blood by this method if his only training is from reading written instructions. Further, injury is much more likely when CPR is performed by an untrained individual. Fractures of the ribs and sternum caused by improper cardiac massage can cause injury to the heart, spleen, liver, and lungs. The American Red Cross and American Heart Association strongly encourage individuals to obtain training that will qualify them to use this technique.

CONTROL OF HEMORRHAGE

Hemorrhages are of two kinds, arterial and venous. *Arterial bleeding* occurs in pulses or spurts and the blood is usually bright red. Since massive arterial bleeding can be fatal in a few minutes, quick and correct action is mandatory. *Venous bleeding* is usually dark and flows smoothly, without spurting. Bleeding injuries should always be examined carefully to determine if they are as severe as they may appear. Many bleeding wounds that at first appear serious may, in fact, be quite minor.

The following steps are taken to control any *major hemorrhage*:

1. Immediately apply direct pressure to the bleeding area! Do not allow severe bleeding to continue while rummaging through packs for sterile dressings; use your bare hand if necessary. When a sterile compress is available, place it directly over the wound. If bleeding continues place additional sterile compresses on top of the old one and continue to apply direct pressure. This stops the bleeding in a majority of instances.
2. If the injury is on a limb, elevate the bleeding extremity. Use pressure points if known.
3. Apply cold packs, if available.
4. If these measures fail, and the wound is on a limb, and *only if the bleeding is severe and life-threatening,* apply a wide (3- to 4-inch) tourniquet. Apply it tightly enough to completely stop the bleeding, and

once the tourniquet is in place, leave it on; do not loosen it. Tag or otherwise mark the victim to alert medical personnel that a tourniquet has been placed, the time of placement, and by whom. *Remember that a decision to apply a tourniquet is essentially a decision to sacrifice that limb to save the life.*

If the wound has bled severely and transportation is planned, it is advisable to pass a tourniquet beneath the extremity without tightening it. It can then be tightened and fastened promptly if bleeding should re-start and cannot be controlled by any other method. This is particularly necessary if the extremity must also be splinted—it would be difficult if not impossible to apply a tourniquet around or under a splinted extremity.

For small lacerations with *minor bleeding* the area should be thoroughly washed and the edges closed with steri-strips, butterfly bandaids, or butterflies improvised from ½-inch strips of adhesive tape. Puncture wounds are not pulled together but are left open and covered with sterile pads. (Sucking chest wounds require special handling and bandaging.) Avulsions (tearing of tissue) and abrasions are simply washed with soap and water and covered with a sterile dressing.

SHOCK

Shock is a profound depression of all body processes caused by the failure of the cardiovascular system to provide sufficient blood circulation. It may follow *any* injury, even a relatively minor one, but bleeding, pain, cold, and rough handling are intensifying factors. The victim feels weak and clammy, the pulse is weak and rapid. Shock actually may be more serious than the initial injury; it must be assumed to exist and treated in every casualty.

The following measures are used both to prevent and to control shock:

1. Place the victim in a supine position (flat on his back) to make the blood which is circulating available to the brain, heart, lungs, and kidneys. If the victim has head or chest injuries, it is desirable to raise him about 15 degrees toward sitting position.
2. Keep the victim warm with extra clothing. If he is badly chilled from exposure to cold, apply heat, but not above body temperatures; otherwise merely prevent heat loss, using material to insulate him from the ground.
3. Minimize shock by controlling hemorrhage, relieving pain and handling gently.
4. Allow victim to drink a weak salt solution (six salt tablets or ½ teaspoon salt per quart of warm water).
5. If the victim has no injuries to the head, neck, back, or legs, it is desirable to raise the legs 8 to 12 inches to deliver an increased supply of blood to the body core.

COMPLETE VICTIM EXAMINATION

This examination is intended to find the additional and sometimes inconspicuous injuries that often cause serious complications: the closed undetected fracture that can become an open fracture when the victim is moved, the spinal injury that causes major spinal cord damage when the victim is helped to his feet. This examination must be a "head-to-toe" evaluation with careful checks for specific injuries. A good 10-point examination starts with the head, as follows:

1. Check scalp for laceration and contusions, beginning at the back of the neck and working to top of head.
2. Check skull for depressions.
3. Check ears and nose for blood and fluid.
4. Check for neck fractures, feel for lumps and bony protrusions.
5. Check chest region for fractures and wounds, look for movement and feel for fractures.
6. Check abdomen for spasms, tenderness, and discoloration.
7. Check pelvic area for fractures.
8. Check all extremities for fractures.
9. Check for paralysis of lower extremities.
10. Check buttocks for fractures or wounds; be cautious if spinal damage is suspected.

FRACTURES

Fractures are classified in two general categories: closed (simple), with no break in the skin; and open (compound), in which a broken bone fragment has penetrated the skin. One or more of the following signs are usually present: pain and tenderness at fracture site, inability to move or bear weight on the affected part without pain, a grating sensation felt or a grating sound heard during motion of the affected part, and sometimes deformity of the limb or body part. The following are general rules for treatment:

1. When in doubt, treat the injury as a fracture.
2. Splint both the joint above and the joint below the suspected fracture.
3. The extremity may usually be splinted in a position of some deformity. If it is apparent that splinting might result in penetration of the skin (in the case of some ankle fractures), or if splinting or subsequent transportation is not practical in that position, a gentle attempt at repositioning may be made by applying traction and then straightening the deformity.
4. Carefully pad all splints. Make sure the splint is the correct size and shape *before* application. Measure the unbroken extremity and use for a pattern.

5. Check splint ties frequently to be sure they do not interfere with circulation.
6. In the case of an open fracture, the bone end should not be left exposed. Before straightening the limb, thereby allowing the bone to slip back under the skin, examine the end carefully for dirt and debris. DO NOT HANDLE the bone end. If it is dirty, rinse with a saline solution of 1 teaspoon salt or 12 salt tablets in a quart of clean, or preferably sterile water. (To sterilize the water boil it for 15 minutes.) In all cases, NEVER allow the bone to dry out — keep it wet. DO NOT attempt to push the bone under the skin, but let it slip back of its own accord when the limb is straightened.
7. Above timberline, splint materials are scarce and a good deal of ingenuity is required to immobilize the fracture. Ice axes, piton hammers or uninjured portions of the patient's own body may be the only splints available.

Fractures of the jaw are held rigid with roller bandages. Place gauze pads or bits of clothing between the teeth before bandaging to allow for drinking or expulsion of vomitus. *Fractures of the collarbone* are held rigid by roller bandages, cravats or triangular bandages, and by immobilizing the affected arm over the chest. In *fractures of the upper arm or humerus*, the weight of the victim's arms helps to overcome the pull of the muscles and reduces pain. The victim's ribs are used as a splint, and the forearm supported in a sling. *Fractures and dislocations of the elbow* are best splinted and supported with a sling in the position of maximum comfort: a position acutely bending the elbow should be avoided, since circulation to the forearm may be cut off. However, fractures of a joint should not be straightened. *Forearm and wrist fractures* are best treated by securing to a splint applied to the inner side of the arm, and then supporting the limb with a sling. For *fractures of the hand or fingers*, the hand is folded around a fluffed gauze bandage and fastened with a cravat, webbing, or triangular bandage. *Fractured ribs* are best immobilized by encircling the chest with three to four cravats or pieces of webbing. They should be tightened as the victim exhales. If pain is not relieved upon gentle compression, nothing should be applied, since there is some possibility that the ribs are fractured inward, and compression may puncture a lung.

Injuries to the pelvis are most frequently of a crushing sort. There is agonizing pain and possible swelling or bruising at the fracture site. Fractures most frequently occur in the front and a great hazard is perforation or rupture of the bladder. In such case it is essential to limit fluids to less than one pint per day. Pelvic fractures are immobilized by tying the legs together at the knees and ankles with a thick pad of clothing between the thighs.

A *fracture of the femur* is difficult to treat because of the powerful thigh muscles. The broken ends tend to be displaced inward and frequently slip over one another, causing great pain. A splint may be improvised, as illustrated, extending from under the arm on the outside of the leg to below the ankle. The splint must be well padded and held in place by strips of cloth or other material. Padding should be placed between the legs and the legs secured together. Under *no circumstances* should a traction splint be attempted; the possibility of causing further damage by impeding circulation is too great.

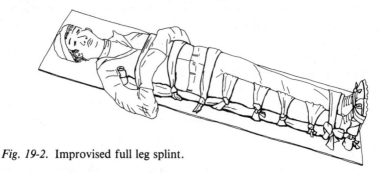

Fig. 19-2. Improvised full leg splint.

Fractures of the leg, ankle, and foot may be treated by splints improvised from ice axes, trees, or by tying to the opposite leg, making sure to loosen the boot lest the swelling impair circulation. Pad all splinting material and between the legs.

INJURIES TO THE HEAD AND SPINE

Injuries to the head and spine give alpine first aiders their worst moments. These portions of the anatomy are so delicate that the slightest mistake may cause further injury or death, yet often symptoms are so confusing it is difficult to choose a course of action. Usually indecision revolves around the question of whether or not the victim can safely be moved, or whether medical treatment on the spot is essential. Many climbers, particularly those who have once undergone the agonies of having to make this life-or-death decision, carry a detailed checklist of symptoms in their first aid kits. The sequence of examination and treatment is important, and must be accurate.

Head Injuries

It is first necessary to control any obvious bleeding. This may be done by direct pressure with sterile compresses. Ten minutes of pressure is usually sufficient to control most bleeding.

Next the first aider must thoroughly examine the victim.

1. *Unconsciousness* means there probably has been some bruising of the

brain tissue by swelling or hemorrhaging, which can create excess pressures within the skull. The length of unconsciousness is roughly proportional to the seriousness of the injury.

2. *Bleeding or secretion of clear spinal fluid* from the ears, nose or eyes is symptomatic of skull fracture. If any is observed, elevate the head to lower blood pressure within the skull and thus lessen bleeding. Caution: ALWAYS suspect a neck injury. Approximately 15 per cent of all severe head injuries are associated with a broken neck (see Injuries to the Spine).

3. *Unequal pupil size or unequal pupilary response* to light indicates possible intra-cranial pressure on the side which is larger or does not react to light. To test for light reaction shade the eye with the hand, then suddenly remove the hand, exposing the eye to bright sun (or to a flashlight). Both pupils should react equally; unequal pupils are an important sign of brain damage.

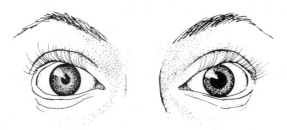

Fig. 19-3. Eyes with pupils of unequal size.

4. *A very slow pulse* or *noticeable respiratory fluctuation* means there may be hemorrhage within the brain and increased intra-cranial pressure.

5. *A headache generalized over the entire head* may be caused by internal hemorrhage.

6. *Disorientation* by the victim as to when, where, or how he got there may be an indication of serious injury.

If the victim has none of the above-listed symptoms and has no indications of spinal injuries, ask him to stand with his eyes closed. Swaying or falling may indicate damage to the brain or to the labyrinth (balancing organ). If he is stable, he may be evacuated by walking, but must be watched during the next six hours for evidence of drowsiness, nausea, vomiting, increased headache, bleeding, or unequal pupils. These may occur in injuries where there is an extradural hemorrhage between the skull and the membrane lining the skull.

If the victim has any of the above symptoms, he should be evacuated

Fig. 19-4. Cervical collar improvised from sweater.

by stretcher. If his condition is serious, a helicopter evacuation should be considered and if his condition is progressively deteriorating, speed of evacuation becomes of primary importance.

Injuries to the Spine

Injuries to the spine may be caused by a blow on the head, a fall, or a blow by a falling rock. If there is any doubt as to a possible neck or back injury, examine for it and, if still in doubt, treat it as if it were a fracture. The victim may be able to assist in defining the area of pain. With a cervical (neck) fracture, there usually is a great deal of muscular spasm and the victim will not want to move his neck. The first aider should check for the loss of muscular and sensory functions in the arms and legs by asking the victim to move them, or by stroking them with a pointed object and asking if any sensation is felt. Always check both right and left sides.

If a fracture of the cervical spine is suspected, splint neck with one pad under the chin to prevent compression of the spinal cord, and others on both sides of the neck to prevent rotation. Alternatively, a cervical collar of rolled ensolite or clothing should be applied, with the center directly under the chin, the objective being to prevent hyperextension or flexion position of the cervical spine. The lateral movements of the neck must also be restricted. For evacuation, log-roll the patient onto his back, being sure his body and head are at all times held in perfect alignment. One person should hold the head and exert slight traction, rotating the head in line with the body as others carefully roll the trunk and legs. EVACUATION MUST BE BY RIGID STRETCHER — not by rope stretcher. If none is available, wait for assistance and proper equipment.

If a fracture of the back is suspected, slowly and gently roll the victim onto his back with one person keeping the victim's legs constantly in line with his body. Put a small pad under the small of the back to hyperextend it, as there is less likelihood of injury to the spinal cord if the back is returned to the natural arched position. If there is any doubt regarding the extent of injuries, EVACUATE BY RIGID STRETCHER.

INJURIES TO JOINTS AND MUSCLES

Sprains

A sprain is a stretching or tearing of ligaments in the region of a joint, followed by hemorrhage, swelling, and tenderness. The most common and distressing type from the standpoint of mountain evacuation is a sprained ankle. If there is pain in the region of the ankle bones or in the region of swelling, the possibility of a fracture is great. It is often impossible to tell without an x-ray if the ankle bones are broken. All severe "sprains" should therefore be treated as possible fractures until proven otherwise. If a sprain has just occurred, the ankle should be elevated and a cold pack applied for 30 minutes to control internal hemorrhage. After that time, if the pain is still excessive, splint as for a fracture.

Strains

A strain is a rupture of the lining covering a muscle, or a tear in the muscular fibers. It is differentiated from a sprain by its occurrence over a muscle rather than in the region of a joint. Localized tenderness is present. Treatment is by warm applications which increase circulation and promote healing.

Dislocations

A dislocation is a tearing of the ligaments around a joint, followed by displacement of the bone from its socket. Most common in mountaineering is dislocation of the shoulder. The shoulder appears more angular, the arm cannot be moved, the muscles are in spasm, and there is considerable pain. A depression can be seen or felt below the tip of the injured shoulder, as compared with the normal side. REDUCTION OF A DISLOCATED SHOULDER SHOULD BE ATTEMPTED ONLY BY TRAINED PERSONNEL, SINCE PERMANENT DAMAGE CAN BE CAUSED BY IMPROPER PROCEDURE.

All dislocations should be treated in the same manner as fractures — by immobilization until medical assistance can be obtained.

HYPOTHERMIA

Many deaths not involving apparent injury have been caused by what the news media refer to as "exposure." Medically, this term is meaningless, for "exposure" is really a condition brought about by a number of factors, one of which, and perhaps the most important, is hypothermia — a lowering of the body's inner core temperature. There are three classes of hypothermia: (1) chronic, usually found in alcoholics, seniles, and others with medical problems; (2) acute, caused by immersion in cold water; and (3) subacute, occurring in healthy persons because of inadequate insulation or subjection to environmental stresses. Only subacute hypothermia and its treatment are discussed in this chapter.

To understand hypothermia it is useful to review some basic concepts of how the body can gain and lose heat.

Body Heat Gain

The body can gain or conserve heat in a number of ways, for example, through the digestion of food: the body produces heat by oxidation of food and tissue at a specific rate while resting (called the basal metabolic rate) or at an increased rate while exercising. The body can also gain heat externally from hot food and drink, the sun, fire, another body, and so on, or internally through muscular activity, either by deliberate exercise or by involuntary exercise like shivering. (Shivering produces as much heat as running at a slow pace or the approximate equivalent to the amount of heat generated from eating two medium-size chocolate bars per hour.) Heat is conserved through constriction of surface blood vessels, which reduces circulation at the skin layers and keeps blood nearer to the central core of the body.

Body Heat Loss

The body loses heat in five ways.

Respiration

A large amount of heat escapes when warm air is exhaled. This cannot be prevented entirely, but can be reduced by covering the mouth/nose area with wool or fur, thereby "pre-warming" the air as it passes through the material.

Evaporation

Evaporation of perspiration from the skin and moisture from the lungs contributes greatly to the amount of heat lost by the body. Although evaporation cannot be prevented, the amount of evaporation (and therefore cooling) can be controlled by wearing clothing that can be opened easily for ventilation or taken off readily, and wearing clothing that will not absorb water, but will breathe, that is, let the water vapor escape to reduce the cooling effect of evaporation.

Conduction

Sitting on the snow, touching cold equipment, and being rained upon are all examples of how heat can be lost as a result of conduction. If an individual becomes wet a tremendous amount of body heat is lost rapidly: deaths have occurred as a result of suspension or immersion in water below 40°F—body temperature could not be maintained. Although not as immediately serious in mountaineering situations, perspiration or rain should never be allowed to saturate articles of clothing, thus seriously reducing their insulating properties.

Radiation

Radiation causes the greatest amounts of heat loss from the body from uncovered surfaces, particularly the head, neck, and hands. Coverage of these areas, therefore, is extremely important in keeping warm.

Convection

The body continually warms (by conduction) a thin layer of air next to the skin. If warm air is retained close to the body, it remains warm. If removed by wind or air currents (convection), the body is cooled. The primary function of clothing is to retain this layer of warm air next to the skin, while allowing water vapor to pass outward, by enclosing air in cell walls or between numerous fibers. Heat is lost rapidly with the lightest breeze unless the proper type of clothing is worn to prevent the warm air from being convected away.

Deaths have been attributed to a loss of body heat at temperatures of 40°F, with 30 mph breeze. Under these conditions, the cooling effect on the skin is equal to that of much lower temperatures due to increased evaporation and convection. At lower temperatures and strong winds, cooling occurs even more rapidly. This is why the victim of an accident situation must have wind protection and a great deal of insulation (dead air space) to ensure that his body heat is retained at a safe level.

Signs and Symptoms

If heat loss exceeds heat gain, and if the condition is allowed to continue, hypothermia results. Table 19-a presents a summary of signs and symptoms keyed to the body's inner core (rectal) temperature. Although the temperatures shown are only approximate, the table provides an indication of how the bodily functions deteriorate with falling core temperatures. Learn to recognize these signs and symptoms and carefully watch yourself as well as others in your party during exposure to cold, wet, and wind.

Treatment

There are four lines of defense against hypothermia: avoidance of exposure, termination of exposure, early detection, and immediate treatment.

Table 19-a. Effects of Hypothermia

SIGNS AND SYMPTOMS

Body Temperature	Symptoms	Observable in Others	Felt by Yourself
98.6 → 95.0°F	Intense and uncontrollable shivering; ability to perform complex tasks impaired.	Slowing of pace. Intense shivering. Poor coordination.	Fatigue. Uncontrollable fits of shivering. Immobile, fumbling hands.
95.0 → 91.4°F	Violent shivering persists, difficulty in speaking, sluggish thinking, amnesia begins to appear	Stumbling, lurching gait. Thickness of speech. Poor judgment.	Stumbling. Poor articulation. Feeling of deep cold or numbness.
91.4 → 87.8°F	Shivering decreases; replaced by muscular rigidity and erratic, jerky movements; thinking not clear but maintains posture.	Irrationality, incoherence. Amnesia, memory lapses. Hallucinations. Loss of contact with environment.	Disorientation. Decrease in shivering. Stiffening of muscles. Exhaustion, inability to get up after a rest.
87.8 → 85.2°F	Victim becomes irrational, loses contact with environment, drifts into stupor; muscular rigidity continues; pulse and respiration slowed.	Blueness of skin. Decreased heart and respiratory rate. Dilation of pupils. Weak or irregular pulse. Stupor.	Blueness of skin. Slow, irregular, or weak pulse. Drowsiness.
85.2 → 78.8°F	Unconsciousness; does not respond to spoken word; most reflexes cease to function; heartbeat becomes erratic.	Unconsciousness.	
78.8°F ↓	Failure of cardiac and respiratory control centers in brain; cardiac fibrillation; probable edema and hemorrhage in lungs; apparent death.		

Avoidance of Exposure

In avoiding exposure one should dress for warmth, wind, and wet. When clothes become wet, they lose about 90 per cent of their insulating value. Wind drives cold air under and through clothing and refrigerates wet clothing by evaporating moisture from the surface. Put on rain gear before you are wet; put on wool clothes and wind gear before you start shivering. Do not be deceived by ambient temperatures well above freezing; most hypothermia cases develop in air temperatures between 30 and 50°F, and water at 50°F is unbearably cold—particularly when running down the neck and legs and flushing body heat from the surface of the clothes. Do not ask how cold is the air, but instead how cold is the water against the body.

Termination of Exposure

If you cannot stay dry and warm under the existing conditions, terminate exposure. Don't be afraid to give up your objective and turn back. Get out of the wind and rain. Bivouac early before energy is exhausted and before coordination and judgment are impaired. Eat sweets which are quickly and easily absorbed and keep continuously active to ensure adequate heat production.

Early Detection

Any time your party is exposed to wind, cold, or wet, carefully watch each other for the symptoms of hypothermia: uncontrollable fits of shivering; vague, slow, slurred speech; irrational actions; memory lapses, incoherence; immobile, fumbling hands; frequent stumbling, lurching gait; apparent exhaustion, inability to get up after a rest; drowsiness (to sleep is to die). Below the critical body temperature of 95°F the victim cannot produce enough body heat by himself to recover. At this point extreme measures must be taken to reverse the dropping core temperature.

Immediate Treatment

Although the victim may deny he is in trouble, believe the symptoms, not the victim. Even mild symptoms demand immediate, drastic treatment. First, prevent any further heat loss by getting the victim out of the wind and rain and into the best shelter available. Then remove his wet clothing and replace it with dry garments, insulate him from the ground, and warm him by the most expedient methods available. If the victim is only mildly impaired get him into a sleeping bag prewarmed by another member of the party who has stripped to underclothing in order to transfer a maximum amount of heat from his body to the bag. (Placing a hypothermia victim in a cold sleeping bag, no matter how much insulation it contains, is not sufficient because the victim's body cannot produce the heat needed to warm the bag and himself.) Well-wrapped, warm (not hot) rocks or canteens also help. Skin-to-skin, chest-to-chest contact is the most effective treatment, the stripped victim in a sleeping bag with another person (also stripped) or if a double bag is available, between two warmth donors. Build a fire, if possible, on each side of the victim. If he is able to eat he should be fed candy or sweetened foods; carbohydrates are the fuel most quickly transformed into heat and energy. If the victim is semiconscious or worse, try to keep him awake. Do not give hot liquids by mouth to the severe hypothermic.

FROSTBITE

Frostbite, or freezing of the tissues, most commonly affects the toes, fingers, and face. It occurs when an extremity loses heat faster than it can be replaced by the circulating blood, or it may result from direct exposure to extreme cold or high wind, as happens with the nose, ears, and hands. Damp feet may freeze because moisture conducts heat rapidly away from the skin and destroys the insulating value of socks and boots. With continued cold or inactivity, the blood circulation to the extremities is steadily reduced, accelerating the freezing process. With adequate equipment, properly maintained and used, frostbite is not likely to occur.

An area of superficial frostbite will look white or grayish, and the surface skin will feel hard, but the underlying tissue will be soft. With deeper involvement the affected area is hard, cold and insensitive. During rewarming large blisters may appear on the surface, as well as in the underlying tissue.

Superficially frostbitten areas are warmed by placing them against warm skin: feet, against a companion's abdomen or in his armpits; fingers, in a person's own armpits. Most emphatically the temperature of the frostbitten area should not be raised much above body temperature, such as by warming near a fire. Such misguided efforts to give speedy relief invariably increase the injury. Further, though the injured part may be snuggled closely, it must never be rubbed, especially with snow, for the additional cooling and the abrasive action of the snow can only cause more damage to already devitalized tissues. Areas of more extensive or deep frostbite, in which the affected area is white, has no feeling, and appears deeply frozen, should be immersed in 99°F to 104°F water until thawed.

If it is not possible to completely and uninterruptedly thaw the deeply frozen area, no attempt should be made to do so; it is better to await medical assistance than risk incomplete thawing and/or refreezing. In some circumstances, callous though it may sound, no attempt should be made to thaw frozen feet, since it is possible for a person to walk on frozen feet and suffer little or no additional tissue damage; once they are thawed he becomes a stretcher case, creating an obvious burden for the party and perhaps incurring considerable pain.

HIGH ALTITUDE PULMONARY EDEMA (HAPE)

Pulmonary edema is the leakage of blood plasma into the lungs, which renders the air sacs (alveoli) ineffective in exchanging oxygen and carbon dioxide in the blood. This condition rarely occurs in healthy people below 9000 feet; the average elevation at which it strikes in the United States is 12,000 feet (the level of onset varies for mountain ranges in other parts of the world).

The early symptoms of pulmonary edema are similar to those of pneumonia, although pulmonary edema is not precipitated by an infection and there is no fever. Within 12 to 36 hours after reaching high altitude the victim of pulmonary edema experiences extreme weakness, shortness of breath, nausea, vomiting, very rapid pulse (120-160), cyanosis (bluish color), "noisy" breathing which progresses to moist crackling breath sounds, and irritative coughing which produces a frothy white or pink sputum and later blood.

If untreated, the victim rapidly moves into the final phase characterized by unconsciousness and bubbles in the mouth or nose. If the unconscious victim is not immediately moved to lower elevation or given oxygen, he will die. All the early symptoms may be mistaken for "mountain sickness" or fatigue, or may pass unnoticed during the night, with the morning finding the victim unconscious in the final phase. The most effective first aid is rapid evacuation to lower altitude or constant administration of oxygen.

HEAT EXHAUSTION

Heat exhaustion may occur either when an individual is exposed to a hot environment or when he overheats (perhaps because of physical exertion). In heat exhaustion, the blood vessels in the skin become so dilated that the blood to the brain and other vital organs is reduced to inadequate levels. The result is an effect similar to fainting. Lack of acclimatization to heat or even minor degrees of dehydration or salt deficiency make an individual more susceptible to heat exhaustion. All or some of the following symptoms may be present: nausea, cold and clammy skin, faintness, weakness, and perhaps a rapid pulse. Treatment consists of rest, in the shade if possible, with plenty of liquid and salt.

HEAT STROKE (SUNSTROKE)

When exposed to excessive sun the body may become so overheated that it is provided too much blood through the cooling effort of the circulatory system. Symptoms are a flushed, hot face; rapid, full pulse; pain in the head; weakness; dizziness. If sunstroke occurs, it is EXTREMELY SERIOUS and requires IMMEDIATE treatment by cooling of the head and body with snow or water; administration of cold liquid should be continued until the body temperature drops to near normal.

THE PERSONAL FIRST AID KIT

Mountaineering first aid begins with the first aid kit, an essential which must be carried *by every person on every trip*. The kit should be small, compact, and sturdy. The contents must be waterproof whether the container is or not.

All mountaineers should have the items listed below in their personal first aid kits, plus any medications they need because of individual medical problems, such as allergies. Parties going on long trips or to regions remote from medical aid may make additions to their group first aid kit. The majority of these require a doctor's prescription and special instructions concerning their use and hazardous side effects.

THE MOUNTAINEERING FIRST AID KIT

Item	Quantity and Size	Use
Aspirin	12 tablets—5 grain	One to 2 every 4 hours, for pain.
Antacid	6 tablets	For indigestion or heartburn
Bandaids	12, 1″	For minor cuts
Butterfly bandaids (or know how to make)	6, various sizes	For closing cuts
Carlisle (Battle Dressing)	1, 4″ (or sanitary napkin)	For large bleeding wounds
Moleskin	½ package	For padding blisters or "hot spots"
Needle	1 medium size	To remove splinters, etc.
Tincture of Benzoin	1-oz. bottle (plastic)	Painted on the skin to make tape adhere more firmly
Antibacterial soap	1 oz. bottle (plastic)	Mild antiseptic for abrasions, cuts

Razor blade, single edge	1	For cutting tape, mole foam, hair, loose bandage ends
Roller gauze	2 rolls, 2″ x 5 yd.	For holding gauze flats in place
Steri-pad gauze	6, 4″ x 4″	For larger wounds
Tape, non waterproof	2″ roll	For securing dressings, etc.
Triangular bandage	1	For supporting arm, protecting dressing from contamination
Prescription medication	As prescribed by personal physician	If carried, each should be stored in a separate container, and clearly labelled as to dosage, expiration date, type of drug and expected reaction
Thermometer	1 (40°F to 120°F)	For measuring temperature
Wire mesh splint	1	For suspected fractures: forearm, wrist, ankle, cervical
Tweezers	1	For removing splinters

Miscellaneous items may include:
    Coins for telephoning in emergencies
    First aid/rescue information, including current telephone numbers
    Pencil and paper, accident report form

COMMON MOUNTAIN MISERIES
Blisters

Blisters result from rubbing of the skin against the socks, either because the boots are too large or laced too loosely, or because the socks are lumpy or wrinkled. To prevent blisters, shoe and sock should be removed at the first sensation of discomfort and the foot examined for reddened skin areas which indicate undue friction. A wide band of adhesive tape, applied smoothly over — and well beyond — the margins of the "hot spot," relieves discomfort and prevents blistering. Application of tincture of benzoin prior to taping makes the tape adhere more firmly and toughens the skin. If preventive measures are not taken in time, a hole may be cut in a piece of moleskin, which is then placed over the blister to protect the area from further direct contact. The moleskin is secured with tape.

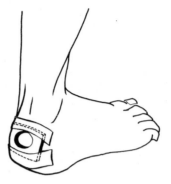

Fig. 19-5. Blister protection. Circle is cut out of pad to keep pressure off blister.

Because of the risk of infection, blisters should not be opened unless absolutely necessary. If it must be done, the area is washed with soap and water and a needle sterilized with a match is inserted under the blister's edge. Fluid is gently pressed out and a sterile bandage applied. If the blister has already broken it should be washed and bandaged in the same manner and carefully watched for subsequent infection.

Headache

Headache in the mountains usually results from inadequate sun-glasses, tension in neck muscles, constipation, acute mountain sickness, or some pre-existing physical condition. In any case of headache, the source of the trouble should be sought and eliminated by better protection of head or eyes, stretching and relaxing neck muscles, or taking a laxative. Aspirin may alleviate the immediate pain.

Acute Mountain Sickness (AMS)

Whenever a person ascends rapidly to an altitude greater than that to which he is accustomed, his system adjusts to new conditions: breathing becomes more rapid to extract the necessary oxygen from the thinner air; the blood increases its proportion of oxygen-carrying red corpuscles. In the extreme case, such as when an airplane pilot climbs thousands of feet in minutes, unconsciousness results. The mountaineer, moving upward slowly but steadily, suffers very uncomfortable but less drastic symptoms. First comes general malaise and loss of appetite, then headache, followed by increasing weakness and lessening of will. If forced by social pressure or inner resolution to continue the climb, the sufferer eventually becomes apathetic, nauseated, dizzy, and sleepy.

Symptoms of mountain sickness can occur even at relatively low altitude. Tourists driving in automobiles to 8000 feet sometimes feel lazy or dizzy, or experience palpitations. Climbers generally have more time to acclimatize, and except for shortness of breath usually feel only minor effects until elevations of 12,000 feet or more are reached. However, in regions such as the Pacific Northwest, where climbers live at sea level yet ascend to over 14,000 feet on a weekend, mountain sickness of greater or lesser severity is the rule rather than the exception.

Proper use of the rest step is the first remedy. Next come rest stops, with forced deep breathing ("overbreathing") to hyperventilate the lungs. Nourishment in the form of the simple sugars in candy, oranges, or fruit juice should be taken.

Muscular Cramps

Leg cramps caused by an accumulation of lactic acid in the muscles and loss of salt through perspiration sometimes make it impossible for a climber to continue. Such cramps appear suddenly, usually after strenuous exertion for several hours; the pain is excruciating. During ordinary activity the blood removes lactic acid as it is formed, but in extended exercise a surplus may build up. Resting, to allow the blood to carry away the lactic acid, is the first step in treatment. Deep breathing, and stretching of the cramped muscle as quickly and completely as possible—painful as this may be—give further relief. Salt tablets should be administered immediately to remove the other cause; indeed, many climbers, after finding their cramps quickly dispelled by salt intake, wisely prevent them by using salt tablets at periodic intervals on any climb if they perspire heavily.

SNOWBLINDNESS

Snowblindness is caused by failure to use adequate eye protection (see Chapter 2) during brilliant sunshine on snow or light-colored rock. The eyes are bloodshot, feel irritated and "full of sand." The treatment is application of cool, wet compresses to the eyes, and then having the patient wear two pairs of dark glasses. Aspirin controls the pain. Occasionally it may be necessary to cover the eyes and lead the casualty out by the hand. Recovery may take two or three days. Snowblindness is not a permanent condition.

SUNBURN

Protection of the skin from the burning rays of the sun is discussed in Chapter 2. At high altitude and on snow nothing but coverage by clothing is completely effective and a degree of burning is inevitable. Lips are particularly vulnerable and some climbers develop severe lip sores unless they exercise special caution. Reflection from snow causes burns in areas not ordinarily affected, such as under the chin, around the eyes, inside the nostrils and ears, and on the roof of the mouth. Lack of a hat when hair is short, thin, or absent may result in scalp burns.

First degree burns with skin reddening and second degree burns with blisters are not uncommon. The climber often miscalculates the intensity of the sun or is simply too weary to take preventive action. As with any burn—from sun, rope, or fire—if the affected area is large, toxic substances absorbed by the body can cause generalized illness.

Sunburn usually is treated on first notice by further applications of sunburn preventive. Sun screens should be used rather than the more common cosmetic suntan preparations. In severe cases, and if there is much swelling, cold compresses should be applied. Aspirin may be taken for pain, and warm, salty liquids administered to replenish body fluids.

Plate 27. Mt. Maude, North Cascades. (Bruce Gaumond)

Plate 28. Calgary Mountain Rescue group lowering climber injured in 40-foot fall on Mt. Rundle, Banff, Alberta. (Patrick Morrow)

20 *

ALPINE RESCUE

ANYONE WHO CLIMBS very often or for very long must expect sooner or later to be involved in misfortune, if not his own, then someone else's. The very nature of the sport rules out much chance of help from casual passers-by; climbers usually must be rescued by other climbers, often at great risk and sacrifice. So high a degree of mutual responsibility requires that every mountaineer be familiar with emergency procedures.

Many times a handful of climbers have effected a difficult rescue speedily and efficiently using only such labor-saving and safety devices as could be improvised from ordinary climbing tools. This chapter approaches the rescue problem from the viewpoint of a small climbing party.

SEARCH

Search is ordinarily not begun until it is reasonably certain the missing person is in need of help. After straying from the route he may recognize his mistake, retrace his steps, and rejoin the party within a few hours. If he is healthy, experienced, well equipped, and has been traveling where injury is unlikely, search can even be deferred overnight.

Under some conditions there should be no hesitation. Immediate search is mandatory if the lost person might have wandered onto steep rock or a crevassed glacier, if a potential physical disability such as diabetes is known to be a factor, if he is fatigued, inexperienced, poorly equipped, or if the one missing is a child. Similarly, if an entire rope team is missing on difficult terrain, after a severe storm, or in avalanche conditions, a search must be started immediately.

A small party may be able to make no more than a hasty search along a limited track. With a half dozen people available there probably can be a perimeter search. If this is ineffectual, a large group must then proceed to thoroughly comb a considerable area.

Regardless of the method adopted, each person must know the full plan before beginning the search. If the party is to divide, each division must know the location of the others. Audible signals such as yodels, yells, and whistles, or visible signs with mirrors or lights, should be pre-arranged. All members must know the rendezvous point and the time at which they are to meet regardless of the success or failure of their efforts.

For safety, searchers should travel in pairs or remain always within earshot of one another. This means that a party of two or three people can cover only a narrow strip of ground. Their best chance is outguessing the lost person, putting themselves in his place and visualizing the logical errors. The most likely places such as the exits of wrong gullies and ridges are checked first. Failing there, the party retraces its original trail while searching about for tracks showing where the lost person wandered off. Once such a point is found the searchers proceed swiftly along the most likely path, watching for footprints in snow, mud, sand, or on footlogs. When such track-showing ground is intermittent, the party fans out at broad intervals, calling to each other regularly and pausing frequently to listen for calls from the lost person. If after several hours no clues at all have been found, it is probably time to seek outside help.

WHEN AN ACCIDENT HAPPENS

When a climber is injured the victim must be reached quickly but not at the expense of additional accidents. The approach should not be made from directly above, as this may invite further injury from rockfall. Calmness is essential: excitement can only frustrate the rescue effort. Under rockfall or avalanche hazard those not needed immediately take cover. On difficult terrain only one or two rescuers should be dispatched to reach the victim, not ignoring the need for belays and anchors.

Competent leadership and strict discipline are requisite to success in alpine rescue. If there has been no recognized leader, then one must be selected to deal with the emergency. Once he accepts the task, companions abide by his decisions without argument, though he should remain flexible enough to consider suggestions.

Urgent first aid should be rendered at the first possible moment: bleeding stopped, breathing restarted, shock relieved, and fractures immobilized. Impending hazards may force the party to move the victim at once to a more sheltered location. However, choice between acceptance of the hazards of the accident site and the risks of moving the victim may be difficult. If he must be moved, methods must be used which do not compound his injuries.

If for any reason an injured person must be left unguarded even for a few minutes he must be tied to the mountain. Too often an injured person left alone has in his confusion fallen or wandered to his death, sometimes untying himself to do so. Companions must anticipate that he may become irrational and secure him so he cannot possibly work free.

When something has gone wrong, swift action may be less effective than correct action. A spontaneous but short-sighted effort has less chance of ultimate success than one more deliberately considered. Therefore, after the initial demands of safety and first aid are satisfied, the leader and party sit down to plan. In the mountains once any person is beyond voice range of companions the party has lost control over his subsequent actions; therefore, there must be no hasty separation. Everything must be thought through to the very end, everything prearranged, including what each member is to do under all conceivable circumstances until he has completely played out his part in the rescue operation.

Every aspect of the situation needs cool analysis: seriousness of the victim's injuries, measures necessary to sustain him during evacuation, terrain and distance to the road, and the strength and resources of the party. Then, and only then, should a course of action be selected.

Evacuation by the Party

There are occasions when a party can successfully perform the evacuation of an injured party member. If the injured person can walk and his injuries are relatively minor, lightening of his pack and moral support may be all that is needed to get him out. Minor but disabling injuries such as a sprained ankle or injured knee may possibly be evacuated by the party also.

It is generally true that a victim will benefit from a period of rest following an injury. The further trauma of immediate evacuation is seldom justified: therefore the inevitable move should be postponed until the victim's condition has stabilized. The victim himself is probably the best indicator of when to start. He should be consulted and his condition closely observed prior to and during transportation. His comfort must be kept foremost in the minds of the party.

Some conditions require immediate evacuation: pulmonary edema, unconsciousness for unknown cause, diabetic coma, and progressively deteriorating conditions such as appendicitis, or whenever circumstances of weather or terrain are life-threatening. Some conditions require that evacuation be delayed until trained rescue personnel arrive (unless such help will be more than 24 hours in arriving): head injuries, neck and spinal fractures, heart attack, apoplexy (stroke), and internal injuries. Evacuation is required but not urgent for all other serious injuries and illnesses.

When Outside Aid is Needed

There are occasions when a party cannot cope with its own emergency. In an area requiring long, difficult technical evacuation (involving long raises or lowers), if injuries are severe, or when the party size, relative condition, terrain and distance to the trailhead combine to make transport difficult, help will have to be obtained. As a general rule 30 or more rescuers are often needed to carry a disabled victim for distances greater than 2 to 3 miles on even the best of trails.

Once it is determined that outside aid will be needed, help should be summoned as soon as the victim is stabilized and it is certain that the persons going for help will no longer be needed at the accident site. In many areas, help by helicopter is usually no more than 3 hours away once word gets to the proper authorities. If a ground party is required, help is usually about 8 to 16 hours away. Therefore, if the party is in an area accessible by helicopter, if the party and victim are sheltered, and if the weather is good, there is little reason to move the victim unless the injuries require doing so.

When help must be requested—from climbers on nearby peaks, from people living or working in the region, or from local authorities—then there must be no hesitancy in making the request. At all times a party should know what help it can expect if its own efforts fail, where and how to get it, and how to co-operate with authorities and rescuers.

Going for Help

Whenever possible, two climbers should travel out together—partly for safety and partly because two people do a better job of obtaining help. Messengers should carry enough equipment to handle their own emergencies but not so much that they cannot move swiftly. Wherever possible marking the trail out will facilitate travel back to the accident site by the rescue party. It is important to remember that the victim and members of the party remaining with the victim are relying solely on the messengers at this point. They are assuming that the message is getting to the proper authorities and that help will soon be on its way; therefore it is doubly important that the messengers travel in a safe manner. The certainty, not the swiftness, of message delivery is the most important factor.

Sometimes it may not be possible to send for help at all, in which case efforts should be made to signal someone visually or auditorily; the victim and party then await rescue. Such situations exemplify the necessity of leaving the intended route and estimated time of return with a responsible person who will notify the proper authorities if the party fails to return.

Once in contact with civilization the messengers call the county sheriff, National Forest or Park Service personnel, or the local authorities in charge of the region, and ask them to relay a message to the local Mountain Rescue group or to provide the needed help themselves. *If evacuation must be accomplished over technical terrain, the authorities must be made aware of the necessity for personnel trained in technical rescue work.*

The messengers' job is not ended at this point. They must make certain messages are sent at once, accurately, and that they reach their destination. Often the organization of a rescue depends upon a chain of communication, messages relayed from person to person via telephone and radio until finally a rescue leader is reached. Along the way vital information may be lost by non-mountaineers who do not understand the words they are asked to convey. In the interest of efficiency and accuracy, the messengers should talk directly with some trusted fellow climber. The line of communication must not be broken. If the rescue leader cannot be personally contacted, then messengers must be insistent with intermediaries to the point of being obnoxious, if necessary. Messages garbled along the way — or simply not forwarded — have directly caused a number of tragic rescue failures.

The party must have a clear grasp of the problem and of its own capacities and needs before deciding how much and what form of aid to request. Once a team has been dispatched to obtain help there is no way to control what they do or say. Excited messengers hurrying to reach the road with little idea of the party's needs only cause confusion.

Enough information must reach the rescue leader so that an effective rescue plan can be devised and executed. A completed accident report form (see example) contains the necessary information and should be filled out in duplicate at the scene of the accident for each injured member of the party. One copy should be sent out with the messengers reporting the accident and given to the responsible agency; the other copy should be retained by the party leader for future reference in making any required reports. In addition, a map with the exact location pinpointed is helpful to rescuers.

Having established contact with the rescue leader, the messengers should remain by the telephone until the rescue party arrives. The rescue leader may need to contact them for further information, to advise them of unexpected developments, or to make progress reports. Careful consideration must be given to the matter of informing relatives of people in the climbing party. In a large party this requires making a written list of names and telephone numbers before leaving the accident scene. It is cruel to keep family members waiting in anxiety for hours or days, but it might be well to await the arrival of the rescue leader so that efforts to

ACCIDENT REPORT FORM

This form is to be completed in duplicate AT the scene of the accident for each injured member of the party. One copy should be sent with those going for help and the other form retained by the leader.

ACCIDENT	Date:	Time: AM ☐ PM ☐
	Quadrangle:	Section:
LOCATION	Exact Location (include marked map):	
	Terrain: Glacier ☐ Snow ☐ Brush ☐ Timber ☐ Rock ☐ Trail ☐ Heather ☐ Easy ☐ Moderate ☐ Steep ☐ Other:	

COMPLETE DESCRIPTION OF ACCIDENT		Ascending ☐ Descending ☐ Roped ☐ Unroped ☐ Rock Fall ☐ Ice Fall ☐ Avalanche ☐ Illness ☐ Excess Heat ☐ Cold ☐ Equipment Failure ☐
	Witnesses:	Other:

INJURED PERSON	Name:	Age:
	Address:	Male ☐ Female ☐
	Phone:	
	Whom to Notify: Relation: Phone:	

INJURIES	Overall Condi-tion	Good ☐ Fair ☐ Serious ☐ Fatal ☐ Unconscious: Yes ☐ No ☐ If yes, length of time:
	Injury 1	Location on Body: Type of Injury:
	Injury 2	Location on Body: Type of Injury:
	Other Injuries	Location on Body: Type of Injury:

FIRST AID TREATMENT	General:	Bleeding Stopped ☐ Shelter Built ☐ Artificial Respiration ☐ Warm Fluids Given ☐ Treated for Shock ☐ Evacuation ☐
	Injury 1	
	Injury 2	
	Other Injuries:	

ON-THE-SCENE PLANS	Will stay put ☐ Will evacuate to trail ☐ to Road ☐ Will evacuate a short distance to shelter ☐ Will send some members out ☐ Other:
PERSONNEL	Number: Inexperienced ☐ Experienced ☐ Intermediates ☐ Advanced ☐ Capability for a bivouac: Yes ☐ No ☐
	ATTACH the pre-trip prepared LIST OF PARTY MEMBERS including names, address and phone numbers to the ACCIDENT FORM BEING TAKEN OUT.
EQUIPMENT AVAILABLE	Tents ☐ Sleeping Bags ☐ Ensolite ☐ Flares ☐ Saw ☐ Hardware ☐ Stove and Fuel ☐ Ropes ☐ Other:
WEATHER	Warm ☐ Moderate ☐ Freezing ☐ Snow ☐ Wind ☐ Sun ☐ Clouds ☐ Fog ☐ Rain ☐ Other:
TYPE OF EVACUATION RECOMND'D	Lowering Operation ☐ Carry-Out ☐ Helicopter ☐ Rigid stretcher ☐ None until specialized medical assistance ☐ Specify:
PARTY LEADER	Name:
MESSENGERS SENT FOR HELP	Names:
FURTHER INFORMATION, IF ANY.	
RECOMMEN-DATIONS FOR FUTURE CLIMBS	Equipment: Leadership: Route: Abilities:

reach the messengers for further information will not be hampered by busy telephone lines. Also, the rescue leader will have had a wealth of experience in dealing with concerned relatives and the public news media.

A last and important function of the messengers is to meet the rescue party at an agreed-upon rendezvous, rested and ready to lead the way back to the accident scene. If they are incapacitated by fatigue or injury it is all the more important that wherever possible the trail be marked on the way out.

TRANSPORT ON TECHNICAL TERRAIN

On terrain so difficult as to require technical climbing, even a minor handicap can render a person incapable of descent without help. With reserve strength and plentiful equipment, a large party may be able to choose almost any route for evacuation, devising elaborate traversing and lifting devices, sending scouts ahead to prepare these in advance of the main party.

The small party has less choice. Though short lifts and traverses can be made, generally the lack of party strength makes it necessary to evacuate by descending the fall line, which uses the least energy and equipment. As a general rule, rescue on class 2-3 terrain is manpower-oriented, and on class 4-5 terrain is more equipment-oriented. Frequently the party must descend by a different (and unknown) route, with hidden dangers. The prime object — moving the victim without further injury — is naturally uppermost in all minds, yet the safety of each individual must never be forgotten. A rescue is inherently more dangerous than a normal climb over the same ground because attention is focused upon the victim instead of upon the surroundings and one's own movements. Therefore, solidly anchored belays may be required both for the victim and for those aiding him, even where superfluous under ordinary climbing conditions. If ropes are in short supply, rescuers can be served by a fixed line to which they attach themselves with prusik slings. Since in a small party the normal equipment may be insufficient for rescue purposes, many climbers carry in their rucksacks — depending on the climb — such emergency items as extra slings, carabiners, a pulley, brake bar, folding saw, snow shovel, whistle, plastic tarp, emergency flares and/or smoke, as well as all the basic essentials described in Chapter 2.

Lowering

A person with slight injuries can climb down under tension from a tight belay, assisted by a companion who helps him place his hands and feet. On snow or ice large platform steps can be prepared. If the victim has no head injury or symptom of shock he can sometimes be allowed to rappel, aided by a rescuer on an adjacent but separate rappel line and always on a safety belay

Seat Harness

If neither downclimbing nor rappelling is possible but the victim still has use of his legs, and no serious upper body injuries, he can be lowered in his seat harness. As a companion pays out the belay line through a braking device, he guides himself down with his feet and hands, again aided by a rescuer on a separate belay line. If there is some doubt about the victim falling over, a chest harness can be arranged to provide upright stability.

Back Carry

If the victim has a minor but disabling lower body injury or is uneasy about being lowered or rappelling, a good lowering method is the back carry. The coil carry method (see Fig. 20-1) utilizes a coiled climbing rope joining rescuer and victim together. A prusik can be run from the lowering rope to the victim's seat harness to take some weight off the rescuer's shoulders and aid in keeping the victim upright. Ideally both rescuer and victim are independently belayed from above. Another method of back

Fig. 20-1. Coil carry.

carry employs nylon webbing to distribute the victim's weight (Fig. 20-2). The webbing should be extremely well padded, especially under the victim's thighs, to prevent cutting in and subsequent circulation loss. The belay set-up for the nylon webbing carry is the same as for the coil carry. A back carry should not be used in a situation involving back or neck injuries, suspected internal injuries, serious head injuries, or other injuries requiring constant monitoring; all of these require evacuation by rigid stretcher.

Fig. 20-2. Nylon webbing carry.

Friction Braking Devices

The versatile carabiner brake is commonly used to control a descent. It can be doubled for very heavy loads, operated from either an upper or lower station, and used for descents of more than one rope length. The braking action is the same as that for rappelling as described in Chapter 9.

The brake usually is placed near the top anchor, but occasionally it can be more conveniently situated below or at one side. In such case, the rope runs from the victim through an upper carabiner or pulley and down to the braking station.

A safety prusik should be attached to the lowering rope below the braking system and also to a separate anchor system. This prusik can be manned by the individual working the braking system if personnel is limited. On a long pitch it is sometimes desirable to tie in additional ropes while the load hangs in midair to allow an uninterrupted descent of several rope lengths. The problem is passing the joining knot around the braking system without dropping the load. Two persons can accomplish this without difficulty. When about 4 feet of rope remain before the knot joining the two ropes together comes to the braking system, the descent is halted (Fig. 20-3). One person holds the rope while the other attaches an additional prusik sling just below the brake and safety prusik and then wraps this sling several times around an auxiliary carabiner anchored above the braking system. The sling is held—it must not be tied—while the load is gently eased onto the prusik by slacking off the lowering rope. The knot is then passed through the braking system *one brake at a time* (the upper brake is released, the knot passed, then the brake reset, etc.). Once the knot has been passed through all the brakes and all of the brakes reset, the sling which is wrapped around the auxiliary carabiner is allowed to slide and the load is slowly transferred back to the lowering rope, permitting the descent to continue. (Note: the prusik sling must be long enough to allow for the slack introduced into the system when passing the knot.)

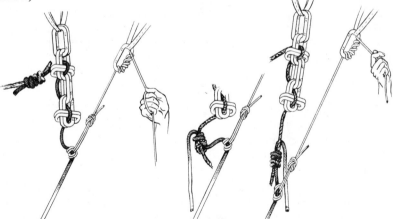

Fig. 20-3. Passing the knot joining two ropes through a carabiner brake system.

Raising

Although lowering puts the force of gravity on the side of the rescuers and thus is preferred whenever possible, there is sometimes no option but to raise a victim up a steep face. In such case the rescuers have a choice of two methods: the prusik system, which depends upon the victim's own efforts, and the pulley system, which can be used to lift even an inert weight. Although they work equally well on steep rock or on snow, these systems are usually associated with crevasse rescue and therefore are described in Chapter 16. The same safety precautions that apply to lowering apply to raising. Backup anchors, safety prusiks, and safety belays are a critical part of any lowering or raising operation.

Traversing

If the descent route must deviate far from the fall line, transport becomes very difficult. A pendulum is useful on terrain where rescuers can traverse overhead. Suspended from an anchored rope, the victim is pulled sideways by a second rope also anchored from above. As tension is gradually released from the first rope he pendulums to a position underneath the anchor of the second rope. The first rope is reanchored farther along for the next pendulum, if required.

Rockfall

Falling rocks are responsible for a large proportion of injuries, and the danger is many times increased during rescue. Loose rock is then a particularly serious hazard because of the many dragging ropes, because the attention of the rescuers is focused on the victim, and because the operation may continue into the night. Anyone working above the victim or other rescuers must be doubly careful. Those below, with small chance for dodging, should wear hard hats and pad vital spots with extra clothing. If possible, sentries should be posted to warn of barrages.

AVALANCHE RESCUE

In the majority of backcountry avalanche accidents, rescue of the trapped victim(s) depends on the actions of the unburied survivors. Organized rescue from afar usually turns into a body recovery operation rather than a live rescue. Statistics show that 50 per cent of buried avalanche victims suffocate if not uncovered within 30 minutes. The unburied survivors must not panic, but must note with respect to fixed objects nearby — trees or rocks — first, the point on the slope where the victim was caught, and second, the point where last seen. As the avalanche moves, the point in the snow where the victim was last seen is followed until the avalanche stops. With three points on the path of the victim located, the probability is good that he lies on or near the line between the two, probably closer to the lowest point.

It is important to keep in mind that sliding snow flows like water, faster on the surface and in the center than on the bottom and at the sides. When an avalanche follows a twisting channel the snow and the victim conform to the turns. Both these facts have obvious implications for searches.

Fig. 20-4. Slab avalanche. Victims are likely to be at accumulation points (marked by Xs).

Regardless of the proximity to assistance a quick scuff search should be conducted immediately. After an escape route has been picked and lookouts posted to watch for further slides, the upper two points are quickly marked. The party hurries down the victim's path toward the lowest point, searching carefully as they go, scuffling their feet through the snow to uncover clues—items of the victim's gear, or his avalanche cord. They look especially carefully around trees or outcroppings which might have stopped him, and scan beneath any blocks of snow that lie on the surface. They shout at intervals, then maintain absolute silence while listening for a muffled answer.

If any loose equipment is found on or near the surface, the buried victim probably lies not far uphill, and rescuers immediately begin to probe and dig in the vicinity. If no equipment is found, the party should mark the observed stopping point of that portion of the avalanche debris where the victim disappeared, and quickly search the area just above, where he is most likely to lie. If nothing is found they begin to probe, using blunted willow wands, taped ice axes, or reversed ski poles. Sharp probes must not be used because it must be assumed the victim is still alive. More systematic probing is best done as a team, not by individuals, and hence may be beyond the capability of the small party except on a very limited basis. However, even a sole survivor *must* carry out a quick search to the best of his ability.

Once the quick scuff search has been carried out, an excruciating choice must be made based on the size of the avalanche area, strength and number of unburied survivors, and the availability of outside help: whether to continue search with full party strength or to send for assistance. Probably the best course, if the avalanche is not too large, is to continue the search with full party strength unless organized help such as ski patrol personnel are near at hand. If the party is large, two people can be sent for help while the rest continue searching. To speed the return trip the messenger must carefully mark the route, especially if snow is falling. Messengers should also be prepared to lead the rescue party back to the scene of the accident.

Whatever the size of the party, the search is not given up as long as there is any hope of success. People have lived for a week in dry snow, and one victim survived burial for some nine hours in wet avalanche debris, his life saved by an air space between big blocks of snow. On the other hand, only one out of six avalanche burial victims survives after being covered for two hours.

Once the victim is found, first aid begins unless there are unmistakable signs of death. As soon as his head is exposed, his mouth and throat are cleared and mouth-to-mouth resuscitation is started. The first aider must check for bleeding and mechanical injuries. Head and spine injuries are common and treatment for hypothermia and shock are an absolute necessity.

Evacuation on Snow

On snow there is a particularly urgent need for protecting the victim from heat loss while administering first aid and planning the evacuation. The victim should be wrapped in extra clothing and insulated from the snow by pads, packs, or ropes. If the victim cannot be moved quickly a trench or low wall should be constructed as a shield from the wind. For overnight stays a tent should be erected or a snow cave dug. If possible, the victim should be moved to a sheltered spot such as below timberline. This should be done as quickly as first aid can be administered and the victim prepared for travel.

Sometimes the victim can be lowered in a sitting glissade position, well wrapped in extra clothing, perhaps riding behind a companion who smooths the track, the two tied together and carefully belayed. If injuries are relatively minor, and the slope not excessively steep, he can be roped in with two or three companions who slide slowly as a team, constantly under control.

The ice axe belay usually is not strong enough for rescue purposes unless two or more are used: if the snow is very hard, the axe will not penetrate; if it is very soft, the axe will pull out. Hip belays are preferable, particularly in very hard or very soft snow. Moats often provide superb anchor positions for lowering. In narrow chutes, belay ropes can be run to both sides. The deadman anchor, the snow fluke, the snow picket or stake, used singly or in combination as described in Chapter 14, also serve as anchors for belayers or for braking devices. The bollard is always worthy of consideration, and a metal ice axe buried in a snow trench at right angles to the pull can be a very strong anchor.

TRANSPORT ON NON-TECHNICAL TERRAIN

In many rescues the hardest job begins when the steep terrain is past and ropes are put away. No longer aided by gravity, the party must carry its burden, very fatiguing work on rough ground. Under some conditions, however, a few simple techniques extend the capacity of the small party so that it need not call for help.

The *four-hand seat* is useful for short distances if the two carriers are the same height. Standing side by side, each grasps his right wrist with his left hand, palms down. Each carrier then grasps the wrist of the other with his free hand to form a seat.

For longer distances the *ice axe carry* is better: carriers wearing rucksacks stand side by side with joined ice axe shafts resting between them in their pack straps; the victim is seated on the padded shafts with his arms over their shoulders.

A strong climber can carry a person on his back for long distances provided the weight is distributed properly. The back carry, described in "Transport on Technical Terrain," works well on non-technical terrain also. Another form of back carry, the *rucksack carry*, involves slitting a large rucksack on the sides near the bottom so the victim can step into it like a pair of shorts.

Another method of evacuation is by rope stretcher constructed and used with or without the aid of ice axes and/or branches as follows:

Place the rope, preferably 150-foot, extended, on the ground, and find the center (Fig. 20-5). From the center make 16 180-degree bends, 8 extending on each side of the center. The distance between the bends should be approximately as wide as the victim and the full 16 bends approximately as long as the victim's length. Bring the rope ends around the sides of the stretcher adjacent to the bends. Tie a clove hitch in the rope section adjacent to each bend and insert the bend. Continue tying clove hitches and inserting bends until all the bends are bound. Leave a small loop between the apex of the bend and the knot. Insert the remaining rope through the loops until the entire remainder is coiled around the stretcher. Snug up the knots, tie off the ends, and pad the area which will support the body from neck to hips.

Someone should try out the stretcher, whether it is constructed of rope

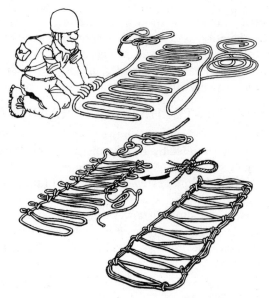

Fig. 20-5. Rope stretcher.

or branches, before placing the victim on it, to determine the need for additional padding or supporting material without causing discomfort to the victim. CAUTION: evacuation by rope or any improvised stretcher is usually very rough on the victim. If there is a chance that further injury will result, WAIT until trained rescue personnel with proper equipment are available to assist.

SPECIALIZED RESCUE EQUIPMENT

Rescue organizations often bring equipment especially designed to make their task easier. Although these items are not standard climbing gear, every climber should know what they are and what can be done with them.

Most important is a rigid stretcher of fiberglass or metal. A well known design is the Stokes litter which has a framework of metal tubing and a wire mesh basket that closely fits the body outlines. The Stokes, although heavy, works well on technical evacuations and general carry-outs. Lighter weight fiberglass stretchers with aluminum framework break down into sections. This type of stretcher works on technical rescues where weight and bulkiness are factors, and are also widely used on snow because they slide easily. Many stretchers have provisions for attaching a wheel or ski for trail or snow carryouts.

For raising or lowering on steep rock or ice there are portable winches. Whether driven by hand or by engine, these have extensive wire cable systems reaching several hundreds of feet. In recent years rescue groups have been using special long (generally 300 feet) low-stretch climbing ropes for technical raising or lowering. These systems are lighter in weight than cable systems and require no specialized equipment to operate other than standard climbing gear.

Radio Communications

Two-way radio communication, when the gear is both light and efficient, immensely facilitates mountain rescue. The main problem is obtaining reliable transmission and reception despite heavy timber, intervening ridges, long distances, and bad weather.

Air Rescue

The international symbols illustrated in Fig. 20-6 are familiar to the majority of pilots and it is well worth a climber's time to jot them down on a slip of paper to be carried in the first aid kit. Symbols should be made 8 to 12 feet in height with lines 1 foot wide.

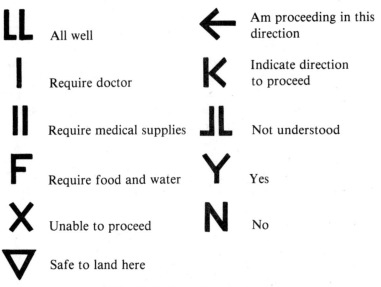

LL All well	**←**	Am proceeding in this direction
I Require doctor	**K**	Indicate direction to proceed
II Require medical supplies	**⅃L**	Not understood
F Require food and water	**Y**	Yes
X Unable to proceed	**N**	No
▽ Safe to land here		

Fig. 20-6. Ground-to-air signals.

The helicopter has revolutionized mountain rescue. It has plucked people from cliffs and glaciers and rushed them to hospitals in hours rather than the days required by ground transport—over and over again meaning the difference between life and death. Therefore a climber should know some of the principles of helicopter operation as well as their limitations.

A helicopter can take on a load either by landing, or when that is not feasible, by hovering and lowering a sling or a stretcher on a cable attached to a power winch. The most important factors governing its ability to evacuate are visibility, wind velocity and turbulence, and air density.

In mountain flight continual visual contact with the ground is essential, and thus in poor weather a helicopter cannot operate. It can maneuver safely in winds up to about 35 mph, a wind of about 10 mph being better than still air. Turbulence which usually accompanies high winds is dangerous, although under some conditions steady breezes are actually helpful. The maximum altitude at which a helicopter can operate is determined by air density, which decreases as altitude and temperature increase; less dense air reduces the lifting force of the rotor blades.

When choosing a helicopter landing zone select an area where a "drop-off" during takeoff is possible rather than a "climb-up." The landing zone should have a 360-degree choice of landing and takeoff directions which allows the pilot to land or take off into the prevailing wind. An area around the touchdown pad at least 75 feet in diameter should be cleared of obstacles such as brush and loose objects, and made as level as possible, with a slope of not more than 10 per cent. The landing area should be clearly marked with colored tape or brightly colored objects, securely anchored. Streamers, plastic ribbon, or smoke should be used to indicate wind direction to the pilot, preferably at the edge or downwind of the area so as not to obstruct his vision. It cannot be overstressed that all loose items near the landing zone should be well secured, especially those used to mark the boundaries. If the helicopter lowers equipment, allow it to touch ground first to dissipate static electricity. If there is a last minute danger to the helicopter, "do not land" should be indicated by moving the arms from the sides horizontally to overhead several times. If the party has no streamers or smoke, members should stand with arms extended toward the landing area with the wind at their backs indicating "landing here; my back is into the wind." The downwash winds from the rotor approach 60 to 100 mph depending on the size of the machine, so do not stand near the edge of a cliff. Watch out for flying debris, use eye protection, and again, have all gear safely secured.

WARNING: Never approach a helicopter unless signalled to do so by the pilot or a crewman and then duck down and always approach or leave from near the front so the pilot can see you at all times. Also, do not approach or leave the helicopter from any side where the ground is higher than where the helicopter is standing. Stay away from the rear rotor; when spinning it is nearly invisible and can kill an unwary stroller. All other personnel should stay at least 75 feet away from the landing area. Be sure to secure the victim and any gear going with him so there are no loose straps, ropes, or clothing, and shield his face and eyes to protect him from flying debris and assure proper respiration. Remember it will take time to secure the victim to the stretcher. Do not let the fact that the helicopter may be waiting rush you in this operation, for the safety of the victim is at stake. Request the pilot to wait or to return at an appropriate time.

RESCUE GROUP ORGANIZATION

In the Alps, with its large corps of professional guides, organized rescue is all part of the business. In North America rescues are carried out largely by amateur organizations. They know their local mountains thoroughly, are able from fragments of telephone information to analyze a situation and decide quickly what action to take, and can direct such action at the accident scene. With the help of a telephone committee they round up the necessary equipment and manpower—volunteers among local climbers, ready to answer a call at any time, ready to finance their own equipment and take time from their jobs.

In most areas, responsibility for rescue now rests with the county sheriff, the National Park Service, or some other comparable arm of government. Volunteer rescue units work closely with such authorities. In the State of Washington, Mountain Rescue Council Units are headquartered in the major cities. Although more people may be peripherally involved, most rescues are accomplished by one telephone calling committee, one rescue leader, and either 18 to 24 stretcher-bearers or one helicopter.

 PART SIX

The Climbing
Environment

Plate 29. *"Yellow Edge"* on Cima Piccolo di Lavaredo, Italian Dolomites.
(*John Cleare*)

21 *

MOUNTAIN GEOLOGY

WHEN CLIMBERS REACH a summit and look out over ridge after
ridge of peaks they may imagine they are on the crest of a gigantic wave
heaved up by a turbulent ocean. Their fancy is not so very wrong, for
even the geologist often likens mountain ranges to stormy seas, though
the storm is inside rather than outside the earth's crust. Nor do the waves
of rock ever achieve the perfect form of waves in water, for as fast as the
mountains rise they are attacked by elements of the very air they have displaced and degraded by the gravity they defy. Sun and frost, water and
wind, tear down the peaks grain by grain.

The tempests in the earth's crust have a duration measured in eons
rather than hours, and man clambers about among the crests and troughs
for too brief a span ever to see — except in imagination — the rise of mountains from plains and their degradation into plains once more. However,
just as the master mariner knows the nature of wind and water so that he
can navigate even in the hardest blow, so does the master mountaineer
know the nature of the more complex storms that toss up the mountains
and tear them down. Some knowledge of mountain geology can make
alpine navigation easier, and climbing a much richer experience than any
mere athletic exercise.

FOUNDATION OF MOUNTAINS: THE EARTH

According to one theory of the earth's formation, the entire solar
system, sun and planets, slowly coalesced from diffuse cosmic dust about
4½ billion years ago. Many scientists believe that as the dust coalesced
the pressure produced in the center of the growing mass and radioactivity

of the interior caused the spinning solid juvenile earth to heat up and melt. With cooling, chemical compounds formed, the heavier ones gravitating inward until ultimately the earth differentiated into at least three concentric spheres. Others believe that this differentiation could not have taken place in the allowable time before the oldest crustal rocks formed at least 3½ billion years ago. It has even been suggested that the outermost layer of the light shell of the earth—the continents with their mountains—began as great splashes of late-arriving meteoric material.

Whatever the origin of the earth, earthquake (seismic) waves show it to have a relatively rigid crust, a layer of rock some 22 miles thick with an average density of about 2.6 (that is, weighing about 2½ times more than water, which has a density of 1). The middle shell has an approximate density of 5, or a good deal heavier than basalt. Virtually nothing is known about the inner core, by far the major mass of the earth. Having a density of up to 17, it could be a nickel-iron alloy, like some meteorites, but many scientists believe that under the extreme pressure and temperature of the earth's center atoms do not have the same characteristics as in the crust, so that the core is a substance utterly unlike any material familiar to man, having the properties of both a highly compressed gas and a tough metal.

The climber is most interested in the outer shell, the crust that crumples and ruptures to form mountains. Though the highest mountains and the deepest valleys are nothing more to the earth as a whole than the scratches and dust on a billiard ball, man is sufficiently small to find the scale impressive.

BUILDING BLOCKS OF MOUNTAINS
MINERALS AND ROCKS

The Minerals

Mountains are made of rocks and rocks of minerals, compounds not broken apart except by chemical action, so that a climber can begin a study of mountain construction by considering minerals as the basic building blocks. Over 2000 are known, but less than 20 are common, and of these, 7 known as the *rock-forming* minerals constitute most of the earth's outer shell: quartz, feldspars, white and black micas, amphiboles, pyroxenes, and calcite. The element silicon is as ubiquitous in rock as carbon in living things, 90 per cent of the crust being either silicon dioxide (*silica*) or compounds of silica and other elements (*silicates*). Among the rock-forming minerals, only calcite does not have silicon in its molecule.

Igneous Rocks

Now and again within the crust, internal friction, heat or radioactive decay, and/or release of pressure creates *magmas*, melts of silicate minerals which on cooling solidify into igneous rocks. If the process is completed deep in the earth with a gradual loss of heat, the minerals crystallize slowly and develop well, forming a coarsely grained *plutonic* rock. If in addition the melt moves upward, propelled by its own lesser density, perhaps dissolving and incorporating the overlying masses, or forcing them aside, an *intrusive* rock results. Should the liquid erupt onto the surface and cool rapidly the mineral crystals have little opportunity to grow and develop, and the rock that results is called *volcanic* or *extrusive*.

Plutonic or Intrusive Rocks

Slow crystallization from deeply buried melts generally means good climbing, since the minerals formed are relatively large and interwoven into a solid mat. Weathering develops protrusions of relatively resistant minerals which either make for a rough-surfaced rock with excellent friction, or, if the resistant crystals are very much larger than the enclosing mat, one with numerous knobby holds. Many of the rock routes in the Cathedral Peak area of Yosemite afford just such crystal climbing.

Pieces of foreign rock included in the plutonic body while it was rising and crystallizing, or clusters of segregated minerals, may weather differently than the main rock mass and form "chicken heads." These delightful features may dot an otherwise unclimbable wall.

Intrusions are variously named according to location and size. Very large masses of plutonic rock are called *batholiths* and small ones *stocks*, being with rare exception in the *granite* family: granite, granodiorite, tonalite, diorite, and others, all similar in composition and formation, differing only in the relative amounts of minerals contained.

There is a core of such batholiths in every major mountain system in the world. In the Alps, Sierra Nevada, North Cascades, British Columbia Coast Range, and most other ranges this core is at least in part exposed, providing some of the finest and steepest rock climbing.

Small bodies are *sills*, forced between sedimentary strata, and *dikes*, fissures which crosscut the strata. Many small intrusive bodies are quickly cooled, and thus may look like extrusive rocks.

Volcanic or Extrusive Rocks

Explosive eruptions, most characteristic of melts with a chemical composition producing rhyolite, eject molten rock so abruptly into the atmosphere that it hardens into loose airy masses of fine crystals and uncrystallized glass. When this ash is bound together, either while still partially molten or after cooling, it is called *tuff*, a weak rock that disintegrates rapidly and erodes easily. Loose ash, or *cinders*, are of no interest whatsoever to the rock climber.

Quieter eruptions with the molten rock flowing from large fissures as *lava* are most characteristic of melts producing *basalt*. The plateau of eastern Washington and Oregon is composed of innumerable basalt flows extruded and accumulated over a few million years. The peculiar "pillow" lavas of Washington's Olympic Mountains are similar, but were formed by basalt spreading out beneath shallow seas.

Volcanoes built almost exclusively of basalt flows have broad bases and gentle slopes, such as Mauna Loa in Hawaii, while those explosive in origin are steep cinder cones. Many are complex, their history including eruptions of flows and ash ranging from basalt to rhyolite in composition. Examples are Fujiyama in Japan and the Pacific Coast volcanoes, from Lassen in California to Garibaldi in British Columbia. On these peaks snow and glacier routes are usually preferred; the nightmarish slopes of shifting cinders and ice-carved cliffs of rotten andesite rarely tempt a climber.

Jointing

In plutonic rocks, joints or cracks are caused by internal stresses such as from contraction during cooling or expansion when overlying rock is eroded away. Some joints tend to follow a consistent pattern throughout an entire mountain and their existence can often be predicted. For instance, when a ledge abruptly terminates the climber does well to look around the corner, for perhaps the joint—and thus the ledge—resumes.

When molten rock extrudes onto the surface of the earth as a lava flow or even when it intrudes into a cold surrounding mass as a dike or sill, the contraction from rapid cooling commonly causes such a profusion of joints that, in contrast to plutonic rocks, the climbing is most treacherous. However, not infrequently the jointing is so regular as to present the appearance of massed pillars, the classic example being the Devil's Tower of Wyoming, where most routes are strikingly vertical.

Sedimentary Rocks

Igenous rocks orginate deep in the earth, but sedimentary rocks are born high on the mountains, where the erosive forces pluck away debris and pass it along to rivers for transportation to places of deposition in valleys, lakes, or arms of the ocean. As sediments accumulate, the underlayers are solidifed by pressure and by mineral cements precipitated from percolating groundwater. Gravel and boulders are transformed into *conglomerates*; sandy beaches into *sandstone*; beds of mud into *mudstone* or *shale*; shell beds and coral reefs into *limestone* or *dolomite*. Sedimentary rocks may also form by direct chemical precipitation (mainly from warm, shallow seas); examples are the Dolomites and the Eiger.

Though in general sedimentary rocks are much more friable than those cooled from fiery magmas, pressure and cementing often produce very solid rocks. Indeed, by sealing up cracks cementing can result in a disturbingly flawless surface, particularly in limestone. Most of the high mountain ranges have some sedimentary peaks. The Canadian Rockies are almost exclusively so, and offer every degree of sturdiness. However, in general sedimentary rocks do not offer high-angle climbing comparable to that of granite.

Metamorphic Rocks

Pioneer geologists quickly became adept at distinguishing between rocks of fiery and aqueous origin, but not so quickly did they recognize that many rocks—though grossly resembling igneous or sedimentary rocks—have been so profoundly changed by heat or pressure that they have become something quite different. These are the *metamorphic* rocks, that is, changed rocks. No rock is fixed in a permanent state; all change in time. Sand does not become sandstone without pressure—and what constitutes a magma if not melted older rocks? Metamorphic rocks bridge the gap between sedimentary and igneous, though on either side the boundaries are ill-defined.

After sediments are solidified they may be subjected to such great pressures and high temperatures, meanwhile being permeated by hot water, that the minerals recrystallize. The bedding may at the same time be distorted by folding and squeezing. Shale is transformed into *slate* or *schist*, sandstone and conglomerate into *quartzite*, limestone into *marble*. The changes may be minimal, producing slightly altered sediments, or so considerable as to produce *gneiss*, hardly distinguishable from igneous rock. Indeed the end result of continued pressure and heat and circulation of hot water is a rock with all the characteristics of granite even though it has never been melted.

Most rocks called metamorphic have a recognizable ancestry in sedimentary rocks, but some can be traced back to an igenous origin. *Greenstone* or *amphibolite* may be metamorphosed basalt or andesite. Even gneiss can be derived from rhyolite or a crushed and squeezed granite, and many of the favorite climbs in the North Cascades are just such gneissic granite.

Metamorphic rocks may have not only joints and bedding, but *cleavage* or *foliation*, a series of thinly spaced cracks imparted to the rock by the pressures of folding. Blackboards were once made from cleaved slabs of slate. Because of this cleavage, the lower grades of metamorphic rocks may be entirely unsuitable for climbing, the mountains quickly wasting away to uninteresting low angles, or if steepened by glaciers, altogether too rotten for pleasure—the rock routes of Mt. Shuksan in Washington State being a prime example. However, the higher degrees of metamorphism or metamorphism of the right rocks provide superb sport. An example of low-grade metamorphism of the right rocks is the Northwest Ridge of Sir Donald in the Southern Selkirks, composed of a durable quartzite sound enough to stand solidly at high angles and yet so well broken by bedding, jointing, and cleavage that rarely is much investigation needed to find the next hold or the next belay. The opposite side, because of incline of the rock bedding, presents loose holds, downsloping slabs and steep, difficult faces with holds weathered off.

MOUNTAIN BUILDING: THE GRAND PATTERN

Two steps are necessary in the building of a mountain. First a land area must rise above sea level. Second, erosion must dissect the crustal protuberance. Both are essential, for mere altitude does not make a mountain. The high plateaus of Colorado and Tibet, not yet deeply eroded, are of little interest to the climber. An understanding of how mountains are built and sculptured will sharpen the climber's perception of mountain forms and the effects they have on climbing strategy and tactics.

The Theory of Mountain Building

Little is known of the *why* behind the crustal motions which produce mountains. The most prevalent theory is that of *continental drift*, in which it is speculated that all continents were once part of a single land mass, gradually separating and set adrift by some force, perhaps one connected with the rotation of the earth. There is evidence, for instance, that Africa, South America, and Antarctica were once joined, ultimately splitting apart and floating to their present positions. The stresses produced in the continental margins, or plates, as they plow through the denser substratum of the earth or drift against one another could give rise to the mountain ranges. For example, there is some evidence to suggest that the Alps, composed of the world's most strongly squeezed rock, have been caught between the crustal blocks of central Europe and Africa.

The Internal Structure

The various horizontal and vertical stresses that act on the rocks of mountains commonly produce complex patterns. However, each kind of stress, if left to itself, would produce a certain ideal *structure*; some ranges can be described in terms of these simple structures.

The first mountain structure to be considered is called with apparent incongruity *plains-plateau,* where sedimentary strata have been lifted upward and dissected without being tilted much from the horizontal. Some sections of the Canadian Rockies evidence such a simple history, but perhaps the best example is the mountain range now being sculptured

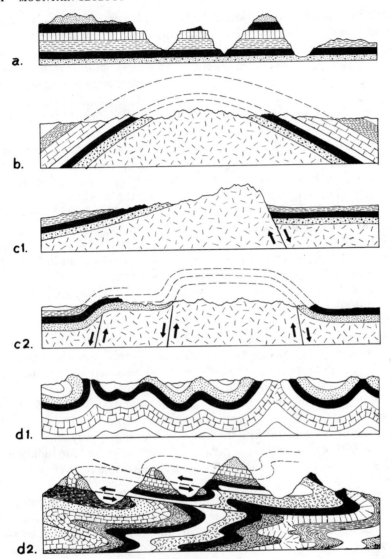

Fig. 21-1. Internal mountain structures.

a. Plains-plateau mountains: Canadian Rockies.
b. Dome mountains, eroded to expose granite core: Raft River Range, Utah.
c1. Fault block mountains, one side faulted: Sierra Nevada, California.
c2 Fault block mountains, deep-seated faults: southern and middle Rocky Mountains.
d1. Fold mountains, gentle folds, highly eroded: Appalachian Mountains, eastern United States.
d2. Fold mountains, tight folds and overthrust fault: Alps.

from the Kaibab Plateau, where the Grand Canyon is the first good cut, so to speak. As erosion progresses in future eons there will be steadily more peaks and less flatland.

A simple upward bulge of the crust forms *dome mountains* such as the Ozarks of Arkansas and Missouri, and in a more complicated way, the Olympic Mountains of Washington and the High Uintas of Utah.

Often accompanying upwarp is faulting, or cracking of the crust into large chunks, resulting in *fault block mountains*. A great variety of forms are created by motion of these chunks along the faults. The ranges of the desert country of California, Nevada, and Utah present most striking instances of faulting; the breakage extends to the surface and often during an earthquake—caused by slippage between the blocks—fresh scarps many feet high develop. Sometimes a block is faulted on both sides and rises or falls as a unit, but the Tetons of Wyoming and the Sierra Nevada are faulted on one side only: along the single zone of faults the range heaves up impressive steep scarps, while on the other side the mass bends but does not break, leaving a gentler slope from the base of the range to the crest. Blocks may drop as well as rise. A clear example is California's Death Valley, which is below sea level and thus most certainly could not have been carved by erosion. The adjacent upfaulted block bears Telescope Peak, 12,000 feet above the floor of Death Valley. Motion is not always merely up and down—slippage along the notorious San Andreas Fault of California is essentially lateral, and elsewhere are instances of blocks that move both horizontally and vertically.

More subtle examples of fault block mountains are the ranges of the Central and Southern Rocky Mountains, from Wyoming to New Mexico, elevated by faulting but with the planes of breakage deeply buried under the surface strata, which are bent above the faults but commonly unbroken—a condition not always easily distinguishable from compressive folding.

Perhaps the most common architectural style is a rococo of complex folds. When erosion strips down the geosynclinal pile that has risen out of the ocean, the folds and contortions are most evident. The Alps are one example of *fold mountains*. The Appalachians are another, but much older; the rocky summits are remnants of resistant strata.

When the squeezing of a range is intense, the rocks of the mountain mass first fold but may then break and parts of the rocks be pushed sideways and override others. Eons later when geologists attempt to decipher the history of the region they may well be puzzled, finding older rocks perched atop younger ones. Isolated blocks of the *overthrust* mass may form when erosion strips away links connecting them with their place of origin. The rocks of the Alps have been shoved to a large extent into foreign locations.

But an overthrust structure may also form in another way. As a large mountain range rises very high, large masses of rock, measured in miles, creep out over the lowlands at the base of the mountain. These may be likened to a landslide, and although their motion may be of a geologic slowness, they may move considerable distances. In the North Cascades Mt. Shuksan (greenschist) overrides younger volcanic rocks on Shuksan arm—part of a very large overthrust originating near what is now the crest area of the Cascades and extending westward to near Bellingham. Almost every range of folded mountains in the world exhibits an overthrust of one sort or another.

Volcanic mountains are in a class by themselves, an exception to the rule that both uplift and dissection are needed to produce peaks. The Pacific Belt includes the Rim of Fire—from Katmai in the north to Aconcagua and Tierra del Fuego in the south, from Rainier and Popocatepetl on the east to Fujiyama and Krakatoa on the west. However, the Pacific has no monopoly on volcanoes; Kilimanjaro in Africa and Etna in Europe are no mean examples.

Mountains can be categorized by ideal structure for convenient description, but most ranges are *complex mountains* with portions that have been simply moved upward without tilting, with other portions folded, domed, and faulted, frequently with a sprinkling of volcanoes. Moreover, the processes described occur both on a large and a small scale. A single gigantic fold may form an entire mountain peak, but there are also folds measured by a rope length, and tiny folds confined within a handhold. A single fault may build a mountain front, but the climber encounters smaller faults that form ledges and gullies.

MOUNTAIN SCULPTURE:
WEATHERING AND EROSION

Having surveyed the processes that elevate portions of the crust, it is time to consider the sculpturing of highlands into peaks and valleys; although the uplift of the mountains has been discussed separately, it is well to remember that the minute a land area rises above the sea, the forces of erosion begin to tear it down. Were it not that uplift gains an edge, the mountaineer would have nothing but broad rolling hills for his pleasure.

Two processes co-operate in carving the mountains. *Weathering*, both mechanical and chemical, breaks the rocks into smaller particles without moving them. *Erosion* encompasses all the activities of gravity, wind, water, and ice which not only break or grind the rocks but transport the degradation products.

Weathering

The consequences of weathering to the climber in choosing his route are considerable. *Chemical weathering* constantly attacks exposed rocks, since many minerals, which crystallized within the hot earth, are unstable at the cooler surface where they are exposed to air and water. Chemical weathering is not uniformly intense on all rocks in all places. Some minerals, such as quartz, are extremely stable, so that quartzite or quartz sandstone are little affected. Feldspars and other complex silicates, on the other hand, break down readily into clays, while calcite dissolves. Water is the prime factor in chemical weathering; a limestone cliff is very durable in a desert but rapidly crumbles in a humid climate. Carbon dioxide and humus acids in solution immensely increase the power of water to dissolve, so that weathering is accelerated in the presence of vegetation, attaining its fastest tempo below timberline in a moist climate.

By way of contrast, *mechanical weathering* is particularly severe high on the mountain peaks, especially *frost-cracking* or *wedging* by water that trickles into minute cracks and in freezing exerts a tremendous expansive force. Many high summits consist entirely of shattered rock; some areas are aptly called a rock ocean. In arctic ranges cracking is so intense that often no unshattered rock is found, merely heaps of loose rubble. In more temperate climates the climber does well to keep in mind that even routes thoroughly "cleaned" by generations of travelers may present new dangers after the freeze and thaw of winter.

Exfoliation does much of the sculpturing in granitic areas: created by pressures built up during cooling and crystallization of magmatic rock deep beneath the surface then released as the rock mass is exposed to the low pressure environment at the surface, its results are quite distinctive. By chemical and mechanical action curved flakes of the surface are loosened and break away from bedrock. A combination of exfoliation at the surface and tension jointing deep in the rock produces the spectacular granite domes of Yosemite Valley. On a smaller scale, exfoliation alone makes the characteristic rounded and flaking boulders often seen on high mountains.

Gravity and Wind Erosion

Gravity does its very best to clean up the peaks, and by rockfall indefatigably clears away fragments loosened by weathering and climbers. More terrifying, though rare, are *landslides*. In December 1963 a series of landslides on the north side of Little Tahoma on Mt. Rainier in Washington delivered some 14 million cubic yards of broken rock to the glacier below, via a climbing route, and sent debris 4 miles down the valley at rates up to 90 miles an hour. Evidence of a recent landslide is an unweathered cliff or slope standing out in sharp contrast to darker and more vegetated surrounding surfaces, or a heap of tangled trees and rocks and earth where a timbered slope has slid from the bedrock. Landslides are usually set in motion when the ground is saturated and thus lubricated with water, such as after heavy rains or when the winter snows are melting, good times to avoid steep and unconsolidated slopes such as those on river terraces and moraines. *Mudflows*, especially wet landslides which act like viscous streams of water, are common on the flanks of volcanoes; climbs of volcanic peaks often begin on gentle ramps of mudflow debris.

All loose soil and rocks steadily *creep* downhill under the pull of gravity. In steep meadows creep produces striking patterns of contoured terraces. These wrinkles in the hillside are usually attributed to animals; actually both game and humans help transform them into "trails," but their origin is quite different.

A special kind of creep promoted by freezing and thawing of ice deep in a pile of coarse rock rubble produces *rock glaciers*. These streams of rock, found in many deglaciated cirques, advance downstream like a glacier and are commonly mistaken for concentric arcs of terminal moraine. Geologists are not agreed as to whether they are actually related to a preceding glaciation or not. Examples abound in the Colorado Rockies.

Wind is least significant of the erosional agents, though playing an important role in deserts, sandblasting rocks into weird forms and impelling sand dunes in their steady march.

Stream Erosion

In all but the iciest or driest ranges, ultimately every particle of every mountain, however it begins its downward journey, enters a stream of water and is ground boulder against boulder, pebble against pebble, grain against grain until — given sufficient time — nothing remains but sand and silt. Meanwhile, the stream carries steadily its burden of milling rubble to the sea, moving the mountains piecemeal to the seeding places of a future range.

Though the highest and most interesting peaks are chiefly carved by glaciers, streams retain an important role. Glaciers rarely if ever originate valleys, rather tending to follow and modify those previously dug by rivers. Actually the digging of the river valley is a complex business. The stream or river saws a notch into the rock, using the rubble it carries for abrasives. As the notch deepens, weathering, gravity, and side streams all work to eliminate the steep walls of the notch, ultimately producing a V-shaped valley. Climbers, whether fording a rushing stream or following a river to its alpine headwaters, constantly must cope with erosional effects of streams. In some places, indeed, such as the cliffs along the

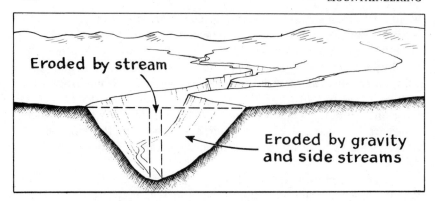

Fig. 21-2. Erosion by a stream.

Great Falls of the Potomac and the impressive Dalles of the Columbia, they find practice climbs on rocks whose steepness is almost entirely due to sculpturing by the load carried in the stream.

Unladen water running downhill gains velocity and thus energy — energy to transport; the swift water seizes hungrily on any loose material until fully *loaded*. If the gradient of the hill lessens, the velocity and energy must decrease; the stream is overloaded and drops its load of sand and gravel, building a new and steeper gradient.

The supreme aim of a stream is to make its bed form a smooth curve from its headwaters to its mouth, or *baselevel*, a curve steep at the upper end, flat at the lower. When the ideal curve is achieved, the stream uses all its energy to carry all the debris dumped into it by side streams and gravity, and the stream is said to be at *grade*. Since perfect grade is elusive, a stream is always in flux, rarely satisfied for long. Lakes and water-falls are particularly abhorrent. To fill the former the stream slows down (it must) and drops its load; to eliminate the latter it speeds up (it must) and picks up more tools to gouge away at the steep face, causing the falls to migrate upvalley, and leaving behind a deep gorge.

Mountaineers soon learn to avoid the temptation of trail-less riverside routes when marching into the hills, realizing that they may arrive at an impasse of cascading water and damp, sheer cliffs. A lake or waterfall acts as a *temporary baselevel*, and the stream above grades itself in re-lation to it, meanwhile trying to remove the lake or fall from the true grade curve.

A river issuing from the front of a retreating glacier is almost invari-ably overloaded, since the melted ice is charged with rock debris picked up by the glacier and the gradient in front of the glacier is very low. The river drops part of its burden, thereby obstructing its own course, moves to a new course and in turn fills that up with debris, finally creating a system of braided channels and the wide plains of gravel commonly encountered below a glacier terminus.

A river flowing at grade may have built itself a flat flood plain. Rejuvenation — by a new uplift of the land or a change of baselevel, such as the elimination of a lake downstream — causes the water to slice deeply into the sand and gravel it had previously deposited, leaving remnants of its abandoned flood plain perched high above the river. Often mountain travelers can make good use of these *terraces* or benches, which provide smooth pathways along the valley. However, such benches are not unmixed blessings, for both the main stream and its tributaries gouge into the old fill, making steep and unstable gravel or sand cliffs that are sometimes troublesome.

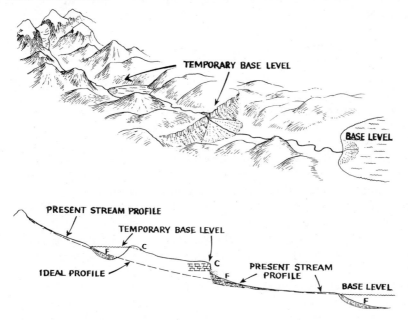

Fig. 21-3. Graded stream profile and baselevels. Stream is cutting at C, filling at F. Dashed line is ideal profile.

Glacier Erosion

Of all erosional agents, glaciers are most significant to the climber. Many mountaineering routes are largely the work of past glaciation; others lie upon the surface of presently active ice. A knowledge of glacier habits is indispensable. The metamorphosis of snow into ice and the formation and behavior of glaciers are described in the next chapter.

The Hierarchy of Glaciers

A *cirque glacier* is one confined to its place of origin, either because it has not yet gathered sufficient mass to venture farther, or because it has retreated from a previously greater extension. As a climbing problem it may be no more severe than a snowfield. If the place of origin is on a steep cliff, a *hanging glacier* results, perhaps consisting entirely of icefalls. When the pressure of increasing snow layers on the underlying ice becomes too great it flows down from the cirque, becoming a *valley glacier*. If ice advances downvalley to the plains beyond the mountain front, a *piedmont glacier* forms. Vast regions of ice lower the average temperature so that more and more snow falls and less melts. The valley glaciers thicken and spill over divides to merge with other ice streams, the piedmont glaciers advance steadily, and ultimately only the highest peaks rise above an *ice cap*.

Features of Glaciers

In the *accumulation zone* of a glacier, annual snowfall exceeds annual melting; in the *ablation zone* melting predominates. The boundary between the two is called the *firn* or *névé* line, though usually it is a wide belt rather than a narrow line. The vitality of a glacier depends on at least as much ice flowing from the upper zone as melts in the lower, and the location of the firn line is a good indication of whether the glacier is advancing or retreating. Many glaciers of the Canadian Rockies, for instance, are chiefly bare ice, *dry glaciers*, with only small patches of snow at their upper limits; these are extremely unhealthy, steadily retreating. If a firn line marches down toward the glacier *front, snout,* or *terminus,* a growth or advance of the glacier may be expected.

The depths of a glacier are solidly compressed and without cracks but the brittle surface layers fracture under the strains and stresses of motion down steep slopes, around corners, and along rock walls. These *crevasses* are rarely deeper than 200-250 feet but even when much shallower, as is usual, they are the major problems of glacier travel (see Chapter 16).

A glacier continually receives debris from its headwall, from its bed which it scrapes and gouges, and from valley sides; it incorporates and carries all this burden along. In the ablation zone the glacier thins and the rubble emerges on the surface; when the ice is entirely melted the debris is dumped in *moraines.*

If the glacier terminus remains in one place for a long time a *terminal moraine* is built, a steep ridge generally concave upvalley in accordance with the usual shape of a glacier front. Deposits along the sides of the glacier, on and off the ice, are *lateral moraines.* When two valley glaciers come together the lateral moraines merge into a *medial moraine.* When a glacier swiftly retreats, debris is widely and thinly scattered, leaving a formless *ground moraine.* The unstable rubble of moraines is usually a nuisance, but sometimes lateral or medial moraines provide easier walking than the surface of the glacier.

Whereas running water sorts sediments so fastidiously that in any one bed particle size may lie within a narrow range, ice carries along particles sized from the *rock flour* produced by milling of rock against rock, all the way to boulders as big as small mountains. Such unsorted deposits are called *till,* the general term for all the material found in moraines. The boulders, when left perched far from their source, are called *erratics.* The flour gives to glacier streams their characteristic opaqueness and when carried in suspension is the *rock milk* which makes fording a blind and chancy job. Within till there are usually inclusions of bedded sand, gravel, and clay, evidence of a vanished river or lake at the margin of the retreating ice.

Land Forms Produced By Glacial Erosion

Few unglaciated mountains have any attraction for the climber. Glaciers deepen the valleys and steepen the slopes, and thus create the sharp relief called "mountainous."

A cirque glacier erodes headward in a complex way. Most of the damage to the rock wall of a bergschrund is done by the freezing and thawing of ice; the loosened blocks fall down into the bergschrund and become incorporated in the glacier. The bottom of the cirque is lowered by the scratching, scraping, and gouging of rock frozen in the ice: a glacier is a giant rasp. Even in the northern Appalachians and the hills of Britain, where glaciation was never prolonged, whatever cliffs exist have been provided by headward cirque erosion, which produces *biscuit-board* terrain, generally gentle of profile interrupted by occasional cirques.

When glaciation is more prolonged and two cirques work toward each other they lower the divide into a razor-sharp *col.* Three or more cirques plucking backward into a common mass of rock make a *horn,* which in

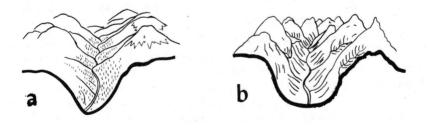

Fig. 21-4. Stream- and glacier-cut valleys.
a.   V-shaped, stream-cut valley.
b.   U-shaped, glacier-cut valley.

ideal form has three cirque walls, three *aretes* separating them, and culminates in a steep sharp summit. The Matterhorn is the classic example.

A distinction must be made between a *valley,* which represents erosion under the leadership of a stream of water or ice, and a *channel,* the actual space occupied at any time by that stream of water or ice. Cross-sections of both river and glacier channels are U-shaped. However, ice moves much more slowly than water, and a glacier requires a much larger channel than a river to drain a watershed. For a given amount of precipitation, a river might have a channel 100 feet wide and 5 feet deep; a glacier might need a channel – the U-shaped valley – 1 mile wide and 2000 feet deep.

Abandoned glacier channels are very widespread in today's mountains and give the traveler some interesting moments. Typically in the North Cascades, the wide flat floor of the U is a swampy tangle of brush and morainal hillocks, and the walls are steep. In many ranges it is not always easy to distinguish a glacier channel from a water-carved valley, for talus and alluvial fans rapidly obscure the U, smoothing it into a V. Such modifications often provide ramps through the cliffs of the U.

Tributary glaciers with their smaller flow cannot keep pace in downcutting with the main valley glacier, and *hanging valleys* are characteristic of ranges once heavily glaciated. Reaching these valleys from below can be as challenging as ascending the peak.

A glacier-cut valley is seldom an evenly graded highway to the alpine country. Most commonly the history of glaciation includes the birth and death of several generations of glaciers which when born as cirque glaciers did not always form at the same elevation. Thus *multiple cirques* are occasionally encountered. In the North Cascades, the upper cirque may still support a glacier, while the steep cliffs of the lower cirque, plucked by vanished ice, are stoutly defended by waterfalls and cedar trees. Mountaineers tend to devalue these pitches with humor, feeling the effort demanded to overcome them is considerably less noble than that needed to scale clean rock crests, but in truth the lower cirque is frequently the crux of the climb.

More commonly the valley is broken into cliffs or *steps* due to differences in rock resistance, the glacier more rapidly eroding the weak rocks than the strong ones. Commonly in jointed granite terrain, large blocks of rock are quarried by the ice, leaving a vertical step along the joint plane when the ice is gone. Steps may also form where several tributary glaciers join a main one, the additional ice volume increasing the erosive power. Any rock protuberance overridden by a glacier, especially one on the edge of a step, is plucked and steepened on the downvalley side and streamlined on the upper side, leaving a *roche moutonée.*

Glaciers, being viscous masses with some strength, have the ability to flow uphill and thus erode a sizable depression in their bed—a feat only achieved by water when it gains extra energy by falling off a cliff to dig a plunge pool. *Grinding down at the heel* is quite typical of glacial erosion and has produced such features as the deep fjords of Norway and British Columbia, long lakes in glaciated valleys such as Lake Chelan of Washington and the Finger Lakes of New York, and the round lakes or *tarns* in evacuated cirques.

Glacial Cycles

World climate has fluctuated radically in past ages. A lowering by only several degrees in mean annual temperature of the atmosphere is sufficient to cause a general advance of glaciers; such fluctuations have occurred many times in the geological past and with them have come ages of ice.

The ultimate reasons for the coming of an ice age are not known exactly, though responsibility has been assigned to a variety of things. Popular for many years have been theories which more or less assign a single cause, such as clouds of dust which shield the earth from the sun, either the passing of the solar system through a cosmic cloud or clouds produced by accelerated vulcanism on earth. Current thought favors more complex relationships which not only involve changes in average summer and winter temperatures due to orbital and rotational eccentricities of the earth, but the configuration of mountain belts and distribution of hot and cold ocean currents.

Whatever the cause, the world is now either in or emerging from a cycle of glaciation, the Pleistocene Ice Age, which is one of the most extensive ever to have occurred. The glaciers were most widespread between 10,000 and 25,000 years ago, at which time a continental ice cap covered all of Canada, most of Alaska, and much of the northern United States. Another reached from Siberia and Scandinavia far south into Europe. The Antarctic cap was thicker and bigger than it is today and extensive systems of valley and piedmont glaciers entwined all mountainous regions of the world.

Subsequent to the time of maximum ice cover, the world glaciers have been in general retreat. The so-called "climatic optimum" of 4000 to 6000 years ago, when all but a few ice caps disappeared, provided warmer and drier climates the world over than have been enjoyed since. Following that period the climate has fluctuated several times, sending mountain glaciers charging down their valleys. Records in Europe show considerable advances in the 16th and 17th centuries. Near Chamonix, the glaciers of the Mont Blanc chain descended into the main valley and overwhelmed several villages.

In the United States the record is less complete. There appears to have been a rebirth and growth of mountain glaciers in the high cirques of the Northwest about 2500–2000 years ago and several resurgences since then. While Europeans explored and settled the New World the ice revived, reaching a maximum in the 18th century; throughout the Northwest mountaineers commonly encounter moraines from that period. Another lesser advance climaxed around 1900, and since then recession has been general and worldwide with but minor exceptions. However, glacier lovers have been excited recently by the general resurgence of ice in the Cascades and Olympics. It would be premature to herald a new age of ice, for so local a phenomenon could be the effect merely of a temporary shift in storm tracks. It would also be unwise to suppose that the Ice Age is over; only time can tell whether contemporary glaciers will increase their dominion or become extinct.

Certainly the world is not so chill as it was earlier in the Pleistocene Epoch, but it is much colder than it has been during most of the geologic past. The Antarctic continent is almost completely submerged in an ice cap of some 5 million square miles and locally almost 3 miles thick. The Greenland ice cap, though only an eighth as large, has been estimated to be almost 2 miles thick. Continental North America is blessed with over 30,000 square miles of glacier, mostly in Alaska and Canada, but also sprinkled in generous samples through the Cascades and Olympics of Washington, and in meager bits through the Rockies and Sierra Nevada.

THE MOUNTAINEER AS GEOLOGIST

It is interesting that much early climbing was done by geologists who sought the secrets of mountain origin. Novice climbers ask what ancient geologic history has to do with their struggle to reach the register book. The devout mountaineer answers that freedom of the hills comes only with understanding. The next handhold, the next belay, the next twist in the route, all express the interplay over millions of years of the forces that both build and destroy mountains. Whether climbers seek their sport high on granite spires that are the remnants of a magma once buried deep in the crust, or navigate the ice avenues of a glacier, they can choose their route with more confidence, and gain a more intimate feeling for the mountains, if they know their history and present state of flux.

Plate 30. Ascending upper Riley's Rib, Mt. McKinley. (Patrick Morrow)

Plate 31. Southeast ridge and summit, Mt. Stanley, Ruwenzori Range, Uganda. (John Cleare)

22 *

THE CYCLE OF SNOW

WHEN CLIMBERS LEAVE behind the rock crags and cliffs and venture into the zone of perpetual snow, they pass from terrain of stable, known, and reasonably predictable character to a region where change is the rule. They enter a world where snow and ice invest high mountains with a beauty foreign to lower peaks, mold their form and character, at the same time presenting some often more strenuous difficulties, unpredictable hazards, and most thrilling moments. The almost infinite variety of conditions which snow and ice can assume at different times of the day and season and in different locales, confronts climbers with an infinite variety of problems. The technique necessary to deal successfully with these elevate the skill of an adequate climber to the craft of a competent mountaineer.

Complete familiarity with the behavior of snow and ice, if attainable, would require a lifetime spent dwelling above the snowline, for the first rule climbers learn is that mountaineering on snow and ice is indeed a craft, and must be learned by direct participation rather than from books. However, apprenticeship will be shortened if one departs for the hills equipped with a basic understanding of the way snow behaves, how it will become ice, and the manner in which meterological factors effect the entire process. The following sections are intended to provide the background for this understanding. Emphasis is placed on fundamentals which will enable mountaineers to face intelligently the problems of snow and ice travel, wherever they may go and in whatever season. Once the basic physical laws which govern snow behavior are understood, logical explanations can be inferred from phenomena observed in the field, a method established for prediction of conditions and a firm foundation set up for the training of an experienced craftsman.

FORMATION OF SNOW IN THE ATMOSPHERE

Snow may occur whenever water vapor is precipitated at temperatures below freezing. The various forms which water assumes during the solid phase of the hydrologic cycle (Fig. 22-1) are discussed in the following sections.

Snow crystals are known to form around centers of foreign matter in the air, such as microscopic dust particles. The first step is collection around the nucleus of a small ice crystal, which grows by the deposition of additional ice from water vapor in the atmosphere. (The transfer of water directly from the vapor to the solid state, or vice versa, is known as *sublimation.*) Recent investigations suggest that minute water droplets (i.e., diameter around 1 micron) may also contribute to the growth of snow crystals. These crystals in general assume a hexagonal pattern, but variations in size, shape, and form are almost limitless. The particular form developed in the atmosphere depends on the air temperature and the amount of water vapor available. When a snow crystal falls through different air masses with different temperature and water vapor conditions, more complex or combined types may develop. Crystals formed in, or falling through, air whose temperature is near the freezing point stick together to become aggregates of individual crystals, or *snowflakes.*

When snow crystals fall through air which contains water droplets, these droplets freeze to the crystal as a *rime* deposit. As the amount of rime on a crystal increases, the original shape is obscured and a rounded ball results, giving rise to the type of snow called *graupel.*

The percentage of water in new-fallen snow prior to settlement may range from 1 to 30 per cent or higher. The average for mountain snowfalls is from 7 to 10 per cent, depending on climate. The lightest snow is deposited under moderately cold and very calm conditions. At extremely low temperatures a fine, granular snow is deposited with somewhat higher densities. The highest new snow densities are associated with graupel or needle crystals falling at temperatures near the freezing point. In general, new snow density increases with air temperature, but density can vary widely in the range of 20° to 32°F (-7°C to 0°C). As air temperature falls, density variations become smaller and lower densities predominate. High winds break up falling snow crystals into small fragments which pack together on deposition to form a dense, fine-grained snow structure.

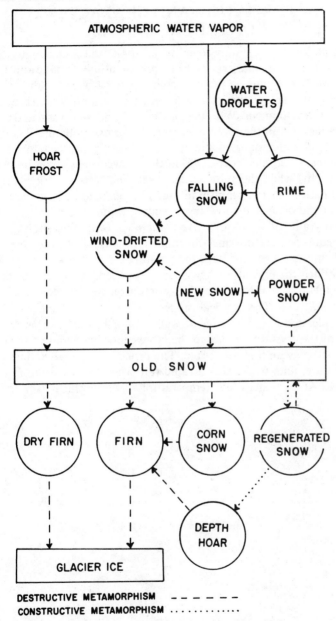

Fig. 22-1. Solid phase of the hydrologic cycle.

FORMATION AND CHARACTER
OF THE SNOWCOVER

Formation of the snowcover is in some ways analogous to the formation of sedimentary rocks. Solid precipitation from the atmosphere (*sedimentation*) builds up the snowcover layer by layer, yielding a stratification that displays the history of weather variations which occurred during its development. With the passage of time, structural and crystalline changes within the snowcover (*metamorphism*) obscure the original stratigraphic differentiation and convert the snow into new forms.

The metamorphic process within the snowcover is a continuous one which begins when the snow is deposited and lasts until it melts. The normal path of metamorphism in Fig. 22-2 tends to destroy the original forms of the deposited snow crystals and gradually converts them into rounded grains of ice (*destructive metamorphism*). This process is also called equi-temperature metamorphism because it is the one which prevails in the absence of large temperature difference within the snowcover. When the crystals of new snow have been altered by this conversion so their original form is no longer recognizable, it becomes, by definition, *old snow*. The physical process causing these changes is not entirely understood, but transfer of water vapor by sublimation from the points of the crystal branches to the more central portions of the crystal appears to play an important role. The process is strongly influenced by temperature, and proceeds at a rapid rate when the temperature is near freezing. At extremely low temperature metamorphism is very slow,

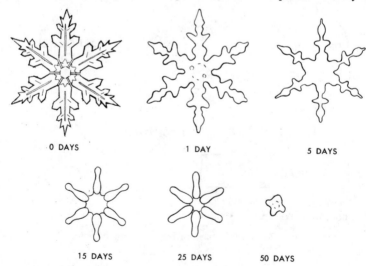

| 0 DAYS | 1 DAY | 5 DAYS |

| 15 DAYS | 25 DAYS | 50 DAYS |

Fig. 22-2. Destructive metamorphism of a snow crystal.

virtually stopping below $-40°C$. All types of crystals tend to approach the uniform conditions of rounded grains as this process takes place, and the snowcover becomes more homogeneous. The rate of metamorphism is influenced by pressure as well as temperature (*pressure metamorphism*), and the weight of additional snowfalls over a given snow layer causes acceleration of the crystalline changes within it.

The destructive metamorphism of the snow crystals results in a reduction of the space a given amount of ice occupies. With this increased density the snowcover shrinks, or settles. *Settlement* is a continuous, visible indication of metamorphism. Rising temperatures cause an increase in the settlement rate.

Constructive metamorphism, or temperature-gradient metamorphism, may also take place in the snowcover. This occurs when water vapor is transferred from one part of the snowcover to another by vertical diffusion and is deposited in the form of ice crystals with different characteristics from those of the original snow. These crystals often have a scroll or cup shape, appear to be layered, and may grow to considerable size (several millimeters in diameter). They form a very fragile mechanical structure which loses all strength when crushed and which becomes very soft when wet. The snow form produced by this type of metamorphism is known as *depth hoar* and is sometimes popularly referred to as sugar snow. The necessary conditions for its formation are a large difference in temperature at different depths in the snow and sufficient air space so that water vapor can diffuse freely. The conditions are most common early in winter when the snowcover is shallow and unconsolidated.

Because of its plastic nature, whenever snow is situated on a sloping surface it tends to move slowly downhill under the influence of gravity. The snow layer deforms internally, the upper layers moving downhill faster than those next to the ground. This internal deformation, called *creep*, proceeds most rapidly at the freezing point and diminishes with falling snow temperature. The entire snow layer also *glides* on the ground if the interface between snow and earth is at the freezing point. If the ground surface is smooth (grass, for instance), gliding is the dominant form of snow motion. The slow combined motions of creep and glide often go unnoticed by the casual observer, but they cause the snowcover to exert enormous forces on obstacles in its path. These forces increase with the square of snow depths and may achieve magnitudes of several tons per square yard. Such forces must be taken into account when designing mountain installations such as avalanche barriers, ski lift towers, and snow sheds. The stresses produced by uneven creep of snow are an important factor in avalanche formation.

Variations in the strength of snow are among the widest found in nature. The hardness of windpacked old snow or frozen firn may be as much as 50,000 times that of light, fluffy new snow. Tensile strength also varies widely. Strength characteristics continually change as a result of metamorphism, and also depend on temperature for a given snow type. When snow is disturbed mechanically and then allowed to set, it undergoes a process known as *age-hardening*. This results in a gradual hardening of the snow for several hours after it has been disturbed. The greatest source of mechanical disturbance in nature is the wind and an increase in hardness is always associated with wind-drifted snow.

SPECIAL FORMS AND FEATURES OF SNOW AND ICE

Certain forms of falling or deposited snow have already been described and their origin explained; there are other special snow and ice forms of interest to the mountaineer.

The term *powder* snow has been so widely applied in the United States to light, fluffy, new-fallen snow that this usage has gained some measure of authority. However, powder snow is also more specifically defined as new snow which has undergone a certain degree of crystalline change, having lost some of its cohesion due to the recrystallizing effects of steep temperature gradients (constructive metamorphism) in the surface snow layers. These changes can occur only during periods of persistent low temperatures. (The widespread phrase among skiers, "cold powder snow," has its basis in fact.) Such snow is loose and powdery, commonly affords good skiing, often better than the original new snow at the time of deposition, and may form dry loose-snow avalanches.

After the advent of melting in early spring, a period of fair weather may be followed by the formation of coarse rounded crystals on the snow surface often called *corn snow*. When this corn snow thaws out each morning after the nightly freezing it offers an excellent skiing and step-kicking surface. These coarse crystals are formed from the alternate melting and freezing of the snow by the diurnal temperature changes during fair weather. The melting each day must be just sufficient to form some free water among the snow grains; if too much melting occurs part of the surface is ablated away, and the process must start afresh with another layer of snow the next day. Only when the same surface layer of snow is exposed to the alternate melting and refreezing does true corn snow develop. For this reason, corn snow formation is less frequent later in the spring and summer, when surface ablation is greater. A surface similar to corn snow is common on summer snowfields, or firn; but this is usually an ice layer exposed and disintegrated by ablation.

Rotten snow is a condition of snowcover, sometimes found in the spring, and characterized by a soft, wet snow in the lower layers of the snowcover which offers little support to the sometimes firmer layers above. In its most pronounced forms it will not support even the weight of a skier. Snow conditions which promise good spring skiing early in the morning, while some strength remains in the diurnal crust, may later in the day deteriorate to rotten snow, the disappointed skiers finding themselves sinking to their knees. This type of snow forms when layers of depth hoar in the lower part of the snowcover become wet and lose what little mechanical strength they originally possessed. This condition frequently allows wet loose-snow or slab avalanches running clear to the ground to occur. Continental climates such as those of the American Rockies are most productive of rotten snow formation, which is much less likely to occur in the more stable maritime snowcovers of the Pacific coastal ranges of the United States and Canada.

Crusts form in several ways. The simplest is the so-called *sun-crust*, which hardens when water melted at the snow surface by solar radiation is refrozen and bonds the snow crystals together into a cohesive layer. This sequence of events can take place at any time of the year, on either snow or firn surfaces, whenever the radiation balance becomes positive during the day and causes melting, followed by a cooling of the snow surface at night to cause freezing. This cooling may be caused by heat loss from the snow surface to air below the freezing point, or it may occur as radiation cooling even when the air temperature is above freezing. In winter and early spring the thickness of a sun crust is usually determined by the thickness of the surface layer where free water is formed in otherwise dry snow. In later spring and summer (firn conditions) when free water is found throughout the snowcover, the sun crust thickness is determined by the amount of cooling at night.

This type of crust might better be included under the more general term *meltwater crust*. Melting due to warm air or condensation at the snow surface, followed by freezing conditions, produces a crust similar to that caused by the sun. The only difference is the source of heat.

In distinct contrast is the *wind crust* caused by mechanical action of the wind, often without the presence of meltwater. Once the surface snow layers are disturbed by the wind, age-hardening is initiated and these layers become harder than the undisturbed ones underneath. Furthermore, the snow crystals are broken and winnowed by wind transport, and the fragments are deposited compactly together when they come to rest, adding a further mechanical process of hardening. The hardening is compounded when the wind provides a source of heat as well as mechanical action, particularly through the medium of water vapor condensation. Even when there is not enough heat to cause melting, the warming of the disturbed surface layer, followed by cooling when the wind dies, provides additional metamorphic hardening.

Rime is the dull white dense deposit derived from freezing of droplets of liquid water on objects exposed to the wind. Rime deposits are always built up *toward* the direction from which the wind blows, and may form large feathery flakes, as well as a solid incrustation, but regular crystalline patterns are absent. This is in contrast to the distinctly crystalline nature of hoar deposits.

Hoarfrost, on the other hand, is formed by sublimation of water vapor from the atmosphere onto solid objects and has distinct crystalline shapes — blades, cups, and scrolls. When deposited on the snow surface, it is known as *surface hoar*, generally produced during a clear cold night when strong radiation and conduction losses can carry away the heat of sublimation from the snow or other surfaces. It is easily recognized by the fragile, feathery appearance of the crystals, which often reach a centimeter or more in length, and the brilliant sparkle of these crystals in sunlight. A heavy deposit of surface hoar makes a very fast and excellent skiing surface.

Crevasse hoar occurs within the snowcover in such enclosures as crevasses. Like surface hoar it is a product of sublimation, but because of a protected location and available free space, it can grow slowly over long periods of time, the crystals often attaining considerable size, sometimes a length of several centimeters. They may assume a cup or scroll shape similar to that of depth hoar, but on a larger scale.

Firnspiegel, or "firn mirror," is the thin layer of clear ice sometimes observed on snow surfaces in spring or summer. Its reflection is so highly specular that under suitable conditions of sunlight and slope angle it produces the brilliant sheen of "glacier fire." Firnspiegel forms when solar radiation can penetrate the surface snow layers and cause melting just *below* the surface at the same time that freezing conditions are prevailing at the surface. Once formed, it acts like a greenhouse, and can permit melting of the snow surface underneath while the transparent ice layer itself remains frozen at the surface. After a clear, cold night, miniature crevasse hoar crystals may be found growing from the underside of this thin ice layer into the hollows which were formed beneath it by melting on the previous day.

Verglas is a layer of thin, clear ice derived from liquid water freezing on a rock surface. A combination of a thaw to form the liquid water followed by a freeze is needed — most commonly encountered at higher elevations in the spring or summer. The water may come from melting snow or firn fields and flow down over the rock, from rain, or perhaps most commonly from the melting of a fresh fall of snow. Radiation cooling can cause the freezing, as well as chilling by air which is below the freezing point. Verglas may also be formed directly by supercooled rain drops freezing as they fall onto exposed objects ("freezing rain," also sometimes called—inaccurately—"silver thaw").

After melting has begun in spring, dendritic *drainage patterns* appear on snowfields, formed in snow—as on the ground—by the runoff of liquid water. However, the flow takes place *within* the snowcover, unlike the surface channels on the ground. As water is formed at the snow surface by melting it percolates downward until it encounters impervious layers (including perhaps an ice layer) which deflects its course, or highly permeable layers which it can easily follow. Much of the water also reaches the earth beneath, and either flows along the surface or else penetrates farther and becomes groundwater. That water which flows along the layers within the snowcover tends to establish a dendritic pattern of channels just as does water flowing on soil. The reason the pattern becomes visible so quickly on the snow surface is that the flowing water locally accelerates the snow settlement around its channels, which in turn are soon outlined by depressions at the surface. The dirt which collects in these depressions absorbs solar radiation and accentuates them further by differential melting.

Suncups (Fig. 22-3) are depressions in the surface of summer firn, varying in depth from an inch to 2 feet or more. They never occur as isolated depressions, but always as an irregular pattern covering an entire snowfield. They form whenever weather conditions combine to accentuate irregularities in the snow surface. There must be motion of air to cause greater heat and mass transfer at points or ridges of the snow surface than at the hollows. The air must be dry enough to favor evaporation (dew point cooler than snow surface). There must be an additional source of external heat; usually this is solar radiation, but need not necessarily be so. Under these circumstances, more heat reaches the points than the hollows, but a larger proportion goes to cause evaporation than melt. Because evaporation of a given mass of snow demands 7½ times as much heat as melt, less mass is lost from the point or ridges as vapor than is lost from the hollows as meltwater. The hollows get deeper faster than the points melt away, and suncups form. Why suncups take the shape and size they do is still unexplained. Once formed, they are further enhanced by differential melting when dirt in the hollows absorbs extra solar radiation. Because the sun is not directly overhead (except in the tropical latitudes), the suncups melt faster on the south sides of the ridges (in the northern hemisphere) and the whole suncup pattern gradually migrates northward across its snowfield. Warm, moist winds tend to destroy suncups by causing faster melt at the high points and edges. A prolonged summer storm accompanied by fog, wind, and rain will often erase a suncup pattern completely. They immediately start to reform with the return of dry fair weather.

Fig. 22-3. Surface features on snow. *Top,* suncups. *Lower left,* nieve penitentes, and *lower right,* sastrugi.

Nieve penitentes (Spanish for "penitent snow" Fig. 22-3) are the pillars produced when suncups are so pronounced that the cups intersect to leave columns of snow standing between the hollows. They are peculiar to snowfields at high altitudes, where radiation and atmospheric conditions conducive to suncup formation are particularly intense, and reach their most striking development among the higher peaks of the Andes and Himalaya, where they may attain a height of several feet, with consequently difficult travel. The columns often slant toward the midday sun.

The surface of dry snow may develop a variety of *erosional forms* when subjected to scouring by winds, minor examples being the small ripples and irregularities on winter snowcover. On high ridges and treeless arctic wastes, where the full sweep of the wind is unimpeded, these erosional features can attain considerable relief. Most characteristic are the wavelike forms, with a sharp prow directed toward the prevailing wind, known as *sastrugi* (Fig. 23-3) from the Russian (singular: *sastruga*), or *skavler*, from the Norwegian. A field of sastrugi is difficult to travel not only because of their depth, which may be as much as several feet, but because like wind crusts they also are usually very hard and unyielding. High winds over featureless snow plains also produce *dunes* similar to those found in desert sand, with the crescentric dune, or *barchan*, being most common.

Cornices (Fig. 22-4) are deposits of wind-drifted snow on the lee edge of ridges or other exposed terrain features. They offer a particular hazard to the mountain traveler because they often overhang to the lee, forming an unstable mass which may break off either from human disturbance or natural causes. Falling cornices, in themselves a large and dangerous mass of snow in motion, in addition are frequent causes of avalanches. Depending on wind and snow conditions, cornices vary from those soft and easily broken to extremely hard structures which remain solidly attached to the mountain throughout the winter. The stability of a cornice is best determined by test or inspection — there are too many complicating factors for advance prediction from consideration of snow and wind data, even if these were available. Probing with an ice axe or reversed ski pole may indicate whether the snow is solid, or weak and poorly compacted. Such probing can also help to locate the crack, if there is one, between a mature cornice and solid snow or bedrock. Where such a space — often hidden by surface drifting — has developed, even a very solid, hard

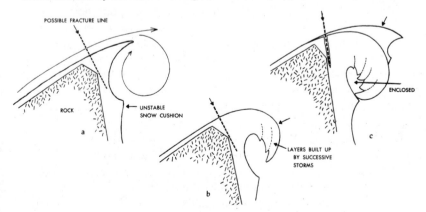

Fig. 22-4. Formation of cornices.

cornice may be on the verge of detaching from the ridge, and great care is indicated. When the climber approaches the cornice from the windward the extent of its overhang and the danger it presents are often hard to judge; in the case of a mature cornice the probable line of fracture may be many feet back from the edge. Though, as with all snow phenomena, it is unwise to generalize too widely, a rather reliable rule is that the fracture line of a well-developed, unstable cornice is usually farther back from the lip than examination from the windward would lead an observer to expect.

Cornices are formed by drifting snow. During storms the precipitated snow furnishes material for cornice formation wherever appropriate eddies form to the lee of ridges. If a snowfield lies to the windward, additional material can be gathered by wind drift. Cornices form during fair weather as well, but here the only source of snow is that picked up to the windward and hence the presence of a source such as a snowfield or other accumulation area becomes essential. As a general, though not universal rule, cornices formed during snow storms are softer than those produced by wind drift alone.

THE FORMATION OF GLACIERS

Discussion to this point has been confined largely to the nature and behavior of a transient winter snowcover. Whenever climatic conditions during the melting season provide a supply of heat insufficient to remove completely the snow deposited during the winter, a certain part of the winter snowcover is carried over to the next season. If the climatic conditions leading to this annual carryover of snow are sustained for a long enough time—that is, accumulation exceeds melt and evaporation losses— the successive annual snowfall will eventually form a glacier.

The process leading to the formation of glacier ice from snow is called *firnification*, during which snow is converted to *firn* (or *névé*) and firn to glacier ice. Firn becomes ice when the air spaces between the grains become sealed off from each other so that the mass becomes airtight. In terms of the processes involved, firn can be more generally defined as old snow from previous years in which destructive metamorphism of the original snow crystals is complete; any further changes lead to the formation of glacier ice.

Part of the ice developed from layers of firn is formed by the refreezing of percolating meltwater each spring when the subsurface layers are still at temperatures below the freezing point. This refrozen meltwater is usually concentrated at certain levels within the snow to form discrete ice layers. Thus, by the time compaction and metamorphism have prepared the general body of a snow layer for conversion to ice, it may already contain irregular bodies of solid ice.

Once ice has been formed, metamorphism does not cease. Through crystallographic changes some of the ice grains continue to grow at the expense of their neighbors, and the average size of the ice crystals increases with age. The mechanical effects of ice flow in a moving glacier influence this growth, so that crystal size can serve only as a very relative indicator of ice age. In large glaciers, where the ice has undoubtedly spent centuries in its journey to the glacier terminus, crystals sometimes are found several inches to a foot or more in diameter — gigantic crystals which have grown from minute snow particles. One way to demonstrate the factors which affect glacier behavior is to follow the steps in the formation and development of an idealized glacier. The formation of a simple valley-type alpine glacier will serve as an illustration.

Consider a mountain in the northern hemisphere presently free from glaciation, and suppose a climatic change sufficient to cause snow to persist from year to year in a sheltered spot on a northern exposure. From the first, snow deposited on the mountainside will tend to flow valleyward in the slow motion of creep. As new layers of snow are added each year, the snow patch will grow in depth (and probably in extent) and the amount of snow in motion will increase. This creeping snow will tend to dislodge the soil or weathered rock beneath it, and the melting, refreezing, and flow of water around and under the snow patch during part of each year will add to the mechanical action of the snow patch on its surroundings. This small-scale process of erosion is known as *nivation*, and will eventually lead to the formation of a hollow where the winter snows can be deposited in deeper drifts. With the climate continuing to favor accumulation of snow each year, the snow patch will continue to grow, and as it becomes deeper its downslope flow will become more pronounced. When the depth approaches a hundred feet or so, the lower layers will be nearing the state of ice, and the increasing pressure of the many layers of firn will cause the plastic flow to accelerate.

In short, a glacier is born. With continued nourishment from heavy winter snows it flows toward the valley as a stream of ice. At some point in this descent of the mountainside it will reach an elevation low enough so that the melting each year will exceed the annual accumulation of snow. Then the excess heat supply left after each annual snowcover is melted away will melt some of the ice which has been carried down from above. Because ice has a much lower reflectivity for solar radiation than snow, it will absorb more of the available heat than snow.

Eventually the glacier will reach an even lower elevation where the supply of heat is sufficient to melt all the ice carried down from above. Until climatic conditions once more undergo a change, this will represent the lower limit of the glacier, also termed the *firn limit* (Table 22-a). The regional snow line, and the firn limits on glaciers, over the earth as a whole vary more widely in altitude than the few examples given.

Table 22-a. Firn Elevation Limits for
Representative North American Mountains or Ranges.

Mountain Range or Massif	Firn Elevation Limits	
	Feet	*Meters*
Mt. Olympus, Washington State	4500–5500	1370–1675
Eastern Cascade Range, Washington State	6000–8000	1830–2440
Sierra Nevada, Oregon & California States	12,000–13,000	3660–3960
Southeastern Alaska	3000–4000	915–1220
Colorado State Peaks	14,000	4270
Wind River Range, United States Rockies	12,000	3660
Glacier National Park, United States	8000–9000	2440–2740
Rocky Mountains, Canada	7000–9000	2130–2740

Glacier behavior varies all the way from stagnant masses with little motion to vigorously flowing rivers of ice which annually transport large masses from higher to lower elevations. The concept of a *glacier activity index* is intuitively obvious in terms of the amount of mass which is added each year in the accumulation zone and the amount removed by melt in the ablation. The larger these quantities are the more mass must be transported by flow through the firn limit; and the greater their difference in elevation, the faster this flow must be.

Temperate glaciers flow both by internal plastic deformation and by sliding on their beds. Velocity distribution is somewhat like that in a river, fastest at the center and surface and slower at the sides and bottom where bedrock creates a frictional drag.

Small polar glaciers present a striking difference in appearance from their temperate cousins; the former look much like flowing molasses, while the latter are rivers of broken ice.

Glaciers do not respond smoothly to changes in climate which alter their mass balance. Often they tend to advance in spurts, overreaching new equilibrium positions and then stagnating in their lower reaches. One reason is that glaciers are unstable in zones of *compressive flow* which commonly occur below the firn limit. Compressive flow occurs when velocity decreases down-glacier and more mass is carried into a volume element on its uphill side than flows out on the downhill side (the difference is removed by ablation).

RECOGNITION OF INSTABILITY
IN THE SNOWCOVER

The first and most common cause of avalanches is a heavy new fall of snow, and this is the first warning sign the mountain traveler heeds. As little as 6 or 8 inches (15 or 20 cm) of new snow may create a hazard; 1 foot (30 cm) or more should always be regarded with suspicion, and greater depths must always be treated with caution.

The total depth of snow existing on the ground affects the development of avalanche hazard. The deeper the snow, the more covered up are terrain irregularities, and the smoother the slide paths. With deep snows, fewer natural obstructions break the surface to hinder the release of avalanches, or reduce their size once in motion.

The rate at which new snow falls is an important factor. A 2- or 3-foot (60- or 90-cm) snowfall spread out over three of four days may produce little hazard, for settlement will often stabilize the snow faster than it builds up. On the other hand, only 1 foot (30 cm) of snow falling within a few hours may become very dangerous, for the stabilizing effects of settlement will not have had time to act. No hard-and-fast rule can be drawn, for conditions vary widely with the type of snow, but snowfall rates greater than 1 inch (2.5 cm) per hour can usually be regarded as a possible source of hazard.

With other factors equal, the development of unstable conditions will become much more likely as wind velocity increases. Wind is one of the prime agents in the formation of slab avalanches, and may build up dangerous conditions even when no snowfall occurs. In this case, hazardous areas are local and generally confined to high-angle lee slopes where heavy wind deposition of snow is taking place. This is not necessarily true when high winds accompany a heavy snowfall. In such cases slab avalanches sometimes may form without respect to exposure, and whole areas of a mountainside, both windward and lee, will become unstable.

The rate at which snow is deposited during a snowstorm is an important key to snow pack stability, though it is difficult to measure in the field. Very high rates of snowfall accompanied by high winds for prolonged periods are almost always followed by avalanche action. Heavy snowfalls of a dense or heavy type of snow (graupel, for instance) must always be suspected as a potential source of avalanche danger, particularly if winds are high. Quantitatively, observations of many storms have shown that snowfall equivalent to $1/10$ of an inch (2.5 mm) of water per hour is about the critical rate of deposition. The greater the rate above this, the more likely it is that hazardous conditions will develop.

Temperature is an important key to both development and duration of avalanche danger. Storms which begin with high temperatures and a damp, sticky type of snow which bonds well to the old snow surface, and then gradually turns to a drier type of snow with falling temperatures at the end, will be less likely to cause avalanching than will a storm which starts with a cold, dry type of snow and then warms up to produce a heavy wet snow toward the end. In the latter case the light snow which fell first provides a poor bond between the old snow and the heavier snow which comes later. The lower the temperature after a storm or high wind, the longer will unstable conditions prevail. Hard slabs formed at low temperatures may remain dangerous for days, or even weeks, if the temperature remains well below 0°F (−18°C). Clear cold weather early in the season when the snowcover is shallow will often lead to the formation of depth hoar within the snowcover. This is not always dangerous in itself, but provides a weak base which may fail to support a subsequent heavy snowfall.

The problems of routefinding in avalanche regions and the general subject of avalanche safety and rescue are discussed in Chapters 13 and 20.

THE HIGHER CRAFT

This chapter has presented in very brief outline some of the characteristics of snow, and how these characteristics affect the formation of glaciers and the stability of the snowcover. The more serious student may continue research by referring to the bibliographies published from time to time in alpine journals, which will serve as a guide to the extensive literature on snow and avalanches. For skiers and climbers who would rather not delve into technical details there is still the best teacher of all−nature itself. An alert observation of snow in its many phases, coupled with at least a rudimentary comprehension of the processes which affect it, can develop within them a better understanding of an important part of their mountain environment, and with this understanding will come the making of better mountaineers.

Plate 32. Observation Rock below Mt. Rainier. (Bruce Gaumond)

Plate 33. South ridge of Snowcrest Mountain, Purcell Range, B.C. (Patrick Morrow)

23 *

MOUNTAIN WEATHER

WEATHER IS OF prime concern to mountaineers, since their comfort and possibly their safety are dependent upon it. Weather can not only change with astonishing rapidity in the mountains, but its patterns and effects may be surprisingly local: hypothermia has claimed victims caught unprepared for wind and rain on exposed alpine slopes, while just a few miles away others have sweltered in lowland summer heat. After an early attempt on the Matterhorn, Edward Whymper reported being driven back by a fierce storm within a cloud high on the mountain; skeptical villagers in the valley below recalled only warm sunshine under clear skies.

At high elevations snow can fall at any time of year; excessive snow-fall brings avalanche hazards to exposed slopes and can force retreat from a major peak, even in summer. Rain, snow, and verglas can present unwelcome problems to the rock climber. Fog can completely frustrate routefinding. Lightning is a particular hazard on exposed peaks and ridges. Climbs of major peaks such as Mt. McKinley frequently require several weeks due to periods of bad weather. Minor emergencies, such as simple evacuation of an injured climber, can become major problems in the face of a mountain storm. Even fair and warm weather can introduce peculiar problems such as melting snow bridges and rising streams which in the afternoon obliterate routes climbed successfully in the morning.

While mountaineers can do nothing about the weather directly, they can learn to recognize signs of impending changes, so that they will not be caught unprepared. Even lacking weather instruments or current Weather Service reports, they can learn much about approaching weather merely by observing clouds. If they have an altimeter, a prognosis can be confirmed through observation of barometric changes: the decreasing pressure, or falling barometer, often announcing an approaching storm, registers on an altimeter as a gain in altitude unjustified by physical progress up the mountain. Barometric changes are easily observed when the party remains at the same elevation, as in an overnight camp or bivouac.

WEATHER FORECASTS

The time to become concerned about the weather is not at the first rumble of thunder, but before leaving home. Local Weather Service observations and forecasts are timely and informative. Weather maps published in newspapers help in anticipating possible developments, but by the time the ink is dry on the newspaper, the weather report is already several hours old. TV weather maps presented with the evening news, on the other hand, are generally based on the most recent information released by the Weather Service, and have the additional advantage of being presented in an easily understood manner. Many include satellite pictures showing cloud patterns over large areas. Other sources of weather forecasts are prerecorded telephone messages and continuous Weather Service reports on the VHF-FM public service band (either 162.4 or 162.55 MHz). In any case, weather signs read in the clouds are more

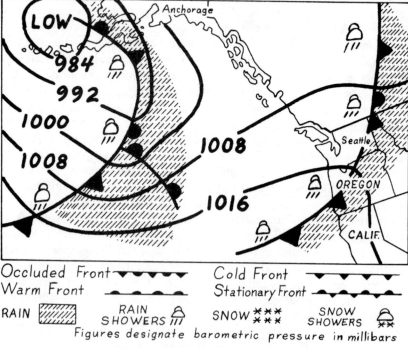

Occluded Front ▼▼▼▼▼   Cold Front ▼▼▼▼
Warm Front ⬤⬤⬤⬤   Stationary Front ▲⬤▲⬤

RAIN ▨   RAIN SHOWERS ⌀///   SNOW ✳✳✳   SNOW SHOWERS ⌀✕✕

Figures designate barometric pressure in millibars

Fig. 23-1. Regional weather map.

meaningful when considered in reference to recent Weather Service forecasts.

Weather at higher elevations in the mountains may be substantially different from weather observed even a few miles away in the lowlands. Low stratus clouds causing an overcast but dry day at home may be forced up mountain slopes, causing a heavy drizzle. Conversely, a cloudy, drizzly day at home may be due to low stratus clouds, or fog, with the mountains rising above this low overcast into clear, sunny weather. While it is sometimes difficult or impossible to anticipate the extent and significance of a heavy overcast, or the weather above an overcast, an aviation weather forecast may resolve these points. Aviation weather observations and forecasts are available on telephone recordings and are also broadcast on the long-wave aircraft frequencies (200–400 kHz and 108–110 MHz). They are especially helpful in identifying cloud levels.

ORIGINS OF WEATHER

In the middle latitudes, major weather patterns are the result of confrontation of cold, relatively dry polar air with warm, moist air of tropical origin. These air masses meet along a *front*, usually identified by clouds, precipitation, temperature change across the front, and a trough of low pressure. Since low-pressure troughs exist along fronts, pressure falls as a weather front approaches and rises after the front has passed. Wind direction shifts clockwise as a cold front passes in the northern hemisphere, and counterclockwise in the southern hemisphere.

Most important weather changes usually accompany cyclonic storms. Development and dissipation of a cyclonic storm is illustrated in Fig. 23-2. As the storm (frontal wave) develops, cold air pushes under a warm air mass, while the displaced warm air rides over the cold air mass. The cyclonic frontal pattern of Fig. 23-2 is characterized by wind movement counterclockwise around a low-pressure center. Winds follow approximately the direction of the isobar lines (isobars are lines connecting places of equal barometric pressure), so that the location of the low-pressure center can often be estimated from the wind direction. However, in mountainous country, wind movement is modified by the shape of the terrain, so that the wind field often bears a complicated relationship to the barometric pressure pattern. This is especially true near mountain passes, where winds attempting to cross the mountains are funneled through the path of least resistance, frequently with increased wind speed and change of direction.

Because a cold front travels about twice as fast as a warm front, the cold front ultimately overtakes the warm front, becoming an occluded front as the warm air is forced aloft by the cold front.

Eventually the storm system is dissipated as the wind circulation is slowed by friction with the earth's surface.

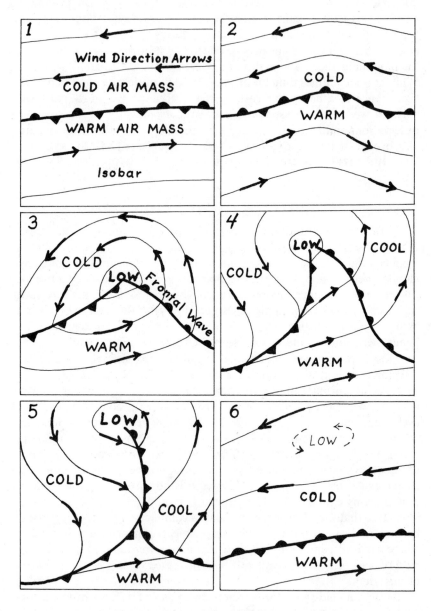

Fig. 23-2. Development and dissipation of a cyclonic storm cell.

FORECASTING WITH CLOUDS

The best way to forecast weather in the mountains, as previously mentioned, is to start at home by reviewing the latest weather maps and Weather Service forecasts. Armed with knowledge of the general weather pattern, mountaineers are better prepared to predict local weather several hours in advance by observing cloud types, pressure changes, and wind direction. Most storm clouds form as a result of the slow ascent of warm air associated with cyclonic storm fronts. As the air parcel ascends, the pressure of the overlying air decreases, causing the air parcel to expand as it rises. The expanding air expends energy as it pushes the surrounding air aside. This energy expenditure causes the temperature of the air parcel to decrease. Cooling of the air parcel eventually allows the dew point of the air parcel to be reached. Further cooling of the air parcel causes condensation of the water vapor which forms the clouds and precipitation associated with cyclonic storms. This phenomenon of sinking air warming by compression (or rising air cooling by expansion) is referred to as *adiabatic warming and cooling,* and is illustrated in Fig. 23-4.

Cloud Types

Clouds are defined by their appearance as belonging to the *cumulus* family, with a billowing shape, or to the *stratus* family, with pronounced horizontal stratification. The two varieties are further classified by their altitude. Examples of clouds commonly seen over mountains are shown in Fig. 23-5 to 23-15.

Cirrus clouds, formed of ice crystals, occur at very high altitudes, usually 20,000 to 35,000 feet in the middle latitudes. They can give up to 24 hours warning of approaching bad weather hundreds of miles in advance of a warm front. Frail, scattered tufts are a sign of fair weather, but prognostic types, such as mares' tails or dense cirrus layers, may be a prelude to approaching lower clouds and finally the arrival of precipitation and the front.

Alto-family clouds are the middle clouds, extending from about 8000 to 20,000 feet. Altostratus sheets or veils and altocumulus clouds should be observed for indication of approaching bad weather. When these thicken, especially if preceded by cirrus clouds, precipitation within 6 to 10 hours is probably indicated.

Stratus clouds are low-level clouds, ranging from the earth's surface to about 8000 feet. If they reach the ground they become fog. Mountaineers frequently find the heavy overcast in the morning is low-lying stratus, or valley fog, which is left behind after a few hours' climbing brings the party to upper slopes bathed in sunlight. *Nimbostratus* is the cloud that yields steady rain.

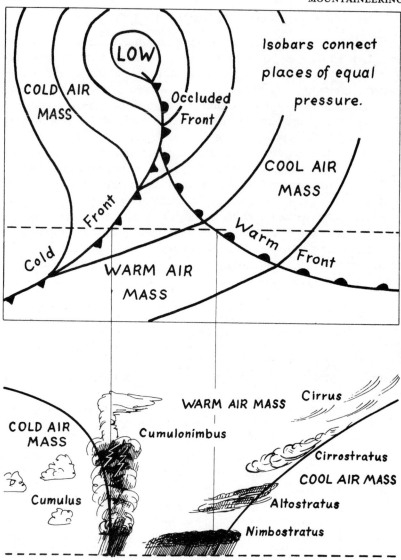

Fig. 23-3. Mature cyclonic storm. *Top,* horizontal profile. *Bottom,* vertical profile taken along dashed line in upper illustration.

Tall *cumulus* clouds with vertical development are formed in moist, unstable air. Cotton puffs of cumulus are fair-weather clouds but should be observed for possible growth leading to *cumulonimbus,* or thunderstorm clouds. Great amounts of energy are released in a cumulonimbus cloud as strong updrafts carry moist air upward for thousands of feet where it condenses, yielding heavy precipitation as snow, rain, or hail. Cumulonimbus activity is typically associated with cold fronts and can occur at any time of year, although more commonly over ridges or peaks on summer afternoons, with thunderstorms, lightning, and heavy precipitation. If a climbing party should find itself in an exposed location high on a mountain during such a storm, it would be wise to retreat to a protected location lower on the mountain where lightning strikes are less likely to occur. In regions of frequent summer afternoon thunderstorms, such as the Colorado Rockies, prudent climbers get an early start to assure being off the peak by early afternoon.

Cloud caps sometimes form above prominent peaks, indicating moisture aloft. A cloud cap is not of immediate concern unless it is descending on the climbing party's objective; in this case a cold and windy summit can be anticipated. A growing and descending cloud cap foretells approaching bad weather. High winds can produce a *lenticular cloud banner* extending downwind from a peak or ridge, sometimes for several miles; such phenomena should be watched for indications of worsening weather.

Cloud development and motion should be observed over a period of time in order to make a rough forecast of future weather events. The following rules apply only in the northern hemisphere and are subject to variations due to local weather patterns.

1. Layered clouds moving from the south generally indicate deteriorating weather. This is especially true if the cloud bases appear to be lowering with time.
2. Broken clouds moving from the north usually indicate the approach of dry, fair weather.
3. Stationary cumulus clouds forming over mountain peaks in the early afternoon during summer often lead to late afternoon or evening thunderstorms.

LOCAL WEATHER PATTERNS

Local weather patterns tend to complicate weather prediction in the mountains but are an important part of local mountain lore. Familiarity with local weather can contribute substantially to the success of a climb. In fact, it is almost impossible to accurately predict weather in the mountains without knowledge of local orographic or terrain effects.

Regional weather patterns can be determined by consulting local meterologists or climbers. Any climber in the Tetons, for instance, should be aware of the predictable summer afternoon thunderstorm and plan to be off the summit before lightning strikes. Winter climbers in New Hampshire's Presidential Range are apprehensive of a "northeaster" bringing in moist air off the Atlantic and resulting in heavy snowfall. Climbers in the

Cascades frequently find that dreary, rainy weather on the western slopes can be avoided by selecting an objective on the sunny eastern side of the range.

Seasonal weather variations are also of interest. Major Himalayan ascents are frequently timed for the brief period between winter cold and the summer monsoon circulation bringing its nearly daily rains. Weather in the Cascades, while generally sunny for several days at a time in summer, frequently has rapidly moving fronts passing through almost daily in winter, almost twice as fast as in summer. Summer weather in the Washington Cascades is subject to occasional thunderstorm activity, imbedded in currents of moist unstable air moving north from the vicinity of California.

Adiabatic cooling and heating of the air occurs as air currents are forced up and over mountain ranges by weather systems. As an air mass is lifted over a mountain range, it cools due to decreasing pressure; as it descends the other side of the range, it warms due to increasing pressure. The drop in temperature with altitude, or dry adiabatic lapse rate, is about 5°F for each 1000 feet. If precipitation accompanies the elevation gain, heat given up to the air through condensation of water vapor reduces the adiabatic temperature drop to about 3°F per 1000 feet.

Knowledge of the adiabatic lapse rate is useful in estimating clothing and equipment suitable for the colder temperatures encountered at a higher elevation. For example, if rain is falling and the temperature is 42°F at one location, the rain will turn to snow about 3000 feet higher. A 15,000-foot summit may be 25 to 40°F cooler than the trailhead at 5000 feet. On the other hand occasionally the temperature increases with elevation (a temperature inversion) resulting in a relatively warm summit.

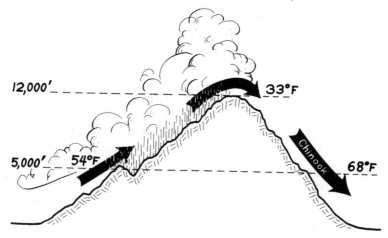

Fig. 23-4. Example of adiabatic lapse rate in an air mass moving over a ridge.

Fig. 23-5. Cloud formations. *Left, Mares' tails cirrus,* earliest warning of possible approaching storm center. *Right,* fair weather *cirrus* over Yakima Peak. (Roger Wilcox)

Fig. 23-6. Fair weather *cumulus* over Mt. Assiniboine. (Austin Post, University of Washington)

Fig. 23-7. Cloud cap on Mt. Rainier, indicating a cold, windy summit. (T.M. Green)

Fig. 23-8. Cumulus dissipating adiabatically over Shuksan Arm. Moist marine air formed clouds as it rose over Shuksan Arm. This is not an indicator of bad weather. (Roger Wilcox)

Fig. 23-9. Mt. Baker rising above *stratus*; fair weather above but foggy below. (Roger Wilcox)

Fig. 23-10. Cumulus congestus over Snoqualmie Mtn. The occluded peaks are wet and foggy.

Fig. 23-11. Cumulonimbus — more commonly observed in congested patterns, the source of lightning storms. (Arnie Hanson)

Fig. 23-12. Sunset under *altocumulus.* Storm passed through the next day. (Roger Wilcox)

Fig. 23-13. Lenticular cloud over Mt. Rainier. A growing and descending lenticular cloud indicates deteriorating weather. (Bob and Ira Spring)

Fig. 23-14. Lenticular altostratus over Tatoosh Range—a growing lenticular cloud pattern which warned of the storm that passed through the next day. (Roger Wilcox)

Fig. 23-15. Banded cirrus over Mt. Baker. Warning of approaching bad weather. (Roger Wilcox)

Chinook winds result from adiabatic cooling of moist air ascending a mountain barrier followed by adiabatic warming as the air parcel descends the opposite side. The temperature drop of the ascending air parcel is reduced due to heat released by condensing water vapor in saturated cloudy air. This condensed water falls out as rain on the windward slope. However, when this air parcel descends the leeward slopes, it still gains 5°F per 1000 feet of descent through drier air. Therefore, there is a net temperature gain by the air parcel upon reaching the base of the leeward slopes. If the quantity of precipitation released on the windward side is large, the temperature of the air parcel on the leeward side is considerably warmer than its temperature on the windward side of the mountains.

Mountain and valley winds are a local weather phenomenon. As the sun warms the slopes, the air near the ground is heated and rises, creating an "upslope canyon" wind; but as the sun sets and the mountain slopes cool by radiating energy to space, the cool, dense air flows back down the slopes into the valleys. Temperature changes and moderate winds may be experienced in the paths of mountain and valley winds. They generally pose little problem except for confusing attempts at recognizing the large scale wind pattern.

FURTHER STUDY

Weather is a complex science, involving a composite of the net effects of multiple contributing factors. Even professionals are so frequently frustrated by its vagaries it is rumored they resort to dart-board forecasting.

It should be apparent that one short chapter can only briefly generalize about mountain weather and its prediction. As a practical matter, however, the preceding information and observations made during the approach to a peak, but *before* the start of any technical difficulties, enable climbers to decide whether or not to go on in the face of developing weather.

APPENDIX I

FOOD REQUIREMENTS FOR CLIMBERS

ENERGY EXPENDITURE IN THE MOUNTAINS

CLIMBING IS ONE of the more strenuous human activities and demands a great deal more energy than the average everyday occupation. The increased food requirement can be calculated approximately by considering the body in its role as a machine.

In city or mountains or wherever, each individual expends a certain amount of energy merely breathing and circulating the blood and otherwise carrying on basic life processes. This *basal metabolism* uses about one "large" calorie per kilogram of body weight per hour, or approximately 1100 large calories per 100 pounds (45 kgm) of body weight per day. (The "large" calorie is the unit of food calculations, equivalent to 1000 "small" calories—the latter being the amount of energy needed to raise a gram of water 1°C in temperature. Throughout this discussion the calorie mentioned is the large one.) The rate of basal metabolism varies with height, age, sex, race, altitude, and other factors, but in relatively insignificant degree. To find the energy requirements for a climb, the amount used to do external work is added to the basal rate.

The activities in Table A1-a are those of "irreversible work," done against friction. Lifting the body to higher elevations is theoretically "reversible work," since the potential energy of the body is increased. Unfortunately the body is incapable of utilizing this potential energy on a descent (except in the undesirable way of falling) and indeed one must work to climb down a mountain, though nowhere near so hard as in climbing up. The efficiency of the body in doing work over and above basal metabolism varies from 20 to 40 per cent. Assuming an average value of 30 per cent efficiency, the *energy needed to raise 100 pounds (45 kgm) 1000 feet (305 meters) of elevation is about 110 calories.*

Table A1-a. Energy Rate Over and Above Basal Metabolism.

Activity	Calories Per Hour Per 100 Pounds (45 kgm) of Body Weight
Walking on smooth level pavement 2 mph (3.2 kmph) 45	
Walking ” ” ” ” 3 mph (4.8 kmph) 90	
Walking ” ” ” ” 4 mph (6.4 kmph) 160	
Eating 20	
Sitting quietly 20	
Driving an automobile 40	
Sawing wood 260	
Swimming 2 mph (3.2 kmph) 360	
Rowing in race 730	
Shivering . . . . up to 220	

Source: Carpenter, T.M., Tables, Factors, and Formulas for Computing Respiratory Exchange and Biological Transformations of Energy. Carnegie Institute. Washington, D.C., 1939.

The final factor in calculating energy requirements is the *specific dynamic action,* or "SDA." During metabolism from 6 to 10 per cent of the calorie content of food is released as heat, and thus is not available for doing work.

Table A1-b. Estimated Daily Energy Expenditure
of 170-Pound (77 kgm) Person at Office Job.

Activity	Calories Per Hour	Hours	Total
Basal metabolism (1100 x 1.7)			1870
Eating	34	1.5	50
Driving automobile	70	1.0	70
Working	90	8.0	720
Leisure and miscellaneous	40	5.5	220
Subtotal			2930
SDA (7% of subtotal)			200
Total			3130

Using such methods the energy expenditure on any proposed trip can be roughly calculated, and thus the food requirements. The "roughly" must be emphasized, since even professional nutritionists vary somewhat in their findings. The standard daily ration of the United States Army is 4500 calories for strenuous work, 3500 for garrison duty.

Table A1-c. Estimated Energy Expenditure of 170-Pound (77 kgm) Climber on Mt. Olympus in Washington State.

To simplify calculation it is assumed the pack weighs uniformly 30 pounds (14 kgm) throughout, making a constant total of 200 pounds (91 kgm). The walking energy rate from Table A1-a is thus multiplied by a factor of 2. In addition it is multiplied by a factor of 1.5 to correct for rough trail. This factor may be several times larger for bushwacking, boulder-hopping, snow-slogging, etc.

Activity	Calories Per Hour	Hours	Total
Day No. 1			
Basal metabolism			1870
Eating	34	1.5	50
Driving (Seattle to road end)	70	6	420
Hike from Jackson Guard Sta. to Elk Lake			
15 miles @ 3 mph (24 km @ 4.8 kmph)	270	5	1350
1600 ft (490 m) elevation gain			350
Pack, unpack, make camp, etc.	100	3	300
Subtotal			4340
SDA			300
Total			4640
Day No. 2			
Basal metabolism			1870
Eating	34	1.5	50
Hike from Elk Lake to summit and return			
14 miles @ 2 mph (22.5 km @ 3.2 kmph)	135	7	950
5400 ft (1650 M) elevation gain			1190
Side trips, camp chores, etc.	100	6	600
Subtotal			4660
SDA			330
Total			4990

Activity	Calories Per Hour	Hours	Total
Day No. 3			
Basal metabolism			1870
Eating	34	1.5	50
Hike to car	270	5	1350
Driving	70	6	420
Pack, unpack, etc.	100	3	300
Subtotal			3990
SDA			280
Total			4270

R.W. Gerard, in *Food for Life,* University of Chicago Press, 1952, estimates that general factory work requires about 3000 to 4000 calories daily. The Juneau Ice Field Research Project, in various reports published by the American Geographical Society, 1949–51, tells of several differing dietary experiments; on one trip it was later calculated that the average intake per man had been 4085 calories per day.

COMPOSITION OF FOODS

The three major food components are proteins, fats, and carbohydrates. Each provides energy, but also other essential values more or less understood at present. In addition the undigestible portion, the pure bulk, has a function. No less important are the trace quantities of vitamins and minerals needed for various vital body processes. All must be supplied in approximately the right amounts to maintain health of body and mind.

Proteins

Proteins are broken down in the digestive process into their constituent amino acids which are in turn recombined by the body to make new proteins, such as muscles and other body tissue. Animal proteins such as meat, milk, cheese, and eggs are called "complete" because they yield exactly the amino acids in the exactly correct proportion the system requires. Cereals such as wheat and oats and legumes such as peas and beans yield varying amounts of amino acids, though their proteins are "incomplete," lacking several amino acids. However, the addition of a little milk or cheese renders vegetable proteins "complete," the combination supplying all essential amino acids.

Protein requirement per day is nearly constant regardless of activity.

The body steadily renews itself, replacing old muscles. Hard work does not accelerate the process, which continues at the same rate during sedentary office work and violent manual labor. The recommended daily allowance is 70 grams of protein, at least half of it *complete*, distributed over the entire day. The body cannot utilize its entire daily requirement at any one meal; amino acids in excess of what can be immediately used, and "incomplete" groups of amino acids, are not stored. Having been rejected for tissue-building purposes they are converted into fuel or stored as fat.

Fats

Fats are used primarily for energy, but also supply the fat-soluble vitamins. In addition there are certain unsaturated fats with an imperfectly understood but apparently vital function. It is recommended that a minimum of 20 to 25 per cent of the total calories be supplied by fat. Major sources are meat fats, butter, margarine, cheese, egg yolks, and nuts.

Carbohydrates

Carbohydrates supply nothing but energy but in a form so easily used that most nutritionists recommend their use for half the caloric intake. Carbohydrates include all sugars, starches, and celluloses, found in cereals, legumes, milk, vegetables, fruits, bakery goods, and candy. Only sugars and starches are digestible by man. Cellulose is digested by the browsing animals but in man passes through the system chemically unchanged, providing bulk, or roughage, in many people seemingly necessary for regular elimination.

Vitamins

Vitamins yield enzymes which catalyze various chemical reactions and physiological processes. The quantities required are small, but when lacking, deficiency diseases result. Vitamins are broadly classified as to their solubility in fat or water, which determines their source. The principal fat-soluble vitamins are A, D, E, and K. The water-soluble vitamins include the B complex and C, found in cereals, vegetables, fruit, and meat both fresh and dehydrated. The fright-propaganda of proprietary drug manufacturers notwithstanding, any ordinary balanced diet supplies enough of all of these. However, body storage of water-soluble vitamins is slight, and though deficiency diseases such as scurvy and beriberi are unlikely to afflict a climbing party, the earlier symptoms of deficiency can occur, such as irritability and mental depression. Thus on any long trip with a possibly unbalanced diet, the inclusion of vitamin supplements (pills, etc.) should be considered.

Minerals

The mineral parts of food include salts of calcium, phosphorus, iron, sodium, copper, chlorine, and a host of other elements, some of whose functions are unknown. All are water-soluble and thus provided by meats, vegetables, and fruits, and in sufficient amount by a balanced diet.

METABOLISM

The mechanism of food usage by the body is extremely complex and not completely understood in detail. All food on digestion contributes to the common metabolic pool. The amino acids needed to build tissue are extracted, the remainder after a further digestive process being contributed to the fuel supply, which also includes the derivatives of carbohydrates and fat. Some of the fuel is used for immediate needs. Some is converted into glycogen, a starch that is stored in small quantities in the liver and muscles and converted to glucose for fuel on quick demand. The remainder is manufactured into body fat for long-term storage.

The end-products of food oxidation for energy are water and carbon dioxide and lactic acid. During hard work these accumulate while fuel dissipates, resulting in weariness. The function of rest is to allow blood and lungs to remove end-products and replenish oxygen and fuel.

Heat is a by-product of work. Virtually all the energy of basal metabolism and specific dynamic action is converted ultimately to heat. Since the body is on the average only 30 per cent efficient in using its "work calories," the remaining 70 per cent are also converted to heat. Together these maintain body temperature. Excessive heat released by metabolism, SDA, and work is dispersed by perspiration. During inactivity in cold weather, metabolism and SDA may not supply enough heat; when the lower limit of the thermostat is touched the body sets the muscles to shivering.

Conditioning

During exercise the body improves its capacity for exercise. Metabolism becomes more efficient, the blood moving more rapidly to carry waste products away from the muscles and bring them new fuel. Glycogen storage is increased slightly, and also the speed of its conversion into energy. The harder a person works today the harder he can work tomorrow.

Before bursts of extreme and extraordinary exertion a simple life is best. How a person feels on a strenuous weekend climb depends partly on how hard he worked on a previous weekend — but also very largely on what he has been doing during the week. A well-balanced regular diet with steady moderate exercise and plenty of rest puts the system in finest tuning. Exotic foods and irregularity of meals and rest upset body chemistry and reduce physical performance for hours or days.

During the climb itself the only physiological requirements are energy and water. Theoretically, then, the most efficient diet during the period of heavy work is sugar and water — and indeed some mountaineers go hours at a time on fruit juice and candy. For various reasons cited herein fats and proteins are generally consumed in addition. Whatever the components, all meals immediately before and during a climb should either be small or followed by a long rest. The blood cannot serve two masters, lungs and stomach; attempting to set a vigorous pace just after a feast causes rubbery legs or stomach upset or both.

Frequency of Meals

Carbohydrates are most rapidly and efficiently converted into energy, and thus starches and sugars most immediately replenish the fuel supply. The rapidity of conversion, however, means that a diet high in carbohydrates requires frequent meals, as many as eight a day.

Proteins and fats are most slowly digested but release their energy over a longer period of time. An egg at breakfast contributes nothing to an energetic start but steadily helps the forenoon struggle. Similarly, peanut butter at noon powers the making of camp at sunset and cheese at supper makes it possible to rise on the morrow. The body can adjust to very infrequent meals when the fat and protein content of the diet is high. Arctic explorers such as Vilhjalmur Stefansson consider one meal a day ample, and only two meals a week no excessive hardship.

Hunger pangs are symptomatic of an empty stomach, not of an empty energy reservoir, since there may still be ample body fat available. Even in the person of average weight this reserve is sufficient to sustain a high level of activity for several days; fasts as long as a month have been made without lasting body damage. During transition from a city diet high in bulk to a relatively concentrated mountain diet it is well to endure mild hunger for a few days while the stomach shrinks; attempting to fill up on concentrated foods leads to obesity, or even illness. Extreme hunger is of course unpleasant, and to be avoided. A meal of carbohydrates passes entirely out of the stomach in one or two hours, while a meal high in fat remains as long as six or seven hours. Bulk in the stomach gives a feeling of satisfaction; foods high in fat and protein "stick to the ribs."

From what has been said, obviously the optimum frequency of meals depends on the kind of food eaten. In addition there are great variations between individuals. Some people work best on almost constant intake of carbohydrates. Others attain top performance with one or two meals a day, high in fat and protein. Every climber should experimentally establish his own best frequency, and limits of variation. Most parties achieve the greatest happiness of the greatest number by planning only the main evening meal in common, letting adherents of the three-squares-per-day and the one-square-plus-constant-nibbles factions adjust the remainder of the diet to individual needs.

Food Efficiency

On a short outing the ratio of calories to pounds scarcely merits consideration, since even with pure carbohydrates (with no water) 2½ pounds per day suffices, a weight relatively small compared to that of equipment. Most overloading of the commissary comes simply from carrying more food than necessary to satisfy the energy requirements of the trip. Another key consideration is choosing foods low in water content, either naturally or through processing. The majority of mountains are quite liberally endowed with liquid resources, and it is pointless to backpack water long distances. Similar objections can be raised to hauling excess metal in the form of cans.

Table A1-d. Energy Values of Food.

	Calories Per Gram	Calories Per Pound
Protein	4.0	1800
Fat	9.0	4100
Carbohydrate	4.0	1800

As is apparent from Table A1-d, an increased proportion of fats in the diet is very desirable on long backpacking trips. A single pound of pure fat very nearly supplies the daily energy requirement, though such a menu is undesirable for various physical and psychological reasons. However, the case of pemmican is instructive, and a climber would do well to read the works of Vilhjalmur Stefansson, including *The Friendly Arctic,* Macmillan, New York, 1953, and *Fat of the Land,* Macmillan, New York, 1956. Pemmican was invented by the Plains Indians, and used on long hunting and war expeditions. Adopted by the early fur traders it made possible the economic penetration of the West, and by a later generation, exploration of the Arctic. Pemmican is composed of equal parts of dried, powdered, lean meat and rendered fat, and despite denunciations by experts who have proved by formula that a man living on pemmican will surely waste away and die in a few weeks, ample testimony to the contrary is provided by the history of the fur trade and Arctic exploration, which cites innumerable instances of men working hard and healthily and happily many months at a time on no other food than pemmican. Genuine pemmican is expensive and rare, but could extend the traditional limit for a backpack trip from approximately two weeks to four without relaying supplies, its equivalent weight being half that of a conventional high-carbohydrate diet.

The virtues of pemmican appear only on a long trip, since like any other unfamiliar diet it requires a period of adjustment. In general it is best for climbers to eat in the mountains approximately the way they do in everyday living to avoid the unpleasantness of physiological conversion. The psychological values of food thus are particularly important on short outings. There is no physical necessity for hot meals, leafy vegetables, spices, and sweets, but if the craving for them is not satisfied morale suffers. This has been most strikingly demonstrated on high-altitude expeditions, leading many expeditions to synthesize from processed foods, at considerable trouble and expense, a diet approximating the one to which the members are accustomed at home. Even during a week in the wilderness it is usually worthwhile to carry a few such luxuries; the food value may be small, but the contribution to pleasure immense.

Table A1-e. Values of Representative Mountaineering Foods.

Food	Energy Value		Composition of Edible Portion		
	Calories per		%	%	%
	ounce	gram	Protein	Carbo-hydrate	Fat
DAIRY PRODUCTS					
Butter	203	7.16	0.6	0.4	81.0
Margarine	204	7.19	0.6	0.4	81.0
Whole milk	18	.63	3.5	4.9	3.9
Whole buttermilk	10	.35	3.6	5.1	0.1
Malted milk, dry powdered	116	4.09	14.7	70.8	8.3
Milk, dry skim	103	3.63	35.8	51.6	0.7
Milk, dry whole	142	5.00	26.4	38.2	27.5
Milk, evaporated, unsweetened	39	1.37	7.0	9.7	7.9
Milk, condensed, sweetened	91	3.20	8.1	54.3	8.7
Cheese, cheddar	113	3.98	25.0	2.1	32.2
Cheese, Swiss	105	3.70	27.5	1.7	28.0
Cheese, processed	105	3.70	23.2	1.9	30.0
FRUITS					
Orange	10	.35	1.0	12.2	Insignifi-
Banana	16	.56	1.1	22.2	cant in
Apple, raw	13	.45	trace	12.0	most
Apple, dried	78	2.75	1.0	71.8	
Apple, dehydrated	100	3.52	1.4	92.1	
Apricot, dried, sulphured	74	2.61	5.0	66.5	

Table A1-e (cont.)

Food	Energy Value		Composition of Edible Portion		
	Calories per		%	%	%
	ounce	gram	Protein	Carbo-hydrate	Fat
Avocado, fresh	49	1.72	1.8	5.6	16.7
Date, dried	78	2.75	2.2	72.9	
Fig, dried	78	2.75	4.3	69.1	
Peach, dried, sulphured	74	2.61	3.1	68.3	
Prune, dried	64	2.25	2.1	67.4	
Raisin	82	2.89	2.5	77.4	
FRUIT JUICES					
Apple	13	.45	0.1	11.9	Insignifi-
Applesauce, sweetened	26	.92	0.2	23.8	cant in
Grape	19	.67	0.2	16.6	all
Grapefruit, sweetened	15	.53	0.5	12.8	
Orange	14	.49	0.7	10.4	
Pineapple	16	.56	0.4	13.5	
Prune	22	.78	0.4	19.0	
Tomato	5	.18	0.9	4.3	
Lemon juice concentrate, frozen, unsweetened	33	1.16	2.3	37.4	
Orange concentrate, canned	63	2.22	4.1	50.7	
Lemonade concentrate, frozen	55	1.94	0.2	51.1	
Fruit cocktail, canned, in syrup	22	.78	0.4	19.5	
VEGETABLES, DEHYDRATED					
Cabbage	87	3.06	14.4	72.5	Insignifi-
Carrot	97	3.42	6.6	81.1	cant in
Potato	100	3.52	8.3	80.4	all
Sweet potato	107	3.77	4.2	90.0	
Tomato flakes	97	3.42	10.8	76.7	
NUTS					
Almond	170	6.00	18.6	19.5	57.7
Brazil	185	6.52	14.3	10.9	66.9
Cashew	159	5.60	17.2	29.3	45.7
Coconut, dried, sweetened	155	5.46	3.6	53.2	39.1
Peanut butter	167	5.89	27.8	17.2	49.4
Peanut, roasted	165	5.82	26.0	18.8	49.8
Pecan	195	6.87	9.2	14.6	71.2
Walnut	159	5.60	14.8	15.8	64.0
GRAIN PRODUCTS					
Breakfast Cereals					
Bran flakes, 40%	85	3.00	10.7	82.1	3.6
Cornflakes	109	3.84	7.9	85.3	Insignifi-
Oatmeal, uncooked	110	3.88	15.0	78.5	cant in
Rice, puffed	113	3.98	6.0	89.5	most
Farina, enriched, uncooked	103	3.63	11.4	77.0	

Table A1-e (cont.)

Food	Energy Value		Composition of Edible Portion		
	Calories per		%	%	%
	ounce	gram	Protein	Carbo-hydrate	Fat
Wheat, puffed	103	3.63	15.0	78.5	
Wheat, shredded	104	3.66	9.9	79.9	
Wheat germ	102	3.59	26.5	47.0	10.3
Other Grains (Uncooked)					
Barley, pearl	99	3.49	8.4	78.8	Insignifi-
Macaroni	105	3.70	12.5	75.2	cant in
Noodles, egg	110	3.88	12.8	72.0	all
Spaghetti	105	3.70	12.5	75.2	
Rice, brown, raw	102	3.59	7.5	77.4	
Rice, white, raw	103	3.63	6.7	80.4	
Rice, precooked	105	3.70	7.5	82.5	
Pancake mix, wheat	101	3.56	8.6	75.7	
Pancake mix, buckwheat	93	3.28	10.5	70.3	
Baked Goods					
Bread					
Rye	69	2.43	9.1	52.1	
White	77	2.71	8.7	50.5	
Pumpernickel	70	2.46	9.1	53.1	
Whole wheat	69	2.43	10.5	47.7	
Boston brown	60	2.11	5.5	45.6	
Cooky, sugar	126	4.44	6.0	68.0	16.8
Doughnut	111	3.91	4.6	51.4	18.6
Fig bar	101	3.56	3.9	75.4	5.6
Triscuit	125	4.41	12.0	?	?
Rye wafer	98	3.45	13.0	76.3	1.2
Logan bread, moist	100	3.52	7.0	60.0	10.0
Logan bread, dry	112	3.95	8.0	67.0	12.0
MEAT, FISH, EGGS					
Beef					
Corned, canned	75	2.64	23.5	0.0	18.0
Dried, chipped	58	2.04	34.3	0.0	6.3
Hamburger, cooked	81	2.85	24.2	0.0	20.3
Pork					
Bacon, lean, cooked	173	6.10	30.4	3.2	52.0
Bacon, Canadian, cooked	79	2.78	27.6	0.3	17.5
Bacon, canned	194	6.84	8.5	1.0	71.5
Ham, smoked	87	3.06	23.0	0.0	30.6
Fish					
Salmon, canned	43	1.51	20.8	0.0	7.1
Sardines in oil, drained	47	1.65	24.0	0.0	11.1
Tuna, canned, drained	47	1.65	28.8	0.0	8.2

Table A1-e (cont.)

Food	Energy Value		Composition of Edible Portion		
	Calories per		%	%	%
	ounce	gram	Protein	Carbo-hydrate	Fat
Processed Products					
Baked beans	35	1.23	6.1	19.0	2.6
Bologna	86	3.03	12.1	1.1	27.5
Chili con carne, without beans	57	2.01	10.3	5.8	14.8
Hash, corned beef with potato	51	1.79	8.8	10.7	11.3
Liverwurst	86	3.03	16.2	1.8	25.6
Luncheon meat, pork	83	2.92	15.0	1.3	24.9
Frankfurter	88	3.10	12.4	1.6	27.2
Vienna sausage	68	2.39	14.0	0.3	19.8
Bouillon cube	34	1.19	20.0	5.0	3.0
Eggs					
Egg, fresh	41	1.44	12.9	0.9	11.5
Egg, dried, whole	168	5.92	47.0	4.1	41.2
CANDIES AND SWEETS					
"Candy bar"	141	4.97	9.2	59.6	25.3
Candy, bulk (hard candy)	139	4.90	8.2	64.2	22.5
Candy, peanut	146	5.14	11.3	60.5	22.2
Chocolate, unsweetened	143	5.04	10.7	28.9	53.0
Chocolate, milk	147	5.18	7.7	56.9	32.3
Chocolate, sweet with almonds	151	5.23	9.3	51.3	35.6
Cocoa mix	111	3.91	9.4	73.9	10.6
Butterscotch	113	3.98	0.0	94.8	3.4
Caramel	113	3.98	4.0	76.6	10.2
Fudge, plain	113	3.98	2.7	75.0	12.2
Peanut brittle	119	4.19	5.7	81.0	10.4
Honey, strained	86	3.03	0.3	82.3	0.0
Jam	77	2.71	0.6	70.0	0.1
Mincemeat	61	2.15	5.3	34.4	6.4
Molasses, cane	66	2.32	0.0	60.0	0.0
Sugar, brown	106	3.73	0.0	96.4	0.0
Sugar, granulated	109	3.84	0.0	99.5	0.0
Ice cream, plain	59	2.08	4.0	20.6	12.5

Source: Adapted from Watt and Merrill, *Composition of Foods, Raw, Processed, Prepared — Agriculture Handbook No. 8,* U.S. Department of Agriculture, Washington, D.C., revised December 1963. This handbook was compiled from all research data available, and is considered by experts to be authoritative. The above table lists several items for which information was derived from other sources. Unfortunately, it has not been possible so far to gain data on the values of the specially-packaged foods which nowadays constitute an important component of the mountaineer diet.

APPENDIX 2

RATING OF CLIMBS

A RATING SYSTEM is intended to give climbers some idea of the level of difficulty they can expect to find on a climb. Different systems have attempted to do this in different ways and as these are used they evolve, sometimes improving and sometimes becoming so complicated that they are unusable. Most current classifications are combinations of several systems. In addition, with few exceptions, these use some sort of numerical sequence to rate a climb, the rationale being that numbers are more precise than words.

When using ratings there are several things to keep in mind. Make sure you understand how the system works, and whether it has changed with time, particularly if the route descriptions are in old journals or magazines. It can sometimes be helpful to know who rated the climb; since ratings are given by humans not computers, human frailties can be interjected into the system. For example, some climbers will intentionally underrate climbs so that those who follow later will be impressed. Fortunately most climbers do attempt to give accurate ratings, and by the time a route is in a guide book, enough people have made the climb to show the rating as a consensus of opinion. Also remember that ratings are given for ideal conditions; unfavorable conditions can cause considerable change in a climb's difficulty.

The descriptions of the rating systems and the comparison tables that follow refer to the systems in use at date of publication.

Yosemite Decimal System (YDS)

This system traces its history back to the 1920s and the Welzenbach System used in Germany. Introduced as the Sierra Club System in the U.S. in 1937, it consisted of six classes, described as follows:

1 — hiking
2 — off-trail scrambling
3 — climbing; rope for beginners
4 — belayed climbing
5 — leader places protection
6 — aid climbing

The system was modified for use at Tahquitz Rock in the 1950s. It was here that the decimals were added to class 5, in an attempt to rate the difficulty of the actual climbing. Originally 5.0–5.9 were set up but as more difficult climbs were done the system developed a problem, because of the closed-end nature of the system. The solution was to ignore the mathematical significance of the decimal and class 5.10 was created. With the rebirth of hard free climbing in the 1970s still harder climbs were accomplished, but considerable time elapsed before class 5.11 was an accepted standard. As a result there was a wide variation between climbs within the 5.10 level, so 5.10 was subdivided into a, b, c, and d. The same has happened with 5.11 and 5.12. By the time 5.13 was reached climbers started subdividing right at the start. Currently 5.13a is the most difficult climb accomplished.

The YDS uses the "A" designation from the NCCS to classify aid climbing rather than the decimal subdivisions of the Sierra Club System. This system rates the "quality" of the aid placements and does not include awkwardness or strenuousness as the Sierra Club System did.

The classification part of the YDS so far described is intended to be an objective rating of the skill required. In order to give an overall rating of the climb the Roman numeral (I–VI) grading system of the NCCS was added in the early 1960s. The grade of a climb takes into consideration length, average difficulty, continuity, exposure, quality of the rock, commitment and other subtle factors.

The experienced climber, having accomplished or attempted free climbs of varying degrees of difficulty in the YDS class 5 range, gains an understanding of the level of difficulty involved. To the beginner, however, these ratings are simply a set of numbers, understandably, easy if rated 5.0 and impossible if rated 5.13. To provide a slightly better understanding within the class for the beginner the following tongue-in-cheek description is provided:

5.0 to 5.4   There are two hand- and two footholds for every move; the holds become progressively smaller as the number increases.
5.5 to 5.6   The two hand- and two footholds are there, obvious to the experienced, but not necessarily so to the beginner.
5.7   The move is missing one hand- or foothold.
5.8   The move is missing two holds of the four, or missing only one but is very strenuous.

5.9   This move has only one reasonable hold which may be for either a foot or a hand.

5.10   No hand- or footholds. The choices are to pretend a hold is there, pray a lot, or go home.

5.11   After thorough inspection you conclude this move is obviously impossible; however, occasionally someone actually accomplishes it. Since there is nothing for a handhold, grab it with both hands.

5.12   The surface is as smooth as glass and vertical. No one has really ever made this move, although a very few claim they have.

5.13   This is identical to 5.12 except it is located under overhanging rock.

National Climbing Classification System (NCCS)

This is the other major system used in the U.S. Its overall grading scheme and aid climbing classification system are the same as described within the YDS. The difference comes in the rating of free climbing. The NCCS uses the letter F followed by a number. There is no tie to equipment as in the old Sierra Club System, just increasing levels of difficulty of climbing, similar to the old Teton rating system, only with more subdivisions. In 1963 when originally proposed, climbs were rated from F1–F10; this has been expanded up to F13 in later years for use at Joshua Tree National Monument.

Union Internationale des Associations d'Alpinisme (UIAA)

In 1968 the UIAA proposed an international scheme for rating climbs, with the hope that it would be adopted world-wide, thus making it easier for traveling climbers to anticipate the difficulty of the climbs for an area with which they were not familiar. Unfortunately for its acceptance in the U.S., Roman numerals were chosen to classify individual pitches, thus conflicting with their use as an overall grade in the YDS and NCCS. Because of this there has been very little acceptance of the system in the U.S. although it is very widely used in Europe. Officially it currently goes from I to VII with + and − designations, but unofficially goes to IX. The system originally had adjectives to go along with the Roman numerals but these are rarely used since they are easily confused with the British system.

Australian System

Developed in the 1970s as a free climbing rating system using Arabic numerals, it is openended and currently goes from 1 to 27.

British System

This system is one of the most confusing, making use of both adjectival and numerical schemes. The adjective very severe (VS) was originally used just as F6, 5.6, V or 13 from the other systems, with a very definite meaning. However as harder and harder climbs were done, extremely severe (XS) was getting overcrowded and running out of adjectives. Exceptionally severe was tried for a while but was not accepted. The solution came in switching to a numerical system which had originally been used at the sandstone areas. This was adopted to rate the objective difficulty of an individual pitch, without regard to exposure or protection, the way a second would see a climb. Currently the scale goes from 1a to 7a although ratings less than 3a are rarely used. The adjective system was then modified to be a rating of the overall difficulty, but not in exactly the same way as a grade is used in the YDS and NCCS; this is because most British climbs are on crags and relatively short in length. It rates a climb more from the leader's point of view, including overall technical difficulty, exposure and how well protected the climb is.

Alpine Rating System

Used primarily in the Alps, this system is an overall grading system similar to the Roman numerals of the YDS and NCCS, and although there are six grades they do not correspond exactly to grades I–VI of the YDS and NCCS. In addition Sup. and Inf. (meaning Superior-Inferior) are used to grade climbs that are high or low in their grade. For individual pitch ratings the UIAA system is used.

Rating on Snow and Ice

It is even more difficult to rate a snow or ice climb. The proponents of the NCCS and those who supported a scheme called the American Classification System (ACS), which was really the YDS with the inclusion of snow and ice routes, tried to say snow and ice could be rated just like rock. In other words there could be F7 or 5.7 ice routes, but this has had very little acceptance. In Scotland ice climbs are rated from I to V, not to be confused with any other system that makes use of Roman numerals. In addition it is used both as an overall grade and for individual pitch rating; for example, a climb may be said to be grade III with moves of IV. This system has been copied in New England as the New England Ice system (NEI) and expanded in Canada to include grade VI because of the length of some of the climbs. In addition Jeff Lowe has suggested combining Scottish grades with the YDS into one system which could be used to rate all climbs. It has yet to receive wide acceptance. For further details, see reference following this appendix.

Table A2-a. Comparison of Free Climbing Ratings.

Welzenbach	YDS	NCCS	UIAA	Australian	British Numerical Pitch	British Adjectival
1	Class 1	F1	I	1		Easy (E)
2	Class 2			2		
3	Class 3	F2	II	3	1 a,b,c	Moderate (MOD)
4	Class 4	F3	− III	4		
	5.0		III	5		Difficult (DIFF)
	5.1	F4	+ III	6	2 a,b	
	5.2		− IV	7	2c, 3a	Very Difficult (V DIFF)
	5.3	F5	IV	8		Mild Severe
	5.4		+ IV	9 / 10	3 b,c	Severe (S)
	5.5		− V	11 / 12	4a	
	5.6	F6	V	13 / 14		Hard Severe
	5.7	F7	+ V	15 / 16	4 a,b,c,	Very Severe (VS)
	5.8	F8	− VI	17 / 18	5 a,b	Hard Very Severe (HVS)
5	5.9	F9	VI	19 / 20		
	5.10a	F10		21		Mild Extremely Severe (MXS) (E1, E2)
	5.10b		VII	22	5 b,c	
	5.10c			23		
	5.10d	F11		24		
	5.11a	F12		25		Extremely Severe (XS) (E3, E4)
	5.11b		VIII	26	6 a,b,c	
	5.11c			27		
	5.11d	F13				
	5.12a					
	5.12b					Hard Extremely Severe (HXS) (E5)
	5.12c		IX		7a	
	5.12d					

Other Rating Schemes

In the past there have been other systems. Some, like Teton Grading System, Appalachian Mountain Club System (AMC), or the American Classification System (ACS), have been incorporated into or replaced by a newer system, while others like the Universal Standard System (US) were so complicated that they were very short-lived. Two other systems are worth mentioning since they sometimes still appear in climbing literature. First the "C" used in aid climbing: this system came about with the clean climbing ethics of the 1970s and merely substitutes the "C" for the "A" if the route is aided "cleanly" (no pitons used). The other is the bouldering system B1, B2, B3 developed by John Gill. At the time of its inception 5.10 was the hardest free climb then done; B1 meant hard 5.10, with B2 being harder and B3 even harder—a route with few if any repeats. Since climbers are doing harder and harder climbs the boulder rating system is on a sliding scale, B1 always being a "hard" version of the highest free climbing standard of the day, with B2 and B3 being relatively more difficult.

Free Climbing Comparison Chart

Comparisons of rating systems as shown in Tables A2a and A2b are approximations. They are intended to permit a reader of a guidebook which uses an unfamiliar system to relate the ratings of that system to one with which he is more familiar.

References

NCCS—includes comparison chart with AMC and Old Teton System: Ortenburger, Leigh, *Summit,* vol. 9, no. 5, May 1963; vol. 9, no. 6, June 1963.
UIAA: Wiessner, Fritz, *AAJ,* vol. 16, no. 2, 1969.
Universal Standard: Carter, Harvey T., *Climbing,* no. 10, November–December 1971.
Bouldering: Gill, John, *AAJ,* vol. 16, no. 2, 1969.
Ice Rating—Lowe system: Lowe, Jeff, *Climbing,* no. 51, November–December 1979.

Table A2-b.   Comparison of Aid Climbing Ratings.

Welzenbach	Decimal	NCCS	
6	6.0	A0	A0 - Fixed
	6.1		
	6.2	A1	A1 - Solid anchor placements
	6.3		
	6.4	A2	A2 - Awkward but solid
	6.5		
	6.6	A3	A3 - Pins can hold short falls
	6.7		
	6.8	A4	A4 - Pins can hold only body weight
	6.9	A5	A5 - 30+ feet of continuous A4

Overall Grades

I - several hours

II - half a day

III - most of a day

IV - long hard day (usually not less than 5.7)

V - 1½-2½ days (usually not less than 5.8)

VI - greater than 2 days

Overall Grades Used in Alps

F - Facile (easy)

PD - Peu Difficile (little difficult)

AD - Assez Difficile (pretty much difficult)

D - Difficile (difficult)

TD - Tres Difficile (very difficult)

ED - Extrêmement Difficile (extremely difficult)

APPENDIX 3

SUPPLEMENTARY READING

Chapter 2: Clothing and Equipment

Doan, Marlyn. *Hiking Light*. Seattle: The Mountaineers, 1982.

Manning, Harvey. *Backpacking: One Step at a Time*. New York: Vintage Books (Random House), 1980.

Winnett, Thomas. *Backpacking Basics*. Berkeley: Wilderness Press, 1979.

Chapter 3: Camping and Sleeping

Doan, Marlyn. *Hiking Light*. Seattle: The Mountaineers, 1982.

Hart, John. *Walking Softly in the Wilderness*. San Francisco: Sierra Club, 1977.

Chapter 4: Alpine Cuisine

Prater, Yvonne, and Ruth Dyar Mendenhall. *Gorp, Glop & Glue Stew: Favorite Foods from 165 Outdoor Experts*. Seattle: The Mountaineers, 1981.

Chapter 6: Wilderness Travel

Hart, John. *Walking Softly in the Wilderness*. San Francisco: Sierra Club, 1977.

Chapter 7: Ropes and Knots

March, Bill. *Modern Rope Techniques in Mountaineering*. Manchester, England: Cicerone Press, 1976.

Smith, Phil. *Knots for Mountaineering.* Twentynine Palms, California: The Desert Trail, 1960.

Chapter 8: Belaying

Leeper, Ed. "Belaying—The European Connection." *Summit,* vol. 25, no. 4, August-September 1979, p. 11.
Leeper, Ed. "Belaying—The Occupational Hazards." *Summit,* vol. 26, no. 3, June-July 1980, p. 20.
Microys, Helmut. "Climbing Ropes." *American Alpine Journal,* vol. 21, no. 1, issue 51, 1977, p. 130.

Chapter 10: Rock Climbing Technique

Livesey, Peter. *Rock Climbing.* Seattle: The Mountaineers, 1978.
Robbins, Royal. *Basic Rockcraft.* Glendale: La Siesta Press, 1971.

Chapter 12: Pitoncraft and Direct Aid Climbing

Robbins, Royal. *Advanced Rockcraft.* Glendale: La Siesta Press, 1973.
Scott, Doug. *Big Wall Climbing.* New York: Oxford University Press, 1974.

Chapter 13: Basic Snow Travel

Gillette, Ned. *Cross-Country Skiing.* Seattle: The Mountaineers, 1979.
Prater, Gene. *Snowshoeing.* Seattle: The Mountaineers, 1980.

Chapter 15: Ice Climbing

Chouinard, Yvon. *Climbing Ice.* San Francisco: Sierra Club Books and American Alpine Club, 1978.
Lowe, Jeff. *The Ice Experience.* Chicago: Contemporary Books, Inc., 1979.
March, Bill. *Modern Snow and Ice Techniques.* Manchester, England: Cicerone Press, 1973.

Chapter 17: Climbing Safety

Accidents in North American Mountaineering. Annual report of the American Alpine Club, 113 E. 90 Street, New York City.
Paulcke, Wilhelm, and Helmut Dumler. *Hazards in Mountaineering.* New York: Oxford University Press, 1973.

Chapter 19: First Aid

American Academy of Orthopedic Surgeons. *Emergency Care and Transportation of the Sick and Injured.* Menasha, Wisconsin: American Academy of Orthopedic Surgeons, 1977.

American National Red Cross. *Standard First Aid and Personal Safety,* and *Advanced First Aid and Emergency Care.* Garden City, New York: Doubleday and Company, 1980.

Hackett, Peter H., M.D. *Mountain Sickness.* New York: The American Alpine Club, 1980.

Houston, Charles S., M.D. *Going High.* Burlington, Vermont: Charles S. Houston, M.D. and The American Alpine Club, 1980.

Mitchell, Dick. *Mountaineering First Aid.* Seattle: The Mountaineers, 1975.

Wilkerson, James A., M.D. ed. *Medicine for Mountaineering.* Seattle: The Mountaineers, 1975.

Wilkerson, James A., M.D. ed. *Hypothermia and Frostbite.* Seattle: The Mountaineers, 1982.

Chapter 20: Alpine Rescue

Accidents in North American Mountaineering. Annual report of the American Alpine Club, 113 E. 90 Street, New York City.

American Academy of Orthopedic Surgeons. *Emergency Care and Transportation of the Sick and Injured.* Menasha, Wisconsin: American Academy of Orthopedic Surgeons, 1977.

Avalanche Handbook. Agricultural Handbook 489, U.S.D.A., Forest Service, 1976.

Fraser, Colin. *Avalanches and Snow Safety.* New York: Charles Scribner's Sons, 1978.

Gallagher, Dale, ed. *The Snowy Torrents: Avalanche Accidents in the United States, 1910–1966.* U.S.D.A., Forest Service, 1967.

Helicopter Operations and Personnel Safety (Helirescue Manual). Washington State Department of Emergency Services, 1976.

The Journal of Winter Emergency Care. National Ski Patrol Systems, Inc.

Kelley, Dennis. *Mountain Search for the Lost Victim.* Montrose, California: Kelley, 1973.

LaChapelle, Edward R. *The ABC of Avalanche Safety.* Seattle: The Mountaineers, 1978.

MacInnes, Hamish. *International Mountain Rescue Handbook.* New York: Charles Scribner's Sons, 1978.

May, W.G. *Mountain Search and Rescue Techniques.* Boulder, Colorado: Rocky Mountain Rescue Group, Inc., 1972.

Perla, Ronald I. *Modern Avalanche Rescue.* U.S.D.A., Forest Service, Wasatch National Forest, Alta Avalanche Study Center, April 1968.

Seattle Mountain Rescue Council Training Manual. Available from the Seattle Mountain Rescue Council, 1978.

Williams, Knox, ed. *The Snowy Torrents: Avalanche Accidents in the United States 1967-71.* U.S.D.A., Forest Service, 1975.

Williams, Paul. *Rescue Leadership.* Distributed by the Mountain Rescue Association, 1977.

Chapter 21: Mountain Geology

Easterbrook, D.J., and D.A. Rahm. *Landforms of Washington.* Bellingham, Washington: Western Washington State College, 1970.

Ekman, L.C. *Scenic Geology of the Pacific Northwest.* Portland, Oregon: Binfords and Mort, 1962.

Jerome, John. *On Mountains.* New York: McGraw-Hill, Inc., 1979.

McKee, Bates. *Cascadia: The Geologic Evolution of the Pacific Northwest.* New York: McGraw-Hill, Inc., 1972.

Milne, Lorus, and Margery Milne. *The Mountains.* New York: Time, Inc., 1962.

Chapter 22: The Cycle of Snow

Atwater, M.M. *The Avalanche Hunters.* Philadelphia: Macrae Smith, 1968.

LaChapelle, Edward R. *Field Guide to Snow Crystals.* Seattle and London: University of Washington Press, 1969.

LaChapelle, Edward R. *The ABC of Avalanche Safety.* Seattle: The Mountaineers, 1978.

Seligman, Gerald. *Snow Structures and Ski Fields.* London: Macmillan, 1936.

Chapter 23: Mountain Weather

Anderson, Bette R. *Weather in the West.* Palo Alto, California: American West Publishing Co., 1975.

Anthes, Richard A., et al. *The Atmosphere.* Columbus, Ohio: Charles E. Merrill Publishing Co., 1978.

Battan, Louis H. *The Thunderstorm.* New York: New American Library of World Literature, Inc., 1964.

Donn, William L. *Meteorology.* New York: McGraw Hill, 1975.

Reifsnyder, William F. *Weathering the Wilderness.* San Francisco: Sierra Club, 1980.

Rue, Walter. *Weather of the Pacific Coast.* Mercer Island, Washington: The Writing Works, Inc., 1978.

Scorer, Richard S. *Clouds of the World.* Harrisburg, Pennsylvania: Stackpole Books, 1972.

* INDEX